WORSHIP AND THEOLOGY
IN ENGLAND

WORSHIP AND THEOLOGY IN ENGLAND

WORSHIP
AND THEOLOGY IN
ENGLAND

FROM NEWMAN TO
MARTINEAU, 1850-1900

BY HORTON DAVIES

PRINCETON, NEW JERSEY
PRINCETON UNIVERSITY PRESS
1962

❖

Publication of this book has been aided by
the Ford Foundation program to support publication, through university presses, of works
in the humanities and social sciences.

❖

HORTON DAVIES is currently the Henry W.
Putnam Professor of the History of Christianity at Princeton University. He was born
in Wales, became an honors graduate in both
Arts and Divinity at Edinburgh University,
and obtained his Doctorate of Philosophy at
Oxford University. Mr. Davies has served successively as minister of an English Congregational Church in London, Dean of the Faculty
of Divinity at Rhodes University in the Union
of South Africa, and Head of the Department
of Church History at Mansfield and Regent's
Park Colleges at Oxford University.

❖

Printed in the United States of America by
Princeton University Press, Princeton, New Jersey

ACKNOWLEDGMENTS

Happily even in this Machine Age no one has yet invented a ready-reckoner for gratitude. Certainly no bibliography can express my obligation to conversations with friendly experts on liturgics in England or the United States.

This opportunity is therefore taken of thanking my colleagues on the Commission of Worship of the United Church of Christ, from whom I have learned much. A stay of nine months in England in 1960 was a series of opportunities to consult distinguished students of worship. In Cambridge I was able to consult my mentor and friend, Dr. E. C. Ratcliff (the Regius Professor of Divinity), the Rev. Cyril Bowles (Principal of Ridley Hall), the Rev. Jack Newport (Tutor of Cheshunt College), and to enjoy the hospitality of many other minds. Many other contacts of much shorter duration proved stimulating. Among them were conversations with Dr. F. W. Dillistone (the Dean of Liverpool), the Rev. C. B. Naylor (Chancellor of Liverpool), the Rev. Michael Henning (Principal of St. Aidan's College, Birkenhead), the Rev. Gilbert Cope (Lecturer in Birmingham University), Dr. John Marsh (Principal of Mansfield College, Oxford), Dr. Peter Murray of the Courtauld Institute of Art in London University, and Mr. H. V. Molesworth Roberts of the Library of the Royal Institute of British Architects. To all these gentlemen I express my gratitude; but the burden of what I have written, or not written, must rest squarely on my own shoulders.

In no formal sense do I thank the Trustees of Princeton University for their steady encouragement of my research. By appointing me a Senior Fellow of the Council of the Humanities for 1961-1962, with a greatly reduced teaching responsibility, as by defraying the cost of typing the manuscript (efficiently undertaken by Mrs. J. F. Helfer), they have made it possible for me to accelerate my studies. In the same way, my colleagues in the Department of Religion have been most encouraging. I am grateful also to the Reference Librarian of Princeton University (Mr. Frederick L. Arnold) for his careful concern, and, especially, to the members of the Princeton University Press, with whom it is a delight to work as well as an education for the book-lover.

Two pleasant assignments were the occasions for the preparation of the final chapter of this book. At the invitation of the Faculty of Theology of the University of Cambridge I delivered a series of lectures in the Spring of 1960 on the history of preaching in England from Wesley to Newman. A similar honour and opportunity were offered by the invitation of President Duke McCall and the Faculty of the Southern Baptist Theological Seminary in Louisville, Kentucky, to deliver the Mullins Lectures in Preaching in May 1961. They were both happy and inspiriting occasions deserving my warm thanks.

Finally, I thank the following publishers for permission to make copyright citations: Messrs. John Murray of London and the Houghton Mifflin Company for extracts from John Betjeman's *Collected Poems* (1958), his *A Few Late Chrysanthemums*, and his *Mount Zion*; and Messrs. Faber and Faber of London and the Harcourt Brace Company for an extract from T. S. Eliot's *The Four Quartets*. I am also privileged, by permission of the Right Rev. Leslie Hunter, the Bishop of Sheffield, to reproduce a hymn written by his father, the late Dr. John Hunter.

Other acknowledgments are made in the List of Illustrations.

H.D.

CONTENTS

Supper: Zwinglian or Calvinist? 6. The Improvement of Praise. 7. Popular Services.

CONTENTS

ILLUSTRATIONS

Following page 50

1. ST. PANCRAS CHURCH, LONDON

   This is the most famous and successful example of an English Greek Revival church. Designed by H. W. and W. Inwood, it was built between 1819 and 1822. Since Greek temples had dark interiors, without galleries; since their exteriors lacked towers; and since Anglican churches needed light and ample gallery space for congregations, but had no need for porticoes and towers except for ornament, the Greek Revival was only superficially *Greek*. In this case, the Ionic portico and the steeple imitation of the Tower of Winds are ingenious adaptations. (See p. 43.)

2. ST. ALOYSIUS CHURCH, SOMERS TOWN, LONDON

   This pre-Emancipation Roman Catholic church, built around 1808, in its scrubbed modesty mirrors the status of Roman Catholicism of that period. Somers Town was a neighbourhood which attracted fugitives from the French Revolution and, at one time, it was reputed to shelter 500 *émigré* priests. Galleries, transepts, and shallow chancel were built at different times. The earliest parts of the building resemble a Puritan meeting-house, except for the omniscient eye of God that dominates the chancel. (*Copyrighted by A. F. Kersting.*)

3. METHODIST CHURCH, BURFORD, OXFORDSHIRE

   This late and interesting example of the Greek Revival was built about 1850, when most new Methodist churches were following the neo-Gothic mode. The adaptable architect planned a lower floor, below street level, for educational and social purposes, and a sanctuary above, approached by an imposing flight of steps. The photograph was taken by Brenda Davies, my wife and partner in ecclesiological espionage.

4. ALL SAINTS, MARGARET STREET, LONDON

   This model church of the Cambridge Ecclesiological Society was designed by William Butterfield in 1849 and became an important centre for Anglo-Catholic worship. Its use of polychromatic brick and wrought iron, the sense of mystery and spaciousness that it evokes, and the single dominating and dramatic high altar, are evidences of Butterfield's inventiveness. (See p. 46.)

5. A PUGINESQUE PANORAMA

This panorama of neo-Gothic churches all built to Pugin's plans is the frontispiece of his book, *An Apology for the Revival of Christian Architecture in England* (1843). The front line of these Roman Catholic churches (reading from left to right) consists of: St. Marie's, Newcastle-on-Tyne; St. Marie's, Stockton; St. George's, London; St. Peter's, Woolwich; and St. Giles's, Cheadle. St. Chad's Cathedral, Birmingham, in which Newman preached, is immediately behind St. Marie's, Newcastle-on-Tyne. (See pp. 26-32, 44-46.)

6. THE CATHOLIC APOSTOLIC CHURCH, GORDON SQUARE, LONDON

Built by John Raphael Brandon in 1852, this imposing neo-Gothic church has the dimensions of a cathedral. It was used for a remarkable experiment in which a richly historical liturgical worship was combined with such charismatic phenomena as "prophesyings" and "speaking with tongues." (See pp. 153-164.)

7. ST. BARTHOLOMEW, BRIGHTON, SUSSEX

This High Church (in both senses) was erected to Edmund Scott's designs in 1874 in the then highly fashionable southern seaside resort. Its polychromatic bricks, mosaic work, substantial walls and altar, were greatly admired. Originally there were seven pendent lamps above the altar, and on it a cross, and flanking the cross on each side a vase of flowers and a candlestick. Its altar, raised on many steps, and its ornaments were considered the paragon of ritualistic correctness. (See Chap. v.)

8. ST. MICHAEL AND ALL SAINTS, CROYDON

Designed in the neo-Gothic manner by J. L. Pearson, the architect of Truro Cathedral, this Anglican church was built between 1880 and 1885, and is one of Pearson's finest works. The lofty and delicate French type of Gothic apse, the use of contrasting textures in brick and stone, the strength and elegance of the vaulting, and the enticing vistas make this an unusually devotional church. "My business," said Pearson, "is to think what will bring people soonest to their knees." (See p. 46.)

9. WESTMINSTER CHAPEL (CONGREGATIONAL)

This vast interior, built between 1863 and 1865, the dimensions of which are 120 feet by 67 feet, with its double tier of galleries, is clearly built for preaching marathons, as the vast rostrum indicates. Its renowned ministers have included Drs. Campbell Morgan, J. H. Jowett, John Hutton, and Martin Lloyd-Jones. It is exceedingly difficult to create a devotional atmosphere in such a vast oval auditorium, lacking Christian symbolism. Many Free Churches were built in the same manner and it is a typical product of an age of powerful preachers. (See p. 56.)

10. MANSFIELD COLLEGE, OXFORD

This happier example of Free Church architecture in the Gothic tradition was built in the perpendicular style by Basil Champneys in 1889. This Congregational Theological College, now an ecumenical study centre, and a Permanent Private Hall of Oxford University, has, by the example of its worship in the College Chapel (the building on the extreme right), raised the standards of worship in the English Free Churches. (See p. 56.)

11. THE KING'S WEIGH HOUSE (CONGREGATIONAL) CHURCH, LONDON

Designed by Alfred Waterhouse, R.A., in his own florid version of Gothic and erected in 1891, this Mayfair church, with its oval auditorium and gallery, has been a notable liturgical laboratory. This was particularly the case under the ministries of Binney, Hunter, and Orchard. It has forsaken its twentieth-century ritualistic deviations and returned to the Reformed tradition under its present minister, the Rev. Daniel T. Jenkins. To him, as also to the emeritus minister, the Rev. Claud Coltman, I owe the kindness of supplying this illustration. (See pp. 56, 221-237.)

12. ROBERT WILLIAM DALE

The great Congregational divine and preacher was renowned for his teaching and practice of "Christian civics." This photograph of him I owe to the kindness of Dale's successor in the ministry of Carr's Lane Congregational Church, Birmingham, and my friend, the Rev. J. Philip Lee-Woolf. (Photograph by R. W. Brown, Birmingham.) (See pp. 322-333.)

13. FREDERICK WILLIAM ROBERTSON

This sensitive expositor of Christian faith and social duty was, perhaps, the greatest pulpit apologist in the history of the Church of England. This likeness of him I owe to the kindness of a former graduate student and friend, Professor Eugene Barth of Albright College, Pennsylvania. (See pp. 311-322.)

14. CHARLES HADDON SPURGEON

This portrait of the remarkable Baptist preacher and philanthropist is by Alexander Melville. It is reproduced (as are also Nos. 15 and 16) by courtesy of the National Portrait Gallery, London, and I gladly thank Miss Christa Dedering, Librarian of the National Gallery of Canada in Ottawa, for her assistance in procuring these photographs. (See pp. 333-341. (*Copyrighted by the National Portrait Gallery*)

15. CARDINAL NEWMAN

This portrait of the great theologian, preacher, and poet is by Emmeline Deane. (See pp. 35-40; 300-311.) (*Copyrighted by the National Portrait Gallery*)

16. JAMES MARTINEAU

This portrait of the great Unitarian philosopher, moralist, preacher, and composer of forms of worship is by G. F. Watts. (See pp. 217-281.) (*Copyrighted by the National Portrait Gallery*)

WORSHIP AND THEOLOGY
IN ENGLAND

INTRODUCTION

THIS VOLUME is the successor to *Worship and Theology in England*, Volume 3, "From Watts and Wesley to Maurice, 1690-1850."[1] Volume 4 continues the inter-confessional history of English worship in its theological context from 1850 to 1900. Although it was originally hoped that a single volume would suffice to cover the eleven decades from the re-establishment of the Roman hierarchy in England in 1850 down to the present, this proved utterly impractical if the theme was to be covered in sufficient depth of detail and as comprehensively as in the previous volume. The sheer bulk of evidence to be sifted and the many mere stereotypes of individuals and movements that a controversial age hands on to the future for revaluation, as well as the new trends and new denominations that came into being, called for a limitation, in this volume, to five decades of religious history.

Staid and stable as the later Victorian Age is mistakenly thought to be from our more vertiginous standpoint, it witnessed a revolution in religious thought and way of life which was far greater than the eighteenth century Christians had encountered in their polemics with Deism. For Deism, while denying the distinctive claims of special revelation implicit in the assertion that Jesus Christ was the Incarnate Word and Lord or the Messiah, yet reasserted the claims of a natural theology and of a beneficent God whose benignant influence was traced in the order of nature and in the conscience of all mankind. The new and enthusiastic apostles of nineteenth century science, natural, biological, and sociological, however, often tried to banish the very conception of God when they did not studiously ignore it, whereas the Deists conceded God the real if limited role of presiding over the laws of the universe. If the eighteenth century problem was the "scandal of particularity"—the acceptance of the universal God but the denial of the Divinity of the Judean Christ—the mid-nineteenth century problem, posed as acutely by science as by Biblical criticism, was rather the acceptance of the example of the heroic Jesus of Nazareth but the questioning of the existence of "Our Father who art in Heaven." The problem is well put in the recent satirical novel of Peter De Vries in the confession and query of

[1] Published by Princeton University Press, Princeton, New Jersey, 1961.

3

a disillusioned theological student: "When I was young, a student I mean, we used to debate whether Christ was the son of God. Now the question is whether God is the Father of Christ."[2] The agony of faith's struggle with doubt is as apparent in Tennyson's great *In Memoriam*, as in the poems of Matthew Arnold and Clough, and in the novels of Mrs. Henry Wood and "Mark Rutherford."

The later Victorian Age witnessed not only a revolution and consequent painful reconstruction of religious and moral thought, but also dramatic changes in aesthetic sensibility, as may be seen in the architecture and art of the period (with its neo-Greek, neo-Gothic, and Pre-Raphaelite movements), a dislocating shift of population from rural to industrial city and town life, a growing awareness of economic inequalities and inhumanities which made hypocritical the claims for brotherhood advanced by middle- and upper-class Christian communities, and an increase in imperial overseas responsibilities which both promoted and hindered Christian foreign missions. In the turmoil and agony of faith's struggle with honest doubt, which gives the period such likeness to our own, two general possibilities lay open to those who could not take the crepuscular path of agnosticism or stand upon the defiant hillock of atheism.

One way that beckoned a Christian individual or community was to reassert the Christian certainties in an age that denied them by looking for a renewal of confidence in a bygone age of heroism as a pattern of restoration. Many Protestants took this path, especially those surveyed in Chapter VI ("New Forms of Primitivism"), by turning to the first or sixteenth centuries of the Christian era for their patterns of renewal. The Oxford Movement took the path of returning to the *traditio quinquesaecularis* for its image of restoration, and the Roman Catholics in England looked back longingly to mediaeval Christendom as *the* "age of faith." Thus for new charismatic denominations as for ancient or established Churches, tradition may be the springboard of presumed advance, as the self-confessed pygmies of the present stand upon the giant shoulders of the prophets and apostles, or the great reformers of the past. It is a case of *reculer pour mieux sauter*. It is, moreover, tradition that provides the ballast of the arks of salvation in the oldest communions, if it sometimes impedes their progress in the stormy waters of the present. The radicals and liberals, of course,

2 *The Mackerel Plaza*, p. 258.

4

think that the traditional vessels, with their historic creeds, hallowed rituals and ceremonials in worship, and their so-called "historic" ministries and polities (with the three-fold order of bishops, priests, and deacons) are arks, not in the symbolical sense, but in the archaeological meaning, and that their journey is an escape, not a "tacking"—in the yachtsman's term. The conservatives can, however, reply that they are following in a route marked out by centuries of satisfied Christian pilgrim-voyagers, and that the vaunted progress of the liberals and radicals resembles not so much a daring adventure as a foolhardy voyage to certain disaster, buffeted by the winds of rationalism and secularism, and shipwrecked on the rocks of Erastianism and materialism. Whatever the nature of the defence of the conservative tendency may be, it is certain that it was and still is a strong and important current in the religious life of England. The first six chapters of this volume are an indication of its strength, warmth, and fertilizing power, as the Gulf Stream in the waters of the Atlantic. They are, therefore, organized under the rubric of "The Appropriation of Tradition."

The second response to the challenge to faith which scientific, historical, literary, and sociological criticism raises in such acute and agonizing form in the period under review is adaptation and theological reconstruction. This liberal impetus to theological revaluation, which was to come to its fullest momentum in the first three decades of the twentieth century, is partly expressed in the terms of "New Theology" and "The Social Gospel." In this book the trend is termed "The Drive towards Innovation" and provides the framework of the last four chapters.

It will be found, however, that neither individuals nor movements can be so conveniently fitted into the categories of conservatism and liberalism, tradition and innovation. For example, the Pre-Raphaelite Movement of this period (the Brotherhood found its name in 1848) may be regarded as, in one sense, another manifestation of the traditionalist's return to the Gothic period—in fact, to an earlier Gothic; yet in its socialism, as shown in the theories of William Morris and in the murals of Ford Madox Brown which honoured the new sons of industrial toil, it was revolutionary. As both tendencies towards traditionalism and modernism may be found in the same movement, so also may they be discovered in the same individual, though in differing proportion.

5

The sub-title of the present volume, "From Newman to Martineau, 1850-1900," does more than record the dates of the greatest influence of these leaders, respectively in the Roman Catholic and Unitarian Churches. It is true that Newman was born in 1801 and died in 1890 and that Martineau lived from 1805 to 1900, but far more important is the fact that they represent in clearest contrast two deeply religious minds, the first strongly traditional in outlook and the second vigorously radical. Yet even here the adjectival terms are far from absolute, for there are forward-looking elements in the mind of Newman and an occasional and significant retrospective look in the eyes of Martineau. One might have guessed that the future Cardinal's pilgrimage which took him from an Evangelical upbringing through twelve years of leadership of the Oxford and Anglo-Catholic Movement to the Roman obedience in 1845 could be fairly described as conservative, *tout court*. Yet the man who repudiated the Gothic overtures of Pugin, because he believed that neo-mediaevalism in religious architecture was a confession of contemporary irrelevancy, is among the "anti-Goths." Moreover, his defence of the idea of development in Christian doctrine, while it leads him to the assertion of the Church's right and duty to declare certain dogmas *de fide*, is explicated on an embryonic analogy that would seem unconsciously to owe something more to the age that produced Hegel's dialectical interpretation of history and religion and Darwin's evolutionary hypothesis, than to the distinctive dimensions of Biblical and Patristic thought.

The same mixture of conservatism and radicalism, though in different proportions, is to be found in Martineau, professor, preacher, liturgist, and Unitarian leader. He, too, might be expected, as the leader of the Unitarian intellectuals, to be in the vanguard of a progressive and left-wing theology, as a kind of theistic Auguste Comte. Yet for all his concentration on the comparative study of religion, and on philosophical and ethical systems, he is more the idealist than the rationalist, the historian rather than the iconoclast, the man of religion rather than the controversialist. Although he was part of that movement which turned to the breadth and inclusiveness of theism (in the non-Christian as well as in the Judaeo-Christian tradition), yet his contribution to liturgics, spirituality, and hymnody is characterized less by dilution of doctrine than by a strong Biblical idiom and insight into the ways of the living God manifested in history. Ecclesiastically he departed from any assertion of the voluntary principle, preferring to see the state recognize a plurality of denominations (as did Arnold of Rugby), and he was the indefatigable foe of sacerdotalism and uniformity. At the same time he believed deeply in personal religion and in the worship of the living God (not of a mere principle or potency), as is manifested in his composition for corporate worship of some of the most memorable prayers of the century.

Although the first six chapters explore the traditional recovery in worship, and the last four explicate the innovational impetus, the coexistence of both emphases simultaneously is indicated in the final Chapter x, "The Power of the Victorian Pulpit." Here the traditionalism of Roman Catholic Newman and of Baptist Spurgeon must be contrasted with the relative liberalism of Anglican F. W. Robertson and Congregationalist R. W. Dale. This is proof, if any were needed, that within the same denomination, as also within the same person, conservative and liberal tendencies are to be found. In these ways, then, while isolating the strands of tradition and of innovation in order to see them the more clearly, we hope that the danger of presenting a new stereotype has been avoided.

If further justification were needed for not providing a synthesis of the traditional and reconstructionist emphases at the conclusion of the book, two more reasons could be given. This synthesis could be found probably only within the mind of one theologian who was greatly in advance of his time—F. D. Maurice —whose *Kingdom of Christ* appeared in its second edition in 1842, and my previous volume in this series concluded with an evaluation of his balanced presentation.[3] More cogent, however, is the second consideration, that ecclesiastical party warfare continued to rage to the very end of the century, despite Maurice's pleas to drop party cries. No larger ecclesiastical synthesis appeared likely while within the Anglican Church the "Ritualists" of the Anglo-Catholic wing (considered in Chapter v) and the Liberal Anglicans of the Broad Church wing (considered in Chapter vii) were at loggerheads, and the Evangelicals cried "a plague o' both your houses."[4] Nor was an accommodation between the Anglicans

---

[3] *Worship and Theology in England*, Vol. 3, "From Watts and Wesley to Maurice, 1690-1850," Chapter xi, "Maurice and the Liturgy as the Symbol of Unity in Church and State."

[4] The important contribution of the Evangelicals to worship is considered in *ibid.*, Chapter ix, "Anglican Evangelicalism: The Spirit and the Liturgy."

and the Free Churchmen likely, when the High Churchmen seemed to flirt with Rome, and the Broad Churchmen with infidelity, and the Evangelicals, who seemed the natural allies of the Free Churches, appeared to be losing their power, while the Free Churchmen themselves were engaged in a campaign for the Disestablishment of the Church of England, for removing the Thirty-Nine Articles as a test for entry to the ancient universities, and for a national system of education in the schools free from credal impositions.

A structure of contrast for this volume is, therefore, a more adequate image of the state of the various tendencies, conservative and liberal, and for the religious partizanship of the period, than any picture of reconciliation would provide. A more synthetic approach will be demanded by the twentieth and ecumenical century; in the latter half of the nineteenth century it is inappropriate.

After this consideration of the general structure of the book, it is suitable to turn to a survey of the individual chapters. The first appropriately deals with the worship of the most ancient of the English Churches, the Roman Catholic Communion, and provides an account of a century of clandestine celebrations of the Mass and of the hidden spirituality of the devotional books of Baker and Challenor, up to the date of the emancipation of the Catholics in 1829, and thereafter of the preparation of Catholicism to emerge from its winter to its "Second Spring" in 1850. It presupposes a knowledge of those factors on the Continent and in England that produced the Catholic reaction and that were considered in Chapter x of my previous volume.[5]

Chapter II shows the transition from the architecture of rationalism (in neo-classicism of the Greek variety) to the romanticism of neo-mediaevalism exemplified by Pugin and his successors, publicized by Ruskin, utilized by Roman Catholicism and Anglo-Catholicism, and ultimately imitated by the English Free Churches, as well as by the Low Church. Theological and ecclesiastical traditionalism was inevitably reflected in architectural traditionalism.

The third chapter surveys the growing dissatisfaction in the English Free Churches with the Puritan tradition of extemporary prayer inherited from the Westminster Directory. It documents the movement towards read prayers, and even to the production of devotional manuals, and towards an ecumenical hymnody by

5 *Ibid.*, Chapter x, "The Oxford Movement: The Recovery of Catholic Tradition."

recovering the treasures of the past. It also considers the depreciation of the importance of the Lord's Supper, possibly in reaction from the Tractarian emphasis on sacramental grace.

Chapter IV includes the survey of Presbyterian thought and practice in Scotland and in England, because the smaller English Presbyterian Church (especially after the defection of so many congregations to Unitarianism in the late eighteenth and early nineteenth centuries) inevitably looked to the larger and more influential Church of Scotland as its model. Moreover, the liturgical movement in that Communion was especially significant as transmitting some of the insights into worship discovered by the Oxford Movement to the Free Churches, their former allies in the days of the seventeenth century Commonwealth who also were increasingly unhappy about the legacy of the Westminster Directory of Worship.

Chapter V follows the fortunes of the often persecuted "Ritualists" (who were in fact "Ceremonialists") who, as the second generation of the Tractarians, fought to introduce and maintain Catholic practices in the worship of the Anglican parish churches and who, in the relative seclusion of their religious communities for women, first, and for men later, introduced a higher ceremonial and ritual than would have been tolerated in the parish churches. This chapter documents the increasingly Catholic trend of Anglican worship.

Chapter VI, "New Forms of Primitivism," is appropriately placed as the last of the group under the rubric "The Appropriation of Tradition" because it is a transitional chapter, paving the way for the second group of chapters, labelled "The Drive towards Innovation." This chapter is, on the one hand, an indication of the restorationism inherent in the justification of the newest denomination, as, for example, in the title of the religious body known as "The *Primitive* Methodists" and is therefore traditional. On the other hand, however, it is an innovation since it repudiates the formality (which it equates with insincerity) of the older denominations in favour of a simple Bible-based, charismatic, Spirit-led worship for a compact "gathered church" group, with a radical world-condemning ethic. Some of the same characteristics are shared by the other new foundations of the period, notably the Plymouth Brethren, the Churches of Christ, and the Salvation Army, though the latter has a distinguishing social compassion for the outsider and—in the Victorian Age—a modernistic musical

9

and military technique for advertisement and for encouragement. The most interesting denomination of all, because it is atypical, is the Catholic Apostolic Church, which combined a charismatic and eschatological interest with a strongly liturgical concern in its worship and which transmitted several of its liturgical recoveries to the twentieth century service-books of the Church of Scotland.

The second division of the book begins with a theological chapter (VII), which attempts, chiefly through the poetry and novels of the period, to recapture the struggle of faith with doubt which the onslaught of criticism from the natural and biological sciences outside the Churches and the literary and historical criticism from within them exacerbated. It is also concerned with the theological reconstruction which was forced on Liberal Churchmen, Anglo-Catholics, and Free Churchmen alike by the mental climate of the age.

The need for a revaluation in theology and therefore in worship inevitably fell more heavily on the denominations which placed their faith in the authority of the Bible rather than in ecclesiastical tradition, and so Chapters VIII and IX deal with English Dissent, which had neither the protection of dogma or creeds nor of an uniform Liturgy comprehensive enough to include various types of theology. Chapter VIII is devoted to the Older Dissent (Baptists and Congregationalists) and particularly to the contributions of such pioneers in worship as Thomas Binney (who lowered the style of preaching from the oratorical to the conversational and raised the standard of worship from the extemporary to the liturgical) and John Hunter, who combined a profound understanding of the traditional liturgical techniques of prayer (Litany, Responses, Collects) with the urgent modern content and a sense of the industrial context of the "Social Gospel." Chapter IX is devoted to the Newer Dissenting denominations, the Methodists and the Unitarians. It shows how the amalgam of Anglican and Puritan traditions of worship in Methodism was variously stressed and how its important hymnody provided creeds with personal warmth. The sections on Unitarianism demonstrate the liturgical fertility of this ever-experimenting denomination and draw special attention to James Martineau's "New Wine" of worship.

The final chapter (X), in that it deals with Victorian preaching in general and with four masters of the pulpit in particular (Newman, Robertson, Dale, and Spurgeon), is a reminder that no account of worship is complete which omits the place of the sermon in the service, as the declaration of the Word of God to men, both as consolation and criticism. In their aid to belief, the doctrinal sermons asserted the contemporary relevance of the Christian faith, the ethical sermons challenged the social complacency of congregations with prophetic insight and zeal, and the devotional sermons (more often devotional parts of sermons) quickened the imagination and spurred the will to the *imitatio Christi* which is the end of all preaching.

Often over-didactic, frequently prolix, the sermon, when it was a living exposition of Divine revelation, was a necessary safeguard against the familiarity, formality, antiquarianism, and aestheticism which may accompany the use of the deepest forms of liturgical worship. Thus the necessary fidelity to the givenness of historic faith in traditional forms of Christian worship is complemented by the immediacy and relevancy of the contemporary proclamation of the Good News in a new day. And so the largely doctrinally conservative Newman and Spurgeon, and the largely doctrinally liberal Robertson and Dale, demonstrate that essential Christianity is renewed by the worship which recalls in ancient words and hallowed actions the creation and re-creation of the people of God and their future destiny, and proclaims through its preaching in the vocabulary of the present, with illustrations drawn from immediate experience, the vitality and urgent relevance of the Gospel in the contemporary situation. In every act of Christian worship, tradition and innovation may be said to play their complementary roles, though in varying proportion.

The practice of supplementing the occasionally formal and arid, official and theological, accounts of worship found in liturgical texts, treatises, and sermons, with illuminating accounts of worship drawn from appreciative or critical poets, novelists, and dramatists of the period, has also been followed in this volume. These borrowings, ranging in scope from Tennyson's *In Memoriam* (the century's longest and most poignant *cri du coeur*) to Bernard Shaw's *Major Barbara*, are given a separate listing in the Bibliography. They enable the reader to feel along the pulse and in the vibrating heart the agonizing issues of the day. Along with the hymnody and architecture of the period, the ritual and ceremonial, ear-gate and eye-gate, they explore the imagination and vision without which not only the people perish, but worship—the re-creation of Christian vision—is mere parrotry. As the theology of the sermons, lessons,

11

and prayers strives to remove doubt, deepen the understanding, confirm faith, and enliven the concern for the neighbour, so worship sensitized by the arts of the imagination perceives the potential saint in the sinner, the Great High Priest ever at His work of intercession and reconciliation, and catches amid the cacophony of the present the symphony of the blessed, conjubilant in adoration.

PART ONE
THE APPROPRIATION OF
TRADITION

CHAPTER I

THE RENASCENCE OF ROMAN CATHOLIC WORSHIP: WINTER AND THE "SECOND SPRING"

I F THE ROMAN CATHOLICS were a penalized minority from 1750 to 1829, the year of their emancipation, they did not become a jubilant and confident minority until 1850, when they could boast not only of having attracted the most distinguished "convert" of the century to their fold,[1] but also of that "Second Spring" and Renaissance of which Newman had preached. Its most evident sign was the re-establishment of the Roman hierarchy in England and Wales, with the metropolitan archdiocese in Westminster and the twelve supporting suffragan bishops, for the true ordering of the faithful. For the greater part of these ten decades from 1750 to 1850, before the arrival of the harried refugees escaping from Revolutionary France, or the more desperate Irish fleeing from starvation and famine, and the hundred Anglican priests who followed Newman into the Roman obedience, the predominant mood was nostalgia.

1. *Pilgrimage from Nostalgia to Hope*

The Vicar of Bray might look back to "Good King Charles' golden days," but Catholic aristocrat and priest recalled the thousand years of English Catholic history from the landing of St. Augustine in Canterbury to their dispossession in 1535 at the rude hands of Henry VIII. In every ancient English city the mediaeval cathedrals were mute testimonies to a glory and a grandeur that had gone. The very names of those great Gothic fanes of the "Old Religion," Canterbury, York, Durham,[2] Winchester, Wells, Ely, Lichfield, Norwich, Gloucester, Chester, Salisbury, and the rest, tolled the knell of long departed days. The nation's shrine, Westminster Abbey, where its heroes were buried and its monarchs anointed at their coronation, was for Roman Catholics little

---

[1] Newman made his submission in 1845.
[2] Durham is, of course, a great Norman fortress of the Spirit.

15

more than a mighty Benedictine Abbey from which the white-robed monks had vanished, like ghosts, into the insubstantial air. The Catholic names in the great pageant of English literature were but a mirror of the decaying fortunes of this faith since the high mediaeval days. Geoffrey Chaucer, depicting in the *Canterbury Tales* the variety of men and women with their mixed motives on pilgrimage to St. Thomas-à-Becket's tomb in Canterbury and to the *civitas coelestia*, and William Langland's *Piers Plowman* with its vision of a spiritually renovated England seen with the mystic's eyes from the Malvern hills, were each witnessing to the precious if precarious mediaeval synthesis of nature and grace, reason and revelation, humanity and divinity, in which England played an honoured part as a significant segment of Christendom, with its own saints and its own variants of the Western Catholic rite, including the Sarum Use. The later Catholic poets image first the gallant but doomed ardours of the Counter-Reformation in England, and then the reluctant compromises and resignation of what Bishop David Mathew has admirably called "a quiescent cultural minority."[3] Southwell and Campion, those urgent Elizabethan lyricists and hunted Jesuit priests, died as martyrs before the gaping crowds at Tyburn gibbet. Crashaw's Baroque inspiration and tortured devotion and conceits manifest, in part, the aspiring agonies and divided loyalties of the recusant's devotion.[4] Dryden's *Absalom and Achitophel* reflects the desperate hope against hope of the Roman Catholic plotters, as *The Hind and the Panther* shadows the resignation of a poet laureate who counts a mutable world well lost for the true and despised faith. Pope's *Essay on Man* mirrors more the Deism of the time than the Catholicism of its witty, envenomed, and unhappy author. It seemed to the Roman Catholic Church in the mid-eighteenth century that, like Cordelia, she must "sit and be silent."

It is John Henry Newman, however, the "lost leader" of the Tractarians, immured in a decent obscurity in the Oratory of St. Philip Neri in Birmingham (so near and yet so far from the acclamations of the university congregations of dons and undergraduates at St. Mary-the-Virgin in Oxford), who most movingly describes the past glory and present insignificance of the Roman Catholics during the three long centuries of post-Reformation win-

---

[3] *Catholicism in England.* (Full information as to place and date of publication is given in the Bibliography.)
[4] See E. I. Watkin, *Catholic Art and Culture*, pp. 132-33.

ter that preceded the "Second Spring." "No longer a Catholic Church in the country; nay, no longer, I may say, a Catholic community;—but a few adherents of the Old Religion, moving silently and sorrowfully about, as memorials of what had been." They were "the *detritus* of the great deluge," and like the early Christians, these poor Irishmen or old Catholic families of England were "a *gens lucifuga*, a people who shunned the light of day." Newman's irony, barely controlling his indignation, then reaches its climax:

"Such were the Catholics in England, found in corners, and alleys, and cellars and housetops, or in the recesses of the country; cut off from the populous world around them, and dimly seen, as if through a mist or in twilight, as ghosts flitting to and fro, by the high Protestants, the lords of the earth. At length so feeble did they become, so utterly contemptible, that contempt gave birth to pity; and the more generous of their tyrants actually began to wish to bestow upon them some favour, under the notion that their opinions were simply too absurd ever to spread again, and that they themselves, were they but raised in civil importance, would soon unlearn and be ashamed of them. And thus, out of mere kindness to us, they began to vilify our doctrines to the Protestant world, that so our very idiotcy or our secret unbelief might be our plea for mercy."[5]

The same nostalgia, combined with a more realistic sense of resignation, can be detected in the preface of Bishop John Cuthbert Hedley's excellently argued *The Holy Eucharist*, which appeared as late as 1907. There he says, with a head inclined over his shoulder which has to be wrenched forward to survey present duty: "When kings have ceased to follow Corpus Christi processions, when magistrates and knights no longer attend high Mass, when Bishops are no longer escorted to their Cathedrals by the chivalry of a diocese, the sheer frequentation of Mass and Communion by the Catholic millions must show forth Christ's earthly Kingdom, embody Catholic faith, and keep before the eyes of Catholics the holy law of the Gospel which the insolent preoccupation of the world is apt to make them ashamed of."[6] In 1907 the Roman Catholic cause was growing and it would not be long before millions in England would affirm their allegiance to the Supreme Pontiff. How different was the situation of the penal days

[5] The "Second Spring" sermon was preached at St. Mary's, Oscott, at the first Provincial Synod of Westminster in 1852 and was published as No. 10 of *Sermons Preached at Various Occasions*. The citation is from the edition of 1892.
[6] Preface, p. xiv.

of the eighteenth century and how much greater then was the temptation to nostalgia!

Using dates as milestones, we may chronicle the change of mood from resignation to the first faint stirrings of hope on to the jubilation of 1850. Lord Hardwicke's Marriage Bill of 1753 fell with equal pitilessness on Recusants and Dissenters alike, requiring that all legal marriages should be celebrated according to the Anglican rite. Nuptial Masses, when they were celebrated, took place clandestinely. The Roman Catholic Sacrament of Matrimony was permitted to be celebrated openly only in 1836. It was not until 1791 that it became legal to celebrate Mass in registered chapels, whose priests had taken an oath of loyalty, and who were sworn to keep the doors open and not to advertise their existence by a steeple or bell. The requirement of the loyalty oath marked the suspicion in which Catholic priests were held and the refusal of steeple and bell was a strong hint that superstition had best keep quiet in the by-ways. Once permitted legally to exist, the impoverished Catholics, given impetus by the five thousand displaced French clergy who were in England by 1797, and the teeming thousands of Irish labourers who crowded into the seaports and manufacturing cities,[7] strained every nerve to build their chapels. Between 1791 and 1814 almost 900 Catholic chapels were opened.[8] In 1829 the English Government granted Catholic Emancipation. The new stirrings of hope were seen in the thirty-five neo-Gothic churches that were built between 1837 and 1845.[9] Moreover, when hope was at high-tide in 1850, the new bishops had on their hands a great and growing problem—that of integrating the labouring Irish and the academic converts (some with advanced Continental devotional tastes) who had followed Newman from Canterbury to Rome, with the staid, unostentatious loyalty of traditional English Catholics.

2. Clandestine Celebrations

The English Protestant can only imagine what Catholic life was like in the penal times if he recalls the similar shifts to which Nonconformist ministers were reduced under the five-stringed whip of the Clarendon Code in the days of Charles II. The only priests

---

[7] E. I. Watkin, *Roman Catholicism in England from the Reformation to 1950*, pp. 145, 158. The largest numbers of Irish emigrants came in 1846 and 1847, but there had been a steady stream for years before then.
[8] *Ibid.*, p. 158.   [9] *Ibid.*

who lived in security were those who were appointed chaplains to noble Catholic families and even these, if Pugin is to be believed, ranked well below the butler, the housekeeper, and the cook, "all in fact well provided except the chapel and the chaplain; no pittance can be too small for the latter, nothing too mean or paltry for the former."[10] Even this security was always liable to be precarious by the occasional removal of the household or the apostasy of the Catholic nobleman. Priests had often to be dressed as laymen, used "aliases" and alibis, and the vicars-apostolic employed code-writing when sending their reports to the authorities in Rome. The Roman Catholic faith was a *religio illicita* and to celebrate the Mass was a criminal offence until 1791.[11] The admirable Bishop Challenor (1691-1781) preached in a contemptible inn at Holborn, while the congregation sat about him at table, each having a pipe and a mug of beer to disguise the fact that they were preparing to receive the Mass. Only in the chapels of foreign embassies in London was the Mass said openly. Elsewhere Mass was said secretly, at midnight, and in an obscure attic in the slums to which entrance was gained only after the password had been given.

A most vivid contemporary account of a clandestine celebration of Mass in 1771, at which Bishop Challenor was the celebrant, is provided by a Mrs. Marlow: "We started from our lodgings at about 5 in the morning to be present for the first time at a Catholic religious service, or at prayers, as it was generally called, for the word Mass was scarcely ever used in conversation. We arrived at a public-house in some back street near the house in which Mr. Horne [the priest] resided. I felt rather frightened seeing some very rough looking people as we passed through the entrance, tho' all were very quiet. . . . We hurried past them, but I could not help clinging to Marlow, having an undefined fear of what was going to happen. We mounted higher and higher. At the top the door of a garret was unlocked and we saw at the far end what seemed a high table, a long chest of drawers with the back turned towards us. A piece of carpet was spread before it by a young man, who pointed us to our seats. In a few minutes the door opened, and the Ven. Dr. Challenor, accompanied by Mr. Horne

<hr />

10 Article in the *Dublin Magazine* (1841) cited in Denis Gwynn, *Lord Shrewsbury, Pugin and the Catholic Revival*, p. 48.

11 It was usual in this period to communicate on eight festivals which were preceded by days of preparation and followed by days of thanksgiving. See E. I. Watkin, *Roman Catholicism in England . . .* , p. 121.

and another priest, entered the garret, the door of which was secured inside by an assistant, who then unlocked some drawers behind what, I found, was then to be used as an altar, and took out the vestments and other things for the service.

" . . . Soon after we heard the door-key turned and several rough footsteps entered the garret, some gentle taps and words were exchanged by a powerful-looking Irishman who kept his post close to it, and those outside, which were passwords of admission. The key was again turned each time anyone entered, and just before the Bishop vested himself to say Mass bolts were drawn also, and no one else could pass into the garret. In the meantime the young man had prepared all that was needed for Mass, taken from behind what was used as an altar, which was covered with a white linen cloth. A crucifix and two lighted candles were placed on it and in the front was suspended a piece of satin damask in the centre of which was a cross in gold lace . . .

"When all was over, I heard the door-key turn once more, and all the rough footsteps leaving the garret. The Bishop, having unvested, remained kneeling before us while the people departed. The two priests, assisted by the young man, replaced the vestments, candle-sticks, and all that was used at Mass, behind the altar, locking it all up carefully, and leaving the garret an ordinary one in appearance as before."[12]

No Roman Catholic chapels were built until the very end of the century, after the passing of the Relief Acts, and these were inconspicuous in appearance and location. Even their interiors lacked side-altars and confessionals, for it was unusual to say daily Mass, and confessions were heard in the priest's lodgings. There were neither statues nor processions, neither votive candles nor tablets. The Stations of the Cross, as well as the service of Benediction, were unknown in eighteenth century English Catholicism. Even when these Catholic rites and ceremonies began slowly to appear or re-appear, largely as a result of the influence of the French émigré priests, they were viewed with suspicion by the English Catholics as "Continental abuses," so unused were they to religion on parade.[13]

In the penal times it was practically impossible for the largely

12 Basil Hemphill, *The Early Vicars Apostolic of England*, 1685-1750, pp. 82-83, cited from Edwin H. Burton's pamphlet on Bishop Talbot, Catholic Truth Society Tract No. 49.

13 *Ibid.*, p. 83.

impecunious Catholics to keep the many holy days of obligation, for the observance of them would prevent men from earning their living on such days. In March 1777 Pope Pius VI confined the holy days of obligation to 12: these were the Circumcision, the Epiphany, the Annunciation, Easter Monday, the Ascension, Whit-Monday, the Assumption, Corpus Christi, All Saints, SS. Peter and Paul, and the Feast of the local Patron Saint.[14]

Yet it was in such days of political and social loss that the foundations of spiritual gain were firmly laid. As with the Puritans in the days of Charles II, so it was with the Roman Catholics in the Hanoverian times. They were sustained by their sacrifices, and their devotional literature, as will be seen, was fed by the purest springs of ascetical adoration and identification with Christ in His sufferings.[15]

3. The Hidden Stream of Spirituality: Baker and Challenor

The remarkable cabin-boy who ran away to sea at fifteen, submitted to the Benedictine Rule, was a chaplain to convicts in Australia, and became Newman's sympathetic diocesan in Birmingham, Archbishop Ullathorne, reveals the secret stream of spirituality that irrigated his soul in Botany Bay in the fourth decade of the nineteenth century. Bossuet he read for the mysteries and festivals, and St. John Chrysostom for moral theology, but for the spiritual life, he wrote, "I had some valuable ascetical writings, especially the best Spanish edition of St. Theresa by Palafox, and Father Baker's Sancta Sophia."[16] Baker and Challenor were the tap-roots of the nineteenth century "Second Spring."

Who was Father Augustine Baker? And what is the importance of his Holy Wisdom? He was a remarkable seventeenth century contemplative in whom the teaching of the fourteenth century English mysticism (of the school of the anonymous author of The Cloud of Unknowing, Richard Rolle, Dame Julian of Norwich, and Walter Hilton's Scale of Perfection) was resuscitated, adapted, and completed for a different age.[17] From the perceptive but prolix

---

[14] Ibid., pp. 183-87.
[15] For the Puritan parallel, see the present writer's The English Free Churches, Chapter IV, "Under Persecution."
[16] Ed. Shane Leslie, From Cabin-Boy to Archbishop: The Autobiography of Archbishop Ullathorne, p. 169. See id.loc. for influence of Coleridge and Scott.
[17] Dom Justin McCann in the introduction to Memorials of Father Augustine Baker and other Documents relating to the English Benedictines, edited by Justin McCann and Hugh Connolly, writes of the Sancta Sophia: "That book resumes

and even repetitive works of Father Baker, the *Sancta Sophia* was compiled by another Benedictine, Serenus Cressy, in 1657. What makes it so distinctive as spirituality, which undoubtedly helped to account for its long continuing popularity among English Catholics, was its combination of ardour with order, its conjunction of aspiration with sheer practical common-sense.

Baker maintains that the normal path of contemplation is by means of aspirations towards the God who is revealed to faith which go beyond the confines of concept or image. At first they are deliberate "forced acts" of the soul, but they become "aspirations" as God helps those who help themselves. The aim of all unitive contemplation for him is not only absorption in the love of God but also complete conformity with the will of God, and holiness consists in the combination. The "inspirations" of the Holy Spirit, however, give illumination only where ethical guidance is sought, and when the moral law and the teaching of the Church fail to give definite leading. This soundly Benedictine and balanced approach to spirituality avoids both the paralysis of scrupulosity and the desiccation of the despondent soul that follows too passionate and agonized a search for perfection. His combination "of a sober prudence in his practical guidance with this boundless aspiration for union with God . . . makes a peculiar appeal to English people."[18] Frequently re-issued, it was fuel to the controlled flame of English Catholic ardour until Bishop Challenor, also in the same tradition, was to provide his own supplementary devotional treatises.

Challenor's is the dominating figure in the winter of Catholicism. Edwin H. Burton, his biographer, remarks on how much English Catholicism, even as late as the early twentieth century, owes to this eighteenth century bishop for the maintenance of the spiritual life. The Catholic version of the Bible (before the Ronald Knox Westminster translation), the popular edition of the *Imitation of Christ*, the form of the "Penny Catechism" learned by children, the English Supplement to the Missal and Breviary with festivals for the English saints, and above all, three handbooks of meditations and prayers, are Challenor's rich legacy from the dark penal days to the brighter future of English Catholicism.[19]

---

and completes the teaching of the most substantive of the fourteenth century, Walter Hilton's *Scale of Perfection*. It is recognised on all hands as the work of a spiritual master" (p. xi).

[18] E. I. Watkin, *Roman Catholicism in England* . . . , p. 82.

[19] Edwin H. Burton, *The Life and Times of Bishop Challenor (1691-1781)*, 2 vols., Intro., p. xxii.

While still a professor of theology at the English College at Douai, Challenor published his *Think Well On't* (1728). This was a short volume of meditations for each day of the month, and four editions of it were demanded in twenty years. The simple, clear, brief, practical meditations are all directed to taming the soul by means of mental prayer. Challenor's themes are sober enough, but his meditations are all infused with a fervent love of God. He considers the ends for which men were created, the benefits of the love of God, and the blessedness of serving Him. He then turns to meditate on Death, Judgment, Heaven, and Hell. Finally, his thoughts are on the evils of mortal sin, the dangers of relapse, the necessity of penance, and the consideration of the sufferings and death of Christ. Here, again, we see that English Catholic piety is characteristically affective and practical, at least until the time of F. W. Faber.[20] The nineteenth century propagandists of Continental Catholic devotions were to find the English school of spirituality insular, chill, and restrained. Yet it is difficult to see how such a charge can be substantiated against the Challenor who wrote in *Think Well On't* these words: "We have this loving and most lovely God always with us; and always in us; why do we not run to His embraces? He is a fire that ever burns; this fire is the very centre of our souls; how is it that we feel so little of its flames? It is because we will not stand by it. It is because we will not keep our souls at home, attentive to that great guest who resides within us, but let them continually wander abroad upon vain created amusements."[21] He also has a heart who does not wear it on his sleeve, or like the Passionists, on his habit. Because Challenor's love was burning at the hearth, he had no need to shout it from the housetops.

His most popular and influential devotional work was published in 1740, the year before his consecration as Bishop of Debra. This work, *The Garden of the Soul*, was intended to supplement the two standard prayer-books of the English Catholics, the *Primer* and the *Manual*, providing not only a collection of prayers, but also

[20] It may be closely paralleled in the Anglican days of J. H. Newman, who wrote: "To be excited is not the *ordinary* state of the mind, but the extraordinary, the now-and-then state. Nay more than this, this *ought not* to be the common state of the mind; and if we are encouraging within us this excitement, this unceasing rush and alteration of feelings, and think that this, and this only, is being earnest in religion, we are harming our minds, and (in one sense), I may even say, grieving the peaceful spirit of God, who would silently and tranquilly work His divine work in our hearts." (*Parochial and Plain Sermons*, 8 vols., Vol. 1, Sermon XX, p. 263.)
[21] E. H. Burton, *op.cit.*, Vol. I, p. 60, where the excerpt is cited.

23

information, instruction, and practical advice. The *Primer*, first published in 1599, was descended from the pre-Reformation Primers or Books of Hours of Our Lady, and contained the Little Office of Our Lady, the Office for the Dead, the Gradual and Penitential Psalms, the Litany of the Saints, and the brief Offices of Holy Cross and of the Holy Ghost. Many prayers (some from the Sarum Primer) were added, also a considerable collection of antiphons, collects, and hymns from the Breviary, together with the story of the Passion as narrated by the four evangelists. The *Manual*, a favourite prayer-book of penalized English Catholics, had been produced by an English priest of Elizabethan days. Its lengthy title also serves as a summary of its contents: *A Manual of Godly Prayers and Litanies newly annexed, taken out of many famous authors, and distributed according to the dayes of the weeke. With a large and ample exercise for the Morning and Evening. Whereunto are added the Hymns and Prayers for the principal feasts of the yeare, with a brief forme of Confession and order to help at Mass.*[22] Challenor himself brought out a new edition of this work in 1758 under the title of *A Manual of Prayers and other Christian Devotions*, itself a proof that he is supplementing not supplanting the existing devotions in his *Garden of the Soul*.

His sub-title for the *Garden* is instructive: "a Manual of Spiritual Exercises and Instructions for Christians who living in the World aspire to Devotion." Clearly, Challenor aims to instruct in Christian doctrine as well as to train the soul in spirituality. The first section of the book is a summary of Christian faith and morality, with a list of the fasts and feasts of obligation for English Catholics. The second section, entitled "A Morning Exercise," provides instructions and prayers for practising the presence of God. The third section comprises the "Ten Meditations" of St. Francis of Sales and these are taken from the first part of the *Introduction to the Devout Life*. Next there follows a section on "Instructions and Devotions for Hearing Mass." This contains a valuable description of the Mass and its purpose, with an explanation of each ceremony's meaning followed by an appropriate prayer. The fifth section consists of "Other Devotions proper to Sundays and Holidays" and includes English translations of the *Te Deum*, other Canticles, the *Pater Noster*, the Athanasian Creed, and several prayers. Section

22 The title as given in the 1637 edition of John Cousturier of Rouen. See *ibid.*, pp. 128 ff., to which I am greatly indebted for information on Challenor's devotional writings.

24

Six provides the first full description of the service of *Benediction* in any English prayer-book. The seventh section provides the Penitential Psalms, while the eighth has "Evening Devotions for Families" in which are included the Litany of the Saints. Section nine supplies "Instructions on the Spiritual Life" and section ten "Instructions and Devotions for Confession with an account of the Examination of Conscience." The eleventh section is concerned with Communion, the twelfth with "Instructions and Devotions for the Sick," and the last furnishes "Prayers for the Dead, the Litany of the Holy Name, and the Mysteries of the Rosary."

Such a volume, when priests were scarce and clandestine and Roman Catholic laymen were few and scattered, was of inestimable value, for it provided information and inspiration for young and old in all circumstances, whether in the Church while at Mass or Benediction, or in the home. This inspired anthology of Catholic spirituality and doctrine, not surprisingly, had been reprinted six times within ten years. The 7th edition of 1757 was augmented by "A Method of Serving at Mass," a modified form of "Acts of Faith, Hope and Charity," "Instructions and Devotions for Confirmation," "The Recommendation of a Departing Soul," and by sections on Jubilees, Indulgences, and the "Jesus Psalter." If imitation is the sincerest form of flattery, *The Garden of the Soul* has been flattered almost beyond belief. It still appears in modern and almost un-recognizable guise in English and American editions, but the title is the same, so great is its prestige. Its influence may be seen from the judgment that "it may be considered as the direct ancestor of such well known and popular books as the *Golden Manual*, the *Church Manual*, and *Vade Mecum*."[23] What is so moving to the modern reader as he turns its pages is the thought that when Protestants and rationalists believed that the international Roman Catholic Church in England had been run to the ground, it lived on underground, fed by the streams of grace of which Challenor was so remarkable a conduit.[24]

In 1754 Challenor published *Meditations for Every Day in the Year*. It was issued anonymously in two volumes at first but it soon became known as "Challenor's Meditations." The ingenuity is in

[23] *Ibid.*, p. 136.
[24] One is reminded of François Mauriac's comment on Graham Greene's *The Power and the Glory*: "We feel it is that hidden presence of God in an atheistic world, that subterranean flowing of Grace which dazzles Graham Greene much more than the majestic façade which the temporal Church still erects above the peoples." (Mauriac, *Mes Grands Hommes*, tr. Elsie Pell as *Men I hold Great*, p. 125.)

the arrangement of the material, so that Christian doctrine and ethics are related to the chief festivals of the Christian Year, and his sources are the Scriptures and the writings of the saints and servants of God.[25] The saints include St. Thomas Aquinas and St. Francis of Sales, the latter being Challenor's chief inspiration. The motive and the dynamic of the author is simply yet profoundly explained: "The love of God must be, then, the great business of your life, and of your prayer; and not any kind of love, but a fervent and perfect love. The school of this love is mental prayer. The Master is our Lord Himself and his holy spirit in your interior. As for time and place, you may exercise yourself in it at all times, in all places and employments; as you have this great Master always near you, even in the very centre of your soul, with both his eye and his heart always upon you."[26]

Moreover, the Challenor who wrote or compiled the three devotional treatises also made time to translate *The Imitation of Christ*, St. Augustine's *Confessions*, St. Francis of Sales' *Introduction to the Devout Life*, and two French treatises, the one Father John Chrysostom's *A Short Treatise on the Method and Advantage of withdrawing the Soul from being employed on Creatures in order to occupy it on God alone* (1765), and the other being Bondon's *Dieu présent partout*, Englished literally as *God Everywhere Present* (1766). As if this were not enough, he completed the two-volume *Memoirs of the Missionary Priest* (1741), "which is the standard martyrology to this day."[27] Most important of all, those who know him best averred that he practised what he preached,[28] and in an age of general religious decay and spiritual indiscipline.

4. The Catholic Revival[29]

Archbishop Ullathorne's autobiography, which was cited earlier for evidence in the nineteenth century for the continued influence of the seventeenth century *Hagia Sophia*, is equally a witness to

[25] For a detailed account of it see E. H. Burton, *op.cit.*, Vol. I, pp. 345 f.

[26] Cited from a letter of spiritual advice written on July 7, 1755 and printed in *ibid.*, p. 355.

[27] E. I. Watkin, *Roman Catholicism in England* . . . , p. 117.

[28] See the remarkable account of his daily devotional life in the Rev. James Barnard's *Life of Dr. Challenor*, pp. 130-33, which is cited in E. H. Burton, *op.cit.*, Vol. I, pp. 118-20.

[29] Chapter X of *Worship and Theology in England*, Vol. 3, "From Watts and Wesley to Maurice, 1690-1850," has treated generally of the factors which promoted a reaction from the previous age and encouraged both Romanticism and a respect for the organic growth of ancient societies and institutions. This background is presupposed in this section.

the impact of the English Romantics as well as of the specifically Catholic novelist, Kenelm Digby, on the young Benedictine monk in Australia. Not only did Ullathorne read to the Sisters who travelled with him from England to Australia Coleridge's *Ancient Mariner*, while they repeated the pious ending to themselves with deep feeling, but he paid a great tribute to both Digby and Scott. "Digby's volumes on Christian Chivalry and on the Ages of Faith," he wrote, "helped much to elevate and refresh the heart amid the din of conflict and the sordid surroundings of a penal settlement. But when I wanted rest and nothing but rest of mind, I not unfrequently betook myself for a few evening hours to the pure humanities of Sir Walter Scott."[30] Scott was a love he shared with Newman, like so many others of his generation.[31]

The leading pioneers in the English Roman Catholic Revival were Kenelm Digby, Ambrose Phillips de Lisle, John Talbot (sixteenth Earl of Shrewsbury), his chaplain Daniel Rock, and Augustus Welby Pugin. In this strangely assorted yet complementary quintet, Digby was the romantic novelist and author of *Mores Catholici* and the *Broad Stone of Honour*, de Lisle and Shrewsbury the patrons with social prestige, Rock the expert liturgiologist, and Pugin the architect. Rock was the single priest among these pioneering Catholic laymen, all committed to the renewal of the faith and culture of the mediaeval ages of faith "in their campaign for Gothic churches and rood-screens, and for reviving the old style of vestments and by replacing orchestral and operatic music with the old Gregorian chant."[32] It is significant that Lord Shrewsbury, Ambrose Phillips de Lisle, and Pugin had each independently (and before the Oxford Movement produced "converts" to the Roman allegiance) set themselves the task of reviving Catholic worship in its beauty and dignity and Catholic faith through missionary expansion in nineteenth century England. Lord Shrewsbury's seat, Alton Towers, and de Lisle's, Grace Dieu, were the centres of the Catholic Revival. In terms of his impact on the face of England's architecture, Pugin was the most influ-

---

[30] Ed. Shane Leslie, *op.cit.*, p. 169.

[31] No systematic study has yet been made of the European influence on the Catholic Renaissance in England, but it is clear that French Catholic piety and the Benedictine liturgical revival had a real, if long delayed, influence. For an objective and yet exciting American Lutheran appraisal of the European liturgical "Second Spring," see B. J. Koenker, *The Liturgical Renaissance of the Roman Catholic Church.*

[32] Denis Gwynn, *Lord Shrewsbury, Pugin and the Catholic Revival*, p. 10.

27

ential, though the enthusiasm, knowledge, and finances of the rest were indispensable.

Though Pugin was by no means the originator of the neo-Gothic ecclesiastical style,[33] he was, along with Ruskin, its great defender and populariser. Moreover, while Ruskin merely conversed and wrote, Pugin did both *and* built Gothic churches and cathedrals. As a youth he attended the services of the sensitive Presbyterian Edward Irving[34] in the Caledonian Church in London (where the minister was remarkable in combining as strong a respect for tradition and liturgy as for the charismatic and pneumatic in worship), and then moved to Salisbury. There he was entranced by the graceful cathedral which lives in the imagination as depicted by Constable,[35] its spire leaping through the uppermost foliage of elms as if nature longed for grace, and rough stone and rude trunk became delicate in their aspirations. What is certain, however, is that the architectural enthusiasm for Gothic in Pugin led to a study of mediaeval liturgy, and ultimately to the faith of the mediaeval "ages of faith."

In 1836 he wrote his belligerent and fascinating book, *Contrasts: or, A Parallel between the Architecture of the 15th and 19th Centuries*. This was a defence of the ultility of the Gothic, as contrasted with the ornamental nature of the stucco of the reigning neo-classical style that covered a multitude of constructional sins. Yet his chief interest in Gothic was its Christian symbolism. In the second edition of this work he called classical architecture "Pagan," claiming that its lines "grovel on the earth," that its "spirit and symbolism are those of death," while "its ornamentation [is] reeking with skulls of animals, sacrificial altars, and foliage" and "in its construction it is a mass of shams, beams of wood being imitated in marble and stone." On the other hand, he maintained that

" 'Pointed,' or Christian architecture, has far higher claims on our admiration than mere beauty or antiquity; the former may be regarded as a matter of opinion, the latter in the abstract is no proof of excellence; but in it alone we find the faith of Christianity

[33] Horace Walpole's mid-eighteenth century Strawberry Hill is an early secular example of neo-Gothic. John Carter, architect of Milner's Roman Catholic church in Winchester (1792), is Pugin's ecclesiastical predecessor. It should be noted that Cork Cathedral, built in 1808, is a neo-Gothic church.

[34] Later Edward Irving founded "The Catholic Apostolic Church" in London. See Chapter VI, *infra*.

[35] Constable's famous "Salisbury Cathedral from the Bishop's Garden" was painted in 1823 for his friend Archdeacon Fisher, and the even more distinguished "Salisbury Cathedral from the Meadows" in 1831.

embodied, and its practices illustrated. The three great doctrines of the redemption of man by the Sacrifice of our Lord on the cross; the three equal Persons united in one Godhead; and the resurrection of the dead are the foundation of Christian architecture. The first— the Cross—is not only the very plan and form of a Catholic Church, but it terminates each spire and gable, and is imprinted as a seal of faith on the very furniture of the altar. The second is fully developed in the triangular form and arrangement of arches, tracery, and even sub-divisions of the buildings themselves. The third is beautifully exemplified by the great height and vertical lines which have been considered by the Christians from the earliest period as the emblem of the Resurrection."[36]

While John Betjeman, in our own day, has castigated Nonconformist imitations of Anglican architecture as "spirelets,"[37] it was Pugin who declared of Anglican neo-Gothic churches that they were "Protestant monstrosities in the garb of Catholic antiquity."[38]

However exaggerated his "Contrasts" may have been,[39] many of his churches and cathedrals were admirable examples of neo-Gothic. One of Pugin's patrons was Ambrose Phillips de Lisle, whose uncle was Bishop of Gloucester, but who nevertheless joined the Roman Catholic Church and devoted his considerable patrimony to the Catholic revival. In 1835 he purchased 227 acres of land, of which 40 were cultivated, in Charnwood Forest and he presented it to the Cistercians, despite Lord Shrewsbury's feeling that a less retiring Order than the Trappists might be more advantageous for popularizing Catholicism in England. Mount St. Bernard, the headquarters of the Trappists, was built according to the plans of Pugin, to de Lisle's evident satisfaction.[40] In 1839, at Lord Shrewsbury's expense, Pugin erected an exquisite small church at Uttoxeter, St. Marie's, of which he wrote that it was "The first Catholic structure erected in this country, in strict accordance with the rules of ancient ecclesiastical architecture, since the days of the pretended

[36] P. 57 of *Contrasts* (second edition). The history of architecture would not substantiate the final sentence of this excerpt.

[37] The reference is to the poem "South London Sketch, 1944" printed in *Bats and Belfries*.

[38] *Contrasts* (second edition), p. 57.

[39] He contrasted, for example, the lovely fourteenth century Gothic church of St. Mary Redcliffe of Bristol with a church in Langham Place, London, which had a round portico surrounded by a balustrade; again, he contrasted St. George's, the Royal Chapel at Windsor, with the theatrical Chapel Royal at Brighton. In short, the Gothic best was contrasted with the contemporary worst.

[40] Cf. letter of Phillips de Lisle to Lord Shrewsbury, cited Denis Gwynn, *op.cit.*, p. 31.

Reformation."[41] Its novelties, for English Catholics of his day, consisted of the priests' seats at High Mass (the *sedilia*), a Gothic holy water stoup near the door, and an arch to support the roof which replaced the usual altar rails, though without the screens which were typical of his later churches. He was particularly proud of having provided a new arrangement for the reservation of the Blessed Sacrament. He wrote: "There is not a tabernacle on the altar which is left entirely free for sacrifice; but the Blessed Sacrament, according to an ancient and formerly general practice, will be suspended over the altar in a pyx, enclosed within a silver dove surrounded by rays of glory."[42] Entirely characteristic of Pugin is the paradoxical emphasis on the functional and the traditional, the uncluttered altar and the traditional pyx, of which Amiens cathedral provided a notable example. St. Marie's Uttoxeter is a distinguished attempt to create a thirteenth century Gothic church with lancet windows and arches, without the tracery that sometimes enriches and often merely distracts the attention.

As Pugin's confidence grew, so did the scope, size, and decoration of his neo-Gothic churches. St. Marie's Uttoxeter had been a moving and modest recreation of the simple dignity of Gothic. His church at Cheadle, the Midland market-town, which was built in 1846, was not only larger in scale, but it proclaimed the Catholic Emancipation from old restrictions by its graceful spire, its rich belfry on the east gable, the lavish decoration on roofs and walls, and especially by its large rood-screen with noble cross and the attendant figures of the Virgin and St. John. The interior richness of colour was equally impressive. His greatest early achievement, however, was the erection of St. Chad's, Birmingham, the first Roman Catholic cathedral to be built in England since the days of the Reformation. Here his life-size figures on the rood-screen dominated the nave and chancel. While he planned and supervised the building of neo-Gothic churches, he did not cease to commend the neo-Gothic style whether in lectures to the priests-in-training at Oscott, where he was styled professor of Ecclesiastical Art and Antiquities, or in the pages of religious magazines, with unexampled verve and contentiousness.

An important, though quieter and therefore frequently forgotten, influence on the Catholic Revival was the Rev. Daniel Rock, the

---

41 *Ibid.*, p. 42, and Bernard Ware, *The Sequel to Catholic Emancipation*, Vol. I, 1830-1840, p. 114.
42 Bernard Ware, *op.cit.*, Vol. II.

domestic chaplain of the sixteenth Earl of Shrewsbury, at Alton Towers. Here Dr. Rock pursued his researches into the history of Western Catholic worship, inspired amongst the elect the study of Catholic antiquity, and published his important liturgiological work, *Hierurgia*. Its nature may be described from its two introductory paragraphs:

"Of the more intelligent and inquiring amongst our Protestant fellow-countrymen, several have occasionally manifested a desire to see a manual which not only contained the prayers, but explained the ceremonies and elucidated the doctrine of the Mass. The purpose of these pages is to fill up such a deficiency in the number of those well-composed and highly useful expositions of Catholic doctrine which we already possess.

"The work is divided into two parts; the first of which embraces the Ordinary of the Mass in Latin and in English, to which are appended notes explanatory of the Ceremonies and of the Ritual of the Liturgy. The second part contains dissertations on the doctrine of the Eucharist as a Sacrifice and a Sacrament; on the Invocation of Saints; on Purgatory; on Images; on Ceremonies; on the Vestments; and the history of their origin and gradual change to the present form; and on several points of ritual and disciplinary observance."

It was far more exciting to build new churches, cathedrals, and monasteries, like Pugin and his patrons, or to enthrall the imagination with accounts of the chivalrous crusaders, the monks, nuns, friars, and hermits of the middle ages, written in the roseate tints of the romancer, like Kenelm Digby; Rock's was the equally necessary, if tedious, task of recovering and explaining the traditional worship of the Roman Catholic Church, which he did with all the resources at his command.

The achievements of those whom their Catholic antagonists called "the Goths" may appear the more considerable, if we reflect on the state of Catholic worship before their advent.[43] It is described with perhaps a dash more of patriotic pride than of realism by

[43] The great need for suitable sanctuaries can be judged from the following report of the Benedictine Bishop of the Vicariate of Wales, Dr. Thomas Brown, on the meeting-place of the Catholics in Merthyr Tydfil in 1841: "The very best place that can be obtained for Catholic worship is a loft reached by a ladder, ill-ventilated, low, narrow, dark, without ceiling, not secure against wet and wind, and running over the public slaughter-house of the town, whence issues the confused bellowing, bleating and screaming of pent-up and butchered oxen, sheep, and swine, and, whence, oftentimes, ascend through the floor, odours exceedingly offensive." (Ed. G. A. Beck, *The English Catholics: 1850-1950*, pp. 276-77, where the report is cited.)

31

Dr. Gradwell in the days immediately before Emancipation (1829), but after the ending of the penal prohibitions, as follows: "As there is but one Mass in a parish, all the parishioners must attend the church at the same time. It is a beautiful and edifying sight on a Sunday or holiday morning to see all the Catholic population of the neighbourhood, rich and poor, to the amount of from 100 to 1000 persons, all assembled in their Sunday dress at the same hour, and all staying the whole time of Divine Service with order, silence, attention and devotion. In some churches the Mass is sung, but except in London and the colleges, without deacon and sub-deacon, because there are none. The service is commonly as follows. The priest reads devotions in the vernacular tongue, *Pater*, *Ave*, *Credo*, *De profundis*, Acts of the Theological Virtues, Litany of the B.V.M., or select Office. Then he reads the Epistle and Gospel of the day, and preaches or leads an instruction on them. Then follows Mass and catechistical instruction, unless the Catechism forms part of the afternoon Devotions and Instructions. For eight days and sometimes more at the eight principal festivals of the year, there is plenary indulgence for those who duly frequent the Sacraments of Penance and Communion. These duties are diligently observed. This common assembling of all together has good effects. It forms the whole congregation into one family, brings them all to the regular Instruction and Devotion, and while it guards them from heresy, infuses the love of Catholic religion and Catholic piety."[44]

While simplicity, devotion, and unity may have marked these Lancashire celebrations of the Liturgy and meetings for instruction in Catholic doctrine, the critical eye of Pugin detected in the Midlands and in the metropolis much that was ugly and unworthy before Pugin's own aesthetic reformation! The senescent Pugin recalled the bad old days to his son-in-law in these unmeasured terms: "Going into Catholic chapels (there were no churches then) what did I see? The very tabernacle a Pagan Temple, the altar a deal sarcophagus, over which a colossal eye with rays looked down from a flat ceiling, artificial flowers under glass shades between the altar candlesticks, costly marbles produced in cheap papers, brackets painted with sham windows supporting nothing; and vest-

---

44 These sentiments are Gradwell's "Home Thoughts from Abroad," for he is writing in Rome a report of English Catholicism as he recalls it in loyal Lancashire. The letter ca. 1820-1825 comes from the Gradwell Letter Book in the Archives of Westminster Cathedral and is cited in Bernard Ware, *op.cit.*, Vol. I, p. 187.

ments, who can describe? In the music gallery soprano and contralto soloists publicly emulating each other, lady vergers in feathers collecting the offertories, High Masses advertised as attractions. Even Bishop Milner's own chapel, he, the Catholic pioneer of the revival, not exempt!"[45]

It may well be that the aesthete in Pugin saw much more of the holiness of beauty than the beauty of holiness which can thrive in the ugliest of surroundings; but it was given to him and his associates to provide sanctuaries, vestments, symbolism, and music befitting the venerable traditions of the ancient Western Rite in England. Moreover, however excessive the mediaeval archaism which dominated the Catholic revival, it was an attempt to be both Roman Catholic and English, whereas, as will be seen, many of the "anti-Goths" were apt to confuse Roman Catholicism with nine-teenth-century Italian religious taste.

5. The "Anti-Goths," or Italianizers

It was the neophytes, the recent "converts" to Roman Catholicism, who, in their attempt to do as the Romans do, made their congregations worship as if their churches were located in the very suburbs of the city on the seven hills. The leader of the Italianate fashions in worship in England was F. W. Faber, the intelligent if mercurial disciple of Newman who became the leader of the London Oratory which sprang from the Birmingham Mother House of St. Philip Neri. W. G. Ward was the leading lay supporter, but the most influential patron of the new fashions was Cardinal Wiseman. The Cardinal's penchant for the flamboyant was exhibited in the jubilant but tactless Pastoral to English Catholics announcing the re-establishment of the Roman Catholic hierarchy in England, which bore the superscription, "From out the Flaminian Gate of Rome," and caused quiescent Protestants to rise like a man to denounce the "Papal Aggression."[46] Wiseman had not concealed his anti-Gothic attitude at the consecration of the Cathedral of St. Chad's, Birmingham, in his criticism of Pugin's great reredos because it placed a barrier between the people and the altar and, in particular, obscured the predominant emphasis

---

[45] From a manuscript in the possession of his son, cited by Bernard Ware, *op.cit.*, Vol. I, p. 101. For confirmation of the theatrical professionalism of so many opera singers who sang in the London Catholic churches during the season, see *ibid.*, pp. 182, 185-86.
[46] Denis Gwynn, *op.cit.*, p. 111.

which Wiseman believed should be given to the tabernacle containing the Blessed Sacrament.[47]

The London Oratory was solemnly opened in 1849, and Newman's *giovani*, as he came to call them half in affection and half in impatience, were given a free hand to Italianize to their hearts' content. Indeed, for a time, Newman seems to have followed the lead of these "angry young men."[48] It was only natural, one supposes, for neophytes who had recently come over from Tractarianism, with its Gothicizing tendencies, to the Roman allegiance, to wish to give excessive proof of their new loyalty by out-Romanizing Rome. It is certain that Faber's exotic fashions alienated the hereditary Catholics whose devotional tastes were more decorous than decorative, in the tradition of the "Garden of the Soul."[49] Faber, as the leading spirit in the London Oratory, would have become, a century later, the patron saint of Wardour Street or Madison Avenue. He and his colleagues, habited in their unfamiliar Oratorian garb, delighted to provoke the bewildered glances of passersby in the London streets. The Oratorian Fathers were tonsured so as to draw the maximum attention to those heads which followed instead of leading their hearts. His most widely publicized (and numerically successful venture) was the holding of a popular daily evening service of worship, with florid and uninhibitedly passionate prayers, English hymns of the same nature (the best of which were written by Faber), and a sermon. The more the crowds thronged these services, the greater was the rivalry between the "Anti-Goths" and the "Goths."[50]

Indeed, it appears that London Catholics were divided for a time into two liturgical parties, commonly known as the "Oratory Catholics" and the "Garden-of-the-Soul Catholics." The former party was modern, Italian, and fervent in its piety and ceremonial; the latter party was traditional, English, and reserved. Not unnaturally the new sons of St. Philip Neri accused the "Goths" of practising a dully formal, excessively archaic, tepid, and wholly

---

[47] In general see Denis Gwynn, *Cardinal Wiseman.* On this particular point see Bernard Ware, *op.cit.*, Vol. II, p. 11.

[48] Louis Bouyer, *Newman, His Life and Spirituality*, pp. 284-85.

[49] Bouyer, *ibid.*, characterizes Faber as "a warm-hearted individual, but something of a dreamer and a rather fantastic one at that . . ." while Ronald Knox in *Enthusiasm*, p. 490, says that Faber, like Whitefield, "has the sacristy type of mind; the religion which absorbs him contrives, somehow, to limit him."

[50] Monsignor Bernard Ware has argued (*op.cit.*, Vol. II, pp. 259 f.) with some justice that the Jesuits who established their famous Farm Street Church in London in 1849 were the *via media* in this dispute.

unattractive type of devotion, while the sons of Bishop Challenor considered the London Oratorians to be unstable in their craving for cultic novelties, credulous in hunting for more miracles to believe in than were necessary to faith, and almost superstitious in their veneration of images and pictures.[51]

6. Newman's Balanced Spirituality

As was earlier suggested, the importunacy of the *giovani* threw Newman off balance for a time, so that he dropped his customary reserve and acumen, scorned the Anglicanism which had reared him, criticized most insensitively the collected edition of the poems of his Tractarian friend Keble, and ridiculed the hereditary English Catholics who had borne the heat and burden of the day as timorous and half-hearted.[52] Even Homer nods, and Newman, too.

There is definite proof that he repented of his rash criticism of English and reserved habits of devotion. In a sermon on "Our Lady in the Gospel" he had said: "I do not wish your words to outrun your real feelings. I do not wish you to take up books containing the praises of the Ever Blessed Virgin, and to use them and imitate them rashly without consideration. But be sure of this, that if you cannot enter into the warmth of foreign books of devotion, it is a deficiency in you."[53] He retracted this statement in a letter of 1866 to Pusey which was printed in *Difficulties of Anglicans*:[54] "I prefer," he wrote, "English habits of belief and devotion to foreign . . . and in this line of conduct I am but availing myself of the teaching I fell in with on becoming a Catholic. . . ." Newman might have added that this has been his preference while still an Anglican.[55]

Newman came increasingly to feel that the defect of Protestant

---

[51] Some insight into the acrimony of the "parties" may be gained from Newman's tart reply to Ambrose Phillips on the subject of Pugin's architecture, "Now is it wonderful that I prefer St. Philip to Mr. Pugin?" and from Pugin's letter to Faber in which he wrote, "A man may be judged by his feelings on Plain Chaunt. If he likes Mozart, he is no chancel and screen man. By their music ye shall know them, and I lost all faith in the Oratorians when I found they were opposed to the old song." Cited in Denis Gwynn, *Lord Shrewsbury, Pugin and the Catholic Revival*, pp. 122-25. See also Ware, *op.cit.*, Vol. II, p. 259 f. and E. I. Watkin, *Roman Catholicism in England . . .* , pp. 183 f.

[52] Newman as Anglican was considered in *Worship and Theology in England*, Vol. 3, "From Watts and Wesley to Maurice, 1690-1850," Chapter X; as preacher he will be considered in Chapter X, *infra*, of the present volume; in this section his views on worship and spirituality as a Roman Catholic receive consideration.

[53] See *Faith and Prejudice and other unpublished Sermons of Cardinal Newman*, edited by the Birmingham Oratory, with introduction by C. Stephen Dessain, p. 95.

[54] Vol. II, pp. 20-22.

[55] See *Parochial Sermons*, I, Sermon XX on "Forms of Private Prayer," p. 263 of the 8-volume edition of 1868.

worship was its subjectivity, its perpetual scrutiny of the feelings, its emphasis on our faith, not on the Object of faith, while the strength of Roman Catholic worship was its objectivity, its steady contemplation of God as revealed in the Incarnation. In aphoristic form he summarized Protestant worship as "invocation" (presumably of a distant Deity) and Catholic worship as "evocation"[56] (presumably of a God who was near in the Mass). The point may be accepted as one of nineteenth century emphasis,[57] even though Deism would better serve as a contrast to Catholicism than historic Protestantism.

Newman's views were expressed more extensively in the following passage: "Divine worship is simply contemplating our Maker, Redeemer, Sanctifier, and Judge; preaching, conversing, making speeches, arguing, reading, and writing about religion, tend to make us forget Him in ourselves. The ancients worshipped; they went out of their own minds into the infinite temple which was around them. They saw Christ in the Gospels, in the Creed, in the Sacraments, and other rites; in the visible structure and ornaments of His House, in the Altar and in the Cross; and, not content with giving the service of their eyes, they gave Him their voices, their bodies and their time, gave up their rest by night and their leisure by day, all that could evidence the offering of their hearts to him. Theirs was not a service of once a week, or some one day, now and then, painfully, as if ambitiously and lavishly, given to thanksgiving or humiliation; not some extraordinary address to the throne of grace, offered by one for many, when friends met, with much point and impressiveness, and as much like an exhortation, and as little like a prayer, as might be; but every day and every portion of the day was begun and sanctified with devotion.[58] Consider those seven services of the Holy Church Catholic in her best ages, which without encroaching upon her children's duties towards this world,

56 See *Loss and Gain* (1848), p. 291. Newman's criticism of Anglican worldliness is found in the same novel on p. 229; of Methodist subjectivism on p. 56; and of formalism in Anglican worship and triteness in Anglican sermons on p. 20.

57 The Pietistical and Romantic Movements found their best Protestant expositor in Friedrich Schleiermacher's massive experiential theology articulated in *Der christliche Glaube nach den Grundsätzen der Evangelischen Kirche* (1821-1822, greatly revised, 1830-1831).

58 This ironical passage is clearly directed at the Puritan tradition with its "days of humiliation and thanksgiving" and at Evangelicalism in the customary terminology for prayer of an "address to the throne of grace." But Newman is forgetting the tradition of family prayer that characterised the daily prayer life of both Puritans and Evangelicals. For evidence on the former, see the present author's *The Worship of the English Puritans* and for the latter, Charles Smyth, *Simeon and Church Order*.

secured them in their duties to the world unseen. Unwavering, un-flagging, not urged by fits and starts, not heralding forth their feelings, but resolutely, simply, perseveringly, day after day, Sunday after Sunday, fast-day and festival, week by week, season by season, year by year, in youth and in age, through a life, thirty years, forty years, fifty years, in prelude of the everlasting chant before the Throne. . . . O great and noble system, not of the Jews who rested in their rites and privileges, not of Christians who are taken up in their own feelings, and who describe what they should exhibit, but of the true saints of God. . . ."[59]

In re-reading such a passage one cannot doubt that for Newman it was the meeting with the Fathers that stimulated his imagination and made corporate worship for him the communion with the saints, as one cannot doubt that in his private devotions he spoke to God *velut amicus ad amicum*. Newman had republished the *Preces Privatae* of Bishop Lancelot Andrewes as one of the *Tracts of the Times*. Their conciseness, comprehensiveness, and Biblical basis were alike the virtues of Andrewes' *Preces* and Newman's posthumously published *Meditations and Devotions*. Undoubtedly, too, the example of St. Philip Neri, with his tender and unaffected approach to His Lord, also had a profound effect upon Newman's spirituality, and he has given moving testimony to it in his great sermon on "The Mission of St. Philip Neri." In one short paragraph Newman has superbly characterized the approach of the school of St. Ignatius and St. Philip Neri: "An earnest enforcement of interior religion, a jealousy of formal ceremonies, an insisting on obedience rather than sacrifice, on mental discipline rather than fasting or hairshirt, a mortification of the reason, that illumination and freedom of spirit which comes from love; further, a mild and tender rule for the Confessional; frequent confessions, frequent communions, special devotion towards the Blessed Sacrament, these are peculiarities of a particular school in the Church, and St. Ignatius and St. Philip are Masters in it."[60]

It is in his *Meditations and Devotions* that the predominant qualities of Newman's spirituality may be discerned: his scrupulous and naked honesty, and his utter reliance on Divine Grace, the longing for fervour which is itself the proof of fervour, and that numinous awe which is not only the sense of all the distance be-

[59] *Lectures on Justification*, pp. 371-90, treats the theme fully.
[60] Preached in the Oratory, Birmingham and published as No. 12 of *Sermons Preached on Various Occasions*.

tween God and the saint, but also an index of the distance between the saint and the average worldling.

One prayer reads: "I beg Thee, O my Saviour, to recover me! Thy grace alone can do it! I cannot save myself. I cannot recover my lost ground. I cannot turn to Thee, I cannot please Thee, or save my soul without Thee. I shall go from bad to worse, I shall fall from Thee entirely, I shall quite harden myself against my neglect of duty, if I rely on my own strength. I shall make myself my centre instead of making Thee. I shall worship some idol of my own framing instead of Thee, the only true God and my Maker, unless Thou hinder it by Thy grace. O my dear Lord, hear me! I have lived long enough in this undecided, wavering, unsatisfactory state. I wish to be Thy good servant. Be gracious to me, and enable me to be what I know I ought to be."[61]

Another tells of his darkness and longing to be radiant like the saints: "Take me and enable me to live the life of Saints and Angels. Take me out of the anger, the irritability, the sensitiveness, the incapability, the anarchy, in which my soul lies and fill it with Thy fulness. . . . In asking for fervour I ask for all I can need, and all that Thou canst give; for it is the crown of all gifts and virtues. . . . In asking for fervour, I am asking for effectual strength, consistency and perseverance; I am asking for deadness to every human motive, and simplicity of intention to please Thee: I am asking for faith, hope and charity in their most heavenly exercise. In asking for fervour I am asking to be rid of the fear of man, and the desire of his praise; I am asking for the gift of prayer, because it will be so sweet; I am asking for that loyal perception of duty which follows on yearning affection; I am asking for sanctity, peace, and joy, all at once. In asking for fervour I am asking for the brightness of the cherubim and the fire of the seraphim, and the whiteness of all Saints. In asking for fervour, I am asking for that which, while it includes all gifts, is that in which I signally fail. Nothing would be a trouble to me, nothing a difficulty, had I but fervour of soul."[62]

The subtle mind of Newman found it difficult to choose between the relative merits of the Classical and Gothic styles in architecture. In a letter written in 1846 from Milan (a year after his "conversion") he writes of the Church of S. Fidelis: "It is like a Jesuit

---

[61] Pp. 470-71.

[62] Pp. 596f. See also Newman's *Meditation on the Feast of All Saints* with its directions for realising the meaning of this festival of the Church. It can also be found in Wilfrid Ward's *The Life of John Henry Cardinal Newman*, Vol. II, pp. 366-67.

Church, Grecian and Palladian—and I cannot deny that, however my reason may go with Gothic, my heart has ever gone with Grecian. I loved Trinity Chapel at Oxford more than any other building. There is in the Italian style such a simplicity, purity, elegance, beauty, brightness, which I suppose the word 'classical' implies, that it seems to befit the notion of an Angel or Saint. The Gothic style does not seem to me to typify the sanctity or innocence of the Blessed Virgin, or St. Gabriel, or the lightness, grace, and sweet cheerfulness of the elect as the Grecian does. I could go into this beautiful Church, and its polished tall pillars, and its smiling winning altar, all day long without tiring. And it is so calm . . . that it is always a rest to the mind to enter it."[63]

We may assume from his implied denials that he found Gothic architecture and the interiors of such churches too dark, complicated, and naive. While he admired the talents and enthusiasm of Pugin and the new "Goths," he seemed to feel that idealized mediaevalism was no way for a modern Catholic to build for the glory of God and the needs of the contemporary worshippers. This becomes clear in his letter to Ambrose de Lisle Phillips, which stresses the need for Christian doctrine to remain ever the same, while discipline and ritual are continually being adapted: "But the Church while one and the same in doctrine is ever modifying, adapting, varying her discipline and ritual, according to the times. . . . Gothic is now like an old dress, which fitted a man well twenty years back, but must be altered to fit him now. It was once the perfect expression of the Church's ritual at those places at which it was in use; it is not the perfect expression now. It must be altered in detail to become that expression. That is, it must be treated with a freedom which Mr. Pugin will now allow. . . . Now for Oratorians, the birth of the sixteenth century, to assume the architecture simply and unconditionally of the thirteenth, would be as absurd as their putting on them the cowl of the Dominicans or adopting the tonsure of the Carthusians. We do not want a cloister or a Chapter-Room, but an Oratory."[64]

The many-sided Newman is known as a master of English prose, as a religious philosopher of the distinction of Pascal as his theory of the development of dogma shows and of the type of Augustine, for his *Apologia* is a kind of *Confessions*. As a preacher he may be

[63] Wilfrid Ward, *op.cit.*, Vol. I, p. 139.
[64] Cited in Bernard Ware, *The Sequel to Catholic Emancipation*, Vol. II, pp. 255-56.

considered an English Bossuet or Fénelon. In the opinion of Döllinger, Newman was a distinguished patrologist and historian. He was a religious poet and hymnologist of distinction as both *Lead Kindly Light* and *The Dream of Gerontius* show. In our own day, as the works of Henri Brémond and Louis Bouyer demonstrate, Newman's spirituality is being appreciated as never before.[65]

7. The Centrality of the Mass

For Newman as for all Catholics of whatever party or none, the chief means of grace are the Sacraments and, supremely, the Mass. For here the Eternal Sacrifice of the Redeemer in which Christ is both the Host and the Victim is presented anew to God the Father Almighty by the whole Church for the remission of sins and that this corruptible may put on incorruptibility and inherit eternal life. In Newman's excessively didactic novel, *Loss and Gain*, he wrote of the meaning of the Eucharistic Sacrifice for him:

"To me nothing is consoling, so piercing, so thrilling, so overcoming as the Mass, said as it is among us. I could attend Masses for ever and not be tired. . . .

"He becomes present on the altar in flesh and blood, before Whom angels bow and devils tremble. This is that awful event which is the end, and is the interpretation, of every part of the solemnity. Words are necessary, but as means, not as ends; they are mere addresses to the throne of grace, they are instruments of what is far higher, of consecration, of sacrifice. They hurry on as if impatient to fulfil their mission. Quickly they go, the whole is quick; for they are all parts of one integral action. Quickly they go; for they are awful words of sacrifice; they are a work too great to delay upon; as when it was said in the beginning, 'What thou doest, do quickly.' Quickly they pass; for the Lord Jesus goes with them, as He passed along the lake in the days of His flesh, quickly calling first one and then another. Quickly they pass; because as the lightning which shineth from one part of the heaven unto the other, so is the coming of the Son of Man. Quickly they pass; for they are as the words of Moses. . . . And as Moses on the mountain, so we too, 'make haste and bow our heads to the earth and adore.' "[66]

[65] The reference is to Brémond's *The Mystery of Newman* and Bouyer's *Newman, His Life and Spirituality*. Great Christian as Newman was, he was yet abysmally blind to the need of his own day for an expression of social justice as the implication of the Incarnation.

[66] Pt. ii, chap. xx, p. 291 (1848).

This mystery of faith transcends all attempts to explain it, but the Eternal Sacrifice of our Lord underlies all Catholic and Protestant worship, witness, and service. Ullathorne, the sound and solid Midlands bishop, who succeeded Wiseman as Newman's diocesan and the metropolitan in Birmingham, knew well that the Mass was the secret of his self-offering. In his *Autobiography* he repeated the solemn words by which he had been consecrated as a priest, with awe and wonder recalling that "for weeks after I seemed to feel the sacred unction coming on my hands, and to hear the words: *accipite potestatem offerre sacrificium Deo, Missasque celebrare tam pro vivis quam pro defunctis*: and the *accipe spiritum sanctum:* and the exhorting words: *Imitamini quod tractatis; quatenus mortis Dominicae mysterium celebrantes, mortificare membra vestra a vitiis et concupiscentiis omnibus procuretis.*" His further reflections on this august formula were the following: "The thought and feeling with which the priesthood elevated me was that of sacrifice, and of sacrifice demanding sacrifice, and making it appear to be the natural life of the priest, whose soul had undergone a transformation into a new order of existence."[67]

It is in such consecration by grace that we may understand how the sap was rising in the sturdy and ancient, if decimated, forest of oaks of the old English Catholicism, of which the only outward evidence was the restoration of hierarchy in 1850 and the cheering statistics which told that although the number of the Roman Catholics in 1780—the dead of winter—had been only 69,316 by 1851 the "Second Spring" had claimed no less than 252,783 souls.[68] As the Oxford Movement had begun the nineteenth century trend in English worship towards the re-appropriation of tradition, the Renascence of Roman Catholicism accelerated it.

[67] Ed. Shane Leslie, *op.cit.*, pp. 117-18.
[68] The Religious Census of March 30, 1851 disclosed this attendance at Mass.

CHAPTER II

ECCLESIASTICAL ARCHITECTURE: FROM GRECIAN TO GOTHIC

TWO GENERALIZATIONS about the religious architecture of England during the nineteenth century are valid. It was a transition from the classical to the mediaeval models, from the Grecian Revival to the Gothic Revival. In this transition Nonconformity was approximately a generation behind the initiative taken by the Church of England in its architectural changes.

1. Anglican Architecture[1]

After England had fought the French wars, there came about a shift in the balance and taste of society, so that "an aristocratic society with bourgeois leanings had become a bourgeois society with aristocratic leanings."[2] The new generation of architects after Waterloo set out to serve these aspirations in two parallel and unopposed movements, since denominated the "Greek Revival" and the "Gothic Revival." Ecclesiastical architecture took over the prevailing patterns in opulent domestic architecture. It is not surprising, however, that in religious architecture the Greek Revival preceded the Gothic, for it was largely only a modification of the Roman Revival characteristic of eighteenth century ecclesiastical architecture, whereas the Gothic Revival required the stimulus of the Oxford Movement[3] to make Protestant and frequently rationalist Englishmen change radically to accept the view that mediaeval Western Catholic architecture was an expression of "the age of faith." Indeed, the Roman Revival lived well on into the nineteenth century.

Its finely-proportioned dignity, simplicity and patrician qualities are subtly evoked by a poem of John Betjeman's:[4]

---

[1] The subject was also treated briefly in Chapters II and XI of *Worship and Theology in England*, Vol. 3, "From Watts and Wesley to Maurice, 1690-1850."

[2] John Summerson, *Architecture in Britain 1530 to 1830*, p. 305.

[3] Nor should the important contribution of the Cambridge Camden Society, founded in 1841, and its influential monthly, *The Ecclesiologist*, be forgotten. See the present author's preceding Vol. 3 of this series, *Worship and Theology in England*, "From Watts and Wesley to Maurice," 1690-1850, Chapter X, section 1.

[4] "Verses turned in aid of a Public Subscription (1952) towards the restoration of the Church of St. Katherine Chiselhampton, Oxon." It is included in *A Few Late Chrysanthemums*, pp. 8-9.

How warm the many candles shine
On SAMUEL DOWBIGGIN'S design
    For this interior neat.
Those high box pews of Georgian days
Which screen us from the public gaze
    When we make answer meet;

How gracefully their shadow falls
On bold pilasters down the walls
    And on the pulpit high.
The chandeliers would twinkle gold
As pre-Tractarian sermons roll'd
    Doctrinal, sound and dry.

From that West gallery no doubt
The viol and serpent tooted out
    The Tallis tune to Ken,
And firmly at the end of prayers
The clerk below the pulpit stairs
    Would thunder out "Amen."

The impetus for new Anglican architecture was supplied by the Act of Parliament of 1818, which provided for the expenditure of a million pounds on the building of churches in London and the Provinces. The first of the Greek churches was erected by Thomas Hardwick, and it was St. Marylebone, built in 1813 and later greatly enlarged. A far more important example of the new style was St. Pancras Church, begun in 1819 and completed in 1822, whose architect was H. W. Inwood. The building, with its great portico supported by six vast columns, is an imitation of the Erechtheum, fragments of which had been brought back from Greece by Lord Elgin. The octagonal steeple with cylindical central column is a combination of elements of the Tower of the Winds and the Choragic Monument of Lysicrates.[5] Less impressive than these two churches were the Grecian style churches of the Commissioners who employed the three architects of the Board of Works—Nash, Soane, and Smirke. Their chief concern was how to crowd two thousand worshippers into a rectangular box with galleries and to make an exceedingly impressive exterior entrance at the west end. In essence, they were more Greek and imitative

---

[5] Summerson, *op.cit.*, p. 317.

and less original and graceful examples of Wren's "auditory" edifices; they represented the last expression of Rationalism. The Commissioners built two hundred and fourteen churches and the great majority of them, one hundred and seventy-four, were in the Gothic Revival style. Most of these, however, succeeded the beginning of the Oxford Movement and were proof that a new conception of worship, in which the sermon was relegated to an inferior position, had supervened.

The enthusiasm for Gothic architecture was a literary rather than an architectural inspiration.[6] Gentlemen like Horace Walpole gothicized their Georgian mansions with pinnacles, battlements,[7] and pointed windows, whereas plutocrats like William Beckford built Gothic palaces like Fonthill (1807). The Romantic movement in the writings of Sir Walter Scott, Victor Hugo, and Goethe changed Gothic architecture from the exotic fancy of the connoisseurs into a profound popular interest. On the Continent the Catholic Revival coincided with the Restoration of 1815 and implied autocratic "Legitimism" in politics, Romanticism in literature, and the Gothic style in architecture. In England Gothic did not have such political associations, but it was certainly an expression of Romanticism and of Tradition in the revulsion from the turbulence of the French Revolution.

The motives for Gothic ecclesiastical architecture on the part of the Commissioners were as much practical as aesthetic, for Gothic could use brick, whereas the Classical style required costly porticoes and pediments of stone. The many Gothic churches built between 1818 and 1833 were sponsored by the Evangelicals. It was only when the Romanticism of Sir Walter Scott yielded to the revived Catholicism of the Tractarians that the association of Gothic with mediaeval religion was asserted. This assertion would, indeed, have made it most unlikely that the English Free Churches would have used a Gothic architectural style, but for the popularization of the view in the writings of Ruskin that the Classical style was rationalist and humanist and the Gothic style distinctively Christian.

The chief publisher of the gospel of Gothic was Pugin, who had an excessively roseate impression of the Catholic Middle Ages. His most effective propaganda was expressed by word and illustration in a volume entitled, *Contrasts: or A Parallel between the Noble Edifices of the Middle Ages and the Corresponding Buildings*

---

[6] Kenneth Clark, *The Gothic Revival: An Essay in the History of Taste.*
[7] Walpole amusingly cited Deuteronomy 22:8 as his authority for these.

of the Present Day; showing the Present Decay of Taste (1836).[8] The Gothic Revivalists in England were not indiscriminate in their approval of all types of Gothic architecture. On the contrary, they deliberately chose to revive the "Decorated" style of Gothic, in preference to the Early "Pointed" or the late "Perpendicular." The former antedated the great symbolical interpreter, Durandus, and the latter was associated with the worldly and Erastian pride of the Tudors. While the judgment cannot be quarrelled with aesthetically, it unfortunately led to great practical difficulties in that it required a subtlety, a precision in detailed carving, and an expertise in craftsmanship that few local masons could command.

The Gothic style was particularly fitted for the expression of Tractarian views of worship, in which two emphases were dominant—the importance of the dramatic altar and the significance of symbolism. For the ecclesiologists of the nineteenth century a church was not an auditory edifice as it was for Wren and the Latitudinarians. It was essentially the sacred place where the altar, on which the sacrifice of the Eucharist was re-presented to the Father, was central and yet remote, at the end of the far-off chancel which divided the people from the priest and the surpliced choir. In the planning of the ecclesiologists symbolical considerations also predominated. The triple division of the church into the two sides of the chancel and long nave represented the Holy Trinity, according to some, while, according to others, the nave represented the Church militant, the chancel the Church triumphant, and the chancel arch the faithful death of the righteous soul.[9] The altar was dramatized by raising the level of the chancel above the nave, and this also had the effect of stressing the significance of the clergy as being in the Apostolical Succession.

The very idea of worship itself had changed from the eighteenth to the nineteenth century. In the earlier century Church men understood by worship the congregation's participation with the clergy in the prayers and praises of the Liturgy. In the nineteenth century, however, worship is thought of as pre-eminently the work of clergy and choir, with the lessons and sermon as an accommodation for the benefit of the laity. The aim of the ecclesiologists is "not so much that the services should be a corporate offering of priest and people, but that they should be offered by clergy and choir in

8 Pugin built sixty-five Gothic churches in the United Kingdom.
9 G. W. O. Addleshaw and F. Etchells, *The Architectural Setting of Anglican Worship*, pp. 204 f.

such a way as to call out from the people an attitude of awe and adoration."[10]

The first Anglican neo-Gothic church was St. Mary's, Bathwick, Bath, built by John Pinch between 1814 and 1820. It is an excellent imitation of the Gothic style, since battlements, finials, and pinnacles are delicate in their upward thrust, and the east end tower incorporates a large east window, a clerestory window above it of equal width, and a topmost section including the belfry, all of admirable proportions.[11] It was another Gothic Revival church of the Provinces, St. George's Edgbaston, Birmingham, the work of Thomas Rickman (1819-1822)[12] which was of far greater distinction than the London neo-Gothic churches.[13] The first Commissioners' church in the new Gothic style to be built in London was St. Luke's, Chelsea, the design of James Savage and undertaken by parochial initiative in 1820. In comparison with the work of Pinch and Rickman it is poorly proportioned. Of the more economical, if not cheap, Gothic churches in London, Charles Barry was the architect, whose best-known essay in Gothic was the Houses of Parliament.

Considering the extraordinary proliferation of Gothic churches in England right down to the designing of the great Gothic cathedral of Liverpool begun in 1903 by Sir Giles Gilbert Scott, it seemed that Augustus Pugin had convinced England that there was only one type of "Christian" architecture and that was Gothic. The name most widely associated with Gothic churches in the three middle decades of the century was Sir Giles Scott, an unequal architect who erected St. Giles' Camberwell, St. Mary Abbotts Kensington, and St. Mary's Cathedral, Edinburgh, on the one hand, and yet perpetrated that essay in industrial rococo, the Albert Memorial. One of the most ingenious of the Victorian Gothic architects was William Butterfield, who was a great believer in modernizing Gothic by using bricks of different surface texture and colouring for making his vast walls more interesting. One of the most intriguing examples of his work is to be found in Keble College, Oxford. G. E. Street and J. L. Pearson proved able to design Gothic fanes with some notable independence, as the former's Royal Courts of Justice and the latter's Truro Cathedral demonstrate. The Gothic

10 *Ibid.*, pp. 208-09.
11 See plate 184 of Summerson, *op.cit.*
12 See Rickman's remarkable book of text and engravings, *An Attempt to discriminate the styles of Gothic Architecture.*
13 See plate 185A in Summerson, *op.cit.*

impulse was not spent even in the last decades of the century, when Bodley, Blomfield, and Sedding carried on the tradition with vigour and dignity. Thus it came about that the oldest and newest Anglican churches were unmistakably Gothic in appearance and classical churches were regarded both as old-fashioned and as worldly in appearance. This Victorian judgment is itself the measure of the overwhelming success of the Gothic Revival.

2. *Dissenting Victorian Architecture in General*

The Dissenting architecture of the period did, indeed, prove imitative of the Anglican, but at least in its very pretentiousness it demonstrated that it had outgrown what has been exaggeratedly called "the squalid sluttery of Dissent." To be sure, the older stereotype was still repeated, but it is a caricature and not the character of Dissenting chapels which Dickens describes when he writes: "It was a little Bethel, a Bethel of the smallest dimensions, with a small number of small pews, and a small pulpit in which a small gentleman (by trade a shoemaker and by calling a Divine) was delivering in a by no means small voice, a by no means small sermon."[14]

The critics cannot at the same time insist that Dissenting architecture was as crudely utilitarian as a warehouse, and a snobbish imitation of the Anglican architecture of a bygone generation. The truth lies closer to the latter alternative, and this is admitted by foe and friend alike. John Betjeman, a present-day architect and Anglo-Catholic poet, pokes fun at the miniature *mimesis* of Dissenting Gothic chapels:

> And calmly rise on smoky skies
> Of intersected wires
> The Nonconformist spirelets
> And the Church of England spires.[15]

B. L. Manning, a percipient Congregational historian, remarks that Dissenting architecture is merely the reflection of the domestic architecture of its period, except when it imitates Anglican styles, and then it is a generation late.[16] Martin Briggs, a Congregational architect, believes that the Gothic chapels of Dissent in Victorian days were an attempt to remove in their days of affluence the sense

---

14 Cited by E. Gordon Rupp in *The Listener*, issue of March 17, 1955, p. 470a.
15 From the poem "South London Sketch" in *New Bats in Old Belfries*.
16 *The Congregational Quarterly*, Vol. v (1927), pp. 290-91.

of social stigma under which they had laboured for so long by building places of worship made to look like the new Anglican churches: "It was thus that the starveling spires, the shoddy tracery and the hideous coloured glass of these mid-Victorian chapels came to be derided more bitterly than the solid Georgian classical chapels or the squat and homely 'little Bethels' ever had been; for the 'Gothic' examples are manifestly pretentious, and snobbery is much more detestable than simplicity."[17]

Snobbishness or a desire to outdo the Anglicans could not, however, have exhausted the motivations of the Free Churchmen who desired to build in the Gothic manner. One of the most distinguished of the Free Church divines of the nineteenth and twentieth centuries, Peter Taylor Forsyth, gave sound reasons for preferring Gothic to classical designs for church architecture. Gothic seemed to him to suggest aspiration and mystery with its upward-soaring lines, while the clarity, compactness, and predominance of horizontal lines in classical architecture reflected a sober and decorous rationality. According to him, the Greek temple was broad and not high. As the eye is induced to travel along its horizontal lines, it satisfies rather than aspires. Classical architecture is stable, not inspiring; calmly confident of its own beauty and grace. On the other hand, Forsyth claims that the Gothic church is "the lovely symbol of man's thirst for the infinite" and "is thrust into a fine question heavenward." It is, for him, the soul of the *Imitation of Christ* projected into stone. Its lines are all vertical and aspiring:

"The pointed arch, reproduced in great and small throughout the whole fabric, the upright line instead of the classical horizontal, the vast height of the pillars prolonged into the roof, the effect produced by bundles of small pillars rolled into one column and carrying the eye upward along their small light shafts, the judicious use of external carving so as to add to the effect of height instead of reducing it, the pinnacles and finials which run up everywhere on the outside, the tower, and still more the spire, placed above all these—the total effect was to make the spirit travel upwards with the eye and lose itself in the infinity of space. The whole building seems chained to earth in fixed flight. . . . It rises like an exhalation from the soil. The fabric seems almost organic and tremulous with life. No architecture like the Gothic so spiritualizes, refines, and

[17] *Puritan Architecture and Its Future*, pp. 38-39.

casts heavenward the substance which it handles. It volatizes the stone. It gives the garment of praise for the spirit of heaviness."[18]

That Forsyth's was not the unanimous Free Church view on Gothic may be seen from the title of a tract by J. A. Tabor, who, with such a name, appropriately beat the old denominational drum, in *A Nonconformist Protest against the Papacy of Modern Dissenting Architecture imitative of Roman Catholic Churches*.[19] It was precisely to meet such prejudice that John Ruskin had bent his endeavours to persuade all Protestants that Gothic architecture was the most Christian form of church building. He wrote, in contrasting contemporary humanist architecture with the Gothic: "The Gothic was good for God's worship, but this was good for man's worship. The Gothic had fellowship with all hearts: it could frame a temple for the prayer of nations, or sink into the poor man's winding stair. But there was an architecture that would not shrink. The proud princes and lords rejoiced in it. It was full of insult to the poor. It would not be built of materials at the poor man's hand; it would not roof itself with thatch or shingle and black oak beams; it would not wall itself with rough stone or brick; it would not pierce itself with small windows where they were needed. It would be hewn of stone . . . it would have . . . in lordly order and of stately size . . . its stairs and pillars . . . its wings and its corridors as if the world were its own."[20]

It is well, however, to remember that there was not an immediate change from the old, grave, white-painted Puritan meeting-houses to the new Gothic. As a preparation for this revolution in Nonconformist architectural taste, there were two other factors. The first was the influence of the Wesleyan Methodist chapels, and the second was the Greek Revival.

The rest of Nonconformity came in time to admire the church buildings of the newest denomination to join its ranks, the Methodist. The squat meeting-houses became longer and wider; they displayed open galleries and plaster of lighter colours; they installed lower pews and built platforms and rostrums where musical displays might be given more advantageously and conveniently. This "questionable taste which substituted the gay Methodistical chapel for the grave Puritan meeting-house is now giving way to a love

---

[18] *Christ on Parnassus*, pp. 183 f.
[19] Published Ipswich, 1863.
[20] *The Stones of Venice*, Vol. III, Part II, section 39.

of ecclesiastical edifices with Gothic columns, arches, vaulted roofs, and lofty spires, called 'Congregational Churches,' " writes a Congregational theological college principal in the year 1872.[21]

The first of the Nonconformist churches to be built in the Greek Revival style was Carr's Lane Chapel, Birmingham, about the year 1820. Between then and 1847 some remarkable examples of the Grecian style chapels had been built by Congregationalists alone. One of the most impressive was Great George Street, Liverpool. This was a great rectangular church with a length of eight wide pilastered windows reaching from the nave to the top of the galleries. Its imposing entrance had a semi-circular roof supported on six Corinthian pillars and approached by an impressive series of semi-circular steps. A substantial dome or cupola completed the appearance of dignity, solidity, and material prosperity that the Liverpool merchants who were its supporters wished it to convey. It is not without significance that the author of an article in the official *Congregational Year Book for 1847* on the architecture of Nonconformist Chapels takes considerable pride in the improvement of the architecture of his denomination. Of the first Grecian chapel, Carr's Lane, Birmingham, he says that "it was the first in the kingdom that combined a due regard for taste and comfort," and he adds, a little smugly, "it is certainly a place of worship which the members of any denomination of Christians might acknowledge as their own with satisfaction and complacency."[22] The same author hopes fervently that "the religion of barns" is passing away from among Nonconformists. His motive is clear in the following admonition: "When money is to be spent for the services of God, we are bound to use it with taste and judgment, so as to attract, rather than repel persons of intelligence and respectability."[23] Thus might any Anglican Latitudinarian have written! The Puritan emphasis on truth was being replaced by tact, the Puritan fear of idolatry by the Victorian Nonconformist fear of not being respectable.

3. Methodism and the Chapels of the People

John Betjeman has a most perceptive essay on the history of Free Church architecture buried in the tenth chapter of his volume *First and Last Loves*. There he characterizes Methodist church-building as "the architecture of enthusiasm" and the "architecture of the

[21] R. Halley, *Lancashire: its Puritanism and Nonconformity*, pp. 437 f.
[22] J[ohn] B[lackburn], *Remarks on Ecclesiastical Architecture as applied to Nonconformist Chapels* in *The Congregational Year Book for 1847*, pp. 150 f.
[23] *Ibid.*

50

1. St. Pancras Church, London

2. St. Aloysius Church, Somers Town, London

3. Methodist Church, Burford, Oxfordshire

4. All Saints, Margaret Street, London

5. A Puginesque Panorama

9. Westminster Chapel (Congregational)

8. St. Michael and All Saints, Croydon

10. Mansfield College, Oxford

11. The King's Weigh House (Congregational) Church, London

14. Charles Haddon Spurgeon

13. Frederick William Robertson

12. Robert William Dale

people." These were, indeed, its essential traits.[24] Built originally as overflow preaching houses when the Established Church was too far away, too inimical, or too small to hold the numbers of Methodist neophytes, they resembled the meeting-houses of the older Dissent rather than the Anglican Georgian churches, except that they were larger, flimsier structures that "did not scorn a bit of carpenter's or plasterer's moulding here and there by way of internal embellishment."[25] These were erected by pious merchants whose pockets were as good as their hearts. They reflected the prosperity of the great provincial cities after the depression following upon the Napoleonic Wars and the opulence of the shopkeepers in a nation of shopkeepers. In exterior, apart from the absence of bells or towers, they might be indistinguishable from the Commissioners' Grecian or Perpendicular of a new Anglican church, or from the similar styles of other city Nonconformist churches. Even their interiors did not greatly differ from an Anglican proprietary chapel built for Evangelicals, where the pulpit dominated the altar. The one obvious difference would be the organ and the mixed choir in close proximity to it. A contemporary account of the Wesleyan Chapel in Stanhope Street, Liverpool, built in 1820 says, "A powerful fine wind organ by Bewsher and Fleetwood gives solemnity to the services; and the 'semi-religious light' falling through an oval window of stained glass, executed by Messrs. Lyon and Son, imparts a sacred shade to the communion-table."[26]

The chapel architecture of the people was rather to be found in the small towns and the country in the mid-nineteenth century. They were not as impressive structures as the city chapels, but they exhibited the loving craftsmanship of their members and their interiors were often a charm and a delight. Pale pink walls, ceilings of Chippendale Gothic, high pews of grained-oak, white gallery-fronts, double-rows of clear-glass sashed windows around three sides of the building, and a fine mahogany pulpit inlaid and moulded on the fourth wall were a not infrequent sight, and two such chapels of the people can still be seen almost in their original and unspoiled state in Bridport, Dorset. They grew more individual-

[24] Cf. Thomas Jackson, *The Centenary of Wesleyan Methodism*, p. 111: "In these buildings of primitive Methodism, elegance of architecture was little studied. They were plain and substantial, intended for use, and not for ornament. The most remarkable circumstance connected with them was the amplitude of their accommodation for the poor. The pulpits also were large, and contained a bench of considerable length for the use of the Preachers who might be expected successively to address the congregations. . . ."
[25] John Betjeman, *First and Last Loves*, p. 97.
[26] *Ibid.*, p. 102.

istic as the century sped on its way. "They are," says Betjeman, "the public equivalent of the parlour mantel-piece." They were the nearest nineteenth century equivalent to the production of the mediaeval guilds.[27] All the members or adherents of the Nonconformist congregations contributed their pennies or their skills. It was truly a communal religious project. The builder would supply the plan and the labour; the builder's merchant the best in tiles, stonecaps, and dressings; the ironmonger provided the iron railings and the lamps; the timber merchant gave the wood; other builders provided window frames and coloured glass; the carpenters in the congregation assembled the pews and the painters did the graining and stencilling; the linen-draper saw to the cushions and the coverings; and when it was all finished the local stationer produced the illustrated account of the opening ceremony. Their aim was to provide for God a home better than the best in the entire circuit; and the pews of pitch pine, the pink or green walls with their geometrical stencillings, the elegant brass lamp-brackets on the pulpit, and the carpeted aisles, all sang to the glory of God in recognition of their conversion and calling, the gift of His Spirit.[28] It was in such chapels that a good deal of individuality and even of idiosyncrasy of expression in architecture were to be found. The absence of imitation, the use of local materials, the freedom from normative canons of taste, and the uninhibited pleasure in gaudiness, all contributed to make this architecture vigorously independent.[29]

It has been admitted that the city churches of Dissent were often an imitation of their Anglican counterparts undertaken a generation later. In addition, however, there was a keen sense of competition among the Dissenters themselves, each denomination in a neighbourhood trying to outdo its fellow denomination. Here, again, the satiric pen of Betjeman has admirably caught this feeling in his poem on Competition, with its accurate list of dates for the improvement:

[27] Compare with Betjeman's enthusiastic view of Methodist country chapels a highly critical account of Cornish chapels ". . . these square naked granite boxes . . . hideous to look at and a blot and disfigurement to the village and to God's earth, are assuredly an insult to every person endowed with a sense of beauty and fitness." This citation is from Chap. XIII of W. H. Hudson's *The Land's End* (1908).

[28] This paragraph owes much to John Betjeman's *First and Last Loves*, pp. 105-06.

[29] In no area was this highly coloured and variegated independence more inventive than in Wales, where Dissenting architecture has the naïve vigour of the Douanier Rousseau's painting. Some outstanding examples have been recorded by John Piper.

	Dates
THE INDEPENDENT Calvinistic	1810

Methodist Chapel is gone,
Dust in the galleries, dust on the stairs,
There was no one to carry it on.

And a Norman New Jerusalem Church   1840
Was raised on the sacred site,
Where they praised the Lord and praised the Lord
By incandescent light.

The Gothic is bursting over the way
With Evangelical Song,
For the pinnacled Wesley Memorial Church   1860
Is over a hundred strong,
And what is a New Jerusalem
Gas-lit and yellow-wall'd
To a semi-circular pitch-pine sea
With electric light install'd?

Crack your walls, Wesley Memorial!
Shine bright, you electrolier!
Your traceried windows may rock with song,
New Jerusalem fall in fear;
Short lived! Short lived! in this world of ours
Are Triumph and Praise and Prayer.
What of Mount Carmel Baptists (Strict),   1875
For they've central heating there?[30]

4. Baptist Architecture

It is extremely difficult to distinguish between the largely similar styles of the Dissenting chapels of the nineteenth century, yet these differences did exist. The earlier Baptist chapels had the simple austerity of the meeting-houses of the Society of Friends, as, for example, Cote in Oxfordshire. No other Protestant denomination, with the exception of the Quakers, gave so genuine an encouragement to the doctrine of the priesthood of all believers. In early Baptist worship this was expressed in the elders' pew. This may well be, as H. L. Short suggests,[31] the origin of the rostrum or platform for several speakers which became so marked a feature

[30] *Mount Zion or In Touch with the Infinite.*
[31] *The Listener*, issue of March 17, 1955, p. 472b of an article "Changing styles in Nonconformist Architecture."

of the Nonconformist preaching chapels of the nineteenth century. The Baptists were, on the whole, very conservative, especially in keeping to the older Puritan and classical types of architecture. The chief innovators were the Methodists and the Unitarians, the chief custodians of tradition the Baptists and Congregationalists. Walter Wilson's description of the interior of the General Baptist Church at Elim Court, Fetter Lane, London, was not untypical of most nineteenth century Baptist churches, though this was built in 1790 and was exceptional in that period in boasting an organ: "It is a square substantial brick building, with four galleries extending round the place; and behind the pulpit is placed an organ."[32] Sometimes the pure functionalism of the auditory type of building was modified by some ornamentation on the front. Such, for example, was the case in the Baptist church built in Newport in the Isle of Wight in 1778, which complacently advertised itself as possessing "comfortable pewes" and a façade "after the Greekan style."[33] The Baptists were late in accepting the influence of Gothic. The most renowned example of the Baptist classical style was the vast "Spurgeon's Tabernacle" built in 1860, with accommodation for 5,000 people and with three tiers of galleries. Hardly less celebrated was Dr. Joseph Parker's "City Temple," a Congregational classical temple built in 1874. The most splendid example of a neo-Gothic Baptist Church was the Coats Memorial Church of Paisley (1893).

5. Congregational Architecture

Congregational church building copied the Anglican styles, moving from Greek to Gothic. This was not surprising, since their city supporters were comfortable members of the middle class. In *The Congregationalist* of 1878, J. A. Clapham has a most illuminating article expounding the attractions and the dangers of the Congregational attraction for Gothic buildings. He believes that the earliest examples of Congregational Gothic were failures because they did not adapt Gothic to the Free Church conception of worship; that is, the wide pillars hid the preacher from the congregation and the side pulpit made him almost inaudible, and the general air of dimness and traditionalism consorted ill with the genius of Congregationalism. He warns that Congregational Church building committees must be on their guard to fulfil the necessary

[32] *The History and Antiquities of Dissenting Churches.*
[33] *The Baptist Quarterly,* Vol. IV (1928-1929), p. 312.

conditions of adaptation, which are the following: "If there be no stone pillars dividing the aisles from the nave, if the galleries be carried round three sides of the building, not being too high (which is the prevailing mistake in Methodist churches), if the roof be underdrawn, and the transepts (if any) not too deep, and the side windows not too small, there is not the slightest reason why the church should not be well adapted for Congregational worship."[34]

Granted these very considerable safeguards, Clapham was even willing to argue in favour of Gothic. It is economical; it is the essential English monumental style, for "the noblest architectural monuments left us by our ancestors are the splendid churches, abbeys, and cathedrals scattered throughout our land." Further, he argues that "as the curved line is more beautiful than the straight line, so is Gothic more beautiful than classical architecture." He even believes that a case can be made out for connecting Liberty with Gothic and Tyranny with classical architecture, since "classical architecture is closely associated with the tyranny of the Stuarts, the declension of the country to a third-rate power in Europe, and the ignoble reign of the Georges. . . ."[35] He leaves the realm of imagination for more sober assertion when he declares that a Gothic church really looks like a church and place of worship. He insists, in condemnation of classic architecture, that "We have been stopped in front of one of the largest classical Congregational churches, and been asked the question, 'What is it?' 'Is it a town-hall?' 'Is it a railway-station?' " Defender and champion as he is of good Gothic architecture, he is contemptuous of "Carpenter's Gothic."

When Congregationalism accepted Gothic, it experimented in all the styles, even if some of the Italian variations of Gothic resembled nothing so much as the more opulent middle class villas of the day. The first large Congregational church in London to be erected in the new Gothic style was Christ Church in Westminster Bridge Road (1872), with accommodation for 2,500 sittings.[36] The striking exterior with its noble spire looks genuinely Gothic, but the interior has the form of a Greek cross enclosing a central octagon. Three arms of the cross are taken up by galleries, the fourth accommodates the Communion-table and side-pulpit. The

---

[34] Vol. VII, pp. 202-07 of article entitled "Gothic Congregational Churches."
[35] The Whig interpretation of history seems utterly impartial as contrasted with this Whig interpretation of architectural styles, and only goes to show how close was the correlation between Victorian Dissent and Victorian political Liberalism.
[36] See figure 8 of M. S. Briggs, *op.cit.*, for illustration of its plan.

question is: Did the architect in adapting mediaevalism for Free Church use entirely change its character? The neighbouring Westminster Chapel (1863-1865) also built for the Congregationalists is only by the use of considerable charity described as Gothic at all, although that was its intention. Its oval brick interior, if it suggests any known type of ecclesiastical architecture, bears some remote resemblance to Italianate Romanesque. The flat ceiling and the immense rostrum and pulpit suggest a conference or concert hall rather than a church. Other romantic, if not definitely Romanesque, experiments in Congregational architecture were Union Chapel, Islington (1876), designed by James Cubitt; The King's Weigh House Church in Mayfair, a notable centre of liturgical experiments, designed by Alfred Waterhouse, R.A., in an oval shape with a gallery completely surrounding it; and Lyndhurst Road, Hampstead (1895), the work of the same architect, but substituting an irregular hexagon for an oval.

Congregationalism also had many examples of the more typical Gothic church structures. Among these were: Albion Church,[37] Ashton-under-Lyne near Manchester, Trinity Church in Woodhouse Lane, Leeds (1900), and the Congregational Church in Otley (1899). Perhaps the finest example of Free Church neo-Gothic building was the work of Basil Champneys in Mansfield College, Oxford in the Perpendicular style. The stone, the carvings, and the proportions are of the best, and of the fine chapel with its statues in stone and its stained-glass representations of the Biblical and ecclesiastical saints of all generations and denominations, Heiler has said that it is "the most Catholic place in Oxford."

These Gothic or near-Gothic buildings were the pride of the Congregational denomination in the nineteenth century, but a modern architect of the same denominational persuasion holds entirely different views. Claiming that they are too pretentious and suggest "the rich man's darling" rather than the "House of God," he insists that they are too costly to build today, and that their conservative outlook and opulently ecclesiastical appearance are a denial of the spirit of Protestant Nonconformity, which would be better served by a modern adaptation of the style of the Puritan meeting-house.[38]

Two novelists provide their vivid accounts of the older Dissenting

---

[37] See plate IX of A. L. Drummond's *The Church Architecture of Protestantism* for an illustration of the interior.
[38] M. S. Briggs, *op.cit.*, pp. 48-49.

architecture, simple, dignified, unpretentious, and humble. William Hale White is probably recalling the Bunyan Meeting Chapel in Bedford of his boyhood as he writes: "We were marched across the road into the chapel, a large old-fashioned building dating from the time of Charles II. The floor was covered with high pews. The roof was supported by four tall wooden pillars which ran from the ground to the ceiling, and the galleries by shorter pillars. There was a large oak pulpit on one side against the wall, and down below, immediately under the minister, was the 'singing pew,' where the singers and musicians sat, the musicians being performers on the clarionet, flute, violin and violin-cello. Right in front was a long enclosure, called the communion-pew, which was usually occupied by a large number of the poorer members of the congregation.[39]

The later Gothic or Romanesque "cathedrals" of the Congregationalists would, with their affluent ornateness, have repelled the poor. Congregationalism "on parade" had a pomp which seemed to have forgotten its ancestry of only a generation before. Mrs. Oliphant pictures this ancestry with a fidelity that must have been painful for the well-heeled members of Westminster Chapel or of Lyndhurst Road, Hampstead, to recall. She is describing a Midland town: "Towards the west end of Grove Street in Carlingford, on the shabby side of the street, stood a red brick building, presenting a pitched gable terminated by a curious little belfry, not intended for any bell, and looking not unlike a handle to lift up the edifice by to public observation. This was Salem Chapel, the only Dissenting place of worship in Carlingford. It stood in a narrow strip of ground, just as the little houses that flanked it on either side stood in their gardens, except that the enclosure of the chapel was flowerless and sombre, and showed at the farther end a few sparsely-scattered tombstones—unmeaning slabs, such as the English mourner loves to inscribe his sorrow on. On either side of this little tabernacle were the humble houses—little detached boxes, each two storeys high, each fronted by a little flower pot— clean, respectable, meagre, little habitations, which contributed most largely to the ranks of the congregation in the chapel. The big houses opposite, which turned their backs and staircase windows to the street, took little notice of the humble Dissenting community."[40] Whether Congregationalism, in going Gothic, lost its

39 *The Autobiography of Mark Rutherford*, Chap. I.
40 Mrs. Margaret Oliphant's *Salem Chapel*, from the first chapter of which the citation is taken, first appeared in serial form in *Blackwood's Magazine* in 1862.

own tradition or not, it must be acknowledged that the journey from "bare barn" to the King's Weigh House symbolized a revolution that took place in the social status and the liturgical ideals of the denomination.

6. Methodist "Gothick"

The earlier Methodist architecture of enthusiasm supported by pious merchant donors, and the smaller country churches of the people, has been considered earlier in this chapter. It remains only to consider the phenomenal attraction the Gothic style had for Methodists during the very time when this Dissenting denomination was most rapidly augmenting its numbers. In this connection, the most revealing document is a work put out in 1850 by the Rev. F. J. Jobson bearing the title, *Chapel and School Architecture, as appropriate to the Buildings of Nonconformists, particularly to those of the Wesleyan Methodists with Practical Directions for the erection of Chapels and School Houses*. It is worth noting that this was an official Methodist publication, consisting of papers once printed in successive issues of *The Watchman* and published on the recommendation of the Methodist Conference of 1849, and it is dedicated to the redoubtable Secretary of the Conference, Dr. Jabez Bunting. Its author, Jobson, had studied ecclesiastical architecture under Edward James Wilson, architect of Lincoln, and a great contributor to the revival of Gothic architecture in England in stone and in print.

Jobson wisely admits that there are several critics of Gothic building and attempts to answer them. To the charge that a spiritual religion does not need forms, he insists "it is no proof of . . . eminent spirituality that men build better houses for themselves than they build for God,"[41] a reply at least as venerable as Richard Hooker. To the second charge that the primitive Christians were unconcerned with the proportions and forms of their places of worship, Jobson replies that this was because they were banned and persecuted, but as soon as the open celebration of their religion was permitted, they began to build no mean temples. To the specific charge that Gothic is an unsuitable style to imitate because Gothic churches were originally built at a time when religion had decayed and become corrupt, he finds it necessary to make a longer reply.

---

[41] *Chapel and School Architecture* . . . , *op.cit.*, p. 7.

He claims there are four major styles of architecture: the Egyptian, Grecian, Roman, and the Gothic. But "Gothic architecture is Christian architecture, as Egyptian, Greek and Roman are pagan."[42] Plainly, the Cambridge ecclesiologists have become the tutors of Nonconformity. Its leading characteristic is the pointed arch. Not only is this a Christian style, but it is also an English style which developed from the Norman domesticated in England by William the Conqueror. Of what the Abbé Suger and Durandus did for the erection and symbolical interpretation of Gothic in France he is entirely ignorant, but the patriotic motif was good propaganda for an expanding imperialistic England.

He distinguishes the Gothic in three classes: the Early English, the Decorated, and the Perpendicular styles. "There is in the Decorative style a greater degree of beauty and of chaste conception apparent, than in any of them."[43] Its greatest English exponent was William of Wykeham, Bishop of Winchester, and it is, he claims, often known as "Pure Gothic." Its leading characteristics are: the expansion and more graceful turning of the pointed arch, the enlarging and dividing of windows into many lights, the window-head filled with flowing tracery (wheels, flowers, and geometrical forms), large and lofty central towers with advanced spires, roofs framed into arches and spandrils (as at Salisbury and Lichfield), vaulted stone groining girded with ribs and bound by the architectural knots of the "bosses," parapets pierced, the interior enriched with complex screen and ornate tombs, the exterior strengthened with flying buttresses. For a Methodist Jobson proved himself an erudite and perceptive antiquarian.

His immediate problem, however, was to prove "the propriety and economy of Gothic Architecture applied to Chapel Building."[44] The Reformation in the contemptuous phrase of John Knox rejected music and organs as a mere "kist o' whistles." But they are now to be found even in Nonconformist chapels. So it will be with Gothic architecture; "it shall, with all its surpassing flexibility and unbounded power of adaptation, be again used in the service of God. It is now reviving; and is, more or less, employed by every Christian denomination."[45] Like the Congregationalist J. A. Clapham, Jobson defends Gothic architecture as a style that proclaims a church to be a church without the possibility of mistake.

He criticizes the inappropriateness of existing Methodist chapels

42 *Ibid.*, pp. 15-16. 43 *Ibid.*, p. 31.
44 *Ibid.*, p. 41. 45 *Ibid.*, p. 42.

for the sacred function of worship; if built in the country, they are like barns; if built in the cities, more like warehouses or factories than houses of God. Others, again, resemble concert-rooms or made-up shop-like fronts. The only possible excuse for them is that they were originally built as temporary and ancillary to the parish churches, and were the churches of fervent and poor hard-working men with more urgent tasks than studying ecclesiastical architecture.

His apologia is summed up by an instructive and illustrated contrast of the "usual style" of building with the "Gothic style."[46] The "usual style" chapel looks exactly like a factory as to sides and roof, but with a sham Grecian front. The latter shows six wide steps leading to a four-columned portico and might be "Town-hall" or "concert-hall" style; certainly it bears no integral relation to the rest of the building, being in the most literal sense a mere façade. The "Gothic style" chapel proliferates with flying buttresses between each lancet window (ten are visible in the view of the front and side); there are four pinnacles looking like newly-sharpened pencils on the front, and pierced and fretted parapets abound. The impression of the "Gothic style" here illustrated is that of wedding-cake fussiness of ornamentation and the conclusion cannot be avoided that had the "usual style" maintained its quiet Grecian qualities in the sides of the building it would be greatly preferable. Happily, the later use of Gothic in Methodist chapels was to be much more restrained and less exuberant[47] in character.

The real importance of this defence of the use of Gothic, as also of J. A. Clapham's essay on "Congregational Gothic Churches," is the clear evidence they give that the views of the Cambridge ecclesiologists (the very "Ritualists" whom every Protestant was up in arms against) had been unconsciously absorbed and reproduced as if they were their own by both Methodists and Congregationalists. In the same way as Ruskin had acted as the mediator of the Oxford Movement to the Nonconformists in its architectural views, so was the Church of Scotland to prove the channel through which the liturgical views of the Tractarians were to find acceptance among the English Presbyterians and Congregationalists.

[46] The idea of contrasted illustrations was borrowed from Augustus Welby Pugin.
[47] Methodist exuberance was also indicated in the numbers, as well as in the styles, of their chapels. In the Conference of 1841, Bunting, alarmed that eight hundred chapels had been built in the previous five years, cautioned: "Fewer chapels and more horses would save more souls. I think we are forsaking our calling. We should preach in barns, the cottages of the poor, and out of doors." (Benjamin Gregory, *Sidelights on the Conflicts of Methodism, 1827-1852*, p. 315.)

7. *Presbyterian-Unitarian Architecture*

The purpose of the hyphen in the above title is to enable us to consider together both those eighteenth century and early nineteenth century chapels which had been erected by Presbyterians but which, by defection of their congregations from Trinitarianism, had come into the hands of the Unitarians, and the nineteenth-century Unitarian edifices. A most charming picture of an old Presbyterian meeting-house in Knutsford, Cheshire, which had come into Unitarian hands, is described by Mrs. Gaskell the novelist, as she recalls the chapel of her youth, Brook Street Chapel, built in 1689, in which Matthew Henry, the famous commentator, had often preached. Characteristically it was placed in a side-street that its secluded site might not draw attention to the despised and often socially proscribed Dissenters of that heroic age.

"The chapel was up a narrow street, or rather *cul-de-sac* close by. It stood on the outskirts of the town, almost in fields. It was built about the time of Matthew and Philip Henry, when the Dissenters were afraid of attracting attention, or observation, and hid their places of worship in obscure and out-of-the-way parts of the towns in which they were built. . . . The chapel had a picturesque and old-world look, for luckily the congregation had been too poor to rebuild it in George the Third's time. The staircases which led to the galleries were outside, at each end of the building, and the irregular roof and worn stone steps looked grey and stained by time and weather. The grassy hillocks, each with a little upright headstone, were shaded by a grand old wych-elm. A lilac-bush or two, a white rose-tree, and a few laburnums, all old and gnarled enough, were planted round the chapel yard; and the casement-windows of the chapel were made of heavy-leaded, diamond-shaped panes almost covered with ivy, producing a green gloom, not without its solemnity, within. . . . The interior of the building was plain and simple as plain and simple as could be. When it was fitted up, oak timber was much cheaper than it is now, so the woodwork was all of that description; but roughly hewed, for the early builders had not much wealth to spare. The walls were whitewashed, and were recipients of the shadows of the beauty without; on their 'white plains' the tracery of the ivy might be seen now still, now stirred by the sudden flight of some little bird."[48]

[48] Elizabeth Cleghorn Gaskell wrote *Ruth* in 1852; the citation is taken from chapter 14.

This delightful cameo of the dignity and simplicity of the early Puritan meeting-house architecture enables us to visualize the great contrast which the elegant Octagon of the Unitarian congregation at Norwich offered with the simpler buildings of the past, and which elicited from the curious John Wesley the following description: "I was shown Dr. Taylor's new meeting-house, perhaps the most elegant one in Europe. It is eight-square, built in the finest brick, with sixteen sash-windows below, as many above, and eight skylights in the dome; which, indeed, are purely ornamental. The inside is finished in the highest taste, and is as clean as any nobleman's saloon. The communion-table is fine mahogany; the very latches of the pew-doors are polished brass. How can it be thought that the old, coarse Gospel should find admission here?"[49]

Indeed, the intention of Dr. John Taylor's cultivated congregation was that instead of the "old coarse Gospel" a humane, advanced, and enlightened theology should be preached there, typical of "mere Christians" not sectarians. They held a competition and required three aspirants to construct models. Thomas Ivory's model was approved and he was ordered to begin the erection immediately at a cost of about £5,000. He may well have been familiar with the new architectural developments on the Continent, where the Germans and the Dutch were experimenting with the *Zentralkirche* ideal of concentrated planning, using the circle and the polygon for that purpose. The dominant feature of the church is a cupola, sustained by round arches which rest on eight fluted Corinthian columns, each a single tree trunk, behind which the gallery extends right round the interior.[50] Whitefield's Evangelical Tabernacle in the Tottenham Court Road was also an octagon, but its roof merely terminated in a turret. This style of building was more usually associated with a liberal and rational type of theology, as in Adrian Street, Dover (1820), and the Octagon in Liverpool (1763-1776). Anglican architecture was not immune from its influence, as may be seen in Bath and in Exeter (Bedford Chapel, 1791).

Pioneers in the use of the Octagon in the eighteenth century, the Unitarians were also pioneers in the use of Gothic among the Nonconformists. For them Sir Charles Barry built a fully Gothic church in Upper Brook Street, Manchester, in 1839 which still

[49] *Journal*, entry for November 23, 1757.
[50] A. L. Drummond, "The Architectural Interest of the English Meeting House" in *Journal of the Royal Institute of British Architects*, London, Vol. 45, Third Series, No. 18, August 15, 1938, pp. 909-17.

stands. Externally Gothic, its interior still had the pulpit in the middle of the end wall with pews fronting it in rows. The first Nonconformist church to have an altar in the chancel (and thus to place the pulpit at the side and emphasize devotions rather than preaching) was the Unitarian Hyde Chapel in Cheshire, built in 1848. It had a fine, slender spire. The same architects, Bowman and Crowther of Manchester, built Mill Hill Unitarian Chapel in Leeds in the same year. This too has an altar in the chancel and is a pioneer in the use of stained-glass windows among Nonconformists. The Unitarians led the way into Gothic and were quickly followed by the Congregationalists and the Methodists.[51]

Apt as we are to imagine that one style of building gave way to another wholly different, as if congregations simply demolished an old-fashioned church to make way for a new edifice, instead of modifying and patching-up, or improving the decoration and furnishing the old, it is instructive to consider the history of a single church building and how it adapted itself to changing fashions in theology and liturgy. The example selected is that of Elder-Yard Meeting-House in Chesterfield, Derbyshire.

In 1774 the windows of this classical building were hung with green curtains and the pews cushioned and lined with green baize. Between 1785 and 1788 the edifice was landscaped and spruce, firs and poplars were planted to improve the approach and surroundings. In 1818 the pulpit was moved from the middle of the long side to the east end, and the chapel is referred to for the first time in the accounts as "Unitarian" instead of "Presbyterian." (The implication is that the sermon was to be briefer and less significant, and that devotions were to become more important.) An organ and choir-loft were added in 1821. In 1838 an oak communion-table was bought and placed in the middle of the chancel. In 1896 the organ was removed to the side and choir-stalls, a communion-table, and reredos were installed. The impact of the influence of the Oxford Movement on this Unitarian church reached its climax in 1927, when a lectern and prayer-desk were introduced.[52] Thus the fabric of a single church is an index of the changes not only of architectural style but, more significantly, of the revolutionary conception of worship which even in Unitarianism

---

[51] The substance of this paragraph is taken from H. L. Short's article "Changing Styles in Nonconformist Architecture" in *The Listener*, London, issue of March 17, 1955, pp. 471-74.

[52] A. L. Drummond, "The Architectural Interest of the English Meeting House," *op.cit.*, p. 916.

had come to place a greater value on prayers than on preaching, on doctrine than on devotions. To a slightly lesser extent, this could also be the verdict on the worship of the whole of Nonconformity in the nineteenth century, as more worshipful churches proved incentives to, if not a deeper, yet a better ordered and more dignified worship among congregations that had previously regarded worship as merely a preliminary to preaching.

CHAPTER III

LITURGICAL RENEWAL IN THE
ENGLISH FREE CHURCHES:
A SURVEY

IT IS PROPOSED in the present chapter to consider the nature of the nineteenth century renewal of liturgical life in the English Free Churches in general and to leave more detailed consideration of the movement within the various denominations to subsequent chapters. The radical revaluation of free prayers was to be the most marked feature of the worship of these Churches in nineteenth century England and this was to lead first to the supplementation of free prayers with read prayers, then to the provision of printed prayers in which both minister and people might join in various congregations, and, finally, at the end of this century and the beginning of the next, to the provision of formularies of prayer by the denominations themselves.

It is appropriate in a general survey such as this to enquire as to the factors that promoted so radical a change of outlook on the part of the heirs of the Puritans and the Separatists, which led them to reconsider the value not only of read prayers but even of a Liturgy, whereas their predecessors wholly rejected the Book of Common Prayer as a "stinted form" in favour of extemporary prayer under the free guidance of the Holy Spirit.

1. *The Causes of the Liturgical Renewal*

1. Undoubtedly, an important negative factor was the abuses to which "free" prayers were subject, and, in particular, their rambling repetitiveness which contrasted so poorly with the consuming attention that was given to the preparation of the sermon. In this there was nothing new, for Isaac Watts himself, in the *Guide to Prayer*, had been as alive to the dangers of spontaneity, pedantry, ostentation, and repetition as the highest of High Anglican critics of Free Church worship. There were also newer and more important elements in the decision in which the spirit of the age played its own part.

2. There can be no doubt that Romanticism played a most

significant role in the depreciation of reason and the elevation of sentiment, the ultimate effect of which was to lower the status of the sermon and to raise the standing of the devotions. Romanticism was variously expressed in the sentimentalism of Jean-Jacques Rousseau, in the Pietism of Lutheranism and Moravianism as expressed in Spener, Francke, and Zinzendorf, and in the popularity of the cult of the Sacred Heart within Roman Catholicism, but it gave an important place to the emotions which predominate over the reason in worship.

3. Another important factor was the recovered sense of the significance of tradition which was so marked a feature of European thought after, first, its disillusionment with and, later, its revulsion from the excesses of the French Revolution. In England Burke's anti-revolutionary views proclaimed a new appreciation for continuity through time-tested institutions and customs, and a deeper conception of society as an organism. The same view was to fashion the Romantic Revival of which the most typical representatives were Sir Walter Scott, Wordsworth, and Coleridge. Scott opened the magic casements of the popular imagination onto the mediaeval scene; Wordsworth rediscovered the eternal freshness and transcendental sublimity of Nature and the fundamental simplicities of human nature; Coleridge, in the *Aids to Reflection*, stressed that religion was life rather than speculation. He also affirmed that the Prayer Book of the Church of England admirably expressed the views that man's greatest felicity is union with God, that the unity of the human race is to be found in the new Adam, Christ, the representative of the Redeemed Race, and that a truly Catholic Church requires forms of worship and sacraments for the expression of its unity with God and man.

4. The spirit of Romanticism and the recognition of the stabilizing power of tradition found their most powerful liturgical expression in the Tractarian Movement, which was to revitalize the worship of English Dissent almost as much as that of the Church of England, despite its excessive antiquarianism, its doctrine of the plenary inspiration of the Caroline divines, and its insensitivity to the constructive possibilities in the political and social liberalism of the day.[1] The Tractarians taught the Evangelicals of the Establishment and of Dissent that the history of the Christian Church from the first century to the period of the Reformation could not

[1] See *Worship and Theology in England*, Vol. 3, "From Watts and Wesley to Maurice, 1690-1850," Chapter x.

be rudely set aside as a millennium and a half of apostasy. They insisted instead that the episcopate, the Creeds, and the formularies of worship had kept alive a sense of fidelity to the Christian tradition in the darkest ages. The Tractarians further denied that the Church was, as the Evangelicals taught, the community of the converted, or, as the Pietists insisted, a radiator for the generating of warmed hearts, or, least of all, as the Latitudinarians implied, the religious branch of the national civil service charged with maintaining the morale of the nation and preventing it from being carried away by enthusiasms whether Nonconformist or Papistical. From them, all Communions were to re-learn that the Church was an independent, Divinely founded and Divinely sustained society, characterized by the marks of unity, catholicity, holiness, and above all, of apostolicity.

Moreover, the Tractarians had a more objective understanding of the nature of Christian faith, rooted as revelation was in history, for they concentrated on the acts of God accomplishing human salvation and on the dogmas of belief rather than on experience or the subjective appropriation of Christian truth.[2] Tractarians also gave sacramental life and liturgy a higher place than Protestantism was customarily prepared to allow them. It taught men to revalue worship in general and the traditional forms of worship in particular, as the historic channels through which the generations of Christians had approached God, as therefore hallowed by powerful associations, as tutors in spirituality, and, by means of the sacraments, as Christ's instruments of healing for the sin-sick soul. It was in contrast with the current subjectivity of Protestant worship that Newman was led to observe that Catholic worship was the "evocation" of God, and Protestant worship only the "invocation" of God. Furthermore, the Tractarian stress on the Incarnation which emphasized the continuity between nature and grace (as contrasted with the Evangelical emphasis on the need for the crucifixion of the ego as proof of the reality of salvation, with the consequence of a radical dichotomy between the two realms), gave a deep significance to the physical and aesthetic sides of human nature. As a result the Sacraments which minister to the soul through the senses were given a higher status in the Christian life,

---

2 Newman criticized Protestant subjectivity thus: "And in this way religion is made to consist in contemplating ourselves instead of Christ; not simply in looking to Christ but in ascertaining that we look to Christ, not in His Divinity and Atonement, but in our conversion and our faith in these truths." *Lectures on Justification* (3rd edn., 1874), p. 325.

and they became the chief channels of Divine grace and the impetus to the sacrificial life which counts the world well lost for Christ.

Finally, in considering the impact of Tractarianism on Dissenting worship, the importance of the emphasis of the second generation on ceremonialism and symbolism in worship must not be forgotten, even if it was at first received with the utmost disfavour. This coronation of beauty in the Establishment was clearly an appeal to the mixed nature of man, spirit, mind, and body, which had been hallowed in the Incarnation. Dangerous beauty had been exiled by Puritanism from its worship, but it was accorded a coronation in Anglican sanctuaries, for it was now believed that there was a holiness of beauty, as well as a beauty of holiness. So powerful was the architectural and artistic impact of Tractarianism that Dissent became ashamed of its sometimes simple and occasionally squalid conventicles. By the mid-nineteenth century there was for Free Churchmen and Anglicans alike only one Christian style of architecture—the Gothic. These cruciform churches, equally distant from the Nonconformist barn and the Evangelical pagan temple of classicism, are the external proofs of the invisible and often reluctantly accepted influence of Tractarianism on the worship of English Dissent. Undoubtedly, the greatest single influence upon the change in worship of the heirs of the Puritans was Tractarianism, however violent were the controversies and the spate of litigation which the mid-century "Ritualists" (who were, in truth, "Ceremonialists") brought upon themselves from their Evangelical opponents.

5. It does, indeed, seem curious that the Evangelicals in the Church of England and in Dissent whose first attitude towards the Tractarians was vitriolic should have come to terms with them by the end of the century in many cases. This *volte face* is to be explained, I believe, by the significant mediating role played by F. D. Maurice[3] in the Church of England in his remarkable apologia for the Prayer Book in his *Kingdom of Christ* (1842)—as important for modern Anglicanism as Hooker was for the Elizabethan Settlement—and by the influence of the liturgiologists of the Church of Scotland in their impact upon English Nonconformists. The point is that however defective English Nonconformity might feel its worship to be, it would not improve it by taking a leaf (or leaves) from the formulary of its traditional foe, the Church

[3] See Chapter XII of *Worship and Theology in England*, Vol. 3, "From Watts and Wesley to Maurice, 1690-1850."

of England. Sharing the same Genevan tradition, English Non-conformists were much more ready to follow the lead of their former Puritan ally, the Church of Scotland, and this they did.[4]

6. A sixth factor has also to be taken into account. It is that two important Communions, representing the new Dissent in England, the Methodists and Unitarians, still retained an affection for liturgical forms of worship, so that the older Dissent (Congregationalists, Presbyterians, and to some extent, Baptists) did not associate a Liturgy exclusively with Anglicanism and Roman Catholicism in England.

The cumulative impact of these six factors was considerable and it is hardly too much to claim with Sprott, the Scottish liturgiologist, that the liturgical renewal of the nineteenth century was a veritable "Second Reformation" in the spiritual life of Great Britain. The manifestations of this renewal will concern us more fully later, but in the meantime we may note some of the more obvious signs.

Not only did read prayers become more frequent, but ministers such as Dr. John Hunter, in his Congregational churches in York, Glasgow, and the King's Weigh House, London, used printed responsive services which had a wide sale when they appeared in print as *Devotional Services*, the first edition appearing in 1882 and the tenth in 1920. Others, less adventurous, were willing to use responsive elements in their services, and it soon became a common practice in certain Free Churches to print a selection of Collects, as well as the General Confession and the General Thanksgiving from the *Book of Common Prayer* in the backs of their hymnbooks so that they might be used by the congregation in public prayer.[5]

The liturgical renewal was mainly expressed in a far greater concern for worship as such, and an unwillingness to relegate it to the inferior status of a mere "preliminary" to the sermon. Individual ministers gave much greater attention to the preparation of their prayers, and to the selection of the items of praise in cooperation with their organists and choirmasters. Indeed, it is a significant fact that during the century organs replaced the fiddles, viols, and flutes of the eighteenth century, and trained choirs were given a place of honour in the service, though this was often as obstrusive as the organ pipes that often resembled gigantic gilded cigars.

4 See Chapter IV, *infra.*
5 See W. D. Maxwell, *The Book of Common Prayer and the Worship of Non-Anglican Churches.*

Largely through the influence of Thomas Binney, the admirable mid-century minister of the King's Weigh House in London, and of Dr. Henry Allon, also a London Congregational minister of the period, it became customary for the Free Churches of the metropolis to augment their hymnody and metrical psalmody with chants and anthems. The liturgical renascence was also seen in the more solemn and more frequent celebration of the Sacrament of the Lord's Supper, and this was interpreted more in the manner of a "Real Presence" than in the memorialist fashion of Zwingli.[6] The minister himself came to discard his look of a prosperous business-man in a nation of shopkeepers, and to wear the grave Genevan gown. But, above all, the revolution of the spirit of worship was symbolically expressed in ecclesiastical architecture in Dissent. The Churches began to look like churches, neither like a city hall or a warehouse in the urban areas, nor a barn in the rural areas. The decoration did not so offensively declare "I believe in Geometry," and in the succeeding century the very stained-glass windows would insist boldly that "I believe in God."

At the same time it must be recognized that social factors as well as purely theological reasons played their part in the liturgical renascence. Dissent was increasing its hold upon the commercial and industrial middle classes of England, and its more opulent members were insisting that Nonconformity should in its palmy days of liberation build what they were pleased to call its own "cathedrals." Thus ornateness for its own sake, or for the cultivated taste it was supposed to indicate, played a part in the "Christianity on parade" which the more flamboyant Italianate architecture of Westminster Chapel or of Lyndhurst Road Church, Hampstead, flaunted. It was too much to expect of human nature that the Nonconformists who had suffered so long from political and legal disabilities should not attempt to emulate the splendour of Anglican worship, in its architectural setting and its praise, however inappropriate this was for the more oracular type of worship that was their own tradition. The result was the intense if rambling prayers of the Puritans, and the bleak austerity and sincerity of the Puritan congregations gathered in the white meeting-house in their sober blacks and greys to hear the marching orders of the Word of God, disappeared. The increase in order and dignity had inevitably been followed by a decrease in spiritual ardour.

---

[6] The sacramental theology of R. W. Dale and P. T. Forsyth are evidence of the deeper respect in which the Lord's Supper was held. See Chapter VII, Sections 7 and 8.

2. The Growing Strength of the Free Churches

It must be recognized that the nineteenth century was a period of great expansion not only for England but also for the English Free Churches. The growing importance of Dissent in the religious life of England can be estimated from the returns made to the House of Lords of the places of worship in towns containing 1,000 inhabitants and more in 1811, as compared with the statistics of the important Religious Census of 1851. It was reported in 1811 that there were 2,665 Anglican churches and chapels-of-ease and 3,457 chapels not of the Establishment.

Of even greater interest are the denominational figures (the Methodists excluded) showing the relative growth and strength of the Unitarians, Congregationalists, and Baptists from 1811 to 1827 in the counties of England. In 1811 the three denominations had 1,583 places of worship; sixteen years later they had increased to 2,157. In 1827 the Unitarians had 204 places of worship, the Congregationalists 1,203, and the Baptists 750. This represents an increase of 368 Congregational chapels, and 257 Baptist chapels; at the same time 247 Presbyterian chapels had become 204 Unitarian chapels.[7] Presumably the two sets of figures are not unrelated, for the more rational of the Presbyterians would join the Unitarians and the more evangelical would join the Congregationalists or the Baptists. Even so there was a considerable increase in the ranks of the Congregationalists and Baptists.

The most interesting figures of all, for the purposes of indicating the strength of the English Free Churches at the mid-point of the century, are provided by the Census Returns of 1851. They record that the attendance at worship on Sunday, March 30th, 1851, was as follows:

Church of England	3,773,474
Wesleyans:	
Original Connexion	907,313
Or, all Wesleyan bodies	1,385,382
Independents	793,142
Baptists:	
Particular	471,283
Or, all Baptists	587,978

This attendance at Divine worship in percentages of the total population was 21 percent Anglican, 7.7 percent Methodist, 4.4

[7] James Bennett, *History of Dissenters in the Last Thirty Years: 1808-1838*, p. 244.

71

percent Congregationalists, and 3.3 percent Baptist. Thus the three major Dissenting bodies together had an attendance at worship which was almost 75 percent of that of the Anglican Church.[8]

The same census reveals the financial strength of the middle-classes of the Free Churches in the astonishing rapidity with which they had increased their number of church edifices in the second quarter of the century. The 1,203 Independent Chapels of 1827 had become 3,244 by 1851; the 750 Baptist chapels of 1827 had become 2,789 by 1851. The Methodists, for whom we do not have any figures earlier than 1851, could boast 11,007 places of worship in 1851 compared with the 14,077 of the Established Church, even though their total accommodation in sittings was less than half that of the Anglicans.

As we have suggested earlier, the growing strength, importance, and respectability of English Dissent had an important influence upon the architecture and worship of the Free Churches. It was not less influential in the changes it brought about in the number and nature of the duties of the ministers. The constant accessions to the Dissenting chapels involved the ministers in much more pastoral visitation and in larger classes of instruction preparing for church membership. James Bennett records in 1839 that there was a general disposition to decline three services of worship each Sunday, and a preference to conduct services only on Sunday mornings and evenings. At the same time, ministers were expected to give several lectures and "as these are designed to counteract infidelity, Popery or Socinianism, and are sometimes delivered on the working days, they form a considerable tax on the minister's time, and on his strength, both physical and mental."[9] The great increase of interest in Missionary Societies required ministers to act as fund-raisers and as advocates of this and other worthy causes in distant pulpits. Even the new Marriage Act had also augmented the work of the ministry since many chapels had recently been registered for marriage and most members intending marriage preferred that their minister rather than a civil registrar should perform the ceremony. It is not surprising that many ministers, having no previous experience of marriage services, used a modification of the form in the Book of Common Prayer. This period also saw the proliferation of religious journals and newspapers among

---

[8] From the article "On the Census Returns respecting Congregational Worship" by the Reverend John Kennedy on pp. 33-47 of *The Congregational Year Book of 1855.*

[9] James Bennett, *op.cit.*, pp. 276 ff.

the Dissenters, and in consequence these provided additional duties for the more learned or ambitious among the ministry. Thus the two services of worship on Sunday, instead of three, were more than counterbalanced by extra services or lectures for religious and charitable organizations (it became the custom during this period to celebrate on a week night the anniversary of the foundation of local churches, a custom which added to the onus of labour). Moreover, in large towns the number of occasional services, such as the solemnization of marriage, added considerably to the burden of ministerial duty.

The pressure of such duties meant that the minister was probably less often in his study than in the old days. In consequence there was a falling off in the theological penetration and devotional fervour of the ministry. Even the old conviction that an Establishment was unfavourable to the development of a vigorous and sacrificial religion—the *raison d'être* of continuing Dissent—was lessening in its intensity. Wilson, writing about the general condition of the Free Churches in 1814, declares that a considerable body of Methodists and Congregationalists "consider the preservation of the Church of England as their best security against the return of Popery."[10] In his judgment this is a view subversive of liberty both to prince and people and a sad declension. He believes that religious apathy is masked by tolerance, and that it is only a "spurious candour" which is responsible for the combination of Anglicans and Dissenters in the foundation and promotion of the Bible Society and the Anti-Slavery Campaign, and that such unity is achieved only by the sacrifice of denominational principle. He alleges that the new generation of ministers sits at ease in Zion and that many of their church members have been trapped by the snares of this world to desert the religion of their forefathers. It is the gravamen of his jeremiad, however, that travelling, lecturing, and sponsoring benevolent and political causes have deflected the ministry from their proper concern, and, as a result, "pastoral duties, at least in large cities, are now out of fashion, and ministers are so completely immersed in business that they have no time either for study or for visiting their people."[11] He further asserts that the younger generation of ministers are more interested in the

---

[10] Walter Wilson, *The History and Antiquities of Dissenting Churches and Meeting Houses . . .* , Vol. IV, p. 547.
[11] *Ibid.*, pp. 550-51.

form than the content of preaching, "wishing to be thought polite.[12] One may well conclude that the pressure of outside duties and the concern for elegance also contributed to the importance of externals in worship among the Free Churches in the nineteenth century.

3. The Development of the New Attitude in Worship

The liturgical renewal in the English Free Churches of the nineteenth century can be traced through three stages: first, there is the radical revaluation of free prayers and the partial use of read prayers; secondly, there is the provision of printed orders of worship for individual congregations under the leadership of a skilled and devout minister; and, finally, there is the compilation of formularies of worship authorized for the use of an entire denomination.

It seemed that the livelier Dissenting ministers themselves had come to realise the bitter truth in Coleridge's view: "Many a proselyte has the Church gained from the Meeting-house through the disgust occasioned by the long-winded preaching prayers of the Dissenting ministers, and the utter exclusion of the congregation from all *active* share in the public devotion."[13] Coleridge had exactly hit upon the two outstanding defects of Dissenting devotions: they were diffusely didactic, as if addressed to an absentminded congregation instead of to God, and as the sole composition of the minister they were unwarrantably sacerdotal for a tradition that claimed to believe in the priesthood of all believers.

4. "A New Directory"

The earliest significant sign of the new liturgical approach in Nonconformity—it is indeed a landmark—was the publication in 1812 of *A New Directory for Nonconformist Churches Containing Remarks on Their Mode of Public Worship, and a Plan for the Improvement of it.* The sub-title indicated that it was "addressed to Dissenting Ministers of all Denominations and to Tutors of Academies." The Prefatory Address, composed by several ministers, reflects the feeling of the authors, who are aggrieved by the improprieties in contemporary Dissenting worship. They particularly

---

[12] *Ibid.*, p. 553. Note also that James Bennett, *op.cit.*, concurs: "But while some fear that the solid divinity of former days is now becoming rare; others think that an excessive attention is paid to artificial method, to brilliancy of thought, and elegance of style."

[13] *Notes on English Divines*, Vol. II, p. 33.

wish to impress upon the tutors of academies the importance of inculcating "upon the youths committed to your care, with greater ardour than ever, the diligent cultivation of the gift of Prayer, which, amidst other less important studies, has been too generally neglected in our seminaries, even by those who have cultivated their talents for preaching with a laudable industry, and with no small degree of success."[14] The title is important as indicating that the Puritan denominations have taken no further common counsel for worship since the Parliamentary Directory of 1645 was prepared over a century and a half before. The timeliness, the thoroughness, and the comprehensiveness of the volume are three indications of its great significance.

It is soon apparent that the judicious authors plead for neither a Liturgy nor for extemporary prayer, but for a combination of both. The need for variety and freshness argues against the constant use of a Liturgy; equally, there are weighty reasons against the constant use of extemporary prayer. The latter deserve detailed consideration since they represent a radical alteration of viewpoint in the heirs of the Puritans. In the first place, extemporary prayer is attended with many disadvantages, especially for the young minister and "such as are not endowed with some very considerable talents" and the naturally modest and self-diffident "will be liable, at least on some occasions, to have their minds discomposed, and constantly to feel their devotion interrupted."[15] This assertion is supported by reference to the facts that on this account many Nonconformist ministers have trod the path to Canterbury, that others left the ministry completely, that others, again, with the concurrence of their congregations have drawn up a Liturgy for regular use, and that yet others have liberty in their preaching but great trepidation in their praying. It is interesting to note the statement: "Some again by reason of their dissatisfaction, or that of their people, with the extemporary mode of prayer (though they have acquitted themselves as well as most of their brethren) have been induced to adopt a Liturgy; and on this ground several Liturgies have of late years been drawn up for Dissenting congregations. But a greater number of Dissenting ministers, from a dislike of Liturgies, have sought the relief they wanted by drawing up Forms of prayer for themselves, and committing them to memory. While others, who have composed the like forms, have preferred the *reading* of

[14] Preface, pp. vi-vii.
[15] *A New Directory*, pp. 5-6.

them; which has of late been a growing custom."[16] Here, then, is positive evidence early in the nineteenth century of ministers going through the first and second stages of the renewed appreciation of Liturgy by composing prayers to be read or even persuading their congregations to adopt a Liturgy.

The authors have no inherent objection to a Liturgy for Nonconformists, and they take pains to point out that the original separation from the National Church was founded not "on a conscientious objection to the public Liturgy itself, so much as on some exceptionable things contained in it."[17] They add that Baxter himself drew up a Liturgy which at least satisfied the Presbyterians. Nevertheless, they conceive that the general opinion of Nonconformists is against an invariable form of worship such as a Liturgy provides. On the other hand, they approve and even applaud the use of forms of prayer composed by ministers themselves, provided they are simple, deeply devotional, and varied. The plan which they approve is: "To continue the use of *Extemporary Prayer* in a certain degree, and so far as all the valuable ends of it will be secured; but with it to make use of those *Forms* of devotion with which we are amply supplied in the Holy Scriptures."[18]

The partial justification for the retention of extemporary prayers is that its sudden abolition would both cause wholesale desertion from the Nonconformist Churches and lead pious souls to consider that their ministers had turned to forms of prayer because they did not possess the gift of free prayer. Free prayer, however, has certain advantages over forms of prayer which are even more cogent reasons for its retention: in chief, its flexibility, its lively way of exciting the religious affections, and the novelty of thought and expression which retain the attention of congregations.[19]

On the other hand, its sole and exclusive use is subject to serious disadvantages. It may lead either to a hesitant and embarrassing interruption of prayer, or to a fatal fluency that produces rapidity of utterance and complexity of sentence structure that are equally difficult for the congregation to follow. Its matter may be over-systematic and pedantic, or it may be chaotic in its mixing up of the moods of prayer. Far from always fulfilling the intention of providing variety and freshness, "the general prayers of some worthy men have so much sameness that they may not improperly be denominated *forms*, though they have not been pre-

16 *Ibid.*, p. 6. 17 *Ibid.*, p. 7.
18 *Ibid.*, p. 13. 19 *Ibid.*, pp. 15-17.

composed."[20] As some prayers are full of clichés, others are too ingenious in their novelty. They may even pursue an *idée fixe* throughout the entire lengthy general prayer. An interesting footnote recalls that one country minister conducting a service in the city gave, instead of a prayer, a disquisition on sin, illustrating it by an enumeration of the mischiefs it had done in heaven, in Paradise, and in the history of mankind![21]

It is clear that the authors expect that their difficulty will be chiefly that of convincing the godly that there are *any* defects in their traditional use of free prayer. For this reason they are careful to catalogue the commonest infelicities of extemporary public prayers. These faults include: the unnecessary specification of the time; the expression of personal political bias; the mentioning of personal and disputatious matters; the use of terms which express a ministerial mock-humility, such as "thy sinful dust" to "the meanest of all thy instruments"; and the making of prayer the occasion of high-flown flattery or individual reproof. Another major fault is that of over-particularizing. In that connection, they give a fascinating glimpse of prayer-customs in English Nonconformity, in uttering the following objection: "We cannot omit this opportunity of entering our protest against the prevalent ludicrous system, in many of our societies, especially in London, of putting up *Bills* to the pulpit with a *long stick*, but more especially at the *close* of the service, when there is scarcely time for the minister to read them; at least without being interrupted in reading the lines of the hymn. . . . When there are cases of moment which require the prayers of the Church, we advise that the minister be acquainted with them before the service begins, that they may be introduced (as they are in the Establishment) in the general intercessory prayer."[22]

Among the remedies they propose are the recommendation that *extempore* prayers be briefer, and they approve Job Orton's suggestion that the long prayer should be divided in two parts, the first to consist of petition and the second of intercession. They further suggest that the following parts of prayer, being of a general nature and thus suitable to the circumstances of all Christian worshippers at all times, are more suitably expressed in a form than extemporaneously: "The adoration of the divine perfections; the celebration of the works of God in creation, providence,

20 *Ibid.*, p. 26.
21 *Ibid.*, p. 27.
22 *Ibid.*, p. 40.

and redemption; thanksgiving for his manifold mercies, temporal and spiritual; confession of sin, in its various kinds and aggravations; supplication for numerous blessings which we all need as creatures, as sinners, as Christians; together with intercessions for mankind at large, for our own country, and for all orders of men."[23]

Among the hints they provide is a proposed Order of Worship consisting of the following essential items:

1. *Introductory brief lections of Scripture* (emphasizing the commemoration of the Resurrection, the privileges of Christianity, and the purpose and benefits of worship)
2. *Short Extemporary Prayer* (thanksgiving for the Resurrection, the Sabbath, worship, and imploring Divine assistance)
3. *General Psalm or Hymn of Praise*
4. *The Old Testament Lesson* (with a few explanatory words at the beginning and practical remarks at the end)
5. *The General Prayer* (the form to be taken from the Scriptures especially from the Psalms, and consisting of the elements of Petition, Confession and Thanksgiving)
6. *The New Testament Lesson* (preferably linked with the Old Testament Lesson)
7. *Short Extempore Prayer* (grounded on some leading ideas of the lessons) and the *Intercessory Prayer* (partly Scriptural and partly free)
8. *Psalm or Hymn* (appropriate to the last lesson)
9. *SERMON*
10. *Hymn or Psalm* (on sermon theme)
11. *Short Extemporary Prayer* (applying the leading ideas of the Sermon)[24]

It deserves notice that the first item of worship is not, as might be expected in the Calvinist tradition, the element of Confession, as it is also in the Anglican tradition: both the Scripture sentences and the first prayer properly express the mood of joyous thanksgiving. Then it is interesting to observe that the authors recommend that forty minutes be spent on the worship and forty minutes on the sermon, so that the entire service shall not exceed an hour and a half. It is recommended also that the forms of prayer included in the order of worship should be printed in full, as "the printing of them will be the more requisite if it should be judged proper that the congregation should bear a *vocal* part in the service, by making a few brief Responses."[25]

23 *Ibid.*, pp. 27-28.
24 *Ibid.*, pp. 82 f.
25 *Ibid.*, pp. 101-02.

Admirable as is the provision of a logically related order of worship comprehensive enough to include lessons from both Testaments and all the moods of prayer, it is not without faults. It is still excessively didactic in making the prayers reproduce the leading themes of the lessons, and it is too restricting to insist that the forms should be derived almost entirely from the words of Scripture. That it is an advance on previous Free Church worship, however, cannot be denied, if the two-fold Coleridgean test be applied. While it is still over-didactic, yet both the insistence on brevity and the inclusion of forms of prayer reduce the didacticism. The strong recommendation that the prayers be printed so that the congregation may join vocally in them is ample refutation of the old criticism of sacerdotalism in which only one voice (that of the minister) is heard in prayer.

The *New Directory* has revolutionary suggestions to make concerning posture. It is argued that it is improper to sit at prayer, while standing for the praise of God. Should it be objected that if the congregation were also to stand for the prayers they would be inconvenienced by standing too long, then let them find relief by kneeling for prayer! The latter posture is recommended "as by far the most decent, and the most friendly to devotion; being the best calculated to preserve the eyes from roving and thereby to keep the mind from being diverted from foreign objects."[26]

On the subject of instrumental music, the *Directory* is conservative, though no disapproval is expressed at the innovation of organs in churches. It is, however, insisted that the organ shall still assist vocal music and not be an obstacle in the way of or a substitute for vocal music. The authors are particularly caustic about the misuse of psalmody whereby the director of music has occasionally chosen a psalm to express his disapproval of the theme or treatment of a sermon. An interesting footnote records: "When a popular preacher appeared in a London pulpit, after he was supposed to have deviated from the orthodox faith, respecting the person of Christ, the clerk gave out the 51st hymn of Dr. Watts . . . entitled 'God the Son equal with the Father.' "[27]

If ministers are searching for source materials for forms of prayer, the authors advise that they consult the *Method of Prayer* by Matthew Henry, *The Guide to Prayer* by Isaac Watts, and *A System of Prayer* by a relatively recent author, William Smith.

[26] *Ibid.*, p. 142.
[27] *Ibid.*, p. 98.

A New Directory has engaged our attention at considerable length both as a portent and equally because no comparable survey of the disadvantages of an exclusive use of either extemporary prayer or liturgical forms, and of the double advantages of combining them, was made during the rest of the century, with the possible exception of the influential work of the American Presbyterian scholar, C. W. Baird. His book, *Eutaxia, or a Chapter on Liturgies*, was published in London in 1856, embellished by an introduction and an appendix by Binney, the distinguished Congregational minister of that centre of liturgical experiments, the King's Weigh House Church, London. The trends revealed in *A New Directory* will prove to have pioneered the liturgical development of the English Free Churches during the century, and they will be overtaken only in its last decade. The compilation of printed formularies of prayer during the nineteenth century will be considered in later chapters devoted to the separate Communions in detail.

The old hard Puritan iconoclasm was, however, an unconscionable time in dying. As late as 1876 a Congregationalist was raising the old objections to forms of prayer as necessarily implying formalism and thus obscuring, if not denying, the intimacy of the soul's approach to God in prayer. He made his plea in the highest terms: "Puritanism has rejected as unnecessary and impertinent the stimulus to religious emotion which Romanism and modern Anglicanism have sought in a sensuous worship, because it has been filled with wonder, and fear, and a 'joy unspeakable and full of glory,' by the immediate vision of God."[28]

The Free Churches were also suspicious of symbolism. Dr. R. W. Dale once delivered a sermon on "The Old Worship and the New" in which the main contention was that symbolism and ceremonial were part of the Judaic dispensation which had been abolished by the one perfect atonement of Christ which has brought Christians into perfect union with God.[29] Furthermore, it was not easily forgotten or forgiven that Nonconformity had been forced out of the National Church because of Anglicanism's insistence that all ministers assent to the Book of Common Prayer as in all things comfortable to the Word of God.[30]

[28] *The Congregationalist*, Vol. II (April 1872), p. 576.
[29] *Discourses Delivered on Special Occasions* (1866), p. 93.
[30] Cf. Henry Allon in *The Ecclesia* (1870), p. 453.

5. *The Lord's Supper: Zwinglian or Calvinist?*

Another sign of the revitalization of worship in the Free Churches was the deepened appreciation of the Communion Service and a desire for its more frequent celebration. J. M. Cramp wrote in 1824 *An Essay on the Obligation of Christians to Observe the Lord's Supper Every Lord's Day*. He deplores the great current diversity of practice in this matter, some religious societies celebrating Communion once a quarter, others every two months, yet others every six weeks. He holds that the majority of Dissenting churches celebrate monthly.[31] He reminds his readers that the early Independents or Congregationalists, as the *Apologetical Narration* of 1643 and Orme's *Life of Dr. John Owen* prove, had the Lord's Supper every Lord's day. Similarly, Smyth, the early Baptist, in his Confession of Faith taught that all Christians were obliged to communicate weekly. At the time of writing Dr. Pye Smith of Homerton is the only Congregational minister known to Cramp who has persuaded his congregation to adopt a weekly Lord's Supper.

J. Sanders Chew preached a sermon in Bond Street Chapel, Birmingham, in 1858, which was afterwards printed as *The Lord's Supper and the Lord's Day: One as Often as the Other*. This makes the same points as Cramp's book but more succinctly. It does, however, provide additional confirmation from a wider denominational range of divines, including Matthew Henry, Isaac Barrow, Bishop Beveridge, Dr. Halley, Charnock, Hook, and Wheatley. Yet a third testimony to the need for a weekly Communion comes from an Irish Baptist. This takes the form of The Circular Letter of the Association of Baptist Churches in Ireland and was printed in Belfast in 1867. One noticeable difference on the part of the author, R. H. Carson, is that he suggests that uncommitted Christians should be invited as witnesses of the Lord's Supper since this is an effective means of witnessing to the death of Christ.[32] Here he was reviving the conception of the Lord's Supper as a converting ordinance, a conviction held by theologians as different as Solomon Stoddard, the grandfather of Jonathan Edwards, and John Wesley.

[31] Pp. 11-12.
[32] R. H. Carson, *The Lord's Supper*, p. 24. An almost complete collection of these Circular Letters of Baptist Associations is to be found in the Library of Regent's Park College, Oxford.

It is rather surprising that along with this desire for more frequent celebration of the Holy Communion went a Zwinglian and memorialist theory of the Sacrament, rather than the older Calvinist, receptionist, and dynamic view. The most recent historian of Victorian Nonconformity, John W. Grant, has written: "About the actual significance of the Sacraments there was never unanimity, but a gradual drift can be discerned from a Calvinistic towards a purely symbolic interpretation."[33] Certainly, there is strong evidence tending in this direction as early as 1833 when the Laodicean and minimal Declaration of Faith of the Congregational Union of Churches founded in the year 1833 asserted that the Lord's Supper was "to be celebrated by Christian Churches as a token of faith in the Saviour, and of brotherly love." A. W. W. Dale records in the *Life of R. W. Dale of Birmingham* that his father was of the opinion that the majority of modern Congregationalists of his time regarded the rite as merely didactic, "a picture lesson shown from the sacrifice of Christ, or as 'impressive'—an appeal to emotions that language unaided could never reach."[34] Even the conservative Baptists were more radical than the Congregationalists in this respect. Their leading minister in Liverpool, Dr. Alexander Maclaren, declared: "All our theories about the meaning and value of this Communion Service must be found within the four corners of that word . . . a memorial rite, and so far as I know, nothing more whatsoever."[35]

True as this is, it is not the whole truth. There were other ministers during the century who held much higher Calvinistic views of the chief Sacrament. The great Baptist preacher of Cambridge, Robert Hall, who died in 1831, held so high a view of the Lord's Supper that Ernest Payne describes it as "almost more Lutheran than Calvinist."[36] In support of this estimate of Hall's sacramental theology, Payne cites several of Hall's writings. The most apposite citation reads as follows: "It is first a feast upon a sacrifice, in which we are actual partakers by faith of the body and blood of the Redeemer offered on the Cross. Considered in this view it is a *federal rite*, in which we receive the pledge of reconciliation, while we avouch the Lord to be our God, and surround His table as part of His family. In its secondary import, it is intended as a solemn recognition of each other as members

[33] *Free Churchmanship in England, 1870-1940*, p. 38.
[34] *Op.cit.*, pp. 358 f.
[35] *A Year's Ministry, First Series*, p. 101.
[36] E. A. Payne, *The Fellowship of Believers* . . . , p. 57.

of Christ, and consequently in the language of St. Paul, 'as one body and one bread.' "[37]

Among Congregational ministers who found Zwinglianism utterly inadequate to explain the conviction of the long Christian centuries that Christ was present in a peculiarly intimate sense at His Holy Table, were R. W. Dale and P. T. Forsyth. Dale insisted that the Sacraments were conveying and communicating ordinances and that Christ gives us His own eternal life in the symbol of His broken body.[38] While the fullest expression of Forsyth's sacramental doctrine emerges only in his excellent *The Church and the Sacraments* (1917), in which he declares that he "holds a mere memorialism to be a more fatal error than the Mass, and a far less lovely,"[39] he had already in 1896 committed himself to the view that the Sacraments were "the most complete and plenary of all the cultic ways of confessing the work of reconciliation."[40] Moreover, however negative the expressions of the sacramental teaching of the undistinguished theologians of the period might be (and Dale and Forsyth were exceptionally distinguished), the Sacrament held for the devout a mystery that could never be dissipated in mere rationalism or didacticism. In this respect religion, as so often, is much deeper than theology.

The question still remains: Why should most of the theologians and ministers of the Free Churches have preferred Zwinglianism to the high Calvinist doctrine of the Lord's Supper? In a necessarily hypothetical answer to this question, several contributing factors may well be kept in mind. This was, in the first place, a period of theological immanentalism, and hence one in which the supernaturalism of the Calvinist theory of the Communion would be less congenial than a purely memorial, didactic Zwinglian theory. Secondly, as Protestant Liberalism advanced, it became fashionable to drive a wedge between the supposedly simple religion of Jesus and the complex theology of Paul, and to claim for the apostle a larger share than his Master in the development of the institutional element in Christianity. It was a part of this trend of thought to claim that Paul had transformed the table-fellowship of the Last Supper into a secret rite on the analogy of the mystery-religions of the Graeco-Roman world. In consequence, a "high" view of this sacrament was tantamount to the endorsement of an

---

[37] *Works*, Vol. III, pp. 61-62, cited Payne, *op.cit.*, chap. IV.
[38] *A Manual of Congregational Principles*, p. 152.
[39] *Op.cit.*, p. xvi (second edition, 1947).
[40] *The Charter of the Church* (1896), p. 245.

old superstition. In the third place, two Christian Communions much admired by the English Free Churches produced admirable examples of Christian character without any need of sacraments. The Society of Friends was a by-word for integrity of life, and the Salvation Army was manifestly imitating the Master in preaching and caring for the derelicts of human society. A fourth factor promoted a "low" conception of the Lord's Supper, while reinforcing its importance as a communal rite: this was the "Social Gospel" which made the Lord's Supper a corporate act for the expression of human brotherhood under the common Fatherhood of God.[41] This was further strengthened by psychology's emphasis on the essentially gregarious nature of man which found expression in the Holy Communion.

Finally, note must be taken of those changes in the administration of the Sacrament which tended to remove the "numinous" associations with which it had been surrounded. Temperance enthusiasts had insisted upon the use of unfermented wine in the Lord's Supper, but a far more striking change was the demand for the individual communion cups in the interests of hygiene, against which the common cup or chalice was believed to militate. Apart from the historical associations of the chalice, the new custom offended against the symbolical unity of the rite which had been admirably expressed in the shared cup but was shattered in the individual cups. Moreover, the act of lifting these diminutive glasses to the lips was unfortunately reminiscent of drinking a toast. These changes in the administration of the Lord's Supper were aesthetically unfortunate and theologically defective.

In 1932 a Congregational minister, A. D. Martin, recalled fondly the Communions of his youth in Lewisham High Road Church, London, in which the older symbolism had prevailed, contrasting it with the less seemly and less moving Zwinglianism and individualism of the Communions in his maturer age: "The outstanding feature of the service was the symbolic acts of eating and drinking, and here a difference emerges. What differentiated this part of the celebration from the present ritual was the beauty and solemnity which marked participation. My childish eyes were fascinated, as I think my man's eyes would be still if the service remained as it was, by the appointments of the table—the many

---

41 J. Morgan Gibbon interpreted the Lord's Supper in terms of social justice, as it provided all Christians with "an opportunity of demonstrating by a sacred significant act the equality of all men in Christ." Cf. *The Lord's Supper: Eden and Gethsemane* (p. 203).

silver vessels drawing to themselves the high-lights of the church, whilst the contrast between the black gown of the minister, as he silently moved to and fro behind the table with its fair white linen, gave just that touch of austerity which the symbolism of the Supper should always include."[42]

Martin then proceeds to ask what has been lost through the administrative changes in the rite. He believes that a subjective or moral influence,[43] rather than a sacrificial, theory of the Atonement is in part responsible for the sense of loss. Equally to blame is the substitution for the old and beautiful chalices of "a trivial and almost grotesque apparatus, an apparatus, too, which is symbolically quite wrong."[44] Thus by the combined efforts of the temperance enthusiasts and the hygienic purists have many Free Churches come "to the unbeautiful stacks of trays with minute cups, suggestive of the laboratory of a chemistry class, or . . . a doll's tea party." The most grievous objection, however, is this: "To partake of a common cup is to symbolize community; to partake of individual cups is to symbolize individualism."[45]

6. *The Improvement of Praise*

Nothing could have been less encouraging to the development of praise than the sad doggerel of the metrical psalmody of the eighteenth century, lined out by the clerk to the congregation who sang one shred of the psalm and waited to hear the words of the next shred before repeating it in song. Whatever defects there might be in the course of praise in the next century, it could not fail to be an improvement on the past. The only considerable defect of the newer emphasis on the choir and the organ was that this tended either in those oratorios so beloved by the Free Churches, still sung in the north of England today, or in the over-ambitious and unduly lengthy anthems, to steal the right of the congregation to sing the common praises of Almighty God. In the accompanying instruments, in the training of the choirs, and in the increased variety of hymns and tunes, there was a considerable improvement in public worship. Some more ambitious

---

[42] *The Congregational Quarterly*, Vol. x (1932), pp. 73-81.
[43] A theory of the Atonement first elaborated by Abelard and strongly revived by the Liberal Protestantism of the later nineteenth century.
[44] A. D. Martin, *The Congregational Quarterly*, Vol. x (1932), pp. 73-81. "The grotesque and trivial apparatus" is a reference to three-tier trays containing individual communion glasses, each of which has a small metal cap on which diced bread may be placed, thus eliminating the Fraction and Libation.
[45] *Ibid.*

metropolitan churches introduced chants and canticles in their worship, but found it difficult to persuade the congregation to join the choir in singing them.

This was the period in which the different denominations issued their own hymn-books and in the course of the century it was common for one denomination to borrow the favourite hymns of another. The Methodists made a wide use of the Congregationalist Watts, as the Congregationalists did of Charles Wesley. Anglicanism also contributed the original hymns of Reginald Heber and William Walsham How, and the admirable translations of John Mason Neale. Cardinal Newman's great hymns, "Praise to the Holiest in the Height" and "Lead, Kindly Light," soon became the favourites of even the most evangelical members of the English Churches. It was, indeed, a period of denominational "lend-lease" in hymnody.

Another characteristic of this century was the tendency of hymns to emphasize contemporaneity—the challenge of the present hour, the joys of social service, and the brotherhood of man under God. It was also a time when hymns were composed that were suitable for the experience of children. However necessary this emphasis was, it cannot be doubted that an expansion of themes was accompanied by a thinning of the theology, and sometimes the objectivity of the mighty acts of God in creation, redemption, and sanctification was sacrificed for the sugary subjectivity and introspection of lyrical spiders forever examining their own insides.[46] But even this was greatly preferable to the formalism and sheer dullness of much eighteenth century praise.

Even the introduction of organs into the Free Churches was not effected without a struggle on the part of the diehards. In the Congregational church of Rugeley, Straffordshire, innovation was undertaken in three stages: in 1840 there was a choir accompanied by a violin-cello; in 1850 they boasted a harmonium; and in 1859 they raised the roof in the inauguration of their pipe organ.[47] In Mosley Chapel, Manchester, they had a pipe-organ as early as 1823, and an obdurate deacon resigned at the "intrusion." The diehards found a spokesman in John Adamson, the minister of Charlesworth. Among his curious arguments against

---

46 A. M. Fairbairn wrote in *Studies in Religion and Theology*, p. 272: "I am grateful that my childhood was nurtured on the Book of Psalms, rather than on the jingling verses that celebrate the 'Sweet Saviour,' or protest how I love 'my Jesus.' "

47 A. G. Matthews, *The Congregational Churches of Staffordshire*, pp. 207 f.

the use of organs in churches are the following: to urge Judaism as a precedent for organs would require us also to introduce dancing in worship; instrumental worship was excluded from worship during the first seven Christian centuries; and the hoary, conclusive irrefutable argument that it "is a custom derived from the idolatrous Church of Rome."[48]

The most advanced liturgical improvement in the Free Churches in the area of praise was, however, the practice of chanting. The great innovator here was Thomas Binney, himself the author of a fine hymn, "Eternal Light." Henry Allon popularized chanting through the publication of a selection of chants in a volume of 1876. A year before this he had proudly boasted: "At the present time the prose psalms are more generally sung and Gregorian music is more extensively used in Nonconformist churches than in Evangelical Episcopalian churches."[49] This was, indeed, a remarkable achievement on the part of the Free Churches. The denominational approval of chanting was given in the officially sponsored *Congregational Church Hymnal*, of 1887, edited by Barrett. Anthems were also introduced at about the same time as chants. Both innovations were undreamed of at the beginning of the century. Clearly, the rising sense of taste and the deepening culture of Nonconformity was insisting on higher standards of public worship.

7. Popular Services

At the same time, even before the visit of Sankey and Moody to England, attempts were made to make both the Gospel and worship more palatable to the masses. As a result chiefly of the Great Exhibition of 1851, a widespread interdenominational attempt was made to relate Christian worship, and especially preaching, to the uncommitted crowds of common people. During the Exhibition the Exeter Hall in the Strand was obtained for the use of such services and they were attended by vast auditories who queued up for admission. In 1855 the great Baptist preacher, Charles Haddon Spurgeon, took the same hall for four months, while his own church was being rebuilt, and he filled it to overflowing. A similarly successful attempt was made at the Surrey Music Hall on the southern side of the Thames.

[48] B. Nightingale, *The Story of the Lancashire Congregational Union*, pp. 125 f.
[49] Thomas Binney, *Sermons preached in King's Weigh-House Chapel, London, 1829-1869, Second Series*, ed. with a biographical and critical sketch by Henry Allon (1875), p. xxxix.

What is most interesting about these ventures is that they were originally undertaken jointly by Anglican clergy and Free Church ministers. If the incumbent of the parish objected, the Anglican clergy could take no public part in the joint services, but were able to indicate their approval of them by sitting on the platform. They also "repeated responses in that part of the Liturgy which Nonconformist preachers, by request, willingly used on these occasions."[50] Clearly, the Free Churchmen had no longer any insuperable objection to a partial use of the Liturgy. This, again, is an achievement that would have been undreamed of in the previous century.

We may notice that evening services and "popular services" had been started, with the advent of gaslight, by the Methodists almost a century before; but the growing industrialism and commercialism of Victorian England had estranged the middle class from the working class, and these popular services were intended to bridge the gap. Some of the services were too spectacular and sensational to advance the cause of true devotions, especially when they tried to organize services in theatres. On such occasions: "The stage became a pulpit, and a crowd of the lower class might be seen in the pit and the gallery; whilst other persons, some as critics and spectators, occupied the boxes. Some of the former indeed made noisy demonstrations, and tore papers in pieces,— amusing themselves with the eddying fragments."[51]

That the rhythmical hymn-tunes of Sankey, the intense preaching of the devout but unsophisticated evangelist Moody, and the military marches played on street corners by the Salvation Army bands were the only truly successful attempts to popularize worship amongst the masses, shows that there is a vast difference between the shock-tactics necessary for evangelism and the slower cultural maturation of the Christian within the Church learned through the art (not the craft) of Christian worship.

The Free Churches, we may conclude, which had hitherto staked their all on "ear-gate" and the sermon, slowly but surely came to value "eye-gate" and worship. Their architecture, their praise, their postures in worship, their increasing use of responsive elements in common prayer, their more frequent and devout celebration of Holy Communion, their gowned ministers and robed choirs, all indicated that they were learning the holiness of beauty,

[50] John Stoughton, *Religion in England from 1800 to 1850*, Vol. II, p. 426.
[51] *Ibid.*, p. 426.

and that in God's worship all things must be done decently and in order. Who the pioneers of the liturgical renewal in worship were in the Scottish and English Presbyterian Churches, and what they did, will be the concern of the chapter that immediately follows.

CHAPTER IV

PRESBYTERIAN WORSHIP, SCOTTISH AND ENGLISH

I. THE WORSHIP OF THE CHURCH OF SCOTLAND

ITHERTO IN THESE PAGES it has proved practicable to
restrict the consideration of worship in each Communion
within the national boundary of England. In the case of
Presbyterian worship, however, such a limitation is utterly artificial; Scottish and English Presbyterian worship are a unity, and
the latter is unintelligible without an understanding of the influence of the former upon it.

1. The Unity of Presbyterian Worship in Scotland and England

Apart from their unity in polity and Calvinistic theology, the
Scottish and English Presbyterians had been liturgically united
since their joint adoption in 1645 of the Westminster Assembly's
Directory for the Public Worship of God in the Three Kingdoms,
more briefly known as the Parliamentary Directory. Since that
time the order of the various items in their worship and their use
of free prayer as well as their high evaluation of learned and theological sermons had been substantially the same in both countries.

Furthermore, with the loss of so many English Presbyterian
congregations to Unitarianism in the eighteenth century, the re-
building of English Presbyterianism in the nineteenth century
had been greatly assisted by Scottish ministers of the Church of
Scotland or the United Free Church. The continuing orthodox
Presbyterian congregations in England were chiefly to be found
in Durham and Northumberland,[1] but their number came to be
augmented elsewhere, especially among the industrial cities, where
the colonies of Scottish immigrants were ministered to by Scottish clergymen of the two larger Presbyterian Churches in Scotland. In the course of the century they were amalgamated with
the indigenous and orthodox Presbyterian Churches to form the
Presbyterian Church of England in 1876.[2] The Scottish influence
had been and continued powerful. Many of the English Presby-

---

[1] "Northumberland has long been the most Presbyterian County of England."
A. H. Drysdale, *History of the Presbyterians in England*, p. 567.
[2] *Ibid.*, p. 625.

90

terian ministers had been trained in the Faculties of Divinity of the Scottish universities of Aberdeen, Edinburgh, Glasgow, and St. Andrews, and reflected the liturgical usages of the Scottish Presbyterian Churches. Their thinking on the theory and practice of worship inevitably manifested their dependence upon the researches of the important Scottish liturgical associations, chiefly the Church Service Society founded in 1865 and the United Presbyterian Devotional Service Association founded in 1882.[3] Moreover, they became familiar with the persuasive writings of the leading Scottish exponents of divine worship, such as Robert Lee, R. H. Story, G. W. Sprott, Thomas Leishman, H. J. Wotherspoon, James Cooper, and C. G. M'Crie.

Furthermore, there was a continuing unity in the worship of the orthodox Dissent in England, which is explicable in part as a result of the common Puritan heritage from the seventeenth century, but also by the fact that many Congregational ministers, for example, prevented until the seventh decade of the nineteenth century from studying at the ancient English universities, elected to undergo theological training in the ancient Scottish universities. In addition, the links of mutual respect between orthodox Dissent in England and Scottish Presbyterianism were strengthened by the frequent award of honorary Doctorates of Divinity by the Scottish universities to leading scholarly ministers of the English Free Churches.

The chief reason, however, for linking Scottish and English Presbyterian worship in a single chapter is that the English Free Churches were enabled to re-appropriate the Catholic tradition in worship through the mediation of Scottish Presbyterian liturgiologists to whom they were bound by ties of history, whereas bitter memories and deep-seated suspicions prevented them from receiving the Catholic inheritance direct from the Oxford Movement. The English heirs of the Puritans came in due time to share the revaluation of worship for which the Scottish heirs of the Puritans were pleading, and which was presented as a form of worship which would combine the advantages of common order with the freedom of the Holy Spirit. Because of the bitter remembrance of the Book of Common Prayer as a legally imposed formulary of worship which had been forced upon their forefathers in

[3] C. G. M'Crie, *The Public Worship of Presbyterian Scotland*, affirms that over a third of the clergy of the Church of Scotland belonged to the Church Service Society in 1892. He also mentions a third liturgical association, founded in 1891, the Public Worship Association of the Free Church.

1662 and which had caused the more conscientious Puritan ministers to become dispossessed Nonconformists, with the loss of so many educational, political, and social privileges, it was not possible to persuade the English Free Churches directly to imitate the worship of the English Church. Yet the same Churches were prepared to listen sympathetically to the Scottish Church because it, too, had suffered under the imposition of the "Laudian Liturgy" in the seventeenth century and yet believed that a greater approximation to a liturgy was necessary. This chapter, therefore, makes the claim that the revaluation of liturgical worship in the Free Churches cannot be explained apart from the astonishing liturgical journey which worship made: from Oxford to London and the provinces via Glasgow and Edinburgh, thus enabling the Oxford Movement of the Tractarians to influence English Nonconformity by way of the mediation of the Scottish Presbyterian Churches.

2. The Need of a Second and Liturgical Reformation

Two incidents only need to be recounted to indicate the desperate need for what Dr. G. W. Sprott called "The Second Reformation"—his title for the nineteenth century liturgical renascence.[4] The first is taken from Wren's Renaissance masterpiece, St. Paul's Cathedral in London. It appears that on the chief day of the Christian year in the chief centre of worship in the metropolis in the year 1800, there was one celebration of Holy Communion at which there was a total of six communicants.[5] If this was the condition of worship in the Church of England, it is not necessary to strain the imagination to depict the slovenly, long, rambling, desultory, repetitive, and windy prayers of the ministers of the Reformed Churches in Scotland and England in the early nineteenth century. This point may be substantiated by one true and revealing anecdote instead of by a mass of dry evidence.[6] It comes from the pen of Dr. Robert Lee, minister of Greyfriars Church, Edinburgh, a great, perhaps the greatest, pioneer of Scottish worship in the nineteenth century.

[4] In his Lee lecture (p. 50), Dr. Sprott had said: "The Second Reformation has done more to revive sound doctrine and strengthen the Church than any other cause." Cited John Kerr, *The Renascence of Worship: The Origin, Aims and Achievements of the Church Service Society*.

[5] Evelyn Underhill, *Hibbert Journal*, Vol. xxx (1932-1933), p. 408 of an article, "The Spiritual Significance of the Oxford Movement."

[6] John Kerr cites Principal R. H. Story of Glasgow University as writing "toward the close of the eighteenth century the public worship of the Church of Scotland had become probably the baldest and rudest in Christendom" (*The Renascence of Worship*, p. 2). Cf. also W. D. Maxwell, who takes a less pessimistic view of the situation in *A History of Worship in the Church of Scotland*, pp. 170, 172-75.

In his famous *Reform of Church Worship* he wrote: "In an Edinburgh Church, much frequented by strangers, especially from England, a gentleman was compelled to stand in the lobby till the devotional services were terminated, and then he was promised a seat. To encourage his perseverance the old woman who kept the door assured him thus: 'Dinna weary, sir, ye'll no hae long to wait; the Doctor's no lang in gettin' through the preleeminaries.' "[7]

Clearly a people, whether Scots or English, who had so exalted the prophetic office of preaching that the prayers had become mere "preliminaries"—a kind of orange or tomato juice that could be dispensed with before the real diet of the strong meat of the Gospel in preaching—and who had made of the Sacrament of Holy Communion a special dessert eaten on rare occasions, were not quickly or easily to be persuaded of the absolute priority of the adoration and glorification of God in worship, despite the fact that the Catechism taught the Scots that "man's chief end is to glorify God and enjoy Him for ever." The very idea of a Liturgy was anathema to the majority who stood proudly in the Puritan tradition. It had become part of the folklore of Scotland and Dissenting England that liturgies were scourges for the scrupulous conscience, the instruments of religious tyranny.

Most Scots schoolboys and every Scottish schoolgirl knew that on the morning of the 23rd July 1637, when the Dean of St. Giles' Cathedral in Edinburgh was reading for the first time the newly imposed High Church Laudian Liturgy, Jenny Geddes threw a stool straight at his head, as a protest on behalf of religious and political freedom. When the story was recounted, it was usually said that Jenny Geddes struck a blow for free prayer. In fact, however, she could be said, with equal truth, to be fighting for the retention of the Scots Liturgy, John Knox's Book of Common Order, which had been used in the same Cathedral that very morning and for many decades before.

Similarly, the English Free Churches (and particularly the major Puritan denominations, the Presbyterians and the Congregationalists) recalled that their forefathers had been forced to leave the Church of England in 1662 because they could not put their hands on their hearts and say that the Book of Common Prayer was in all things conformable to the Word of God. When, however, the story of "the Great Ejection of 1662" was recounted, it was forgotten that the English Presbyterians, headed by Richard

[7] Cited John Kerr, *op.cit.*, pp. 20-21.

Baxter, had asked for comprehension within the Church of England, if only certain minor modifications were to be made in the Anglican formulary of worship. It was also forgotten that Richard Baxter had prepared his Reformed Liturgy (sometimes called the *Savoy Liturgy*) as a possible alternative to the Prayer Book to be used by Anglicans and Presbyterians at the Restoration.

3. *Prejudices and Criticisms To Be Overcome*

Worship, then, needed re-organizing and renewing, but great obstacles stood in the way, of which inaccurate folklore and the prejudices based upon it made up a large part. It is not surprising, therefore, to learn that the liturgical pioneers of Scotland were under a constant barrage of accusations and insinuations. With monotonous regularity the Church Service Society was being charged with many and often incompatible crimes. These are worth considering because they were to become very familiar also in England. The reformers in worship were accused of being a society for the subversion of the Church of Scotland; they were crypto-Catholics intent upon Romanizing the Reformed Church; they were sacerdotalists—they were, incongruously, also sacramentarians; they were assassins of the sermon![8] The two main charges against them, which they had the greatest difficulty in rebutting, were: first, that they intended to introduce a Liturgy into Scotland; and, secondly, that they were aping episcopacy.

The Church Service Society, the most significant of all the Scottish societies for the promotion of the liturgical revolution, took the first criticism so seriously that it issued a special report on its aims designed to mitigate suspicion. Its careful words on this issue were: "Whether the introduction of a Liturgy is desirable and possible, or undesirable and impossible, the Society does not even propose to discuss. Upon that question there may be within it diversity of opinion; but on this point there can be none—That the introduction of a Liturgy into any Church whose worship has not been hitherto liturgical must be a measure long considered, slowly matured, and ultimately carried, not by any private association of clergymen, but by the public, official and constitutional action of the Church herself."[9]

The second charge—that of aping episcopacy or copying Canter-

---

[8] These charges are detailed in full, with confirmatory citations from critics, on pp. 19 f. of *ibid*.

[9] Kerr, *ibid*., prints the report in full on pp. 53-60; the citation is from p. 53.

bury—was one that, unless deflected, could be equally damaging to the reformers of worship in the Church of Scotland and in the English Free Churches, for the former were proudly independent and the latter feared guilt by association. Even an active member of the Church Service Society, such as Dr. Thomas Dykes, found it wise to warn against too much imitation of the foreigners and Sassenachs south of the border and when he made the protest in 1890 there was considerable point in it. This was the canny story which he recounted to bring his fellow countrymen to a just appreciation of their own Scottish heritage: "A clever Englishwoman once went into one of our parish churches and the whole service was so much like what she had heard in England, with some differences, that she was very much surprised. When she came out, she was asked what she thought of it and she said she preferred Scotch broth to Mock-turtle."[10]

A less witty but much more erudite and balanced reply to the criticism was made by Dr. G. W. Sprott. He argued that the Scottish Church was heir to the universal and Catholic Christian tradition of worship from the Primitive Church onwards, and that the English Book of Common Prayer is a skilful anthology of many devotions gathered from many centuries and many lands to which the Scottish or indeed any other Church has equal rights of access. His actual words were these: "The English Liturgy is taken from the Greek and Roman sources which are as much the heritage of the Church of Scotland as that of England; and, further, what may be said to be peculiar and special to the English Liturgy was borrowed from the other Reformed Churches, e.g. the General Thanksgiving was composed by a Presbyterian, other portions being taken from the foreign liturgies on the Continent."[11]

Of course, the fullest answer to this criticism, as of the former one, was provided by the studies and publications of the Church Service Society. When it was founded in 1865 it set itself to improve the public worship of God in a two-fold way: first, by studying the ancient and modern liturgies of many branches of the Church of Christ, both Catholic and Reformed; secondly, by providing annotated reprints of former Liturgies actually used in Scotland and by producing modern forms of worship for the celebration of the Sacraments, for regular Sunday use, and for such occasional ordinances as marriages and burials, based upon sound historical study. The historical studies resulted in the publication of the

[10] *Ibid.*, p. 144.   [11] *Ibid.*, p. 19.

following series of volumes of reprints: *The Book of Common Order, Commonly Called "Knox's Liturgy"* edited by G. W. Sprott; *Scottish Liturgies of the Reign of James VI* also edited by Sprott; *The Westminster Directory* edited by Thomas Leishman; *The Second Liturgy of Edward VI* edited by H. J. Wotherspoon; *The Liturgy of 1637, Commonly Called "Laud's Liturgy"* edited by James Cooper. The constructive volumes issued under the aegis of the Church Service Society included: *Daily Offices for Morning and Evening Prayer*; commemorative orders of worship for important public occasions as on the Diamond Jubilee of Queen Victoria or the Quatercentenary of John Knox; and a Children's Service Book prepared by Professor James Cooper. *Euchologion*, the most important publication, however, deserves detailed consideration.

4. *"Euchologion, a Book of Common Order"*

This notable liturgical compilation first appeared in 1867 and its chief compilers were G. W. Sprott of North Berwick, R. H. Story of Roseneath (later Principal of Glasgow University and friend of Edward Irving, from whose Scottish Church in London the Catholic Apostolic Church with its remarkable Liturgy was to spring into being), and Principal Tulloch of Edinburgh University. While it was not an official publication of the Church of Scotland, it was a representative publication, as the distinction and high offices held by two of its compilers indicate. Moreover, the form for the celebration of Holy Communion was used by the General Assembly of the Church of Scotland from 1890 to 1923, and this indicates the Church's official approbation of the compilation.[12] No book since the Parliamentary Directory had comparable influence on the worship of English-speaking Presbyterianism, as it went through edition after edition.[13]

The first edition in 1867 did not consider the order of the various items of worship, the compilers contenting themselves chiefly with providing materials for prayers and forms for Baptism and the Lord's Supper. The demand for a second and expanded edition in 1869 provided an occasion for supplying four complete services for public worship, and forms for the admission of catechumens and for ordination. The third edition of 1874 included orders of

---

[12] W. D. Maxwell, *A History of Worship in the Church of Scotland*, p. 177.
[13] The eighth edition in 1905 was edited by G. W. Sprott, and has, in addition to an invaluable historical preface, an appendix of fourteen pages indicating the sources of the various prayers.

service for morning and evening for five Sundays, an order for adult Baptism and an alternative exhortation for use before Holy Communion. The fourth and fifth editions, appearing in 1877 and 1884, supplied a revised Lectionary, and services for the visitation of the sick, the admission of elders, the laying of a foundation stone, and the dedication of a church. The Nicene Creed appeared in the Communion service, with the Apostles' Creed as an alternative. The sixth edition of 1890 included the Litany and more prayers for the Christian year and the natural seasons. The seventh edition of 1896 made some important changes, which a later generation felt to be unfortunate in their mistaken imitation of the order of the Anglican Prayer Book. It was, in fact, determined to change the order of public worship: the Lord's Prayer was to be said by minister and congregation at the close of the first prayer, and the intercessions and thanksgiving were to precede the sermon. It is significant that Sprott comments on these changes, as follows: "From this resolution there were dissents, the chief reason, besides the departure from Primitive and Reformed usage, being that the order of the Communion which is the normal service of the Church should be followed as closely as possible at other times. The old order was, however, printed as an alternative."[14]

The successive editions of *Euchologion* were ample justification for the labours of the Church Service Society and it became otiose only in 1923 when the General Assembly's Committee on Aids to Devotion produced an official directory in *Prayers for Divine Service*. There is no reason to dissent from Sprott's evaluation of the influence and values of the book: "It has done much to improve the worship of the Church, to check the ignorant innovations of innovators on their own account, and to preserve sound doctrine in a time of unbelief. The Society has kept many in the Church who, but for it, would have gone over to Episcopacy, and at the same time, by building bridges, bevelling distinctions, and levelling up, it has made a large contribution to Christian reunion."[15]

The best evidence of the Catholicity of the volume is a brief consideration of the many sources from which it was taken.[16] The First Morning Service is drawn chiefly from Calvin's Liturgy in Strassburg and Geneva. The First Evening Service is taken from the American German Reformed Liturgy, with the addition of two

14 *Euchologion, a Book of Common Order*, eighth edn., edited by G. W. Sprott, introduction, p. xxi, n. 2.
15 *Ibid.*, intro., p. xxii.
16 All references in this paragraph are to the eighth edition of 1905.

collects composed by Professor John Bright of Oxford. The Second Morning Service is drawn from a variety of sources, including Dr. Robert Lee, the Book of Common Prayer, and Bishop Jeremy Taylor. The Second Evening Service makes use of the same sources as the previous order, with the addition of intercessions founded chiefly on the Liturgy of St. Basil. The Third Morning Service uses the Liturgy of the Catholic Apostolic Church, Jeremy Taylor and the Anglican Prayer Book. The Third Evening Service borrows the Confession of Archbishop Hermann of Cologne, and the prayers of Archbishop Laud and Bishop Jeremy Taylor, with collects from the ancient Sacramentaries, and elements from the Prayer Book. The Fourth Morning Service uses an Anglican invocation, a confession that is part Calvin and part John Knox, supplications from the Greek and Latin rites, intercessions from the Catholic Apostolic Liturgy itself modelled on oriental forms, a prayer of illumination from Dr. Lee, and a prayer after the sermon from the Prayer Book. This service of itself illustrates the comprehensive range of the sources of the prayers. The Fourth Evening and the Fifth Morning and Evening Services use, in addition to the sources previously mentioned, the Liturgy of St. Clement, commemorative prayers composed by Dr. Martineau, the distinguished Unitarian scholar, and selections from Bright's Ancient Collects, as also from the prayers of St. Augustine, Luther, and Bersier. In all these services only five new prayers were provided, and each of these was Biblical in thought and diction.

Considering these ten orders of worship for Sundays and the collection of supplementary prayers that follows, the real genius of *Euchologion* is seen to consist in the combination of ancient and modern prayers in a manner that is not in the least incongruous or inharmonious. It took brave men to raid the different treasuries of the Greek, Roman, Anglican, and Reformed rites, and to include the very controversial riches of Irving's Catholic Apostolic Liturgy, since the more sober members of the Church of Scotland considered that he had apostatized from the Church of Scotland in his search for a community that would combine the traditional and the charismatic in its worship. It required equal courage, recalling the losses of Presbyterianism to Unitarianism in England, to use the great spiritual resources of Dr. James Martineau. Humility was needed to borrow from the prayers of Professor Shields of Princeton Theological Seminary and from *The Book of Common Worship* of the Presbyterian Church, U.S.A. The compilers were clearly conscious of the old charge of aping episcopacy because, while they make a considerable use of the Book of Common Prayer (and proudly point out that its superb Prayer of General Thanksgiving is the work of Edward Reynolds, the Presbyterian minister who became Bishop of Norwich in 1662), they are careful to indicate that many of the prayers which they take from Anglican sources are themselves only translations from more ancient Liturgies of the East and West.[17]

5. The Communion Order in "Euchologion"

The most important single service in *Euchologion* was "The Order for the Celebration of the Lord's Supper, or Holy Communion." It followed on the prayer after the sermon and began with an Exhortation compiled chiefly from the older Book of Common Order, with some paragraphs from the Book of Common Prayer. The Exhortation concluded with the venerable τὰ ἅγια τοῖς ἁγίοις translated as "Holy things which are for holy persons." The alms were then received and the minister and elders brought in the elements in solemn procession to the communion table, during the singing of a paraphrase, in the Scottish equivalent to the Eastern Church's "Great Entrance." The minister then saluted the people with the grace, read the words of institution (I Corinthians 11: 23-26) as a warrant, and gave a brief address on the meaning of Holy Communion, afterwards setting apart the elements to their sacred use, while taking the paten and cup into his hand. Then followed the Nicene Creed (1905, in earlier editions the Apostles' Creed) in the form of a prayer, with the introductory phrases: "Almighty and eternal God, with Thy holy Church throughout all the world, WE BELIEVE. . . ." Then followed the prayer of approach and confession, the *Agnus Dei* and the prayer of the veil. The Eucharistic Prayer proper, or Consecration Prayer, begins with the *Sursum corda*, continues with thanksgiving for providence and Redemption, and leads into the *Sanctus*; then follow the Epiclesis, the Oblation, and the Lord's Prayer. Because of its departure

[17] Far from aping episcopacy, members of the Scottish liturgical associations were occasionally given to comparing the inadequacy of the Anglican Communion Order with the fullness of the Eastern rites. At a Scottish Church Society Conference in 1894 Dr. John MacLeod said: "The absence of a direct invocation of the Holy Spirit in the consecration, the introduction of the intercession for the whole Church militant previous to the consecration, the absence of any true commemoration of the Holy Departed—all these constitute defects so great as to make it impossible to accept the Anglican service in its present form otherwise than as the example of a meagre, disordered, and defective Eucharistic order." *The Church Service Society Annual*, No. 1, May, 1928, p. 31.

from the Anglican rite and return to the Eastern rites, the Epiclesis deserves to be cited in full: "And we most humbly beseech Thee, O merciful Father, to vouchsafe unto us Thy gracious presence, and so to sanctify with Thy Word and Spirit these Thine own gifts of bread and wine which we set before Thee, that the bread which we break may be to us the communion of the body of Christ, and the cup of blessing which we bless the communion of the blood of Christ."

Then follows the repetition of the manual actions of Christ in the Fraction and Elevation of the chalice, preceded by the words— so characteristic of the Biblical fidelity of the Scottish rite—"According to the holy institution, example and command of our Lord Jesus Christ, and in remembrance of Him, we do this. . . ." It should be noted that since in the Anglican rite these actions take place during the reading of the words of institution in the form of a prayer they are not seen by the people and thus the prophetic symbolism of the actions is lost. The celebrant communicates first, and afterwards the elders and people are communicated. Then the *Pax* is given. A short exhortation to thanksgiving succeeds, followed by a prayer of thanksgiving and a rich intercessory prayer for the Church militant and a thanksgiving for the Church triumphant. The Eucharist closes with *Nunc Dimittis* or *Gloria in Excelsis* and the Benediction.

As in the other orders of service in *Euchologion*, there is a remarkable blending of Eastern, Anglican, and Reformed traditions. The hortatory material and the repetition of the manual actions at the Last Supper before the eyes of the congregation, as the formula for communication, are drawn from the Westminster Directory. The considerable Eastern influence, as seen in the form of the Eucharistic Prayer, and especially in the *epiclesis* and in the comprehensive intercessions for the Church militant and the remembrance of the Church triumphant, were mediated through the Liturgy of the Catholic Apostolic Church. They serve to corroborate the judgment of J. W. Baird that "Any obvious modern influence on Presbyterian forms of service is not Anglican, but rather derives from the 'Liturgy' of the 'Catholic Apostolic' Communion—a marvellous treasury of devotion which we find it difficult to credit as having been compiled only a few years after the beginning of the Oxford Movement."[18]

18 Article "The Service of Holy Communion" in *The Church Service Society Annual*, No. 1, 1928-1929, May, p. 32. Cf. W. D. Maxwell, *A History of Wor-*

The Scottish rite is no mere anthology of other rites and has its own distinctive excellence. While it retains the Eastern Orthodox ceremony of the "Great Entrance" (as also the *epiclesis*), yet it does not use other ceremonies such as lights and incense; moreover, the whole Communion Order differs from the Eastern Orthodox Eucharist in that all is done within the sight and hearing of the people. It differs from the Roman rite in using the language of the people, in its adherence to Scriptural precedent, and in its invocation of the Holy Spirit upon the elements. It differs from the Anglican usage in having an *epiclesis*, in using a prayer of confession at the beginning of the order, and in placing the fraction, libation, and intercession after the consecration. It differs from the Greek, Roman, and Anglican rites in refusing to incorporate the Words of Institution in the Consecration prayer; in this it follows most of the ancient liturgies, and in the Scots rite the words are accompanied with the solemn actions of the Christ who spake them.

6. *Other Scottish Liturgiologists*

Important as was the work of the Church Service Society, it would be entirely erroneous to give the impression that it alone was concerned with the improvement of Divine worship in Scotland in the nineteenth century. To begin with, there were other important Presbyterian liturgical associations in the field. The Devotional Service Association of the United Presbyterian Church formed in 1883 published a service-book entitled *Presbyterian Forms of Service* in 1891 with subsequent editions in 1892 and 1899. The Public Worship Association of the Free Church was formed in 1891 and published *A New Directory for Public Worship* in 1898 which included prayers as well as directions for worship. The Church Worship Association of the United Free Church formed in 1901 published an *Anthology of Prayers* in 1907, which was reissued the following year, and produced a *Directory and Forms for Public Worship* in 1909.

In addition to these societies for the improvement of public worship among Scottish Presbyterians, there were remarkable individual contributions to the Second Reformation. Chief among these was *The St. Giles' Book of Common Order* prepared by Cameron Lees and in use in the cathedral from 1884 to 1926. It was re-

---

ship in the Church of Scotland, p. 179: "It was influenced in much by the rite of the Catholic Apostolic Church, but is by no means derived from that rite, and it follows the Directory closely."

markable in providing a service-book for every day in the year, although at Communion the *Euchologion* Eucharistic order was used.[19] Another important work was compiled by H. J. Wotherspoon and entitled *The Divine Service, A Eucharistic Office According to the Forms of the Primitive Church* (1893).

Several important books and pamphlets appeared on the history and theory of worship throughout the latter part of the century in Scotland. Many of these had an important effect upon the Presbyterians in England and guided them in their liturgical reforms. The work of Bonar, Bannerman, M'Crie, and Wright are especially worthy of brief consideration. Andrew A. Bonar, under the anonymous description of "A Minister of the Church of Scotland," did for the Scottish Church what Baird accomplished in *Eutaxia* for American Presbyterians, that is, convinced them that there was no historic antagonism between Presbyterianism and Liturgy. His book, appearing in Edinburgh in 1858, was entitled, *Presbyterian Liturgies with Specimens of Forms of Prayer for Worship as Used in the Continental Reformed and American Churches; with The Directory for the Public Worship of God Agreed Upon by the Assembly of Divines at Westminster; and Forms of Prayer for Ordinary and Communion Sabbaths, and for other Services of the Church.*

His work is important as preparing the way for the Church Service Society's work, in its description of the innovations of Dr. Robert Lee of Greyfriars Church in Edinburgh who was Scotland's liturgical pioneer, in his diagnosis of the defects of existing Scottish worship (which he maintained were didactic prayers and over-emphasizing the sermon),[20] and, above all, in insisting on the need for special forms of worship for the Sacraments and occasional ordinances as well as for a hymn-book. His most effective way of rebutting the charge that the Presbyterian Church should remain content with free prayer as alone in its true tradition was by presenting irrefutable evidence of the existence of Continental and American Reformed Liturgies. He particularly emphasized the need of a service-book for scattered and ministerless congregations

---

[19] Cf. *The Church Service Society Annual*, 1953-1954, article by C. T. Thornton.

[20] On the over-emphasis of the sermon he says: "Churches are too often converted into scenes of rhetorical exhibition on the part of the minister. . . . The vacant parish thus often becomes the locale of a mere preaching match; in which the people sit in judgment, and wherein pictorial delineation and loudness of voice, with a due admixture of animal excitement, are likely to be esteemed far above a more sober, thoughtful, and unpretending style of discourse" (p. 6).

in the English-speaking colonies and for families who could not attend church as in winter in the Highlands, who otherwise had recourse to the Book of Common Prayer. Such a service-book would also provide and maintain orthodox views of Baptism and the Lord's Supper "in these times, when Romanism and Puseyism are making such strides."[21]

D. D. Bannerman provided a moderate defence of liturgical worship, moderate because he would by no means exclude a place for free prayer, in *The Worship of the Presbyterian Church with Special Reference to the Question of Liturgies*.[22] An able introductory chapter insists that the ideal of Presbyterian worship has five characteristics: it is spiritual, Scriptural in requiring the positive authority of God's Word, it makes the Word of God central in worship, requires full congregational participation, and is both simple and elastic—that is, capable of adaptation to circumstances and emergencies.[23] He believes there is a place for liturgical forms in Presbyterian worship provided they are not made compulsory and that they do not lead to the absolute exclusion of extemporary prayer. He admits that the practice of extemporary prayer is daunting to young ministers, but that it has often established a true spiritual sympathy between minister and people.

The great value of the book is its judicious estimate of the values and dangers of an exclusive dependence upon either liturgical or extemporary prayer. On the whole he favours an optional liturgy like the old Scottish Book of Common Order. It would raise the standard of devotional taste in public prayer.[24] It would give the people a more direct share in the devotional part of worship, as distinguished from the praise.[25] It would supply a great need "on special occasions, at sea, in India, in the colonies."[26] It would be a practical defence of the rights of Christian people in connection with the administration of Baptism and marriage, for parents and the bridegroom and bride would know what vows they had to make

---

[21] *Ibid.*, p. 55. [22] Published in Edinburgh, 1884.
[23] He makes (pp. 24-25) a great point of the unsuitability of a liturgy for emergencies, citing an experience of Phillips Brooks. Apparently a large American Episcopal Convention was gathered when news came of a great city being gutted by fire, and consequently of thousands of people homeless and exposed to danger. It was agreed to adjourn the meeting and join in prayer until a fatal difficulty emerged—there was no form of prayer in the Liturgy suitable for such an emergency. So the assembled bishops had to use the Litany "laying before God almost every woe but the woe of a burning city." Bannerman's source is *The Catholic Presbyterian*, Vol. VII, p. 54.
[24] *Ibid.*, p. 76. [25] *Ibid.*, p. 77. [26] *Ibid.*, p. 78.

before making them.[27] It would enlarge the devotional experience of minister and people by making available the devout thought of the ancient and Reformation Liturgies.[28] Finally, it would make the people realize more than they do "the true unity of the Church of Christ in what is best and highest in all ages of her history."[29]

M'Crie and Wright provided two solid and substantial histories of the worship of Scottish Presbyterianism. C. G. M'Crie's work appeared in 1892 and was entitled *The Public Worship of Presbyterian Scotland*. Alexander Wright's volume appeared in 1895 and was entitled *The Presbyterian Church, Its Worship, Functions and Ministerial Orders*. M'Crie shows that it was possible at the end of the century to be appreciative of the work of such reformers as Robert Lee without being blind to their faults. The approach was sober, historically sound, and mature. For example, he maintains that Lee had little respect for Catholic usage and that the spirit of his prayers was rationalistic rather than mystical or tender. The contributions to liturgical reform of each of the three Presbyterian Churches in Scotland are carefully recorded and analysed.

Wright's book is an even more admirable history of the worship of the Scottish Presbyterian Churches written "to promote an improvement in the ritual of the various branches of the Presbyterian Church" and to show that such are in accord with the use and wont of the Reformed Church of Scotland.[30] He gives an account of the reforming predecessors of Robert Lee, of the various attempts to produce an adequate Scottish hymn-book, and a fully-documented record of the aims of the various liturgical associations in Scotland, including the important Scottish Church Society which had been founded only in 1893. This, he claims, represented the views of the advanced High Church party in the Church of Scotland. Their aims were three-fold:

"To defend and advance Catholic doctrine as set forth in the ancient creed, and embodied in the standard of the Church of Scotland;

"Generally to assert Scriptural principles in all matters relating to Church order and policy, Christian work and spiritual life throughout Scotland;

"To consider the Church's attitude towards many of those social questions which are at present forcing themselves upon the minds of all thoughtful men."[31]

---

[27] *Ibid.*, pp. 78-79. [28] *Ibid.*, p. 79. [29] *Ibid.*, p. 81.
[30] *Ibid.*, p. 33. [31] *Ibid.*, p. 271.

This society the author evidently disliked, since he criticized its Romanism, Episcopacy, and Ritualism. Moreover, he considered the view of one of its members, Dr. John MacLeod of Govan, namely "that the celebration of the Holy Communion is the distinctive ordinance of Christian worship," to be entirely "prelatic."[32]

His own views approximate those of M'Crie. Far from demanding the exclusive use of a Liturgy, he asks "simply for the restoration of the union of liturgical and free prayer."[33] His requests are, in fact, essentially moderate, for he wants no more than that congregations should at stated times rehearse the creeds, recite the Lord's Prayer, respond "Amen" to the minister's prayer, and commemorate the chief festivals of the Christian year associated with the birth, death, resurrection, and ascension of Christ.[34]

7. The Effects of the Scottish Liturgical Renaissance

The study and work of four Scottish Presbyterian liturgical associations, the impact of the successive editions of *Euchologion*, and the plethora of literary treatments of the subject of worship, as well as the examples of the reverent conduct of worship by so many ministers changed the whole attitude towards worship in the Scottish Presbyterian Churches, and profoundly influenced the discussion of the same theme in the Presbyterian Church of England, and even among English Nonconformists generally.

The differences could be seen in the nature and length of the prayers, the place of the offertory, the dignity of the church marriage service and of the form of ordination to the ministry, the provision of services for the dedication of churches, the improvement of the burial services, the regular observation of the Christian year, the more frequent celebration of Holy Communion, and in the restoration of old churches. Prayer ceased to be rambling and repetitious and there came to be a generally accepted division of prayer into confession, thanksgiving, supplication, and intercession, though no particular sequence was agreed upon. The offertory was no longer relegated to a place at the door of the church in which the departing worshippers furtively deposited their pelf; instead it was given a place in the service and was consecrated to God's use. Marriage services, with their solemn vows, were so improved that the older custom of marriage in private houses was

---

[32] *Ibid.*, p. 278.
[33] Alexander Wright, *The Presbyterian Church, Its Worship, Functions and Ministerial Orders*, p. 278.
[34] *Ibid.*

105

becoming less frequent. In the ordination service it became customary for a senior minister to deliver the charges to both minister and people, and for neighbouring ministers to attend in their robes and hoods. Services for the dedication of churches and for burials were innovations.[35]

It became increasingly common to celebrate the birth, passion, resurrection, and ascension of Christ and the donation of the Holy Spirit to the Church at Pentecost. Holy Communion, which had been celebrated annually in remote country areas, and quarterly in the cities and towns, was frequently celebrated monthly. Under the impact of various ecclesiological societies, many historic and ancient Scottish churches were restored, among them Old Grey-friars and St. Giles', in Edinburgh, St. Mungo in Brechin, Dunblane Cathedral, King's College in Aberdeen, St. Vigean's, and Paisley Abbey. Fine new churches also were built, including the parish church in Govan, the Barony Church in Glasgow, St. Oswald's in Edinburgh, and New Greyfriars in Aberdeen. Instead of being mere auditories for preaching, they became sanctuaries for worship. All this amounted to nothing less than a revolution in worship, which has continued in a remarkable way in the Church of Scotland of the twentieth century, in which the Reformed and Catholic heritage, the joint importance of sermon, Sacrament, prayers, and praises has been maintained in balance.

The proof of the effectiveness of the liturgical renaissance in Scotland is to be seen in words written by a moderate who trembled in 1895 because he felt the liturgical sense was over-developed in the Presbyterian Churches in the Scotland of his day: "Though no liturgy has yet been sanctioned by the Assembly of the Established Church, there is a growing feeling in that Church for one, and in many congregations prayers are read by the officiating minister, from Sabbath to Sabbath, and free prayer almost abandoned. And in several churches of pronounced advanced type certain festivals have been reintroduced, such as Christmas, Good Friday, Easter, and the choir, in Anglican fashion, have become habited in surplices. Doubtless the tendency in many congregations is towards a highly advanced ritual, and the danger exists on the part of many

---

[35] Dr. Sprott began the custom of holding burial services; there was none, for example, for the distinguished Dr. Robert Lee of the Greyfriars Church. This was due to the old Puritan prohibition which reacted against the insincere custom of the Established Church in the early seventeenth century of committing even vagabonds to the grave "in sure and certain hope of everlasting life" and of eulogizing the dead to fantastic heights.

ministers and others to rush to extremes and to leave behind much that is distinctively Presbyterian in the fresh and unrestrained and somewhat feverish rush to have a service which will commend itself to the aesthetic tastes and culture of the advanced wing of Presbyterianism."[36] The fear was groundless, but its very existence was proof that the Church of Scotland was recovering its Catholic heritage in worship.

II. THE WORSHIP OF THE PRESBYTERIAN CHURCH OF ENGLAND[37]

A study of the history of the worship of the Presbyterian Church of England in the nineteenth century would seem to indicate that there was little widespread will to liturgical improvement, and that the Church's concern for a revised edition of the Westminster Directory was as hotly denied as it was asserted, because it took the appropriate Committee of the Synod from 1882 to 1898 to produce an agreed revision, and even this was not submitted to the approval of individual Presbyteries in the Church. The distinct impression is obtained that the liturgiologists of the Church were few, that they were driven to argue for a revision because of the inadequacies of the Old Directory to meet the new demands for burial and marriage services, and that their arguments drew upon those of Scottish writers and upon Scottish precedents.

1. The Inadequacy of the Old "Directory"

Before the agitation for a revised Directory of worship arose, the worship of the English Presbyterian Church seems to have been unprogressive. In 1882 a Synod enquiry under the chairmanship of Dr. Monro Gibson was undertaken into the condition of worship in the churches. The results indicated that of the 279 churches replying 218 confined themselves largely to metrical psalmody rather than included hymnody and that 61 congregations did without any musical instruments in their praise. The report acidly describes the general nature of English Presbyterian worship as "repulsive" to persons of taste.

36 Alexander Wright, *op.cit.*, p. 264.
37 In the ensuing part of this chapter the writer is greatly indebted to a manuscript essay loaned to him by the late Rev. J. F. Marquis (a learned archivist of the Presbyterian Church of England), which he had prepared under the title of "What we *Used to do* in Church: The Revision of the Westminster Directory, 1882-1898." The documentation of this manuscript, with its summaries of the proceedings of the Synod's Committees on Public Worship, has proved an invaluable source for the history of English Presbyterian Worship.

The inadequacy of the Directory was chiefly and most acutely felt in the matter of services for marriages and burials. The Westminster Directory presupposed that these ordinances were the concern of the State, not of the Church. Furthermore, until 1836 marriages could be solemnized only in Anglican churches in England; after that date the presence of a Registrar was necessary and the service was illegal unless held in an edifice licensed for the purpose. The Directory provided even less assistance for Nonconformists on the matter of burials, since it reacted strongly against Roman Catholic abuses and laid down the following prohibition: "praying, reading, and singing, going to and at the grave, have been grossly abused, are in no way beneficial to the dead, and have proved many ways hurtful to the living; therefore let all such things be laid aside." After interment, all that was allowed to Christian friends was that they might retire to a convenient place, where the minister, "if he be present, may put them in remembrance of their duty." It was not until 1880 that a bill became law which gave a right to inter in parochial cemeteries after forty-eight hours notice had been given to the incumbent. In several parishes the Anglican clergy were obstructive over a considerable number of years.

It was the removal of these disabilities in burial arrangements in 1880 that led Nonconformists to wish to show that they could conduct dignified burial services, as the Act demanded. Until the Presbyterian Church of England was to authorize its own form of burial, its ministers were content with either importing the burial service from *Euchologion* or using the burial order compiled by the English Congregationalist, Dr. Henry Allon. It was the pertinacity of the Rev. A. L. Henderson of Durham, and later of Camphill, that finally succeeded in getting the Synod to appoint a committee to consider the need for providing occasional services for which no directions were provided in the Directory.

2. The Work of Exploration

This Committee of 1885 and 1886 was a small and exploratory group, but it consisted of men who held the view that "it is desirable to prepare a revised Directory on the lines of the Westminster Directory and along with this forms of service provided for optional use on special occasions, as marriage, burials, ordination of office-bearers, reception of young communicants." The committee further

108

believed that from such a revision "the Church would gain in the completion, concord and decorum of her services."[38]

It began its work by sending out a questionnaire to the churches asking for an account of their customs in worship. The results of the scrutiny of 200 answers are interesting. It was clear that printed forms of worship for the Lord's Supper, marriages, burials, and the reception of new communicants were very generally used, but that, in all, 24 different printed forms were in use. This liturgical chaos provided the committee with a strong argument for an official series of forms for these occasional services. Variety also characterized the celebration of the Sacraments. One congregation celebrated the Lord's Supper every fortnight, 22 celebrated monthly, 34 celebrated every two months, 89 celebrated quarterly, and 10 celebrated only twice a year. The enquiry also revealed the disturbing information that Baptism in private was the predominating custom. There were also considerable diversity in the conduct of regular Sunday services in the morning and evening. All but 30 of the congregations had two Scripture lections in the morning service, but the practice was most uncommon in the evenings. One hundred and eighteen congregations only repeated the Lord's Prayer at either the morning or evening service, but none repeated the Apostles' Creed. Very few congregations repeated the Creed even in the Communion service. The committee felt that the only reasonable conclusion it could come to was to recommend the Synod to appoint a Special Committee "with instructions to proceed with due care and deliberation in the direction of revising the Westminster Directory, and preparing forms or specimens of service adapted to special occasions."

3. *The Drafting and Debating of the Revised Directory*

The Chairman of the Committee, Dr. Donald Fraser of Marylebone Presbyterian Church, was ably assisted in the production of various drafts of the revision by his secretary, Moinet, and by two keen collectors of liturgies, Principal Dykes and Mr. Rodger. They went quickly and enthusiastically to the work, but every order of service was hotly debated in the Synod. There was a clear and acute division of opinion. On the one hand there were, says Marquis, "some going back beyond Puritanism to Knox and Melville, and others taking their stand on the Nonconformist practice

[38] Cf. Dr. Donald Fraser's article on "Confirmation" in *The Catholic Presbyterian*, Vol. VII, p. 118.

of their day, which they believed to be the true, long-standing, evangelical way of ordering Public Worship."[39] In the Synod of 1891 an evangelical eagerheart, the Rev. S. R. Macphail of Canning Street, Liverpool, tabled an amendment remitting the draft to the committee and urged his brethren to intimate "that no Synodical approval has been given to the present printed draft." Macphail printed an enlarged version of his speech, with that of his seconder, Mr. T. M. Douglas, as *Liturgical Proposals to Presbyterians of England Tried by History, Experience, and Scripture*. His criticisms were acutely phrased and admirably set in order. He deplored the archaic and ritual expressions of the draft, its lurking Catholicity, and the offensive and untrue echo of the Prayer Book words of committal in the burial service. His greatest wrath was reserved for the requirement that the Apostles' Creed should be recited in either the Communion or Baptismal services, claiming that "it is now a commonplace that the present form of the Apostles' Creed was not reached until the 8th century." His final comment on this point is: "A Creed equally open to Arianists, Romanists, and ourselves, is extremely unsuitable for use in God's worship." Evidently not a glimmer of Ecumenism had penetrated the complacency of his denominational doctrinal darkness.

The death of Dr. Donald Fraser, and the Synod's lack of confidence in Moinet, his successor, led the redoubtable Macphail to move that an entirely new committee be appointed for the revision. A debate in which incendiarists on both sides participated led to adjournment for a year. A reconstituted committee started on its revisionary work only in 1894.

The work of the committee was not concluded until 1898, but even then the controversy was not over. True to form, Macphail had his objections to offer. This time he criticized the service for "The Dedication of a Church Building" as it did not, in his judgment, add anything to the holiness of the edifice. The motion was defeated, probably from indifference rather than from conviction. The rest of the book was approved, but with important changes. For instance, the prayers in the baptismal and admission services were reduced to mere directions, but the forms for marriage, burial, and dedication were retained substantially in their integrity. A lectionary was also drawn up, being chiefly the work of the Rev. D. Matheson of Putney.

[39] Page 11 of the typescript of the Rev. J. F. Marquis.

4. *The Publication of the Revised Westminster Directory of 1898*

The work of twelve years was completed with the publication of the Revised Directory in 1898, but it can have given little satisfaction either to its promoters or to the obstructionists. The latter had not succeeded in preventing its being published, but the former—its promoters—could not describe it as the official Liturgy of the Presbyterian Church of England. It was never submitted to the presbyteries for approval or disapproval, and wisely, for its reception would have been a divided one. Hence it was acknowledged by the Presbyterian Church of England as containing forms which might be found useful and might be used if found expedient. The only official part of the Revised Directory was the formula for ordination which was sanctioned in 1892. But even if this was less than the promoters of the revision hoped for, it was more than had been achieved by the Church of Scotland by the end of the nineteenth century. *Euchologion*, however wide might be its influence, was the publication of the Church Service Society, not of an official Committee of the Church of Scotland. Indeed, it is very doubtful if *Euchologion*, with its wide use of the ancient Greek and Latin rites and the modern Catholic Apostolic Liturgy, would ever have been as advanced liturgically as it was if it had been the compilation of an official and cautious Committee of the Church of Scotland. At least the Revised Directory represents a common optional norm for the worship of English Presbyterians, and this was considerably more than the English Baptists or Congregationalists had achieved.

What pattern of worship emerges from a consideration of the Revised Westminster Directory of 1898? The shape of the regular Sunday Morning Service, which could be abbreviated considerably for the shorter Evening Service, was as follows:

Invitation to worship with suitable Scripture Sentences
Prayer of Invocation
Psalm or Hymn
Prayers of Adoration, Confession and Petition for Pardon
Old Testament Lection
Hymn of Praise (suitable for Children)
(Optional Children's Address)
New Testament Lection
(Optional recitation of Apostles' Creed)
Prayers of Thanksgiving, Supplication, Intercession and
the Lord's Prayer

111

Psalm or Hymn
> Announcements
> (Optional Prayer for Illumination)
> Sermon and brief prayer at conclusion
> Offertory

Psalm or Hymn
> The Blessing

The form for the celebration of the Lord's Supper is rather disappointing, especially if compared with the richer and more comprehensive fare provided by *Euchologion*. It consisted of the following parts:

> Exhortation and Fencing of the Tables
> Hymn (during which the minister and elders take their
>> places at the Table)
> Hymn, Psalm or appropriate passages of Scripture
>> Prayer of Approach
>> The Eucharistic Prayer, including an *epiclesis*, oblation,
>>> and optional *Tersanctus*
>> The Distribution of the elements
>> Brief Exhortation (optional)
>> Prayers of Thanksgiving, Intercession for the Church
>>> Militant, and remembrance of the faithful departed
> Psalm or Hymn
>> Offering for the Poor
>> The Blessing from Hebrews 13:20-21.

In comparison with the most advanced thought and practice in the Church of Scotland, this is a bare Communion rite. It lacks the "Great Entrance"; the order of the parts of the Eucharistic Prayer is curious and it contains no *Sursum corda*; the Institution narrative is not required as a warrant; the manual acts of Fraction and the Elevation of the Cup, so important a feature of fidelity to the Lord's own acts in the Last Supper in the Scottish order, are missing. Yet when all is said by way of criticism, this is a considerable advance on the rare and perfunctory exhibitions of naked memorialism which were all too common before the publication of the Revised Directory of 1898. A beginning was made in 1898 which was to grow to liturgical maturity in the ensuing century. Furthermore, the Presbyterian Church in England was not, like the Church of Scotland, an Established Church with many important and cultured city parishes avid for liturgical experiment, nor did it have the ancient liturgical traditions of the Church of Scotland to look back to for encouragement. It was a heterogeneous group of recent traditions and it found its natural affinity with the Evangelical Dissenters who would have pronounced its moderate Revised Directory of 1898 a dangerous flirting with Rome. It had at least the notable distinction of having produced the only denominationally approved optional service-book of all the heirs of the Puritans in the British Isles in the nineteenth century. And this it had done against acute opposition.

CHAPTER V

THE CATHOLIC TREND OF ANGLICAN WORSHIP: THE "RITUALISTIC" CONTROVERSY AND THE RELIGIOUS COMMUNITIES

THE DEVELOPMENT OF ANGLICAN WORSHIP in a more Catholic and often Roman Catholic direction in the second half of the nineteenth century is attested by two significant movements: the "Ritualistic Controversy"[1] and the rapid growth of Religious Communities. The Anglo-Catholics, who may be regarded as the second generation of the Tractarians, and more ceremonially inclined, propagated their views militantly in the Ritualistic Controversy when under attack from Evangelicals, and more peaceably in the Religious Communities, where ascetical spirituality and the revival of the daily offices of the Breviary and of Eucharistic devotions could be practised in relative independence from the secular arm. Thus in war and peace, in parish controversy and monastic quietude, the Catholic trends of worship were advanced.

The Ritualistic Controversy was a dramatic testimony to the determination of many Anglo-Catholic priests to adopt the liturgical practices of the pre-Reformation Church in England and, in not a few cases, the extra-liturgical devotions of the post-Tridentine Roman Catholic Church in Western Europe. They clung to their advanced ceremonial the more tenaciously when they were attacked by noisy mobs, testy bishops, and litigating Evangelicals. The first thunders of the approaching storm were heard in 1844 in St. Sepulchre's Church, Cambridge, where in the process of restoration a stone altar was erected by eager parishioners against the will of the incumbent and the church-wardens, and the con-

---

[1] The following note on the term "Ritual" (from p. 1168b of *The Oxford Dictionary of the Christian Church*, ed. F. L. Cross) is pertinent: "Strictly, the prescribed form of words of a liturgical function. By common usage, the word is also employed, in a derogatory sense, of the accompanying ceremonial. In the nineteenth century the term 'Ritualist' was commonly used of those who introduced or reintroduced Mediaeval or modern Roman Catholic ceremonial practices into the Church of England."

114

troversy was not concluded at the end of the century, for during its last decade the devout Bishop of Lincoln, Edward King, had to stand trial before the Archbishop of Canterbury for his alleged deviations from the liturgical norm of the Prayer Book.

The controversy over ritual and ceremonial became a national issue with the formation in 1859 of the English Church Union by the Anglo-Catholics to provide legal support for the prosecuted ritualistic priests, and with the foundation of the Church Association by the Evangelicals in 1865 to prosecute the ritualists. The unremitting struggle was most acute between 1871 and 1882 when four priests, held to be contumacious by the civil court whose authority they would not recognize, were imprisoned.[2] It proved, however, to be a Pyrrhic victory for the Evangelicals, since a fair-minded public was as revolted by the vindictiveness of the prosecutors as it was full of admiration for the courage of the Anglo-Catholic priests, most of whom were esteemed for their self-denying devotion to their parishioners in some of the foulest slums of the metropolis.

This late and almost reluctant expression of admiration by a public easily roused by the cry of "No Popery" would never have been given to men who were thought to be effeminate, aesthetic, or esoteric, and it helped to win respect for their doctrines of which the ceremonial was the expression. At all events, however bitter the controversy and however unsuitable it was for the mysteries of the Christian faith to be discussed in rationalistic fashion, the attention of an increasingly secularized nation was turned to the question of the most suitable worship of the Divine Majesty.

It was also, of course, a lamentable failure of Christian charity that the house of the English Church, divided against itself, presented to the nation. To some degree tension is inevitable in a "bridge church" claiming to be both Catholic and Reformed, and the seventeenth century had witnessed strain between the "Papistical" and the "Puritanical" wings. Furthermore, where truth is felt to be at stake, tolerance must seem to be the virtue of the uncaring. The point must be made that both Anglo-Catholics and Evangelicals fought so bitterly only because they cared so passionately for the truth of religion, however differently they were to define it.

It was emphatically no storm in a ceremonial tea-cup; no trivial

2 These were Tooth, imprisoned in 1877; T. P. Dale and R. W. Erraght, imprisoned in 1880; and S. F. Green, imprisoned between 1881-1882.

choice between a "tuppenny coloured" or "penny plain" worship, determined on temperamental or aesthetic grounds; least of all was it a passing whim for this item of ecclesiastical millinery or that device of liturgical stagecraft. It was basically a theological struggle, a contest between Catholic and Protestant conceptions of Divine Grace, the Sacraments, the nature of the Church, and therefore of the type of worship appropriate to such conceptions.

This is plainly to be seen in both the "Gorham Case" (1847-1850) and the "Denison Case" (1853-1858), which owe their acerbity entirely to High and Low ideas of the nature, respectively, of Baptism and Holy Communion. In the former case, Phillpotts, the High Church Bishop of Exeter, who, with the Tractarians, believed in "Baptismal Regeneration" as being effected by the Rite, refused to institute Gorham to the living of Brampford Speke because the latter held that Baptismal regeneration might precede or succeed the Rite, but was not invariably tied to the Rite itself. In the "Denison Case" the High Church Archdeacon Denison, and a Fellow of Oriel, taught the doctrine of the "Real Presence" in the Eucharist, affirming that the Body and Blood of Christ are supernaturally and invisibly present in Holy Communion by virtue of the act of consecration, that both parts of the Sacrament, outward and inward, are received by all who communicate, and that worship is due to the Body and Blood of Christ present under the forms of bread and wine. Archbishop Sumner's Commission of Inquiry insisted that a "receptionist" doctrine of Holy Communion was required by the formularies of the Church of England, and that Denison's contention that to "all who come to the Lord's Table, whether worthily or unworthily, the Body and Blood of Christ are given and by them received" was directly contrary to the doctrine of the Church of England.[3] Here again, there was a conflict between a High Church Catholic and a Low Church or Evangelical doctrine of the Sacraments.

What might seem to be strictly ceremonial issues also had their doctrinal overtones or implications. An apparently trivial vestiarian issue, such as whether a clergyman should wear a black gown or a surplice in the pulpit, became important when each garment was interpreted as a theological party badge. While there was ample authority for the insistence of Bishop Blomfield of London

---

[3] For the Gorham case see J. C. S. Nias, *Gorham and the Bishop of Exeter* and for the Denison case, see F. Warre Cornish, *The English Church in the Nineteenth Century*, Pt. II (1910), pp. 130-32.

that all his diocesan clergy should wear the surplice as demanded by the Book of Common Prayer, yet the fact that it had not been used for over two centuries by the vast majority of English clergymen, and the more serious consideration that in the use of the gown the English Church approximated the attire of Reformed ministers on the Continent and of orthodox Dissenting divines in England, made its retention a proof of the Protestantism of the Church of England. So, obviously, the disuse of the gown and the substitution of a surplice were interpreted as an approximation to the usage of the Roman Catholic Church. An apparently minor ceremonial issue—whether the clergy should be permitted to employ the eastward position (facing the altar, with their backs towards the worshippers) in the celebration of the Holy Communion—became an important one because of its implications. For the Anglo-Catholics who used the eastward posture, this was a sign that the Eucharist was a sacrifice, the clergyman a priest, and the communion-table an altar, all of which the Evangelical denied on Protestant grounds.

To the uninstructed, or, better, the bewildered layman, on whom fell an avalanche of tracts and counter-tracts and whose ears were confused by discordant episcopal, judicial, and parliamentary pronouncements, these issues might well seem exaggerated and grossly partisan. For many of the clergy, however, they were the cause of deep heart-searching and perplexity. Indeed, those for whom the Erastianism of the Church of England, ultimately in the control of the English Parliament, was intolerable, sought refuge in the Roman fold by the hundreds, or, in the Free Churches by the handful.[4] At the end of the century not even an armistice had been reached and the inconclusive debates on the Revised Prayer Book of 1927 and 1928 were a proof that agreement had not been reached even then on the permissible limits of ceremonial in the Catholic and Reformed Church of England.

The victory, though unacknowledged by Mr. Kensit and his *circumcelliones*, lay with the Catholic party, who, however some bishops might remonstrate with them and even on occasion force them to seek a more congenial diocesan under whom to serve, taught their catechisms and illustrated their doctrine with high

---

4 Between 1840 and 1899 no less than 446 Tractarians joined the Roman Catholic Church, including the future Cardinals Newman and Manning. Archdeacon Manning was one casualty of the Gorham Judgment and another was the Hon. the Rev. Baptist Noel, Daniel Wilson's successor at St. John's, Bedford Row, who became a Baptist minister. Cf. G. R. Balleine, *A History of the Evangelical Party in the Church of England* (revised edn. of 1951), p. 185.

117

ceremonial at the end of the century. The highest of High Church liturgical observances, as will be seen, were practised with less opposition because they took place in the private oratories of the religious communities, with an impressive spirituality. The most signal proofs of this Anglo-Catholic victory lay in the abandonment by the Church Association of its policy of persecution[5] and in the revolution in architecture and ecclesiastical furnishings accepted by the Evangelicals themselves. The desertion of the Greek architectural manner to erect cruciform neo-Gothic edifices, the surrender of the gown for the surplice in the pulpit and even its use for members of the choir, as well as the placing of a simple cross on the communion-table and the use of distinctively Christian decorative emblems, and more frequent Communions, were eventually to become common practice among Evangelicals. The first Tractarians, no less than Charles Simeon, would have been amazed to witness the liturgical "right turn" that the Church of England had taken by the end of the century.[6]

1. *The Causes of the Ceremonial Revival*

It is commonly asserted that the first generation of Tractarians, especially their leaders, Newman and Pusey, were uninterested in ceremonial and ritual. Had not Pusey protested that "the leaders of the Tracts always deprecated it, especially any revival of disused vestments"?[7] Did he not refuse to adopt the eastward posture when celebrating in Christ Church Cathedral until 1871? Had he not written of this ceremony that it "seemed certainly against the rubric" and that "Dear Newman consecrated to the last at the North End"?[8] Did they not both remonstrate with Bloxam of Magdalen when he was infuriating the Bishop of Oxford with his tactless wearing of idiosyncratic vestments embroidered with a cross? All these statements lend considerable colour to the view that the Tractarian leaders were uninterested in ritual and ceremonial. Certainly, it would seem that theirs was a policy of first things first—

---

[5] *Ibid.*, pp. 231-32.

[6] It should be recognized, however, that the Evangelicals won a victory, also, in the increasing frequency of Evening Communions, to which many of the Anglo-Catholics objected (although Dr. Hook of Leeds was a supporter) because they could hardly be fasting Communions. In 1869 sixty-five London churches adopted the practice and by 1879 the number was increased to 262. In 1881 a hundred of the 261 churches of the predominantly Evangelical diocese of Rochester had Evening Communion. Cf. *ibid.*, p. 193.

[7] Letter to Bishop Tait in R. T. Davidson and T. W. Benham, *Life of Archibald Campbell Tait, Archbishop of Canterbury*, Vol. IV, p. 211.

[8] Letter to Scott cited in *ibid.*

a concentration on the revival of Catholic doctrine and Church order (especially the apostolical succession), and the Sacramental life.

Yet there is also another side to the picture, which would suggest that in the institutions which were more their private concern than their public responsibility they were greatly interested in ceremonial. Newman was plainly interested in the refurnishing of his retreat in Littlemore chapel. Pusey, in building St. Saviour's, Leeds, at his own cost, hoped to provide a model centre of revived Catholic church life, with the appropriate inward and outward expression in its worship. The truth seems to be that they felt that rash innovators in ceremonial would alienate the bishops by flouting their authority and bring into jeopardy the doctrinal and sacramental matters which were primary. Moreover, perhaps both Pusey and Newman retained enough of their Evangelical heritage to suspect that religious aestheticism might only too easily lead to a neglect of the inner transformation of the soul. It is inconceivable that before long a return to Catholic ceremonial would not become inevitable, however awkward and inconvenient that might prove in view of the almost universal English suspicion of Roman Catholicism, which was to be re-awakened by the defection of Newman, Wilberforce, Ward, and Manning to Rome and the re-establishment in England of the Roman Catholic hierarchy in 1850. The stranded Pusey, who like an Atlas had to bear the whole world of the Oxford Movement on his shoulders since Newman's departure, took as his motto, *Festina lente.*

If Oxford appeared cautious and even subtly devious, Cambridge was characteristically direct. Little was heard of the Oxford Archaeological Society, but the Cambridge Camden Society, founded by Trinity men, soon familiarized English Churchmen and enthusiastic laity with the whole range of pre-Reformation ritual and ceremonial in England. Formed in May 1839 by John Mason Neale and Benjamin Webb, its aim was to study ecclesiastical art and in 1841 it published its researches in a monthly periodical, *The Ecclesiologist.* No less than 189 numbers of this periodical were issued between November 1841 and December 1868. It succeeded in stimulating an avid, informed, and deepening interest in church architecture as the setting for traditional Catholic worship and thus stimulated the liturgical and ceremonial revival of the Anglican Church of the later nineteenth century. Indeed, it was Cambridge's most significant contribution to the Catholic revival.

119

Its new name, "The Ecclesiological Society" (adopted in 1846), showed that revived Catholic Churchmanship was its aim, not mere antiquarianism, as the earlier name "Camden Society" might have suggested. The absorbing interest of the second generation of Tractarians in vestments, incense, lighted tapers, chanting and intoning, the careful observance of fasts and festivals, genuflexions, crossings, candles, flowers and crosses on the communion-table, the reservation and adoration of the Eucharist, is partly to be accounted for by the work of the Ecclesiological Society. It is no accident that Dr. Neale,[9] its co-founder, erudite hymnologist, liturgiologist, historian of the Eastern and Western Churches, was in the centre of the ritualistic controversy, since he was also the founder of St. Margaret's Religious Community at East Grinstead, and the leader of the two major movements for the dissemination of Catholic principles in Anglican worship.[10] Sir Kenneth Clark, in a modern tribute to the Ecclesiological Society, wrote: "It is doubtful if there is a Gothic church in the country, new or old, which does not show their influence."[11] Not only was practically every neo-Gothic church built under their impetus and inspiration, but even the restoration of the mediaeval churches was on lines that they recommended.

The primary cause of the increasing desire for Catholic ceremonial was quite simply that Catholic doctrine can be most effectively taught through Catholic ceremonial. *The Tracts for the Times* created a sympathy towards Catholicism by eliciting a desire to approximate Anglicanism to its pre-Reformation traditions and to the unity of mediaeval Western Christendom. Thureau-Dangin is surely right in claiming that the Oxford Movement inevitably drew nearer to Rome "by seeking out the lost meaning of liturgical symbolism, by renewing the obliterated theory of the supernatural and of mystery, by enlarging the narrow horizon of piety and devotion" because it created "in souls and minds, hearts and imaginations, needs which the existing ceremonial could not

---

[9] See "The Cambridge Anglo-Catholics," being Chap. IV of S. L. Ollard's lively, popular account of *The Anglo-Catholic Revival*, pp. 50-63; also Dean J. W. Burgon, *Lives of Twelve Good Men* (2 vols., 3rd edn., 1889). An important doctoral dissertation, prepared under Dr. Ray Petry's direction at Duke University by James Floyd White, entitled *The Cambridge Society and the Mediaeval Revival in the Church of England during the Nineteenth Century*, is summarized in *Church History*, Vol. XXIX, No. 2 (June 1960), p. 207.

[10] Important organizations for the spread of Catholic principles in the English Church were The Confraternity of the Blessed Sacrament, The Federation of Catholic Priests, and, of course, The English Church Union.

[11] *The Gothic Revival* (2nd edn., 1950), p. 238.

satisfy." He is equally perceptive in recognising that the profession of the doctrines of the Real Presence and the real Sacrifice in the Eucharist made it "impossible to be satisfied with the bare and denuded churches which at the best were but preaching halls, where there no longer was an altar, and where, behind the high-backed pews, the pulpit, and the reading-desk, one could hardly catch a glimpse of the plain wooden table upon which on very rare occasions the Communion Service was celebrated, without honour, and often without decency."[12] Where the imagination had been aroused to proclaim Catholic truth, that imagination could not be satisfied until the churches had recaptured the symbolism of the ages of faith and worship and ceremonial resembled the Sarum use, or more modern Roman Catholic devotions. A high doctrine of the Sacraments inevitably produced an emphasis on adequate preparation by fasting and confession, the arts of mental prayer, and the asceticism that was the proof of sacrificial living. With equal inevitability the supreme life was, in technically correct terms, the religious life, whether it was to be in brotherhoods and sisterhoods combining the *opus Dei* with works of mercy or in religious communities that were dedicated exclusively to contemplation.

It may, of course, be asked: If the ritualists (or at least some of them) wished to go so far towards Rome, why did they not go the whole way and accept the Roman allegiance? One part of the answer is that many Anglo-Catholic priests and not a few of the earlier religious communities did. Another part of the answer is that many devout ritualists believed that they could work more effectively for the re-union of the Church of England with the Church of Rome by teaching Roman Catholic doctrine in the Church of England. Others, again, were arrested in their Romeward progress by a series of events, notably the declaration of Papal Infallibility of 1870 (a victory of an Ultramontanism which was repugnant to their view of the English Church as well as to the ancient Orthodox Churches of the East), and the declaration of the invalidity of Anglican orders.[13] The very freedom which they enjoyed, after the end of litigation, proved more attractive than the Roman bondage, and the more sober English tempera-

[12] *The English Catholic Revival in the Nineteenth Century* by Paul Thureau-Dangin, revised and re-edited by Wilfred Wilberforce (1914), Vol. II, pp. 428-29.

[13] I owe these suggestions to the Rev. Dr. E. C. Ratcliff, Regius Professor of Divinity in the University of Cambridge.

ment found the more florid manifestations of Italianate piety less to their liking than they had imagined. Whatever the reasons, at the end of the century, in the hyphenated term "Anglo-Catholic" the first element became increasingly more significant than the second, and this indicated a greater loyalty to the English Church than had characterized the more contumacious and Romanizing ritualists, who did not scruple to substitute the Roman Canon of the Mass for the Consecration Prayer of the Prayer Book, or (in some cases) even to introduce Benediction and Exposition of the Sacrament.[14]

2. The Leading "Ritualists"

The first "martyr" to ritualism in London was the Rev. W. J. E. Bennett, who became vicar of St. Paul's Knightsbridge in 1850 and by his industry built the daughter church of St. Barnabas, Pimlico, which included a rood screen, a stone altar, stained glass in every window, and richly gilded mural ornaments. Bennett's innovations in those early days included preaching in a surplice, the chanting of Psalms and Services, the intoning of the prayers, the procession and recession of a surpliced choir to and from a highly decorated chancel, the closing of the chancel gates, bowing to the altar, the eastward position, a cross on the communion-table, and candles on it which were lit during the Communion. He also vested the altar with coverings appropriate to the different seasons of the church year and decorated it with flowers. In 1900 most of these might have passed without notice, but in 1850 the coincidence of these innovations with the national outcry against "Papal Aggression" incited by Lord John Russell's inflammatory "Durham Letter" of November 4th was enough to set violent crowds onto the "Puseyite priests" for the next few Sundays. Two hundred per-

---

[14] See the *Report of the Royal Commission on Ecclesiastical Discipline* (1906) and especially its list of ten practices, both illegal and "clearly inconsistent with the teaching of the Church of England as declared in the Prayer Book," including: the interpolation of prayers and ceremonies belonging to the Canon of the Mass, the adoration of the Reserved Sacrament, Corpus Christi processions with the Sacrament, and Benediction with the Sacrament, and the observation of the festivals of the Assumption of the Blessed Virgin Mary, and of the Sacred Heart. See also Peter F. Anson, *The Call of the Cloister* (1955), pp. 57, 63, 99, 172, 178, 345-46, 351-52, 363, 380, 403, 422, 431, 443, 493. It is worth noting that the researches of Father Thurston, S.J., and Dom Gregory Dix have shown that the Eucharistic devotions thought to be so "Italianate" and modern by their critics originated in the popular mediaeval religious practices of Germany, Scandinavia, and the Low Countries before they were known in Italy. See Thurston, "Benediction of the Blessed Sacrament" in *The Month* (issues of June-Sept. 1901) and Gregory Dix, *A Detection of Aumbries* (1942), pp. 47-60, and Benedict Steuart, *The Development of Christian Worship* (1953), pp. 265-66.

sons tried to force their way into St. Barnabas' Church on November 17, 1850, and were restrained only by policemen in plain clothes placed among the congregation. On the next Sunday, Bennett, with more courage than tact, proceeded to defend his ceremonial innovations, only to be muffled by the coughing, hissing, and stamping of the objectors. Bennett, who despised the mob who baited him and regarded his bishop as a mere Erastian, persisted in these innovations, with the inevitable result that he resigned his living at the request of Bishop Blomfield in 1851.

His successor, the Hon. and Rev. Robert Liddell, attempted to quiet the situation by a few changes in the ornaments and ritual of the service, but to little effect. He was involved in the action of Westerton (churchwarden of St. Paul's) versus Liddell which went before the Consistory Court, then on Liddell's appeal to the Court of Arches, and finally on appeal to the Judicial Committee. The conclusions of the Judicial Committee were such as to give comfort and dissatisfaction to both ritualists and Evangelicals. The ornaments rubric held to regulate Anglican vestments was that of the First Prayer Book of Edward VI and of Act 2 and 3 Edward VI, c.l., and it was held not to apply to furniture and decoration employing symbolism, to the considerable chagrin of the Evangelicals. Crosses (though not crucifixes) were held to be lawful decoration, but not if attached to or placed on communion-tables. Credence tables were also permissible. On the other hand, a stone altar was held to be illegal in the Church of England; the communion-table must be of wood and movable. This difference in Eucharistic furniture was held to be necessary to distinguish between the doctrine and ritual of a transubstantiatory sacrifice, requiring an altar, which was rejected at the Reformation.

Another doughty ritualist, who had been a curate at St. Barnabas', Pimlico, was the Rev. Charles Lowder[15] who became mission priest at St. George's in the East, near the London Docks, in July 1856. Here, with the aid of priests, including A. H. Mackonochie, laymen, and Sisters of Mercy, he attempted with great success to minister to the spiritual and social needs of the desperately poor and often vicious souls of that squalid and sordid part of London. Incited by the employers of sweated labour and the brothel-keepers of the neighbourhood, the ritualistic services in St. George's in the East became a bedlam of bawling and blasphemy, in which books

15 See S. L. Ollard, *The Anglo-Catholic Revival, Some Persons and Principles*, pp. 65-69.

and cassocks were hurled at the altar and the clergy were kicked and spat upon. On September 25, 1859, Lowder barely escaped being thrown into the dock. What were his offences? Ostensibly, the use of Eucharistic vestments, the cross on the altar, the surpliced choir in the chancel, the turning eastward at the end of the sermon, and the chanting of Matins, Evensong, and the Litany. In fact, however, it most probably was that self-denying spirituality which, in its search for the buried image of Divine Royalty in the most dirt-encrusted coins of a derelict humanity, infuriates the exploiters. It is significant that Bishop Tait of London withdrew his early opposition to Lowder and his colleagues, convinced that their sacrificial service for the poor outweighed the inconvenience of their ritualistic deviations from the Prayer Book. He declared of Lowder's associate, "I have not a better man in my diocese than Mr. Mackonochie."[16]

As ritualism increased, the disappointed Evangelicals founded the Church Association to prosecute the ritualists, finding that the bishops preferred not to act as ecclesiastical policemen and judges in cases where men showed apostolical zeal. This body, nicknamed "The Persecution Society," was later to boast of having spent £80,000 and of having obtained sixty decisions against the ritualists.[17] The first prosecution was directed against A. H. Mackonochie, the vicar of St. Alban's, Holborn, who was more advanced in his ceremonial than any of the preceding ritualists had been, but also as dedicated a man as any of them. The son of a colonel of the Indian Army, the friend of Charles Marriott while at Oxford, he had served under William Butler of Wantage, who had founded the important Community of St. Mary the Virgin in 1848. This man was never free from prosecution from 1867 to 1882 when Archbishop Tait, then on his death-bed, suggested that he should exchange the living of St. Alban's with St. Peter's, London Docks, to avoid further litigation.

Mackonochie was no aesthete; he appreciated forms only as they were moving demonstrations of Catholic truth. His favourite book was the *Spiritual Exercises* of St. Ignatius Loyola and he regularly concentrated his meditations before a large painting of the Crucified Christ.[18] His spiritual ideal and indeed his achievement was that of the mediaeval or Counter-Reformation ascetical saint. He

[16] F. Warre Cornish, *op.cit.*, Vol. II, p. 136.
[17] See Thureau-Dangin, *op.cit.*, Vol. II, p. 466.
[18] F. Warre Cornish, *op.cit.*, Vol. II, p. 136, and Thureau-Dangin, *op.cit.*, Vol. II, pp. 467 ff.

was an immensely skilled confessor and his widely attended Sung Masses were a vigorous proclamation of his faith and veritable means of grace to thousands. One of the first priest-associates of the Confraternity of the Blessed Sacrament, he aimed in all his ritual to pay the honour due to the Person of Jesus Christ in the Blessed Sacrament of His Body and Blood.

There were four charges presented against him when the case of Martin versus Mackonochie came before the Court of Arches in 1867. He was charged with having elevated the paten and chalice, and with bowing, kneeling, or prostrating himself before the consecrated elements; with using lighted candles on the communion-table during the celebration of Communion, although they were not necessary to provide light; with the ceremonial use of incense during the Communion Service; and with mixing water with the wine in the Communion (intinction or the Mixed Chalice).[19]

Sir Robert Phillimore, who gave judgment on March 28, 1868, decided against the elevation of the paten and chalice, and the use of incense during a Communion Service although "an ancient, innocent and pleasing custom" and that intinction was permissible if not done during the service. He did not, however, consider it illegal to place two lighted candles on the communion-table or for the priest to kneel or prostrate himself before the consecrated elements during the prayer of consecration. The appeal was made to the Judicial Committee of the Privy Council, which declared that standing is the only lawful posture during the prayer of consecration, except that kneeling is permitted when receiving the Sacrament, and held that lighted candles are illegal as ornaments.

The Mackonochie case is important for three reasons: it shows that the Anglo-Catholics had made strong ritualistic advances in a Roman direction in the twenty years from 1850 to 1870, that the legal interpretation of obsolete formularies and rubrics was extremely uncertain as the differing judgments of the Court of Arches and the Judicial Committee of the Privy Council plainly showed, and, most important, that an ultra-ritualist could win the approval of a moderate bishop because of the undoubted spirituality that prompted his liturgical innovations and the integrity of life that adorned the faith he held.

There were others, many of them hardly less eminent than Mackonochie, who faced the same opposition and endured the same official mistrust and consequent lack of preferment. Such were

[19] F. Warre Cornish, *op.cit.*, Vol. II, p. 138.

Purchas of Plymouth (associated with another ritualistic *cause célèbre*[20]), West of Plymouth, Sharp of Horbury, Wagner of Brighton, and Carter of Clewer in the same succession as Keble of Hursley, unregarded but faithful High Church priests. It is significant that one of their number, A. H. Stanton, when he was on the eve of leaving Oxford to join Mackonochie, was warned by Bishop Tait that he must never expect Church preferment if he carried through this resolve.[21] Forty-five years later, in 1907, he was still assistant curate at the church to which he was first licensed. Despite mobs, episcopal inhibitions, parliamentary legislation such as *The Public Worship Regulation Act of 1874*, imprisonments, and the condemnation of the Court of Arches and the Judicial Committee of the Privy Council, the Anglo-Catholics had won freedom for most of their distinctive ritualistic claims and thus changed the character of the worship of the English Church in many parishes.

Perhaps, from their point of view, the most important judgment that went in their favour was the decision of the Court of Arches in 1870, confirmed by the Privy Council on appeal in 1872, that it was lawful for an Anglican clergyman to teach the objective, actual, and spiritual Presence in the Eucharist. By an irony of history it was the first ritualistic "martyr," the Rev. W. J. E. Bennett, who was now vindicated in the suit brought by the Church Association. Before long a distinguished Tractarian, R. W. Church, was to become the Dean of St. Paul's Cathedral, by the advocacy of Gladstone, and it was thought that he later refused the Primatial See of Canterbury.

But the crowning proof of the moderate acceptance of the Tractarian ideals as a permissible Anglican alternative was the translation of Edward King to the See of Lincoln in 1885, even though an attempt was made to embarrass him by requiring him to attend a trial before Archbishop Benson of Canterbury in February 1889. At this trial he won a notable moral victory, and gained a reasonable liberty for Anglo-Catholic ceremonial, including the eastward position during the first part of the Communion Service, a carefully defined permission for the Mixed Chalice, and the right to use two lighted candles on the Holy Table throughout the service,

[20] The Judicial Committee of the Privy Council in 1871 hearing the case of the Rev. John Purchas (1823-1872), vicar of St. James', Brighton, declared that Eucharistic vestments, the eastward position, the Mixed Chalice, and Wafer Bread were illegal, thus reversing the judgment in Purchas' favour given by the Dean of Arches. The judgment was disobeyed by Purchas and many others.

[21] S. L. Ollard, *op.cit.*, p. 75.

even when not wanted for light, and permission to sing the *Agnus Dei* after the consecration prayer.[22]

3. *Changes of Ceremonial in Anglican Parish Churches*

It is appropriate to consider next the chief developments in Anglican ceremonial from 1850 to 1900. What had begun as revolutionary innovations in 1850—namely, the surpliced clergyman and choir, the use of chants and canticles, the intoning of the service, the processionals and recessionals of the clergyman and choir to and from the chancel, the embellishment of the Holy Table with frontals and a cross, and the provision of stained-glass windows and mural decorations exhibiting the Communion of Saints— soon became commonplace sights in the proliferating neo-Gothic churches in the course of the half-century. Having familiarized their congregations with one set of innovations, the ritualists were now prepared to go further.

To appreciate the more rapid Rome-ward direction of ceremonial and ritual developments in this period, it is necessary only to turn to such popular Anglo-Catholic volumes as the first two editions of the *Directorium Anglicanum, according to the Ancient Uses of the Church of England*, the first edited by J. Purchas in 1858, and the second by F. G. Lee in 1865, or to Charles Walker's *The Ritual Reason Why*, the first edition of which appeared in 1866 and the second in 1868, which provides full rubrical directions for the Canonical Hours "as used in our Sisterhoods and religious houses."[23] It is clear that by 1865 Anglo-Catholic altars had six candlesticks (compared with the two of 1858), a cross, and two flower vases, and some were provided with riddel curtains, while others had two standard candlesticks on the pavement. As yet there was no provision for the Reservation of the Sacrament in either pyx or tabernacle. The sources of the inspiration seem to be Pugin and the Pre-Raphaelites, rather than "the Ancient Uses of the Church of England" indicated by the full title of the *Directorium*.

The state of the ritualistic churches in 1866 is thus described by Thureau-Dangin:

"The Services were inspired by the pre-Reformation traditions or by existing rites of the Roman Church. This was, above all, true of the Eucharistic Service, in which the chasuble, alb, stole, mani-

---

22 G. K. A. Bell, *Randall Davidson, Archbishop of Canterbury* (2nd edn., 1938), Vol. I, p. 148.
23 P. 233.

ple, amice, the five canonical colours, the position and gestures prescribed by the ancient rubrics, the prayers of the Missal—in a word, the whole ceremonial of the Mass was employed. The crucifix, statues of saints, and sometimes holy water, were introduced. Confession was restored to its place of honour. On the eve of festivals the clergy were sometimes obliged to spend the night hearing penitents. Confraternities encouraged various Catholic devotions, especially to the Blessed Sacrament. Manuals were printed for the use of clergy and laity in order to initiate them into this form of religious life. Clergymen took a pride in styling themselves priests; several wore cassocks and were tonsured; even ecclesiastical celibacy began to have its votaries who formed the higher section of the Association of the Holy Cross. The Church Congress, held at York in 1866, was made an occasion for religious art, at which magnificent Church vestments, chasubles, altar frontals, crosses, mitres, crucifixes, and images of saints were displayed for the inspection of the clergy."[24]

This picture would probably be truer of the extremists than of the more moderate sons of the Tractarians, and it would be a fairer account of the extremists if dated some ten years or more later.

This qualification may be confirmed by the curious fact that Thureau-Dangin seems to agree so closely with the liturgical customs alleged to be practised by ritualists in the Protestant propaganda of that notorious exaggerator, Walter Walsh, in his *Secret History of the Oxford Movement* (1897).[25]

It was of this type of worship that the Evangelical Lord Shaftesbury had written, as he seethed with indignation, "It is the worship of Jupiter and Juno. . . . Do we lead souls thus to Christ or to Baal?"[26] With greater control, and less temptation to choler being a Broad Churchman and a don, Jowett of Balliol had written to a friend: "If you walked abroad you would be greatly astonished at the change which has come over the churches in London; there is a sort of aesthetico-Catholic revival going on."[27] The surprise of both Evangelical and Broad Churchman is the measure of the High Church advance towards Catholic ceremonial. No doubt if

---

[24] Thureau-Dangin, *op.cit.*, Vol. II, pp. 443-44.

[25] They purported to describe clandestine rather than open practices. See especially pp. 373-410 for a catena of citations illustrative of ritualistic teaching.

[26] See Edwin Hodder, *The Life and Work of the Seventh Earl of Shaftesbury*, p. 618.

[27] See *The Life and Letters of Benjamin Jowett*, ed. E. Abbott and Lewis Campbell, Vol. I, p. 381.

they had entered some of the private chapels of the Anglican Religious Communities their reactions would have been apoplectic. The opinion of the Anglo-Catholics held by most Evangelicals and by many Broad Churchmen, by the Queen and by "Punch" in its anti-Ritualist caricatures, as well as by the Roman Catholic novelist Compton Mackenzie in his trilogy, beginning with *The Altar Steps*, was unfavourable in the extreme. The attitude was expressed in pithy, if prejudiced, manner by Lord John Russell in a letter to Queen Victoria in 1850: "Dr. Arnold said very truly, 'I look upon a Roman Catholic as an enemy in his uniform. I look upon a Tractarian as an enemy disguised, a spy.' "[28] For this dislike the Anglo-Catholics, however devout, courageous, and convinced, must bear part of the blame. They, as well as their opponents, did encourage a party spirit within the Church of England; they were excessively rigorist, as in refusing Holy Communion to all who did not come to it fasting; they often appeared to worry overmuch about fussy details of vestments and ornaments; and their devotions in many cases appeared to be more suited to the more demonstrative popular Italian temperament than to the reserved English. But to regard them as merely Roman Catholics in disguise was to be unaware of two features in their teaching, which were quite distinctive. Under the leadership of Gore they welcomed the newer Biblical and scientific studies which Rome at that time strongly proscribed, and they were greatly concerned to express the implications of the Incarnation in a more just ordering of society, as the examples of Gore himself, Frere, Kelly, Stewart Headlam, and Basil Jellicoe attest.[29] In due course, they would come to stress the "English Use" in contrast to a mere imitation of contemporary fashions in Roman popular devotions.

Beside Thureau-Dangin's picture of the ritualists at worship in 1865 should be set Canon Roger Lloyd's careful portrait of a typical Anglo-Catholic congregation at High Mass some forty years later.[30] The time is eleven o'clock in the morning, the place any ancient parish in an English sea-port hard by the docks, and the congregation is mixed, socially and educationally. It is composed of many poor children and a few poor adults from the parish, detachments of soldiers from the local garrison, some officers from

[28] Ollard, *op.cit.*, cites this on pp. 73-74.
[29] See Gore's later summing-up, *Anglo-Catholicism Today*, chap. 3, on "Some Necessary Modifications" (of the Oxford Movement).
[30] *The Church of England in the Twentieth Century* (Vol. I, 1900-1918; Vol. II, 1918-1939), Vol. I, pp. 140-44.

the ships in port, some nurses from the local hospital, and the rest have come from the suburbs. Most of them are young women, and there is a scarcity of middle-aged and elderly men. The worshippers, and even the children among them, know exactly how to behave in the House of God and their intentness is a proof of the value they attach to honouring Almighty God. While the congregation gathers, there is "controlled bustle" behind the scenes, as the scarlet-cassocked serving boys (later to don lace cottas) bring in tapers to light the candles, and as the large choir of men and boys put on cassocks and surplices, and the priest vests himself.

The service begins with a most impressive procession:

"First comes the cross-bearer, and then the young boy with the incense, his left hand on the shoulder of a tiny boat-boy, his right hand swinging the censer by its long silver chain. Clouds of incense eddy softly at each step. He is followed by the choir-boys and the men; and all, having been properly trained, bear their part with a deep reverence. Then come the servers, and finally the priest, wearing a cope heavy with magnificence, the ends of which are ceremoniously held clear of his walking feet by two little boys. As he passes down the aisle, the people in the nearest pews bow.

"Presently the procession winds back into the chancel, and as the last verse of the hymn is sung, the priest's attendants divest him of his cope, and put on him his Eucharistic vestments. He then places more grains of incense into the censer, and the liturgy is ready to begin."

Here, also, every enrichment of the visual arts and of music is used to the full both to enhance the honour of the Sacrament and to instruct the people: "There is a ceremonial Gospel procession with candles and incense. There are appropriate hymns—plenty of them. There is a sermon. There is the solemn censing of the priest, choir, preacher, and people. At the supreme moment there is the ceremony of the Kiss of Peace. Every detail has been lovingly cared for. Nothing which might help impress upon the people that this is the Service of services, and the church where the Blessed Sacrament is none other than the Court of Heaven."

Criticisms can, indeed, be made of this Communion as a spectacle rather than a participation in the benefits of the Sacrifice of our Lord (for there may well have been no communicants), of the rushing through the spoken parts of the Liturgy which renders them inaudible, and of the sermon as possibly not a declaration of the judgment and mercy of the living God. But that it is a devout, glad, splendid, edifying, and beautiful corporate tribute of worship suitable to the Divine Majesty is undeniable.[31] Moreover, in Newman's phrase, it is "an evocation" rather than an "invocation of God."

4. Ritual and Ceremonial in Religious Communities for Women[32]

While the ceremonial revival was chiefly to be seen in parish churches, the most striking advances in ritual as well as ceremonial were to be sought out only by the initiated and the trusted in the sequestered chapels of religious communities that were such a remarkable manifestation of Anglo-Catholic spirituality in the second half of the nineteenth century. To be sure, there were also signs of liturgical vitality in the English cathedrals,[33] under the leadership of Hamilton of Salisbury, Benson of Truro, and Church of St. Paul's, and Howson of Chester, but their fullest development was to await the inspiration of Bennett of Chester in the next century.

Whatever indirect inspiration the promoters of the revival of religious communities in the English Church derived from the Evangelical pursuit of holiness[34] (and Pusey, Newman, Wilberforce, R. M. Benson, and G. H. Wilkinson had strong Evangelical antecedents), the direct inspiration came from Catholic sources, with the single possible exception of the House for Deaconesses founded at Kaiserwerth by the Lutheran pastor, Fliedner, in 1837. The leaders of the Oxford Movement in their Patristic researches had re-discovered the adamantine orthodoxy and ascetical strength

[31] Furthermore, not only do the present High Church theologians and liturgiologists insist that a Mass without communicants is an impoverishment, but High Churchmen have included (and still include) some of England's most distinguished and successful preachers, such as H. P. Liddon, Dean Church, Dom Bernard Clements, and the Rev. Sir Edwyn Hoskyns.

[32] The major authorities consulted on this subject have been Peter F. Anson, in his thorough survey entitled *The Call of the Cloister, Religious Communities and kindred bodies in the Anglican Communion* and his admirably illustrated *Fashions in Church Furnishings, 1840-1940*, and A. M. Allchin's *The Silent Rebellion: Anglican Religious Communities, 1845-1900*, which gives a clear account of the theological motivations of the founders of these communities.

[33] For the reform of nineteenth century cathedrals, consult E. B. Pusey, *Remarks on the Prospective and Past Benefits of Cathedral Institutions* . . . , W. K. Hamilton, *Cathedral Reform. A Letter to Members of his Diocese*, E. W. Benson, *The Cathedral: Its Necessary Place in the Life and Work of the Church*, ed. J. S. Howson, *Essays on Cathedrals*, and B. F. Westcott's article in *Macmillan's Magazine* of Jan.-Feb. 1870.

[34] Bishop W. H. Frere, co-founder of the Community of the Resurrection with Bishop Charles Gore, wrote of the Anglican communities "in many ways it would be true to state, that the Evangelical movement gave the spirit, and the Catholic movement the form, for this revival." (*English Church Ways*, p. 79.)

of such great leaders of the Church as Saints Athanasius and Augustine, Benedict and Basil, Ambrose and Gregory the Great. In their mediaeval studies they were enthralled by the pageant of the revived splendours of the Benedictine ideal and especially by the towering figure of St. Bernard of Clairvaux, the confessor of kings, the preacher of a crusade, the adviser of Popes, the hammer of heretical Abelard, a passionate mystical writer and a superb example of Christ's "athlete" in asceticism. They could not fail to be attracted by the God's troubadour, St. Francis, and St. Dominic, founder of the other great order of Friars, whose preaching order trained the greatest theologian of the Middle Ages, St. Thomas Aquinas. All these were men (and many notable women were of the company of the mediaeval saints) who strove to obey our Lord's counsels of perfection, in the discipline of a regular community life, and the Tractarians claimed kin with them through the mediaeval Church in England, which they romanticized excessively.

When, however, the founders of the Anglican religious communities for women (which preceded and greatly outnumbered those for men) drew up their rules, it was to seventeenth century France that they turned, and particularly to the writings of St. Francis de Sales and St. Vincent de Paul. Pusey, Butler of Wantage, and Neale of East Grinstead visited the Roman Catholic religious communities in France and Ireland in order to get practical help for their communities.[35] Moreover, the Camden Society was influential in determining the design of the conventual buildings of the sisterhoods of the nineteenth century, and it is significant that Butterfield and Street, respectively, were the architects of St. Saviour's, Osnaburgh Street, London, for the first women's community (the Sisterhood of the Holy Cross) and of the convent of the Society of St. Margaret in East Grinstead.

Social factors also played their part in the foundations, for the first community was designed as "a religious rule for the purpose of relieving distress."[36] The duties of these Anglican Sisters of Mercy included visiting the poor and sick in their own houses; the visitation of hospitals, workhouses, and prisons; feeding, clothing, and instructing destitute children; giving shelter to distressed women of good character; and assisting in the burial of the dead.[37] The Community of St. John the Baptist in Clewer had as its chief work of mercy the care of unmarried mothers, while the Commu-

[35] See A. M. Allchin, *The Silent Rebellion*, p. 38.
[36] *Ibid.*, p. 62.   [37] *Ibid.*

nity of St. Mary the Virgin at Wantage, which saw its task as primarily educational, was urged by Manning to undertake penitentiary work. The Society of St. Margaret in East Grinstead, founded at about the time of Florence Nightingale's great work at Scutari in the Crimea, naturally turned for its work of mercy to nursing the sick poor in the many scattered villages of the neighbourhood. Strong as the claim of relieving the sick and destitute was in the foundation of communities, even more dominant, however, was the impulse to a deep spirituality, nourished by corporate worship.

The chief significance of the Anglican religious communities was as houses of spiritual devotion.[38] Here provision was to be made for frequent Communion and for regular confession. Here it would be possible to recover the full meaning of liturgical prayer, by means of the Breviary offices, of which Matins and Evensong were but a surviving remnant in the Book of Common Prayer. Here it would be possible to practice the more developed kinds of mental prayer. Here, by the provision of retreats, and the example of a gracious godliness, the understanding of the spiritual life in the English Church at large might be increased. Here responsible only to a sympathetic bishop, and unaffected by the curious prejudices of churchwardens, the cruel fickleness of the mob, and beyond the reach of the Court of Arches and the Judicial Committee of the Privy Council, and especially of the "Prosecution Society," advanced experiments in ritual and ceremonial might be made. In fact, all these intentions were fulfilled in the religious communities.

The ritual and ceremonial at the Community of St. Mary the Virgin (founded in 1848) in Wantage were far more restrained than in the Society of St. Margaret at East Grinstead (founded in 1855), as reflected in the attitudes of their founders, respectively, W. J. Butler and J. M. Neale. Butler, an early Tractarian, was to dissent strongly from the individualism, excessive Romanism, and canonical disobedience of such later ritualists as Mackonochie of Holborn, disliking "enforcement of fasting communion, making confession a matter of salvation, or at least a duty for every soul, besides a heap of ritualistic practices, some of the queerest kind."[39] He believed that the Church of England was a true branch of Christ's Catholic Church, with a right to lay down for her chil-

[38] *Ibid.*, pp. 55 f.
[39] A. J. Butler, *The Life and Letters of W. J. Butler*, p. 139, cited in *ibid.*, p. 92.

133

dren what they ought to believe and do, and that "in her Prayer Book her teaching and will are found."[40] From the outset the Wantage Sisters recited the Day Hours of the Sarum Breviary, using the English translation made by the Rev. Albany Christie in 1845, while daily also attending the Prayer Book Offices of Matins and Evensong in the parish church.[41] They were the first Anglican community to revive plain-chant. A reflection of their eminently sober and dignified ideal of worship may be found in the novels of Charlotte M. Yonge, who had been an associate of the Community in 1868, and whose novels, especially *The Three Brides* (1878), contain warnings against excessive ritualism. They attest that she had learned Butler's lesson well.

Neale, the co-founder of the Camden Society at Cambridge, was ready to go far beyond the liturgical norms permitted by the first Tractarians. He introduced the East Grinstead Sisters to the entire range of Catholic instruction and religious practice. Daily Communion was begun in 1856; a year later, permanent Reservation of the Sacrament was introduced, a custom then unknown in the Anglican Church. By 1859 Benediction and Exposition were introduced—those extra-liturgical Roman rites intended to repair the dishonour endured by Christ in the midst of His creatures. Neither Butler nor Carter of Clewer (founder of the Community of St. John the Baptist in 1851) attempted such innovations. Although the Sisters daily used a translation of the Sarum Breviary, as at Wantage, Matins and Evensong were recited in East Grinstead only on Sundays. Moreover, the Sisters were the first to use an English translation of the Night Office.[42]

Their claims for practising advanced ritual and ceremonial are equalled only by those of the Community of St. Mary at the Cross, Edgware, known as "The Sisters of the Poor," who were founded in 1865 by a notable ritualist, the Rev. H. D. Nihill. Not only were they familiar with the rites of Exposition and Benediction, but they were the first Anglican Community to recite the Day Hours in the Latin of the *Breviarium Monasticum*, which they did

40 A. J. Butler, *op.cit.*, p. 204, cited in Allchin, *op.cit.*

41 Anson, *The Call of the Cloister*, pp. 245 f. where the author, a Roman Catholic, declares that the Wantage Sisterhood "has done more to encourage liturgical worship than any other Anglican community."

42 Allchin, *op.cit.*, pp. 107 ff. and Anson, *The Call of the Cloister*, pp. 337 ff. The Clewer Sisters from 1858 used *The Day Hours of the Church of England* as their Office Book, an adaptation of *Occasional Offices for the Hours of Prayer*, compiled by F. G. Lee and Canon H. P. Liddon, when the latter was Vice-Principal of Cuddesdon, and intended for the use of the ordinands there.

134

almost from the time of their foundation.[43] The central importance of the Blessed Sacrament, to which all the advanced foundations paid homage, was vividly emphasized in the title of one Community, that of "The Community of Reparation to Jesus in the Blessed Sacrament." These, also known as the Mission Sisters of St. Alphege in Woking, reflected the views of the Anglo-Catholics of the late sixties, consequent on the founding of the Confraternity of the Blessed Sacrament in 1862, whose first President was Carter of Clewer.

In such religious communities the central source of inspiration is the Divine Liturgy and all the works of mercy are incitations of Divine Grace. Thus Neale taught the Sisters: "Look at the whole service rendered to God by this House, day by day, as one Liturgy, one Celebration. As the greatest, and highest, holiest Sacrifice of all is once daily offered here in Celebration, so all that you do, do actively, or bear passively, in the course of one day is so far, that day's Liturgy to your Lord."[44]

5. Worship in Religious Communities for Men[45]

Although the pioneering Society of St. John the Evangelist was founded in Cowley, Oxford, in 1865, it was only in the last decade of the century that Benson's great example was followed, and three other important men's communities came into being: the Community of the Resurrection (1892) which moved from Oxford to Mirfield, Yorkshire; the Society of the Sacred Mission (1894) of Kelham, Newark; and the Society of the Divine Compassion (also founded in 1894) in Plaistow, London.[46] The relative tardiness of these foundations is explained by the fact that the Church already provides in the office of the priesthood ample opportunities for a dedicated life for men, such as are not available to women.

[43] See Anson, *The Call of the Cloister*, pp. 399-402.
[44] Allchin, *op.cit.*, p. 109.
[45] From Anson's Appendix (in *The Call of the Cloister*) entitled "List of Religious Communities and Kindred Bodies in the Anglican Communion in Order of Foundation (1) Great Britain and Ireland" (pp. 590-94), the following computation has been made. Of 31 male communities founded between 1842 and 1953, 15 are extinct, 5 have been received into the Roman Church, and 6 remain. Of 82 communities for females founded between 1845 and 1952, 21 are extinct, none have seceded to Rome, and the rest remain loyally Anglican.
[46] In the present century important new foundations were the Anglican Benedictines of Nashdom (1914), and the Society of St. Francis of Cerne Abbas (1921). The former community is widely known, chiefly through the lively erudition of Dom Gregory Dix, whose chief work is *The Shape of the Liturgy*. The Oratory of the Good Shepherd, Cambridge, "a Society of Priests and laymen living under a Rule, which can provide as large an element of common life and discipline as the conditions of the works of the members permit" was founded in Cambridge in 1913.

However, the foundation of brotherhoods was made the easier because of the sisterhoods that preceded them, because the growing recognition of the insidiousness of increasing secularism in the last decade of the century required sterner measures for the cultivation of the spiritual life, and because Gore and the Cambridge Trio (Lightfoot, Westcott, and Hort), under the delayed influence of F. D. Maurice, taught a Biblical and social Catholicism relevant to the scientific and sociological thought of the times.

Richard Meux Benson,[47] the founder of the Society of St. John the Evangelist when Vicar of Cowley, a poor suburb of Oxford then, was planning to form a Collegiate Society in the northwest province of India when Bishop Wilberforce of Oxford begged him to remain. On this act of renunciation the Society was based. Benson did not give his Society a rule until twenty-five years after it was founded, so fearful was he of legal and spiritual petrifaction. His interesting, practical, and eclectic rule is said to be a combination of some aspects of the Lazarists of St. Vincent de Paul (hence the title "Mission Priests") with the Benedictine emphasis on the primacy of the Divine Office as the *Opus Dei*.[48] Certainly, his own deep spirituality based on the Liturgy and reflected in three series of *Instructions in the Spiritual Life* (published respectively in 1927, 1935, and 1951) as well as his book *The Religious Vocation*, which appeared in 1939, the many retreats and missions which the community held, and their concern for the underprivileged at home and abroad, showed how firmly based the first Anglican Brotherhood was. If Benson's aim can be put into a single capsule, it might be his own wise saying: "Others study so as to cavil. We study so as to worship."

The austerity and order of this community compared very favourably with the ardours, ecstasies, and eccentricities of Father Ignatius's contemporary attempt to revive Anglican Benedictine monastic life in St. Dunstan's Priory, Norwich, and later at Llanthony Abbey.[49] The diet was frugal in the extreme, the life in the House and among the poor parishioners was Spartan, and so was the setting of the worship in the ugly iron church in which the Eucharist was celebrated each morning according to the Book

[47] See H. F. B. Mackay, *Saints and Leaders*, pp. 237 f. and M. V. Woodgate, *Father Benson of Cowley*.

[48] See Anson, *The Call of the Cloister*, p. 79, n. 2, for an interesting communication to the author on the probable sources for Benson's rule.

[49] See Donald Attwater, *Father Ignatius of Llanthony: A Victorian* and *Kilvert's Diary* (1870-1871, edited by William Plomer in 1938), pp. 77-78, 219-25.

of Common Prayer, and in the bleak chapel above the Mission House, with its deal fittings painted a dull browny-red, where the *Day Hours of the Church of England* were recited. It was not until 1896 that G. F. Bodley's fine Church of St. John the Evangelist was built, when some ceremonial compensation was offered for those priests who were the living embodiment of their vows of celibacy, poverty, and obedience. Even so, it was built when Benson had ceased to be Superior, while on a nine years' absence from England. It was not austere enough to suit his ideals, and he confessed to a dislike of incense and ceremonial additions. It was not until the next century that the practice of Reservation was begun in this Society. Clearly, Father Benson, like Butler of Wantage, valued reserve in emotion and ceremonial, and devotion to the Prayer Book tradition.[50]

The great contributions of the Community of the Resurrection to worship and theology, and the remarkable liturgical leadership that has emerged from the Society of the Sacred Mission, belong to the twentieth century. The very titles of the writings of Walter Howard Frere, co-founder of the Community of the Resurrection and Bishop of Truro, are a sufficient index of his important contributions to liturgiology.[51] His co-founder, Charles Gore, Bishop of Birmingham and Oxford, concentrated chiefly on dogmatic theology, but his *Reflections on the Litany* (1932) and *The Church and the Ministry* are more directly concerned with worship. Father Gabriel Hebert's *Liturgy and Society* (1935) has brought distinction to himself and the Society of the Sacred Mission, for first introducing to England the ideals and practices of the Continental Liturgical Movement in a manner that was both vigorously relevant and spiritually sensitive. He has widened the horizon of the Church of England by his translations of and introductions to important Swedish works in liturgiology and theology, such as Yngve Brilioth's *Eucharistic Faith and Practice, Evangelical and Catholic* (1930). The last title is a portent of the Ecumenical Movement which has made possible in our own day a link between the Lutheran churches and the Church of England which would have proved unimaginable for the Tractarians who objected so strongly to the projected estab-

[50] See M. V. Woodgate, pp. 162 f.
[51] Notably, *the Use of Sarum* (2 vols., 1898-1901), Proctor and Frere, *A New History of the Book of Common Prayer* (1901), *Some Principles of Liturgical Reform* (1911), *Studies in the Early Roman Liturgy* (3 vols., 1930-1935), and *Walter Howard Frere: a collection of papers on liturgical and historical subjects*, ed. J. H. Arnold and E. G. P. Wyatt (1940).

lishment of a joint Prussian-English episcopate in Jerusalem. "Evangelical" and "Catholic" were the party labels of bitter opponents in the nineteenth century; in the twentieth century they may be complementary emphases in the coming Great Church.

The contribution of the religious communities of women to worship, especially in the days of the ritualists, has been seen to be the provision of a liturgical laboratory for advanced experiments in Catholic and even Roman Catholic practice.[52] The contribution of the religious communities of men to worship, in accordance with their generally later foundation, has been to prove that a more sober, thoughtful, and sacrificial English spirituality can be more easily domesticated in the Church of England. But in all there has been a notable testimony to the priority and the power of the Liturgy for the greater hallowing of humanity and the transformation of society. Such communities are the trophies and testimonies of Divine Grace, and they have effectively helped to raise the standard of parish worship and ceremonial in their contemplative life, just as their undemonstrative acts of mercy (themselves a reflection of the Divine Mercy) have helped to raise the level of society. Their aim and their achievement in a cacophonous, hurried, and materialistic world has been that of the Dominicans: *contemplari et contemplata aliis tradere.*

[52] However inconvenient these practices may have been for diocesans, and particularly for the Primate, it is significant that Benson, the Archbishop of Canterbury, wrote of the Sisterhood of St. Augustine at Kilburn, whom he had just visited: "The idea of 'putting down Ritualism' which a large number of these magnificent bodies are sedulously propagating with every advantage worldly and spiritual, with their own saintly lives first and foremost! 'Agree with thine adversary quickly' is rather the course that now seems practicable." (A. C. Benson, *Life of Edward White Benson*, Vol. II, p. 273.)

CHAPTER VI

NEW FORMS OF PRIMITIVISM

THE DOMINANT TREND of worship in the nineteenth century, following the lead of the Oxford Movement, was to return to the Catholic tradition of the Great Church of the first five centuries, with an emphasis on the historic faith enshrined in the Creeds, on the authority of the apostolical succession of the ministry, on the architecture of the ages of faith, and on the sacramental life and Liturgies of long ago. There was also a partial reaction expressed in a simpler and naïver form of Protestant primitivism which aimed at a return to the supposedly less institutional and more charismatic worship of the New Testament Church. It was manifested in the foundation of new denominations, and the impetus was evangelical rather than ecclesiastical. In fact, much of its inspiration was a reaction from the supposed rigidity, complacency, and even traditionalism of the existing communions and from the rationalism and sophistication of the age.

This stream of primitivism led to the foundation of the following religious movements: the Primitive Methodists (1812), the Plymouth Brethren (1827-1830), the Catholic Apostolic Church (1835), the Disciples of Christ (founded 1833,[1] established in Britain 1843), and the Salvation Army (the organization began in 1865 but was first known under a military designation in 1879). Small and often humble in origin, they became important in the later nineteenth century.

1. Common Characteristics

Different as these organizations were in origin, social composition, success, and even in their ordinances of worship, they have many significant characteristics in common. Each was marked, in the first place, by a strong Biblicism. The Primitive Methodists would not have come into being if Wesleyan Methodism had allowed its founders, Hugh Bourne and William Clowes, to emulate their Master who had preached the Sermon on the Mount, for they were expelled for encouraging open-air revivalistic gatherings,

---

[1] Originating in the U.S.A. in 1811, when the first independent congregation was established it became a separate denomination there in about 1833. The denomination was introduced into England in 1843. See Einar Molland, *Christendom*, p. 298.

and for years they existed as a congeries of simple Bible-reading and preaching fellowships. The Disciples of Christ have a similar origin, also, except that their American founders, the Campbells, in their zeal to reap the fields of the revival white unto harvest, found the Presbyterian insistence on the long training of a learned ministry too slow to meet the exigencies of a Western frontier situation requiring rapid mobility. It is significant, however, that in their protest against a constricting tradition, they refused creeds and confessions of faith, the easier to be guided by the New Testament alone.

The Plymouth Brethren, too, were extremely conservative in their Biblical fidelity and their Anglican evangelical leaders felt it necessary to cut the painter that hitherto had bound them to the Church of Ireland, so that they could recover the simplicities of the New Testament, without a specially ordained ministry and with regular Lord's Day meetings for the Breaking of Bread and Bible study. In the case of the Salvation Army, it was, like Primitive Methodism, a break away from the Wesleyan fold in order to concentrate on the reviving of Christianity among the social lepers of the industrial areas, many of whom would have never thought to enter a bourgeois city Methodist Church.

Even in the admittedly unique combination of the traditional and the charismatic in the life of the Catholic Apostolic Church, there was an insistence upon the reviving of offices and customs of the Apostolic Church which Christendom had allowed to fall into desuetude, and a great deal of detailed typological exegesis of the Scriptures provided the rationale of its worship and polity.[2] Ever since the Reformation (and, indeed, before it), reformers large and small have turned to the Bible in general and to the New Testament in particular, on the presumption that the earliest was the purest form of the Church, and have attempted to revive its radiant faith, its fervent hope in the immediate Second Coming of the Lord, its closely knit fellowship, its enthusiasm for spreading the Gospel, and even some of its charismatic practices such as "prophesying" and "speaking with tongues," which were believed to be directly inspired by the Holy Spirit. The revolt of the charismatic against the institutional is a phenomenon frequently found in the history of Christianity and the nineteenth century, like the

[2] See J. B. Cardale's *Readings upon the Liturgy and other Divine Offices of the Church* (2 vols., 1874), Vol. I, pp. 204-363, a section entitled, "A Dissertation upon the Types of the Law."

seventeenth, provides much evidence of it. The Bible was the text-book of revolution.

In the second place, three of these five new religious organizations exhibited a marked charismatic character. The Primitive Methodists, under the leadership of Hugh Bourne, who had been favourably impressed by the accounts an American evangelist, Lorenzo Dow, had given him of the American camp meetings, determined to introduce camp meetings in England. The first of these took place on the hill, Mow Cop, in 1807, where during one afternoon and evening there were four preachers simultaneously appealing for conversions in passionate extemporary pleading, supported by a band of praying men and women, devoutly seeking the intercession of the Holy Spirit. Lively choruses of hymns, and the "Amens" and "Hallelujahs" of the crowd, encouraged both the preachers and the potential converts, as a "gospel by incantation" was proclaimed. It was not until 1861, when the charismatic spirit had cooled, and warm evangelical fellowships had subsided into a denominational organization—and one with a considerable social and intellectual respectability by that time—that the Primitive Methodists drew up a service-book. Even then, it was for the permissive, not obligatory, use of their ministers.[3] Up to this time "forms" and "spirit' would have been considered antithetical, not complementary, terms and conceptions.

The Salvation Army was eager in its evangelistic and social work to be as unlike a Church as possible, and to this end it employed what the complacent were disposed to consider sensational methods of attracting attention. Its processions in military uniform with banners, its bands with their bugles, trumpets, drums, and tambourines, its street-corner testimony meetings punctuated with rousing choruses and joyful interpolations, all were as opposed to the dignity of a Liturgy, as life to death.

But it was the Catholic Apostolic Church, first under the leadership of Edward Irving and then under Cardale and Drummond, which went furthest in the charismatic direction, on the one side, as it did in the institutional-liturgical, on the other side. Here were introduced as a regular part of the worship both *glossolalia* (the speaking with tongues) and "prophesyings" (weird warnings

---

[3] *Forms for the Administration of Baptism; the Solemnization of Matrimony; Maternal Thanksgiving after Child-birth; Administration of the Lord's Supper . . . drawn up by the Order of the Primitive Methodist Conference . . . for the use of such Primitive Methodist Ministers as may require them . . .* (1861).

and forecasts given by spirit-possessed prophets either during or immediately after the lections and sermons). These invasions of the Holy Spirit, as they were supposed to be, were a deliberate revival of the gifts of the New Testament Church, devoutly sought and deeply appreciated. An indication of the common concern for a charismatic rather than a predetermined form of worship is to be seen in the fact that four of the five denominations (the Catholic Apostolic Church being the exception) used free prayers in preference to a Liturgy. And even the latter Church made way for the imperious demands of those claiming the inspiration of the spirit despite its hierarchical government and fixed service order, and the admonitions of St. Paul to the Corinthian Church which suffered from over-indulgence in the *charismata*.

As a third common characteristic, it may be noted that the rebirth of the impetus to revivalism in the nineteenth century was connected with the conviction of the impending Second Advent of Christ which made it a matter of the greatest urgency to snatch brands from the burning. This was the original concern of the Salvation Army and it formed an important part of the credo of the Plymouth Brethren, who regarded themselves as a "remnant" which had separated for the sake of a greater dedication to holiness from the mixed multitude of the Established Church in Ireland. Nowhere was the Adventist fervour more potent than in the Catholic Apostolic Church, which feverishly determined to restore the Apostolate and all the ordinances which a lethargic Christendom had allowed to fall into abeyance, so that the true Church of Christ might be ready to greet her Spouse at His Second Coming, arrayed as a bride in the virginal purity of holiness. There is probably some correlation between this belief in an imminent Second Advent and the increase in political convulsions in the mid-nineteenth century.

Though apparently contradicted by the formation of new denominations, an ecumenical impetus was a fourth characteristic of some of these new religious organizations. The Catholic Apostolic Church and the Disciples of Christ (often known as the Churches of Christ) were deeply interested in the reunion of Christendom. The former, though they believed they had restored the lost orders of the ministry and the full ordinances of the Church of Christ, were far from considering themselves to be the only Christians. They recognized all baptized persons as fellow-Christians and prayed for all Churches and their ultimate unity in the bonds of the Holy Spirit. The Disciples of Christ, for their part, believed that it was through the rejection of tradition and the return to the New Testament that the unity of the Church was to be recovered. The mistake, they felt, had been to make other conditions than those of Christ Himself for entry to the Kingdom, and this accounted for the bewildering variety of Christian denominations.

What is not to be expected in a charismatic primitivism is a renewed appreciation of the Sacraments and an appreciation of ceremonial. It is this fifth characteristic which makes many of the new denominations founded during this century so absorbingly interesting. The single exception appears to be the Primitive Methodist Church in its earlier phase of growth, though, as we have seen, it also came to appreciate forms as every sect does when it develops into a denomination with a trained ministry and common worship. What is chiefly remarkable is that the Plymouth Brethren, the Disciples of Christ, and the Catholic Apostolic Church, all insisted on the celebration of the "Breaking of the Bread," the Lord's Supper, and the Eucharist, each Lord's Day (these were the terms they used for the Communion) as the central and distinctive mark of the corporate activity of Christians.

Only two of the new denominations emulated the Oxford Movement in a concern for ceremonial. These were the Catholic Apostolic Church and, surprisingly, the Salvation Army, which had first permitted and then abolished the celebration of the Sacraments. This final common characteristic of the new denominations was the rectification of an unfortunate tendency in post-Reformation Protestantism to elevate preaching and depreciate the Sacraments. It is all the more astonishing that it should have been characteristic of denominations which generally had a strong evangelical concern. While the stress on the Lord's Supper can be attributed in part to the return to Biblical foundations (and wholly so in the case of the Disciples of Christ), it is probably to be associated also with the sacramental impetus of the Oxford Movement and the Romantic and Gothic revivals in literature, art, and architecture.

After these introductory generalizations our study now turns to the specific and distinctive contributions made by each of the new denominations to worship, treating them in chronological order.

2. *The Primitive Methodists*

This off-shoot of the Wesleyan Methodists, which was reunited in the British Methodist Church in 1932, came into being because two earnest evangelists, Hugh Bourne and William Clowes, de-

manded a greater freedom for evangelistic work among the un-
reached than the Methodist discipline of the day would permit.
Joining their forces, they formed the Primitive Methodist Church
in Staffordshire in 1812. It is supposed that they took the name
from John Wesley's final charge to his Chester preachers, in which
he had urged them to preach the gospel in the streets and lanes
and under the hedges, adding, "and this is the way the primitive
methodists did."[4] Bourne declared as his conviction that "The Lord
appointed us to labour at large in promoting open-air worship and
the converting work."[5] It is certain that in taking the name they
did they recalled the vigorous open-air preaching of Wesley and
Whitefield to the uncommitted, and determined to follow them.
After all, were not the Methodist pioneers themselves following
the greater example of the Preacher of the Sermon on the Mount?

They were not the only dissatisfied Methodists who felt that
complacency had paralysed the committed, for there were at the
same time companies of "Tent Methodists" at Bristol, "Band Room
Methodists" at Manchester, and "Quaker Methodists" (afterwards
"Independent Methodists") at Warrington.[6] In considering the
strongly charismatic emphasis of the denomination in its origins,
it is significant that Hugh Bourne had not only read the great
Quaker apologist, Robert Barclay, and was in friendly touch with
the Quakers, but that, like them, he exhibited a natural Christ-
mysticism, sought for Divine leading at every crisis of his life,
and recognized the value of women ministers, one of whom may
well have been the prototype of Dinah Morris in George Eliot's
Adam Bede. The chief influence in Bourne's determination to com-
mence camp meetings on the American model was undoubtedly
Lorenzo Dow (1777-1824), who came to England to report on
the camp-meeting movement in the United States in 1805 and
remained until 1807. Before the name "Primitive Methodist" was
assumed in 1812, Bourne's followers were, indeed, known as the
"Camp-Meeting Methodists," and Dow himself was present at the
first famous camp meeting held under Bourne's direction on the
summit of Mow Cop in 1807. This form of meeting, held for a

---

[4] See *Proceedings of the Wesley Historical Society*, Vol. XXVI, pp. 78-79, article
by F. F. Bretherton on "Wesley's Last Visit to Chester." See also, J. T. Wilkinson, *Hugh Bourne 1772-1852*, pp. 92 f.

[5] Wilkinson, *Hugh Bourne*, p. 67, citing the A text of Bourne's manuscript
autobiography now in the Library of Hartley-Victoria Methodist Theological College, Manchester.

[6] H. B. Kendall, *History of the Primitive Methodist Church* (rev. edn., 1919),
p. 14.

whole day in the open, was definitely designed for those who were unattracted by the routine approach of the Church, and was pronounced by the Wesleyan Conference to be "highly improper and likely to be of considerable mischief."[7]

The enthusiasm it generated may be felt in the description given by William Clowes in his eye-witness account of the Mow Cop meeting held on May 31st, 1807:

"The morning was unfavourable; it was rainy. . . . On my arrival at the hill about six o'clock, I found a small group of people assembled under a wall, singing. I immediately joined them, and several of us engaged in prayer. When we had concluded the singing and praying services, a Peter Bradburn preached the sermon, and an individual from Macclesfield followed with another. The people now began to be strongly affected . . . and kept increasing in larger numbers; but as they came from various places to the hill, many were at a loss to know to what point they should make. . . .

"Accordingly a Mr. Edward Anderson from Kilham, Yorkshire, unfurled something like a flag on a long pole in a conspicuous position, which became the centre of attraction. It was about this time that I stood up on the stand to address the people, by giving a statement of my Christian experience. . . .

"The first day's preaching on Mow Hill presented a most magnificent spectacle. Four preachers simultaneously crying to sinners to flee the wrath to come; thousands listening affected with 'thoughts that breathed and words that burned'; many in deep distress, and others pleading with Heaven in their behalf; some praising God aloud for the great things which were brought to pass. . . .

"The Camp-meeting continued full of glory and converting-power . . . the power of the Highest continued with undiminished force and effect until the close, which took place about half-past eight o'clock in the evening."[8]

The seething crowd, the earnest leaders who had gathered from many adjacent counties, the companies of intense men and women of prayer, the shouts of joy over reclaimed sinners and the agonies of repentance, the lurid preaching made doubly impressive as the torches threw sinister shadows—all this was the impressive background of the interior psychological drama of the soul, in which

---

[7] Ed. F. L. Cross, *The Oxford Dictionary of the Christian Church*, p. 1106.

[8] Pp. 23-25 of J. T. Wilkinson, *William Clowes 1780-1851*, from the unpublished manuscript of Clowes's *Journal* in the Library of the Hartley-Victoria Methodist College, Manchester.

grace fought with the powers of darkness in a contest of eternal significance. Such is elemental charismatic worship.

The camp meeting had a freshness and urgency that recalled the first Quakers and the earliest Methodists, or even the thirteenth century Franciscan friars in England. It was a revival of the field-preaching of Whitefield and Wesley, but with three significant changes. Instead of relying on the impact of one preacher, the Primitive Methodists used several preachers at the same meeting. Furthermore, their impassioned appeals for conversion were pointed and much briefer than those of Whitefield and Wesley. Finally, the preachers were supported by praying-circles. In brief, the camp meetings were an effective demonstration, not of the power of a popular preacher, but of the priesthood of all believers.[9]

The enthusiasm of the Primitive Methodists proved contagious among the common people. They were almost always to be found in the open-air, and their chosen places of worship and preaching were the country common, the town cross, and the city streets. Walking in procession and singing hymns, they were the fore-runners of the Salvation Army in using this method of attracting public attention. Like them, too, they were persecuted for their faith. At Camberwell a group of hooligans pelted them with stones, let guns off in their proximity, and mocked their temperance endeavours by offering pots of porter to their converts. At Westminster three desperadoes, dressed up as devils, terrified the faithful. At York a sadistic opponent turned a riderless horse loose in their midst, causing the greatest fear and confusion.[10]

In the early years it seems that the leaders of the Primitive Methodists were fearful of changing from an evangelistic movement into a sober and possibly complacent denomination. This would account for two features in their life: their unwillingness to build elaborate churches and their reluctance to channel the Holy Spirit in prescribed forms of worship. Their first building for worship was erected, not in the shape of a chapel, but in that of a house: "The building measured sixteen yards long by eight wide, and was galleried half-way . . . it was furnished in a plain manner; the walls were not coated, and it had no ceiling. . . . In the erection of it the house form was chosen in preference to the chapel form, so that if not wanted, it would form four houses, according to the plan on which houses were usually built in Tunstall . . . because

[9] H. B. Kendall, *op.cit.*, pp. 17-18.
[10] J. T. Wilkinson, *William Clowes 1780-1851*, pp. 59, 68.

it could not be known whether or not the connexion would be of any long continuance."[11]

Although the economic motive predominated in the narrative, written some time after the event, presumably to account for an early meeting-house looking less like a place of worship than existing chapels of the Primitive Methodists at the time of writing, yet there was also a deliberate unecclesiastical simplicity involved and a sense that it was highly improper for a denomination committed to open-air conversions to build elaborate sanctuaries for indoors worship. The early charismatic emphasis is also seen in the reluctance to celebrate the Sacrament of the Lord's Supper. Bourne's *Journal*, for example, frequently refers to love-feasts and very rarely to Communion services. (In this, too, the Primitive Methodists were following early Wesleyan practice.)

The first large-scale Lord's Supper was celebrated at the Annual Conference on the evening of Saturday, June 12, 1841. Bourne notes that "the room was well set out. At one end stood a table, on which the elements were placed; and on either side and at the end of the table were placed several forms at a suitable distance, for the people to kneel while partaking the Sacrament."[12] This is an interesting indication that the Primitive Methodists were attempting to approximate the Wesleyan usage, rather than to imitate the table-fellowship characteristic of Presbyterian and Congregational worshippers, in which the characteristic posture was sitting, rather than kneeling. Bourne's account is full of details, as befitted an important denominational celebration of the Lord's Supper, which was presumably a model for all the local fellowships.

It reads:

"After singing and prayer, one of the brethren stood up and spoke of the first institution of the feast of the passover. . . . He next spoke of our Lord continuing it in the Christian Church. . . . He then took up a plate from the table, which had on it a number of unleavened cakes, and held it up in the presence of the people. . . . Then, setting down the plate, he took up a cake and broke it in the presence of the people, using the words of the apostle, where he speaks of the body of Christ being broken for us. This made a deep impression.

"He then took up a bottle (there were four on the table) and

---

[11] J. T. Wilkinson, *Hugh Bourne*, p. 88, citing Petty's *History of the Primitive Methodists*, pp. 30-37.

[12] J. T. Wilkinson, *Hugh Bourne*, pp. 153-54, citing *The Primitive Methodist Magazine*, 1841, pp. 353-55.

he poured it into a cup, and spoke of the blood of Christ which was shed for us. He observed that it was prepared in a way similar to that which the Jews prepared their passover wine. . . . So nearly following the footsteps of our Lord in His instituting the Sacrament gave great satisfaction.

"A quantity of bread was immediately broken into small pieces on one of the plates: and the three appointed to minister took the Sacrament. A number then came forward and kneeled at the forms placed there for that purpose: and one administered the unleavened bread and another the unleavened wine, the cup of blessing. The other, during this, broke an additional quantity of bread to be in readiness; and gave other needful assistance. When these had partaken, a verse was given out: and whilst it was singing[13] they rose from their knees and returned: and a number more took their places. In this way they proceeded until all had partaken in obedience to the order of our Blessed Lord."[14]

It is most instructive, as a study of the morphology of enthusiasm in a sect as it becomes a denomination,[15] to compare the Communion Orders of the Primitive Methodists with that of the Wesleyan Methodists as they had developed at approximately the same time.[16] In this case, the choice of permissive orders of worship is itself an indication that the Pentecostal freedom of charismatic worship can no longer be maintained, but it is also indicative of a desire to preserve as much of the charismatic character of its origins as possible, as will be seen. The Wesleyan Communion Order clearly reveals its Anglican origin in its use of collects, responses, the exhortation, the Decalogue, the General Confession, the Comfortable Words, the Sursum Corda, Preface and Proper, Sanctus, and in its prayers of Humble Access and Consecration, as also in its use of the Anglican words of delivery.

In direct contrast, the Primitive Methodist Order omits all collects, responses, and traditional prayers, and removes from the Words of delivery all associations of the "Real Presence." Its distinctively charismatic character, however, is seen in three ways.

13 Singing a verse of a hymn while communicants arrived at or departed from the Communion-table was also a Wesleyan Methodist custom.
14 J. T. Wilkinson, *Hugh Bourne*, pp. 153-54, citing *The Primitive Methodist Magazine*, 1841, pp. 353-55.
15 Here it may be noticed that we differ from Troeltsch in regarding a "denomination" as a stage intermediate in development between a "sect" and a "church."
16 We are comparing the Primitive Methodist *Forms for Administration of Baptism*, etc. (1861) with the *Order of Administration of the Lord's Supper and Baptism . . . as used by the Wesleyan Methodists* (1848).

The service begins with either a "Brief Address" or the reading of the Matthaean Institution Narrative. It permits a set or an extemporary prayer to follow after a hymn, and allows the service to end with a brief exhortation and a short prayer, followed by a verse of a hymn or the Benediction. Finally, an important rubric indicates that "the communicants may receive the elements at the communion rails or in the pews, sitting or kneeling as may be most convenient or agreeable to the respective societies."[17]

It is essentially this flexibility and freedom allowed to the ministry of the Primitive Methodists in celebrating the Lord's Supper which is the last remainder of charismatic worship in a service-book. By extemporary prayers, exhortations, and the selection of verses from appropriate hymns, the Conference hoped to prevent that familiarity which breeds contempt and to secure for their ministers the right to respond to the leading of the Holy Spirit which gives a literally incalculable freshness to the most solemn rite. The Wesleyan Order, it is true, allowed for the free choice of hymns and for a concluding extemporary prayer, but these were always additional (never substitutes or alternatives) to the uniform order of the rite which must be followed in its completeness. The compromise rubric is interesting testimony to a struggle among the various societies in which some were advocates of the Wesleyans who knelt beside the Lord's Table to receive Communion, and others were advocates of the Genevan (Presbyterian and Congregational) mode of reception, sitting in the pews as guests of the Lord.

In one respect the Primitive Methodists were truer trustees of Wesley's legacy of worship than even the Wesleyan Methodists—this was in their retention of the Convenant Service, in "A Form for Renewing our Covenant with God." The preface to it indicates that it was valued as being "calculated to deepen religious impressions, to strengthen our pious resolutions, and to quicken our desires after larger measures of Scriptural holiness."[18] In one particular it was probably an improvement on the original Wesley Covenant Service: its first part was designed for penitent sinners and its second part for Christian believers and disciples. It was a comprehensive dedication: "Covenant with Thee; we dedicate ourselves afresh to Thy service. We would consecrate ourselves unreservedly unto the Lord: our bodies and our souls, and all their

[17] *Forms for the Administration of Baptism*, etc. (1861), p. 38.
[18] *Ibid.*, p. 47.

powers; our time, our talents, our property, our influence, and all we have and are, would we devote to Thee."[19] Here, if anywhere, in this renascent Puritanism, with its total commitment, its burning sincerity, and its refusal of adventitious aids in worship, is the immense strength and enduring simplicity of Primitive Methodism, and the proof that even in accepting forms of worship the Spirit of God would not be quenched.

3. The Plymouth Brethren[20]

The iron-ration of this evangelical denomination (the metaphor is appropriate because the Plymouth Brethren number so many generals and other military officers in their disciplined communities) is the Bible. Its naïve New Testamentalism represents the strongest protest against worldliness in churchmanship, ritual, ceremonial, and organization. It has no ordained clergy and is apparently out of communion with all other Christian groups. Comte's new religion was described as "Roman Catholicism without Christianity," and in view of its rigid uncharitableness one is tempted to define this denomination as Protestantism without Christianity. Its chief founder, John Nelson Darby, was exactly contemporaneous with Pusey, the leader of the Tractarians after Newman's secession, and originally shared many of the Tractarian views. Darby's dissatisfaction with the Anglican Church in Ireland, of which he was a clergyman, was due to both the Church's subservience to the State, and the fact that few of the clergy and of the members gave evidence of converted lives.[21]

Clearly, it was another case of the Spirit versus the letter, the charismatic protest against the institutional. There was, however, in their origin, a concern among Plymouth Brethren for the unity of Christ's Church. Darby and some Dublin friends, disturbed by the denominationalism of the day, paradoxically resolved to create a new denomination consisting of Christ's true "Remnant," as unecclesiastical as possible in form. After a detailed and thorough study of the New Testament, they decided to "meet on the Lord's

[19] *Ibid.*, p. 51.
[20] Founded in Dublin in 1827, they transferred their headquarters to Plymouth in 1830.
[21] Of the Irish Church he said, ". . . I was looking for the body of CHRIST (which was not there, but perhaps in all the parish not one converted person) and collaterally, because I believed in a divinely-appointed ministry. If Paul had come, he could not have preached (he had never been ordained); if a wicked ordained man, he had his title and *must be recognised as a minister; the truest minister of Christ unordained could not.*" (Cited p. 18 of W. G. Turner, *John Nelson Darby.*)

Day to break bread as in the early days of Christianity." A present-day apologist sums up their convictions as the discovery "that intelligently to worship the Father in Spirit and truth, and direct responsibility to serve the Lord, while awaiting His return, compose the proper sphere of the believer's aspirations here on earth."[22]

The original charismatic conception of their worship is clearly defined by Darby: "To worship in spirit, is the powerful energy of communion which the Spirit of God gives (in contrast with the forms and ceremonies—with all the religion of which the flesh is capable)—and in the true nature of Him whom we worship."[23] Such a pneumatic emphasis will obviously be iconoclastic. That can be seen in the utter rejection of all instrumental music in worship. Darby expresses his detestation of music in a letter to a friend which for its extremism invites comparison with Tertullian (also a lawyer turned theologian) in his Montanist days: "Harps and organs down here began in Cain's city when he had gone forth out of the presence of the Lord. In point of fact artistic musicians as a general rule are not a moral class. The imagination is at work, not the conscience nor the heart. . . . If I could put a poor sick father to sleep with music, I would play the most beautiful I could find. But it only spoils any worship as bringing in the pleasure of sense in what ought to be the power of the SPIRIT of God. They cannot go really together, save as water may take away the taste of wine."[24]

Such "angelism" is not only a denial of the Incarnational principle, but also a refusal to accept the goodness of God's creation, or to see the artist as capable of Divine inspiration, and, indeed, it conceives of salvation in a niggardly and diminished way as precluding the sanctification of the senses. It inevitably leads to a tense, critical, scrupulous spirituality that has little kinship with Him "who came that men might have life and have it more abundantly." It presumes that grace must always be antagonistic to nature.[25]

As might be expected, even though the Lord's Supper is given a central place in the cultus, and renewed each Lord's Day, its doctrine is Zwinglian. It has a two-fold importance, each pedagogi-

[22] W. G. Turner, op.cit., p. 33.
[23] J. N. Darby, On Worship, p. 16.
[24] Cited W. G. Turner, op.cit., pp. 40-41.
[25] This is positively affirmed in the following letter to a friend of Darby's who had asked his opinion about an organ voluntary: "This is a poor plea, and putting nature instead of grace, which has even boldness to enter into the holiest." W. G. Turner, op.cit., p. 40.

cal: it is a memorial of the Sacrifice of Christ offered to and accepted by God as the foundation of all relationships to Him, and it is the proof of Christ's love for His own.[26] What could not have been predicted, however, was that the Plymouth Brethren had no desire to re-introduce *glossolalia* or "prophesyings" (as indubitably New Testament practices) into their worship.[27] This may be accounted for by St. Paul's insistence that the overriding criterion in worship was "edification," or by the fact that Darby's Anglican inheritance would have made the disorder of "speaking with tongues" repugnant, or even by the upper middle-class status of some gatherings of Plymouth Brethren. Their charismatic worship was certainly never rhapsodical.

Charismatic their worship certainly was, for it is a central conception with them that it is the Holy Ghost who presides in their assemblies. In this their unecclesiastical and group worship has obvious parallels with that of the Society of Friends. The Brethren, moreover, insist that their simple meeting-places shall resemble rooms, not churches or chapels. In one other respect, also, they resemble the Quakers: they have no pulpit, believing that the elevation of one minister in a pulpit would be a dishonouring of the Holy Spirit and of the company of believers who share the Spirit.[28]

Admirable as is the idea of a purely Spirit-directed worship, it is quite unpractical. This the Brethren have reluctantly admitted in having set times for worship and in using hymn-books which are humanly composed. We may, however, do their teaching a severe injustice unless we recognise that the movement in its origins was very different from its subsequent and highly controversial development. The initial attraction of the movement was its repudiation of any ecclesiastical pretensions and its desire to merge sectarian distinctions in the simple gathering of all believers to Christ around the Lord's Table, its aversion to divisive theological systems, and the humility, zeal, and even sanctity of its disciples, who included Müller, the founder of a celebrated orphanage,[29] and Tregelles, a

26 J. N. Darby, *On Worship*, p. 29.

27 *Ibid.*, footnote to p. 24.

28 The germinal idea for the fellowship was that of Groves: "This, I doubt not, is the mind of God concerning us, that we should come together in all simplicity as disciples, not waiting on any pulpit or ministry, but trusting the Lord will edify us together by ministering to us . . . from ourselves." Hastings, E. R. E., ii, p. 843.

29 See the very fair evaluation, entitled *Plymouth Brethrenism: its Ecclesiastical and Doctrinal Teachings; with a Sketch of its History* (2nd edn., London, 1874). There is a copy of this anonymous pamphlet in the Cambridge University Library.

distinguished Biblical scholar. A perceptive judgment on this charismatic sect, as also upon many others, is that of Rabbi Duncan who affirmed that "if a body without a soul is a carcase; a soul without a body is a ghost."[30]

4. The Catholic Apostolic Church

The leaders of this Church made the most comprehensive attempt to return to the teaching and practices of the Primitive Church during the whole of the nineteenth century, for they conceived that it must be charismatic and institutional, prophetic and priestly in its ministries, and this is what accounts for its interest and for its impact on worship. Other ecclesiastical revivals concentrated on the charismatic (as the Plymouth Brethren, the Primitive Methodists, and the Salvation Army) or on the institutional (the Oxford Tractarians and the Cambridge Ecclesiologists), but only the Catholic Apostolic Church decided to revive both aspects of primitive Church life.

The importance of the worship of the Catholic Apostolic Church can be seen from the fact that eminent liturgiologists of different communions have expressed their admiration for its Liturgy, which has had a significant influence upon the development of the Liturgy of the Church of Scotland.[31] Heiler says: "It is undoubtedly one of the finest and fullest forms of Christian worship. Indeed, of all liturgies of today it comes perhaps nearest to the Primitive Church."[32] D. H. Hislop maintains that it is the one Liturgy of modern times "which contains all the virtues and escapes almost all the blemishes of the Prayer Book," and remarks that it makes great use of Oriental prayers of mystical passion and is characterized by a sense of the imminence of the advent of the Spirit which gives to it "a fresh and living freedom."[33]

It was once, in popular parlance, known as the "Irvingite Church" and certainly Edward Irving, the former minister of the "Scots National Church" in Regent Square, was one of its founders. It is to him and to Henry Drummond that its "apostolic" or charismatic character is due, but the "Catholic" element in its name and its nature is more certainly the contribution of J. B. Cardale, a

---

For a thorough theological exposition and evaluation of J. N. Darby's teaching see C. B. Bass, *Backgrounds to Dispensationalism*.
30 Cited *ibid.*, p. 35.
31 See W. D. Maxwell, *An Outline of Christian Worship*, pp. 159-60.
32 *The Spirit of Worship*, p. 109.
33 *Our Heritage in Worship*, p. 212.

retired lawyer and liturgiologist. Edward Irving (1792-1834), although he had been the assistant of the great Chalmers at St. John's, Glasgow, came as a virtually unknown preacher to the metropolis in 1822. Within a year his commanding eloquence made him so famous that Canning referred admiringly to a sermon of his in the House of Commons.

Irving had come to the conclusion that the Second Advent of Christ was imminent and that the spiritual gifts so generously bestowed on the Apostolic Church of the first century were not exceptional, but that only the absence of faith had prevented their continuance through all the Christian centuries. In this belief he was greatly strengthened by Drummond, the Member of Parliament for West Surrey, who convened a gathering of those interested in the apocalyptic writings in both Testaments at his country house in Albury, Surrey, to which Irving came. There the assembled "prophets" re-affirmed their conviction that the imminent return of Christ would be heralded by the restoration of the lost spiritual gifts of tongues and of "prophesying." Irving's ministerial colleague, Scott, also shared this belief and was convinced that the gift of tongues had already been restored to a woman in Scotland who, although given up for dead, was marvellously restored by faith, and enabled to speak "with tongues" and to "prophesy."[34]

In 1831 Irving was able to report the gift of tongues and prophecy in his own congregation. It was partly the disorder thus introduced into the worship of his church and partly his unorthodox doctrine of the Incarnation that our Lord assumed an unredeemed human body for our redemption that caused Irving to be delated and ultimately discharged from the ministry of the Church of Scotland by his home Presbytery of Annan in 1833. In describing these charismatic phenomena, therefore, it is most important to include two accounts of the restored Apostolic gifts, one by a critic and one by Irving himself.

The critic is the Rev. Dr. J. A. Alexander who attended a service that Irving conducted in 1833. He pays tribute to Irving's trumpet-like voice and deep sincerity in reading the Scriptures and in prayer, but thinks his Biblical interpretation allegorical and even fanciful. While Irving was expounding the thirty-ninth chapter of *Exodus* and explaining the "ouches" of the breastplate as symbolizing the rulers of the church, "he was interrupted in a manner rather startling. . . . Just as Irving reached the point I have mentioned

---

[34] See Margaret Oliphant, *The Life of Edward Irving, Minister of the National Scotch Church, London, illustrated by his Journals and Correspondence*, pp. 362-63.

and was explaining the ouches; the elder of the church who sat in the chair . . . burst out in a sort of wild ejaculation, thus: 'Taranti—hoiti—faragmi-santi'; 'O ye people—ye people of ye Lord, ye have not the ouches—ye have not the ouches—ha-a-a; ye cannot hear—ye cannot hear!' This last was spoken in a pretty loud whisper, as the inspiration died away within him. When he began, Irving suspended his exposition and covered his face with his hands. As soon as the voice ceased, he resumed the thread of his discourse, till the 'tongue' broke out again 'in unknown strains.' "[35]

With this must be compared Irving's own description and interpretation of the power of tongues: "The whole utterance, from the beginning to the end of it, is with a power, and strength, and fulness, and sometimes rapidity of voice altogether different from that of the person's utterance in any mood; and I would say, both in its form and in its effects upon a simple mind, quite supernatural. There is a power in the voice to thrill the heart, and overawe the spirit after a manner I have never felt. There is a march, and a majesty, and a sustained grandeur in the voice, especially of those who prophesy, which I have never heard even a resemblance to, except now and then in the sublimest and most impassioned moods of Mrs. Siddons and Miss O'Neil. . . . And when the speech utters itself in a way of a psalm or spiritual song, it is the likest to some of the most simple and ancient chants in the cathedral service. . . . Most frequently the silence is broken by utterance in a tongue . . . sometimes occupying only a few words, as if it were filling the first gust of sound; sometimes extending to five minutes or even more, of earnest and deeply-felt discourse, with which the heart and soul of the speaker is manifestly much moved to tears, and sighs, and unutterable groanings, to joy, and mirth, and exultation, and even laughter of the heart. So far from being unmeaning gibberish, as the thoughtless and heedless sons of Belial have said, it is regularly-formed, well-proportioned, deeply-felt discourse, which evidently wanteth *only the ear of him whose native tongue it is* to make it the very masterpiece of powerful speech."[36]

We can only observe, as Canon Sydney Smith did, watching two Edinburgh fishwives shouting at each other across a street, "Clearly they cannot agree; they argue from different premises."

[35] H. L. Alexander, *Life of Joseph Alexander*, Vol. I, pp. 290-92, cited in P. E. Shaw, *The Catholic Apostolic Church sometimes called Irvingite, a Historical Study*, pp. 49-51.
[36] M. Oliphant, *op.cit.*, p. 431. For other accounts see the *London Times*, issue of November 19, 1831 under the heading, "Disturbance at the National Scotch Church," and the account of a sympathetic observer, Mrs. Hamilton, in *ibid.*, pp. 426-27.

Irving's premises were the faith-filled Apostolic Church of the first century, Alexander's the Church of the cautious and rational nineteenth century.

Nonetheless, Irving had gathered round him a congregation who shared his apocalyptic and charismatic convictions, and when he was ejected from the National Scotch Church, several hundreds of them followed him to the new church in Newman Street. Here architectural provision was made for the new orders of ministry. Baxter, an early supporter of Irving, reports on the appearance of the interior:

"The room adapted for their meetings was fitted up in the usual style of pews and galleries, as in a church; instead of a pulpit, however, there was constructed at the upper end of the church a raised platform, capable of containing perhaps fifty persons. In the ascent to this platform are steps; on the front of the platform are seven seats; the middle seat is that of the angel; the three on each side of the angel are elders. Below them, on the steps, and in a parallel line, are seven other seats, belonging to the prophets, the middle seat being allotted to Mr. Taplin as the chief of the prophets. Still lower, in a parallel line, are seven other seats appropriated to the deacons, the middle seat being occupied by the chief deacon. This three-fold chord of a seven-fold ministry was adopted under the direction of the utterance. The angel ordered the service, and the preaching and expounding was generally by the elders in order, the prophets speaking as utterance came upon them."[37]

Up to this point Irving had been the leader of the new movement, but he was soon to be sadly aware of the fact that having encouraged an uncontrollably charismatic ministry of prophets, he could soon be unseated by a prophet. He returned to his own flock, after his deposition by the Annan Presbytery, to discover that he was deposed there as well. He was reappointed on the merely "spiritual" authority of one of the ecstatics who had merely requested it in a "prophecy."[38] Even so, it was a tamed authority he held, for he was now under the authority of the "apostle" of his area.

[37] Cited from Baxter's pamphlet "Irvingism" (1836), p. 11, in M. Oliphant, op.cit., p. 507. The Mormon Temple at Kirtland, Ohio, has three rows of seven elevated seats at each end. Perhaps both faiths found their blue-print in the Book of Revelation.

[38] J. G. Simpson, art. in Hastings Encyclopedia of Religion and Ethics, vii, p. 424 b, declares: "From the moment that Irving acknowledged the utterances of the prophets as the authoritative voice of 'the Spirit' his function towards the society practically ceased. Making no claim to exceptional endowments on his own behalf, he became a follower rather than a leader." See also M. Oliphant, op.cit., chap. xviii.

The first two to be appointed were those powerful and wealthy lay personalities, Drummond and Cardale, to whom the Catholic Apostolic Church owed its emphasis on the "Catholic" side. If Irving, who died in the next year, laid down the foundations of the Church, certainly Drummond and Cardale were wholly responsible for its superstructure. They soon began to find fault with the limitation of the worship to the metrical psalms approved by the Church of Scotland, and added impressive Gregorian chanting and ancient Hymns and Canticles of the Early Church to the Puritan diet of praise. It is chiefly to Cardale that the elaboration of the remarkable ritual and ceremonial of their worship is due.

The development, however, would not have been possible without the theology that undergirded it. This still owed to Irving its Adventist character, its conception of the Church as the community of Christians in heaven and on earth, and its insistence upon the centrality of the Incarnation. Moreover, even if Irving had over-emphasized the reality of the struggle of our Lord with sin by insisting that Christ assumed an unredeemed nature in which He had to overcome the power of original sin, it had the effect of en-couraging men to follow their Lord as One who had overcome their temptations and sufferings, and who had taken up on high a profound sympathy and experience of manhood which was for-ever after a part of the Divine Nature. Irving, too, believed in the efficacy of the Sacraments[39] of Baptism and the Eucharist.

It was left to others, however, to develop the doctrine of the Eucharistic Sacrifice and the "Real Presence" to the point where it became necessary to "reserve" the Sacrament, and to make of Con-firmation or "Sealing" a new and important rite. It was also the others who gave the higher ranks of the restored four-fold ministry a dignity appropriate to their status in the hierarchy in the Liturgy. And, however much Irving was given to allegorical exegesis of the Old Testament, he more than met his match in Cardale, who was able to deduce all the details of the restored cultus from the hints and foreshadowings provided in the Mosaic dispensation, and interpreted by prophecy, until it required two lengthy volumes to explain all the esoteric significance of the Liturgy in his *Readings upon the Liturgy and Other Divine Offices* (1874).[40]

It seems as if the death of Irving in 1834 left the "apostles"

[39] See *ibid.*, p. 291.
[40] The chief proof-texts were Exodus 25:9; 26:30; 27:8; Acts 7:44; Ephesians 4:12-16; Hebrews 8:5; I Peter 2:5; I Timothy 3:15.

free to develop the Liturgy in a direction that bore little resemblance to its Scottish and Presbyterian parentage. The monthly celebration of the Sacrament of the Lord's Supper became, in June 1836, a weekly celebration. The apostles prepared a temporary Liturgy which was lithographed and a copy was sent to each of the "angels" (local ministers) in 1838. This, the first draft of the later more impressive Liturgy, shows an interesting development towards the hieratic character of the Eucharist of the Early Church.[41]

After the presentation of the elements by the Deacons to the Elders, and a prayer of Confession (followed by the Absolution), and a further prayer beseeching the Divine acceptance of the Church's gifts and faith and interceding on behalf of the Universal Church and all orders of the ministry, there is a commemoration of those who have departed in the faith. Then follows an Act of the Consecration of the Bread in four parts: first, the Angel takes the Bread, reciting the Corinthians Communion narrative; then there is a Blessing "which should be commemorative of His mercies in Creation and Redemption, and specially that the Lord Jesus is not only our Sacrifice for sin, but our heavenly bread—And should include a petition that God would bless the Bread, and by the Holy Ghost make it to us the flesh of Jesus Christ";[42] and the conclusion of the prayer, when the people are sufficiently instructed, is to be the *Ter-Sanctus*; finally the manducation is to be accompanied with the words, "He blessed and brake it and said, Take eat, this is my body, etc." The Act of the Consecration of the Cup begins by the recitation of the second part of the Corinthians Communion narrative; it proceeds with a prayer of Blessing on the Cup, giving thanks for its benefits and beseeching "that it may by the Holy Ghost be made to us the blood of Christ."[43] The people's response, when they are sufficiently instructed, is to be the *Gloria in Excelsis*, and the words of administration are to be "This cup is the New Testament in my blood, etc." The Communion ends with a Psalm of Praise concluding with the *Gloria Patri* and the Blessing.

Even this rudimentary set of directions for the Eucharist shows an interesting combination of the Scottish Presbyterian Order and of Eastern Liturgies. Of Scottish provenance are the use of the Corinthians institution narrative and the Biblical fidelity in the words of manducation (as contrasted with the Book of Common

41 P. E. Shaw, in *The Catholic Apostolic Church sometimes called Irvingite, A Historical Study*, prints the documents in full, pp. 102 f.
42 *Ibid.*
43 *Ibid.*, p. 105.

Prayer); typically Scottish also are the division of the narrative into two parts and the exact reproduction of the order of the events of the narrative in the blessing first of the bread and then of the cup, a faithful imitation of the Dominical institution of the Sacrament. Not less Scottish is the use of a concluding psalm of praise. The Eastern influence can be seen in the variety of prayers of intercession (especially the commemoration of the saints), the linking of thanksgiving for Creation with gratitude for Redemption, and, particularly, in the *epiclesis*,[44] though the double invocation of the Holy Spirit is a peculiarity of this particular rite.

More permanent provision for a Liturgy was made in 1842 at Albury Chapel, Drummond's Surrey home, and a year later permission was given for all the churches to use it, if they so wished. A second revised edition appeared in 1847 and a third in 1850. The changes are not very significant, however.[45] What is important is the increasing elaboration of the ceremonial. In 1838 altars were set up in the churches, and in 1842 such vestments as the cope and the chasuble, as well as the surplice, were introduced. The year 1847 was notable for two innovations: the practice of "sealing" was adopted, by the laying-on of hands of the apostles for the impartation of the Holy Ghost, and chrism or consecrated oil for healing the sick and for ordinations was introduced. In 1852 use was made of the symbolism of lights: there was a light before the altar as long as the Sacrament was reserved on it,[46] and there were two lights on the altar when the Eucharist was consecrated on the Lord's Day. In the same year incense was introduced, not for censing the congregation, but as a symbolical offering to God during the prayers of intercession. Finally, in 1868 the practice of holy water was adopted.[47] Evidently the Catholic emphasis had taken precedence over the Protestant and charismatic character of the worship of the movement.

Those who attended such worship were attracted by its awesome sense of mystery and by its ceremonial magnificence. W. E. Orchard, later to become a distinguished liturgist, was greatly

---

[44] That is, the invocation of the Holy Spirit upon the elements that they may become the Body and Blood of Christ.

[45] The liturgical changes were all made upon a two-fold principle: all had to be in accord with Holy Scripture and the worship "must gather up into itself every pure and precious thing which had been developed in the Church in all past ages through the guidance of the Spirit of Christ" (H. C. Whitley, *Blinded Eagle, An Introduction to the Life and Teaching of Edward Irving*, p. 77).

[46] The reservation of the Sacrament during the week was adopted in 1850.

[47] For fuller information on these ceremonial developments see P. E. Shaw, *op.cit.*, pp. 107-08.

impressed when he visited the Catholic Apostolic "cathedral" in London. He wrote: "I wandered into the Catholic Apostolic Church in Gordon Square at the hour of their Evening Service. The Service began with the ceremonial lighting of the sanctuary lamps, which were then swung up into the lofty chancel, to the accompanying of the hymn, 'Hail! gladdening light!', and, in those days, at some point in the Service incense was offered. The impressive building and the high ceremony produced the combined feeling that it was not perhaps the right thing to do, but, nevertheless, that it was mysteriously attractive; for I remember taking friends there afterwards to see it."[48]

Some indication of the deep spiritual quality of the rite may be given by two citations, one from the Good Friday Meditations, and the other from a prayer for the Festival of All Saints, because these were the most distinctive and original services of the Catholic Apostolic Church. The Fifth Prayer or Meditation on Good Friday has a deeply moving simplicity that recalls the *Imitatio Christi*:

"Condemned as a malefactor, Lord Jesu, Lamb of God, Thou didst go forth to the place of death, bearing Thy cross; until fainting through pain and anguish, they took it from Thee, and laid it on Thy disciple to bear, not in pity for Thy suffering, but that Thou mightest be ready to bear fresh torment. They pierced Thy hands and Thy feet, they nailed Thee to the cross. Thou wast lifted up between heaven and earth, as utterly unworthy, and abhorred and rejected of all. Yea, the transgressors with whom Thou wast numbered, who were crucified with Thee, they mocked and reviled Thee. All but Thy mother and Thy beloved disciple, and the faithful women with them, looked upon Thee with hatred and derision. None gave Thee love nor pity, Who wast full of love and pity for all.

"O Lord, we behold Thy sufferings, and we mourn; our eyes, our eyes run down with tears; we weep in the bitterness of our souls; for Thou wast wounded for our transgressions, Thou wast bruised for our iniquities. And above all we mourn, that although we have been made partakers of Thy grace, our sins have pierced Thee anew; we have seemed to count Thy sacrifice a vain thing; we have forgotten that we were cleansed from our old sins. They who nailed Thee to Thy cross knew not that they crucified the Lord of Glory; but we have known Thee, and yet have crucified Thee

48 Orchard, who was then a Presbyterian, records his impressions in *From Faith to Faith*, pp. 49-50. C. F. Andrews gives a sympathetic picture of the Birmingham congregation in Chap. iv of his *What I Owe to Christ*.

afresh, and put Thee to open shame. We have made void Thy mercy, and have kept back from Thee Thy reward. Yet, Lord Jesus, let not Thy mercy fail; and, as in Thine hour of agony Thou didst pray for them that put Thee to death, so for us also do Thou intercede. Behold, we wait before Thy cross; we adore Thee, O Thou that wast crucified. Draw us unto Thee, conform us to Thine example, and now and henceforth let us take up our cross, and follow Thee in this world, looking for our reward in the regeneration, in the kingdom of Thy glory."[49]

With this tender, if diffuse, prayer should be compared the following terse and rapid prayer, spurred on by a longing that re-captures the New Testament expectation: "Take to Thyself, O Lord Jesu, Thy great power, and come again, and reign; come into the midst of Thy people and save us, for Thou only art our deliverer; Thou only art the Saviour of the body as well as the soul: bring with Thee all those who sleep in Thee; give unto them again their bodies, for Thou art the Resurrection and the Life. Hide not Thy face from us any more, we beseech Thee."[50]

It is not only in the quality of the prayers, whether borrowed widely and adapted from Roman, Eastern, and Anglican sources or original in composition, or in the majesty of the ceremonial, or even in the architectonic of this Liturgy, that its supreme value is to be seen. It is also in its comprehensiveness. For the Catholic Apostolic Church had introduced into its service-book many items that went beyond the hope of even the most fervent Anglo-Catholics in the 1928 Revised Prayer Book. The proliferation of its Special Occasional Services is an indication of the rich profusion of spirituality.

There are services for the Receiving of a Catechumen, the Dedi-cation of Catechumens, the Benediction of New Communicants, the Renewal of Vows, the Committing to Pastorship; an impressive group of Benedictions for Newly Married Persons, for Works of Charity, for a Door-keeper, for Singers, for Deacons and Dea-conesses, and for Furniture, Vessels, and Vestments. There are forms for the Consecration of Churches, Altars, and Table-Altars. There are also many forms of ordination for the several ranks of the sacred ministry. There are twelve offices for private occasions, including the Benediction of a House, a Ship, and Holy Oil, and a Commendation for a Departing Soul. There are Forms for cele-

---

[49] *The Liturgy and Other Divine Offices of the Church*, pp. 148-49.
[50] *Ibid.*, pp. 182-83.

brating the Eucharist in times respectively of Calamity, Sickness, Scarcity, and War. All these are in addition to longer and shorter forms for the Eucharist and for Morning and Evening Prayer, as well as for Baptism. In addition, there are impressive services for Christmas, Easter, Pentecost, and All Saints, the chief Feasts and Festivals. One cannot but be impressed by the liturgical largesse of the Catholic Apostolic Church, and by its attempt to hallow the entire lives of its members in the Church and in the world. The triumphant notes of adoration and eager expectation were sounded throughout these services, which represent an enrichment of the resources of the worship of Christendom.

Impressive as these liturgical contributions are, they are not flawless. The Church had staked everything on the fulfilment of its hope of the imminent Second Coming of Christ, with the result that, on the death of the last apostle in 1901, its members could live only in the afterglow of a great hope.[51] Apocalypticism defeated Irving; in the end it also destroyed the Catholic Apostolic Church, which had made no provision for evangelical enterprise during the supposedly brief interim between time and eternity. This, incidentally, is also a criticism of its worship, which did not keep a proper balance between the preaching of the Word and the celebration of the Eucharist. The lengthy and brilliant sermons of Irving gave place, on his decease, to ten or fifteen minute homilies, and the Church became so wrapped up in its own interior life that it had no message for the teeming millions of an industrial society. It hugged itself to death. It was conspicuously the Church of one race and of one class in society, through the absence of missionary concern. To this extent it lacked the Catholicity in its social composition that it sought in its worship.

In its fascinating attempt to combine the charismatic and the traditional (which it saw as twin aspects of a revived apostolic age), it failed to see the antagonism of these principles. Internal dissension between the apostles and the prophets was inevitable. While apostles are the rulers, their power can be challenged by those prophets who claim to have direct revelations from heaven. If the apostles decide whether the prophets are speaking Divine truth or not, then revelation is subject to the misinterpretations of

[51] Yet in its prime, during the Census of 1851, the Catholic Apostolic Church had 30 congregations and 6,000 tithing members.

men and the prophet's authority is called in question. Thus the charismatic and legal principles of authority were inevitably brought into bitter competition.[52]

Moreover, there was a naïve archaism inherent in the entire movement. It was assumed that the Apostolic age was to be imitated in every way, despite the changed conditions and the different modern way of understanding the ways of God to man. In the first century of the Christian dispensation the evidence of the presence of the Holy Spirit was sought in abnormal, mysterious, and violent phenomena, while in the nineteenth century, in which the sense of the immanence of God was paramount, the influence of the Holy Spirit was sought rather in the quieter ethical transformations of character. Words of Dean Inge may fitly be applied to the charismatic phenomena sedulously cultivated by Irving: "Generally it is by the small voice, not by the earthquake, wind or fire, that God speaks to us. And the wish to empty ourselves that God may fill the void is a mistake. It is when we are most ourselves that we are nearest to God."[53]

Furthermore, so much of the allegorical exegesis of Scripture on which the new forms of worship were constructed was far too subjective and esoteric to appeal to anyone except the inner circle of devotees and the office-bearers whose standing was aggrandized in the Liturgy. The Catholic Apostolic Church was a brilliant failure to join two incompatibles and, in the political, intellectual, and social storms of the nineteenth century, appeared as a religious and aesthetic escape-hatch.

Its abiding significance, however, is to be seen as an auxiliary of the Oxford Movement, though unacknowledged, which helped to restore to the people of Britain many of the forgotten treasures of primitive devotions, placing in the most conspicuous light the glory of the Incarnation, the Church's need to be ever-vigilant for the return of her Lord, the doctrine of the Eucharistic Sacrifice and the Eucharist as the norm of Christian worship, and a ceremonial that is an apt reflection of the inspiration of the Divine Artist. Its immediate and direct influence was greatest on the worship of the Church of Scotland, which, through the *Communion Office* of Dr.

---

[52] Edward Miller, *The History and Doctrines of Irvingism, or of the so-called Catholic and Apostolic Church* (2 vols., 1878), Vol. I, p. 89.

[53] *Faith and Knowledge* (pp. 167 f.) cited A. L. Drummond, *Edward Irving and His Circle*, pp. 271 f.

John MacLeod of Govan, was to enrich the *Prayers for Divine Service* and ultimately to add to the comprehensiveness and depth of the Communion Order of *The Book of Common Order* of 1940.[54]

5. The Churches of Christ, or Disciples

The Churches of Christ, or Disciples, were originally known as Campbellites, and are chiefly of interest to us as another significant example of nineteenth century primitivism or restorationism. While their numbers are relatively small in Britain, they form a considerable and important denomination in the United States.[55] Indeed, the first congregation was set up in the United States of America in 1811, as part of the great attempt to convert the thousands of westward-moving settlers. Alexander Campbell, their founder, was a respected and energetic Presbyterian minister, who was unable to persuade the Presbyterian Church to accelerate its programme of ministerial training to meet the great need for Western evangelists. His sympathizers were organized in a separate denominational organization in 1833 and were first established in England in 1843.

The Churches of Christ trace their descent to the views of John Glas, who seceded from the Church of Scotland in 1728 in consequence of his belief that a national Church was unscriptural and that a truly Biblical Church should consist of independent religious communities of convinced believers. His son-in-law, Sandeman, propagated the views of Glas in New England, where he was a vigorous solefideist who adopted some interesting New Testament customs such as that of members washing one another's feet. (In more bizarre fashion, Glas had insisted on celebrating the love-feast or *agape* with broth.) The Churches of Christ, however, dropped the unusual customs and adopted the basic and enduring characteristics of their predecessors.

Long before the Oxford Movement, the Glasites, Sandemanians, and early Disciples of Christ had insisted that the Lord's Supper was the central act of Christian worship. Reacting from the excessive didacticism and dependence upon sermons that characterised the Presbyterians, they restored the weekly celebration of the

[54] See W. D. Maxwell, *A History of Worship in the Church of Scotland*, pp. 175-76. See also Chapter IV, Section 4, *supra*. The important Mercersburg movement in the Evangelical and Reformed Church in America was also influenced by the Catholic Apostolic Church. See J. H. Nichols, *Romanticism in American Theology* (Chicago, 1961), pp. 231, 301.

[55] They have approximately 90,000 members in Britain and 1,900,000 in the U.S.A. See W. G. Baker's article "Disciples of Christ" in *Weltkirchen Lexicon Handbuch der Oekumene*.

Sacrament to its rightful position as the distinctive corporate act of worship of the Church. In England this practice was inherited from the Baptist Churches which had been influenced by McLean, from which the Churches of Christ took their English origin. If the Lord's Supper is central, this does not mean that it is celebrated with an elaborate ritual and ceremonial. On the contrary, says William Robinson, "Without elaborate ritual, then, and without vestments, Churches of Christ have found very satisfying, this worship centering round the Lord's Supper, conducted with dignity, simplicity, and quiet reverence, witnessing to the bond of fellowship which unites the members of the 'beloved community' to one another and to their Divine Head, and which joins the Church on earth to the Church in heaven."[56]

That such a simple celebration can also be deeply devout worship may be confirmed from William Robinson's own Eucharistic hymn now included in *Congregational Praise*,[57] the official hymnbook of the English Congregationalists. Vitiated by memorialism, Dissenting hymns have generally been weakest when written for sacramental occasions. Robinson's is a splendid exception:

> Thee we praise, high priest and victim,
>   Of our hearts the shepherd-king;
> Living, dying, rising, saving,
>   Now let alleluias ring.

> Here, as priests before Thine altar,
>   We are met to worship Thee;
> All Thy saints, on earth, in heaven,
>   Humbly bend the adoring knee.

> Here we see the mystery telling
>   Of Thy wondrous love for men,
> Here set forth in sacred symbol
>   Love beyond our widest ken.

> Lo! in adoration bending,
>   We receive what Thou dost give;
> Join the angels' song unending,
>   Feed by faith on Thee and live.

56 *What the Churches of Christ Stand For*, p. 90.
57 No. 312. *Congregational Praise* appeared first in 1951.

Praise to Thee, eternal Saviour,
Praises from the earth ascend;
Praises from the saints in heaven,
Alleluias without end.

In these verses we find, so rarely conjoined in evangelical devotion, the doctrines of the priesthood of all believers and the communion of saints. The Lord's Table is centrally placed by the Churches of Christ and this, rather than a central pulpit, has always been characteristic of their emphasis as well as of their furnishings.[58] For them the Communion is the regular, corporate, and central act of worship every Lord's Day. Preferring the term "real action" of God to "Real Presence," they interpret the Sacrament ethically rather than metaphysically.[59]

They follow the Baptists in restricting Baptism to believers, assured that there is no positive warrant for paedo-baptism in the New Testament. Taking the New Testament as their guide, and avoiding tradition, which they believed to be responsible for the fissiparousness of the Christian Churches of their day, they refused all creeds and confessions. Their typical trait remains what Campbell intended it to be when he wrote in 1843, "The distinguishing characteristic is a restoration of the ordinances of the new institution to their place and power."[60] They have been in a remarkable way both evangelists and sacramentalists, with a deep concern for the re-union of a divided Christendom.

6. *The Salvation Army*

This important organization, as widely respected for its social as its religious concern, began in 1865 and was first known by its present designation in 1879. The closest parallel to it among the movements studied in this chapter is the Primitive Methodist Church.[61] In each case there was a break away from the restrictive discipline of official Methodism[62] in the interests of untrammelled

---

58 Robinson, *What the Churches of Christ Stand For*, p. 87, footnote.

59 See W. G. Baker, *op.cit.*

60 *Christian Messenger*, Vol. VII, p. 39 (1843), cited Robinson, *What the Churches of Christ Stand For*, p. 84. For the rich understanding of the Lord's Supper, see also William Robinson, *A Companion to the Communion Service; a Devotional Manual.*

61 See J. H. Rigg, *A Comparative View of Church Organizations, Primitive and Protestant* (3rd edn., 1897), p. 320, for confirmation of this judgment.

62 Bourne and Clowes broke away from Wesleyan Methodism and William Booth from the Methodist New Connexion.

evangelism; in each there was a determination to bring the Gospel to the poverty-stricken masses; in each there was the use of open-air meetings; and both groups manifested a gaiety that not even persecution could cloud.

Yet in three respects the Salvation Army deviated from the norm of religious primitivism during the century. It was unique in its social concern as in its rejection of sacramentalism, and it was highly unusual in combining an evangelistic outreach with a love of ceremonial. Bernard Shaw paid wry tribute to these three characteristics in a speech he put into the mouth of Cusins, the classic who is in love with *Major Barbara*, the daughter of the armaments peer, from whom the play takes its name:

"I am a sincere salvationist. You do not understand the Salvation Army. It is the army of joy, of love, of courage; it has banished the fear and remorse and despair of the old, hell-ridden evangelical sects: it marches to fight the devil with trumpet and drum, with music and dancing, with banner and palm, as becomes a sally from heaven by its happy garrison. It picks the waster out of the public house and makes a man of him: it finds a worm wriggling in a back kitchen, and lo! a woman! Men and women of rank, too, the sons and daughters of the Highest. It takes the poor professor of Greek, the most artificial and suppressed of human creatures, from his meal of roots, and lets loose the rhapsodist in him; reveals the true worship of Dionysos to him; sends him down the public street drumming dithyrambs. [*he plays a thundering flourish on the drums*]."[63]

William Booth, the founder of the Salvation Army, formerly a minister of the Methodist New Connexion, then an evangelist, decided to devote himself entirely to the poverty-stricken and drunk of the East End of London in 1865. Two years before he had been to observe a movement in Walsall known as the "Hallelujah Band,"[64] consisting of ex-pugilists, drunkards, and gamblers, who took part in revivalistic meetings as the dramatic "trophies" of salvation. He returned to London with the conviction that the working-classes were most effectively influenced by their own flesh and blood.

In its early days the Salvation Army was not very different from any other revivalistic group, except perhaps in its enthusiasm for the down-and-outs. Its distinctive features, such as its military

---

[63] *The Complete Plays of Bernard Shaw*, p. 478. *Major Barbara* was written in 1905.

[64] For a detailed and official account of the origins of the Salvation Army, see Robert Sandall, *The History of the Salvation Army, Vol. I: 1865-1878.*

organization, its military ceremonial, its exploitation of music, and its rejection of Sacraments, were gradually developed.

At first "the Christian Mission" merely adopted the ordinances of the Churches to which its earliest leaders were accustomed, and this is particularly true of the Sacraments of Baptism and the Lord's Supper. Why, then, were they abandoned by Booth in 1882? With an emphasis akin to the Quakers, Booth held that the inner essence of a Sacrament could be observed without retaining the outer form. The purpose of Baptism was to testify to the inner cleansing of the Holy Spirit: this, he believed, was better attested by conversion than by paedo-baptism. Similarly, he insisted that the Scriptures presuppose that the death of Christ should be remembered at every meal, not restricted to a ceremonial meal. Furthermore, the conflicting views held in the Churches about the nature of both Sacraments seemed to argue that it would be wise to avoid any possibility of acrimonious discussion by abolishing them. Besides, it could not be argued that they were necessary to salvation, since only faith and repentance were the pre-conditions of conversion. It perhaps only needs to be added that the orthodox administration of it might prove a snare to souls who had been addicted to strong drink.[65] Whatever the reasons, theological or utilitarian,[66] the Sacraments were banished.

T. H. Huxley had scathingly referred to the Salvation Army's charismatic emphases as "corybantic Christianity." It may be supposed that Huxley had in mind the rhythmic choruses, the beating of drums and tambourines, the blowing of trumpets, the shouted "hallelujahs," and the embraces of the converts. It is surely better to characterize it, with St. John Ervine, as "the Elizabethan note in religion."[67] Ervine saw, as Huxley did not, that the squalour of industrial city life for working men was so appalling that only an attraction equivalent to the public house in providing gaiety and friendship could ever be religiously successful, and that "the damned could only be drawn from hot sin by hot religion."[68] The expert in the art of advertising religion was Booth's henchman, Elijah Cadman. On learning that the Supreme Pontiff had died,

---

[65] This rather unconvincing argument is adduced by Sandall, *ibid.*, Vol. II (1950), p. 133. The English Free Churches avoided this danger by the use of unfermented grape juice.

[66] Bramwell Booth in his article on the "Salvation Army" in Hastings' *Encyclopedia of Religion and Ethics*, xi, p. 158a, insists that practical outweighed doctrinal considerations.

[67] *God's Soldier: General William Booth* (2 vols., 1934), Vol. I, pp. 260 f.

[68] *Ibid.*, p. 264.

he gathered a great crowd in the streets to hear him preach "The Pope's Funeral Sermon."[69] Booth was to lean on him as he did on Railton for the idea of a military organization for his recruits and for the choice of appropriate regalia.

The English, aristocrat and working-man alike, have a keen sense of ritual and ceremonial, which can be seen on the most exalted scale in the installation of a Knight of the Garter in Windsor, and in a humbler scale in the least pretentious local Masonic lodge. Evangelical Christianity, hitherto almost tone-deaf and certainly colour-blind, was first to exploit the common love of sound and colour in the practices of the Salvation Army. Booth gave his soldiers banners of vivid red, blue, and yellow symbolising "Blood and Fire"; he dressed them smartly in military uniforms, and commanded them to noise abroad their assurance of salvation while processing to the accompaniment of drums, trumpets, bugles, flutes, and tambourines.

Booth recognized the immense importance of music, claiming that "Music is to the soul what wind is to a ship, blowing her onwards in the direction in which she is steered."[70] He argued that if secular music belonged to the Devil, then there was all the more reason for Christians to plunder it from him. "I rather enjoy," he said, "robbing the Devil of his choice tunes, and, after the subjects themselves, music is about the best commodity he possesses." He was strongly critical of many of the sentimental hymns of the day: "I am sick of singing sentimental rubbish that had no connection with the soul's immediate interests. It won't do a man good to set him for ever and ever singing about the bright and beautiful streets and stars and streams of Paradise. . . ."[71] This gusto and gaiety of the founder was fully reflected in the Army as a whole. It broke through the cordons of reserve and decorum in a riot of joyous righteousness, and proved that charismatic fervour and ceremonialism were, after all, perhaps compatible. Its strongly social concern has made it an international movement and guaranteed its relevance in our own day. It was the most successful of all the century's forms of religious primitivism, perhaps because it was the least archaic in its outlook.

[69] *Ibid.*, p. 254.
[70] The Christmas issue of *War Cry*, 1880, cited in Sandall, *op.cit.*, Vol. II, p. 112.
[71] St. John Ervine, *op.cit.*, Vol. I, pp. 390-91.

PART TWO
THE DRIVE TOWARDS
INNOVATION

CHAPTER VII

FAITH GRAPPLING WITH DOUBT:
THE THEOLOGICAL REVOLUTION

IT IS A FALSE STEREOTYPE that presents the Victorian Age as a period of unruffled calm, or even as a succession of mere storms in a teacup. It was rather a period of explosions—of political, social, moral, scientific, and religious revolution. "Change and decay in all around I see" is a Victorian expression for a Victorian experience. The Repeal of the Corn Laws, the passing of the Reform Bill, the extension of the franchise and of free public education, and the publication of Karl Marx's *Das Kapital* were seismic shocks that shattered the eighteenth century order of English society. The onset was partly met by the Christian Socialists, under the guidance of F. D. Maurice, who significantly came into being in 1848, the very year that the Communist Manifesto appeared in the very same city of London, and partly by the combination of Christian and radical reformers who were ultimately to help to produce the modern compromise of the "Social Welfare State."

An even profounder earthquake, from the volcanic upthrust of the natural and social sciences, was to shake English religion to its foundations. This would involve thoughtful Christians in an agonizing encounter with doubt, as well as replace the ethical imperatives of the Christian Gospel for many thousands with the pleasure calculus of Utilitarianism or the sanctified competitiveness of a Social Darwinism in which, as Bishop Gore said, "it is a case of each for himself as the elephant said when it danced among the chickens." Well might the second half of the nineteenth century be designated "The Age of Honest Doubt." Unless we can feel along the nerves these shocks of doubt, it will be almost impossible either to understand the problems of reconstruction with which theology was faced, and which it still encounters, or to evaluate the impact of the newer theology on the development of Christian worship. In this attempt to stand in the quaking shoes of the mid-nineteenth century theologians, the poets and novelists will be found most perceptive guides, both to the warfare of science with religion, and to the conflict of the newer historical studies with the older supernaturalism.

173

1. *Science Throws Down the Gauntlet*

Science was to make its triple onslaught on religion in the fields of the natural, the biological, and the social sciences. The antagonism between the natural sciences and religion was, of course, not a new phenomenon, for the Copernican world-view had destroyed the older geocentric view of the universe, and the Newtonian physics had attenuated the concept of miracle in the Christian doctrine of providence by stressing the "laws" of the inorganic universe. The newer natural science, however, had two major influences on the Christian cosmogony. In the first place, not only, as Hazlitt complained, had the heavens grown afar off and become astronomical, but the Lamarckian version of the evolutionary hypothesis for the origin of man, as popularized in Robert Chambers' *The Vestiges of the Natural History of Creation* (1844), had superannuated the Deity in favour of sheer chance. Then, in the second place, Lyell's *Principles of Geology* (1830-1833) had conclusively shown that Ussher's dating of Creation as early as 4004 B.C., must be pushed back millennia, as demanded by the aeons necessary for the stratification of the earth from slowly cooling and liquefying gases to solids, and by the fossils of plants and animals that had existed millions of years before Christ. The geo-centric universe had gone, now the seven days' story of creation had also to go, as *Genesis* retired in favour of Geology.

It was, however, the implications of the natural sciences for the Christian doctrines of Creation and Providence, hinted at in Lyell but fully expounded in Darwin's epoch-making *The Origin of Species* (1859), that were even more disturbing. To the older idea of an immutable law operating in the inorganic universe, there was now added the frightening concept of "inexorable development" proceeding throughout the organic sphere as it moulded and modified living species.[1] Moreover, this idea arrived exactly when there had come into existence an avid reading public increased by popular education and the means of satisfying it by more economical methods of printing and publishing. Thus the researches of the scientists, instead of being discussed in the ivory tower or withdrawn laboratory by the cognoscenti, rapidly found their way in books onto the tables of the average Victorian household to the consternation of their simple faith. Darwin's challenge lay in drawing attention to the disteleological aspects of Nature: the callous

[1] Basil Willey, *Nineteenth Century Studies, Coleridge to Matthew Arnold*, p. 82.

discarding of entire species, the prodigal waste of fecundity, the internecine war between the species, the descent of man from the apes, and the possibility of man's being replaced by some higher beings, reducing him to the status of a fossil of the future. The basic problem for religion was how the blind Life and Force revealed in organic Nature and assuming consciousness in man could be equated with the Divine Fatherhood and the assurance of eternal life in the Gospel. Not only was God's face clouded by the assumptions of the new science, but man himself was forced to bite the dust, as he, who, according to the Psalmist, was created "a little lower than the angels" was now seen to be a little higher than the apes. The social sciences, under the combined influence of Marx, Comte, and Spencer, began to treat man, not as "made in the likeness of God," nor as the unique master of Nature holding dominion over the beasts of the field, but as the victim of heredity and environment, whose common charcteristics were much more important than his individuality, who could be manipulated economically, educationally, and sociologically by a knowledge of the laws that governed him. The industrialists, who had made a "hand" of a person, were not slow to claim that Darwinism ruled in the field of technology where only the fittest survive, presumably to become captains of industry.

It is in writings of the poets and novelists of the period that we can best experience the agonies that faced the honest Christian believer, who could neither retreat into the dogmatic enthusiasm of Protestant Fundamentalism or the dogmatic orthodoxy of the infallible Roman Catholic Church, nor accept the iconoclasm of rationalistic atheism. As Matthew Arnold, the chief critic of the century, said in 1875: "Two things about the Christian Religion must be clear to anyone with eyes in his head. One is, that men cannot do without it; the other, that they cannot do with it as it is."[2] The theologians, as will be seen later, were reluctantly facing the same problems as the literary artists and the less articulate people, and they gave their guidance in *Essays and Reviews* (1860) and in *Lux Mundi* (1889), to take two representative essays in Anglican theological reconstruction.

2. *"Nature Red in Tooth and Claw"*

A. N. Whitehead, with great perceptiveness, selected, as representative longer poems of their times, Milton's *Paradise Lost*, Pope's

[2] From the preface to *God and the Bible*.

Essay on Man, Wordsworth's *The Excursion*, and Tennyson's *In Memoriam*.[3] Tennyson's greatest poem appeared appropriately in 1850, the year in which he succeeded Wordsworth as Poet Laureate. While it pre-dated Darwin's masterpiece by nine years, it had taken full stock of both Lyell's researches and Chambers' popularization of new scientific concepts, and therefore of the idea of evolution, which Darwin was to systematize and explain with his biological observations. The poem is a tribute of homage to his dead friend Arthur Hallam, and it is appropriately concerned with the themes of immortality and Divine providence, and the reconsideration of human nature and destiny in the light of the scientific thought of the time. Each problem is discussed with urgent anxiety. Lyell, in particular, emphasized that many species of creatures had been doomed and that their mortuaries were ancient strata of the earth, and Tennyson saw immediately that this diminished the likelihood of immortality and made it more difficult to derive the beneficence of God from the consideration of Nature, as Addison had found possible, for example, in his hymn "The spacious firmament on high." Tennyson found these implications underlined in Chambers, but also the hope that evolution was keeping in store a nobler type of humanity, as the crown of the species.

The antagonism of Nature and Providence, of Science and Religion, is most movingly expressed in the following verses from Section LV:

> Are God and Nature then at strife,
>   That Nature lends such evil dreams?
>   So careful of the type she seems,
> So careless of the single life;
>
> That I, considering everywhere
>   Her secret meaning in her deeds,
>   And finding that of fifty seeds
> She often brings but one to bear,
>
> I falter where I firmly trod,
>   And falling with my world of cares
>   Upon the world's great altar stairs
> That slope thro' darkness up to God.

---

[3] In *Science and the Modern World*. Professor Willey, while endorsing Whitehead's selection of poets, would substitute Wordsworth's *Prelude* for the *Excursion*, and I would be inclined to add Eliot's *Waste Land* as a representative poem of the early twentieth century.

I stretch lame hands of faith, and grope
And gather dust and chaff, and call
To what I feel is Lord of all,
And faintly trust the larger hope.

Even the conclusion that Nature preserves the type, if not the individual, has to be jettisoned, on further reflection:

"So careful of the type?" But no.
From scarped cliff and quarried stone
She cries, "A thousand types are gone:
I care for nothing, all shall go.

"Thou madest thine appeal to me:
I bring to life, I bring to death:
The Spirit does but mean the breath:
I know no more." And he, shall he

Man, her last work, who seem'd so fair,
Such splendid purpose in his eyes,
Who roll'd the psalm to wintry skies,
Who built him fanes of fruitless prayer,

Who trusted God was love indeed
And love Creation's final law—
Tho' Nature red in tooth and claw
With ravine shriek'd against his creed—

Who loved, who suffer'd countless ills,
Who battled for the True, the Just,
Be blown about the desert dust,
Or seal'd within the iron hills?

No more? A monster then, a dream,
A discord. Dragons of the prime,
That tare each other in the slime,
Were mellow music match'd with him.

O life as futile, then, as frail!
O for thy voice to soothe and bless!
What hope of answer or redress?
Behind the veil, behind the veil.[4]

4 In *Memoriam*, Section LVI.

177

Tennyson continues to stumble in this grey dusk of doubt until the star of hope appears in Section CXVIII, where he senses that there is a controlling unity of physical and moral law in the universe:

Contemplate all this work of Time,
  The giant labouring in his youth;
  Nor dream of human love and truth
As dying Nature's earth and lime;

But trust that those we call the dead
  Are breathers of an ampler day
  For ever nobler ends. They say,
The solid earth whereon we tread

In tracts of fluent heat began,
  And grew to seeming-random forms
  The seeming prey of cyclic storms,
Till at the last arose the man;

Who throve and branched from clime to clime
  The herald of a higher race,
  And of himself, in higher place,
If so, he type this work of thine

Within himself, from more to more;
  Or, crown'd with attributes of woe
  Like glories, move his course, and show
That life is not as idle ore,

But iron dug from central gloom,
  And heated hot with burning fears,
  And dipt in baths of hissing tears,
And batter'd with the shocks of doom

To shape and use. Arise and fly
  The reeling Faun, the sensual feast;
  Move upward working out the beast,
And let the ape and tiger die.

Tennyson's faith was hammered out on the hard anvil of doubt, and he could contemplate the easy complacency of the orthodox only with shame. He rebutted with the utmost contempt the convenient claim of the orthodox ostriches, with heads in air or in sand, that doubt itself is devil-born, with the ringing *apologia*:

178

There lives more faith in honest doubt,
Believe me, than in half the creeds.[5]

His fullest re-affirmation of faith was the last to be written, although it was published as the Prologue to *In Memoriam*. But he knew, as early as Section XXXVI, that the principles of morality are not dynamic enough to live by, and that the total rejection of supernaturalism in Christianity as so much mythological embroidery, which was the plea of Strauss's *Leben Jesu* (1835-1836), as later of Renan's *Vie de Jésus* (1863), and Seeley's *Ecce Homo* (1866) and the concentration on Jesus as an idea, not as an historical person, would make the *imitatio Christi* an idle fancy. Deeds beget deeds, but dreams only provoke reveries:

> For Wisdom dealt with human powers
> > Where truth in closest words shall fail,
> > When truth embodied in a tale
> Shall enter in at lowly doors.

> And so the Word hath breath and wrought
> > With human hands the creed of creeds
> > In loveliness of perfect deeds,
> More strong than all poetic thought.

His faith, fighting doubt, made the final defiant and honest affirmation:

> Strong Son of God, immortal Love,
> > Whom we that have not seen Thy face,
> > By faith and faith alone embrace,
> Believing where we cannot prove;

> Thou wilt not leave us in the dust:
> > Thou madest man, he knows not why;
> > He thinks he was not made to die;
> And Thou hast made him: Thou art just.

> Thou seemest human and divine,
> > The highest, holiest manhood, Thou;
> > Our wills are ours, we know not how;
> Our wills are ours to make them thine.

5 *Ibid.*, Section XCVI.

Our little systems have their day;
 They have their day and cease to be:
 They are but broken lights of Thee,
And Thou, O Lord, art more than they.

We have but faith: we cannot know;
 For knowledge is of things we see;
 And yet we trust it comes from Thee,
A beam in darkness: let it grow.

Let knowledge grow from more to more,
 But more of reverence in us dwell;
 That mind and soul, according well,
May make one music as before,

But vaster, We are fools and slight;
 We mock Thee when we do not fear:
 But help Thy foolish ones to bear;
Help Thy vain worlds to bear Thy light.[6]

As the century was to grow older, the findings of science would appear to contradict not only theology but even the popular trust in freedom and progress. James Thomson seemed to anticipate the desolation of the *Waste Land* in *The City of Dreadful Night*:

I find no hint throughout the Universe
Of good or ill, of blessing or curse;
 I find alone Necessity Supreme;
With infinite Mystery, abysmal, dark,
Unlightened even by the faintest spark,
 For us, the flitting shadows of a dream.

In due time the scientific approach was so victorious that it could almost be assumed that all reasonable men were noble agnostics, like T. H. Huxley, Darwin's bulldog. H. G. Wood has described the immense practical benefits of applied science—as leading to an immediate concentration on means, and letting the ends take care of themselves because they were disputable, so that the scientist can be described "as sedulously paying court to Madam How and becoming sceptical about the existence of Lady Why."[7] Moreover, the very idea of dogma became repellent to scientists since all their hypotheses are necessarily provisional and subject to

[6] *Ibid.*, the Prologue.   [7] *Belief and Unbelief since 1850*, p. 47.

revision in the light of further facts. By contrast, the dogmas of the theologians seemed to claim an irreversibility the scientists could regard only as misguided, if not arrogant. In comparison, how modest seemed to be their own tentative views, subject to verification by experiment!

3. *The Challenge of Literary and Historical Criticism*

The natural and biological sciences were, by implication, criticizing the accepted Biblical account of the Creator, but they cast no direct aspersions on the Redeemer, nor on the record of His life as narrated in the pages of the New Testament. The direct attack on this, the central citadel of faith, came from historical and literary criticism. The second attack followed hard on the heels of the first, as may be seen from the fact that *The Origin of Species* of 1859 was succeeded by *Essays and Reviews* in 1860, a book whose seven authors were castigated by the orthodox and the obscurantists as *septem contra Christum* and as "the seven extinguishers of the seven lamps of the Apocalypse," although they were six loyal Anglican clergymen and a pious layman.

The development of historical studies in the nineteenth century, especially in Germany, sooner or later would have demanded that the laws of evidence should be applied to the Biblical record. In 1858, in fact, Buckle's *History of Civilization* had already applied the historical method to the records of Christianity. This method had been profoundly influenced by natural science and consequently causation tended to replace the categories of purpose or Divine judgment. During the same period archaeology produced reconstructions of civilizations, as Schliemann excavated the ruins of Troy, Sir Arthur Evans the Minoan culture, and Sir Flinders Petrie the glory of ancient Egypt; the comparative study of religion showed that Christianity was not as unique as had hitherto been assumed in Christian apologetics. All these studies led to acute difficulties for faith. Finally, when literary criticism was applied by clergymen to the sacred documents of Christianity, it was felt by the conservative majority of Christians that the Church's most desperate foes were those of her own household. Newman, for example, had declared that Liberalism was the half-way house to atheism.

The value of *Essays and Reviews* was that it brought these doubts into the open and attempted to allay them by showing how little the methods of historical criticism were able to affect the citadel of the central doctrines of the Christian faith, whatever inroads they appeared to make in the outworks.[8] It was, in effect, a Liberal theological *Tract for the Times*, emanating from Oxford, and carrying on the approach of Arnold, after the eclipse of Liberalism under Newman. It made the shrewd point that, apart from accommodation to the newer knowledge, orthodoxy would be synonymous with ignorance. The chief exemplar of the new approach was Benjamin Jowett, who wrote the crucial essay "On the Interpretation of Scripture." Jowett argued that the Scriptures demanded to be interpreted by the same rules of evidence and the same criteria of criticism applied to other literature. In consequence, he urged the necessity of discarding two traditional and obscurantist types of interpretation, which presupposed that the Scriptures were uniformly, verbally, and mechanically inspired and that their authors were merely the passive penmen of the Holy Spirit.

These untenable older views were the mystical and allegorical interpretation practised by Origen, Ambrose, and others of the Fathers, as well as by the Oxford Tractarians, and the literalism so beloved by the Evangelicals. The allegorical and mystical interpretation introduced an element of subjectivity which forced the Scripture to mean what the exegete intended it to mean, and it refused to face up to the variety and apparent contradictions of Scripture by pretending that these did not exist, or by avoiding them altogether. The Evangelical interpretation of Scripture in its literalism confused imagery with statements of fact, and poetry with prose. Furthermore, it refused to recognize the variety of literary forms in that library of writings that constitutes the Scriptures. In the Old Testament, for example, there are myth and legend; contemporary memoirs and later interpretations; poetry, proverbs, law, and prophetical oracles.

The newer literary criticism of the Old Testament might be tolerated, as showing the progressive appropriation of revelation by the people of God (a theological use of the concept of evolution), provided that the authority of the crown and climax of the Divine revelation—the Incarnation—were not to be weakened. But, suppose that the methods of literary criticism were applied to the New Testament, would it not also cease to be the inspired Word of God

---

[8] In *Democracy and Liberty*, Vol. I, pp. 424-25, Lecky wrote that *Essays and Reviews* marked the increased range "of permissible opinions on religious subjects" which had hitherto been confined to small circles, and which were henceforth to be "familiar to the great body of educated men."

and merely be the testimony to a first century faith? In fact, it proved impossible to insulate the Old Testament from the New, even when the critical views were limited to the Old Testament alone, because Christ had accepted certain views of the authorship of parts of the Old Testament which the critics had exploded.

This issue was raised in the Gospel of St. Mark, in the twelfth chapter, where Jesus appealed to Psalm 110 as a word of David in order to demonstrate that the Messiah must be more than David. If David, as the critics contended, did not write this Psalm, the argument is untenable and Christ is convicted of error. The result was that the Incarnation had either to be given up, or radically re-interpreted. The latter view was taken ultimately by Charles Gore in *Lux Mundi* (1889), where he argued that God could only become man in Jesus Christ by accepting the limitations of the first century world view, and that this was the great paradox of the self-emptying of grace. Others, in great distress, felt they had no alternative but to give up the doctrine of the Incarnation and therefore the uniqueness and authority of Christianity.

Literary criticism was also reinforced by historical criticism— the attempt to reconstruct the Jesus of history, by removing the legendary accretions which had grown about Him, and by presenting Him as an unhaloed Galilean prophet. One of the most radical attempts, Strauss's *Leben Jesu* (1835-1836), had been translated into English by Marianne Evans ("George Eliot"), and Ernest Renan's modernist *Vie de Jésus* (1863) was also translated into English, while Seeley presented anonymously his reverent but unmiraculous Christ in *Ecce Homo* (1866).

Here, again, the agony of those who found it impossible to accept the Christian doctrine of the Incarnation because they believed the historical grounds were insufficient to support it is movingly mirrored in the literature of the time, particularly in the novels of Mrs. Humphry Ward[9] and of William Hale White.[10]

[9] For the life of Mrs. Humphry Ward, see Mary Augusta (Arnold) Ward, *A Writer's Recollections* and Janet Penrose Trevelyan, *The Life of Mrs. Humphry Ward by Her Daughter*. A useful monograph is J. Stuart Walters, *Mrs. Humphry Ward and the Trend of Ethical Development since Robert Elsmere*.

[10] For an evaluation of the life and thought of William Hale White, two distinguished American studies should be consulted: Irvine Stock, *William Hale White (Mark Rutherford), A Critical Study* and Wilfred Stone, *Religion and Art of William Hale White ("Mark Rutherford")*. See also Mrs. Dorothy V. White, *Last Pages of a Journal, with Other Papers by Mark Rutherford*. I have attempted a fuller analysis of the "theological" novels of Mrs. Ward and Hale White in *A Mirror of the Ministry in Modern Novels*, Chap. VI.

4. Mythology and Demythologizing

Mrs. Humphry Ward's *Robert Elsmere*, which appeared in 1888, was the most widely read and discussed Victorian novel on the theme of religious doubt and theological reconstruction. So alarmed were the orthodox by this novel that Gladstone felt it necessary to write an essay-review of it in *The Nineteenth Century* full of admiration for its honest intentions but gravely questioning the adequacy of its reconstruction. It is the account of how Robert Elsmere, a former Oxford don and Anglican vicar, reluctantly resigns his living because he can no longer hold the creed of his Church, and how he devotes his remaining years to the foundation of a new Company of Jesus, "The Order of Brotherhood," in the London slums, honouring and following Jesus as leader but not as Lord.

For our restricted purposes, it is less important for its fine portraits of the sturdy Evangelicalism of Elsmere's wife and of the ascetical doubt-trampling High Churchman, Father Newcome, than for its documentation of the failure of Elsmere's orthodoxy and his attempted reconstruction of religious thought. Elsmere has all the attitudes that the good Liberal could demand in the way of regarding Christianity as the inculcation of morality and compassion, and he can even go part way with the Tractarians in appropriating the aesthetic, if not the doctrinal, thrill of tradition. He prepares to enter his Surrey parish with the moral and social ardour of the Christian Socialists, and is assiduous in reading up "the history, geology, and botany of the Weald and its neighbourhood, or spending his quick brain on village sanitation."[11] When not visiting the sick or perplexed souls of his community, he encourages the lads of the village as naturalists. (He is a veritable reproduction of the Vicar of Eversley, Charles Kingsley.)

His fault, however, is that he has never fully investigated the intellectual and historical foundations of his beliefs. When he informed an Oxford tutor, Langham, that he is considering the ministry as a vocation, the latter replied sardonically that "one may as well preach a respectable mythology as anything else." Pressed by Elsmere for a definition of mythology, the tutor replied, "Simply ideas or experiences personified"—a thoroughly Hegelian answer. Elsmere retorted: "To the Christian facts have been the medium by which ideas the world could not otherwise have come at have

---

[11] *Robert Elsmere* (2 vols.), Vol. I, p. 124.

been communicated to man. Christian theology is a system of ideas, indeed, but ideas realized, made manifest in facts." The tutor replied drily: "How do you know they are facts?"[12]

The basic problem is, therefore, one of historical evidence. It is the agnostic squire, savant, and historian of ideas, Wendover, who urges Elsmere to undertake an investigation into the documents on which the case for Christianity rests. Elsmere has been led to accept evolution in his naturalist's studies, and it is clear that he must accept the validity of the same conception in his historical studies. A lengthy conversation between Elsmere and the squire allows the latter to propound his thesis that eras of history are only to be understood by studying them in the light of the dominant ideas and intellectual preconceptions of the age. Wendover then exemplifies this thesis from the early history of Christianity: "In the first place, I shall find present in the age which saw the birth of Christianity, as in so many other ages, a universal preconception in favour of miracle—that is to say, of deviations from the common norm of experience, governing the work of *all* men of *all* schools."

He goes on to urge that the testimony of the times must be read in the light of this, and with the result that "the witness of the time is not true nor, in a strict sense, false. It is merely incompetent, half-trained, prescientific, but all through perfectly natural. The wonder would have been to have a life of Christ without miracles. The air teems with them. The East is full of Messiahs. The Resurrection is partly invented, partly imagined, partly ideally true—in any case wholly intelligible and natural, as a product of the age, when once you have the key of that age."[13]

This key, indeed, unlocks the history of ideas, but it also locks out Christianity from serious consideration on naturalistic grounds. The next three months of doubt were the blackest and bitterest days of Elsmere's life.

He was then forced to join the company of the historical reconstructors, and when light came in his darkness it would take the form of "the image of a purely human Christ—a purely human, explicable, yet always, wonderful Christianity. It broke his heart, but the spell of it was like some dream-country wherein we see all the familiar objects of life in new relations and perspectives."[14] Mrs. Ward is fully alive to the fact that Elsmere's is a typical case: "And meanwhile half the tragedy of our time lies in the perpetual

[12] *Ibid.*, p. 99.　　[13] *Ibid.*, Vol. II, pp. 18-19.　　[14] *Ibid.*, p. 24.

clashing of two estimates of life—the estimate which is the off-spring of the modern spirit, and which is forever making the visible world fairer and more desirable in mortal eyes; and the estimate of St. Augustine."[15]

An immediate consequence of Elsmere's doubt is that he must give up his living as vicar of the parish. Although other Liberal Churchmen might continue in the ministry, undertaking its humane and charitable work while refusing assent to its dogmatic system, this was an impossible course for him. Before undertaking his settlement work with a group of Unitarians in the London slums, Elsmere visits Grey, his old Oxford tutor and mentor, who expresses the agony of the Victorian doubter and also his stoical courage and honesty: "I know very well, the man of the world scoffs, but to him who has once been a Christian of the old sort, the parting with the Christian mythology is the rending asunder of bones and marrow. It means parting with half the confidence, half the joy of life!" He offers Elsmere the bleak consolation that the path of doubt is God's pedagogical method: "It is the education of God! Do not imagine it will put you farther from Him! He is in criticism, in science, in doubt, so long as the doubt is a pure and honest doubt, as yours is." Henceforward, "God is to be sought in the soul of man, in the verifications of experience, and in the sacrificial giving of Christian love," and "All things change—creeds and philosophies and outward systems—but God remains."[16]

As Mrs. Humphry Ward is the chronicler of Anglican doubt, William Hale White (or "Mark Rutherford," to use his literary pseudonym) is the recorder of Dissenting doubt in his novels. If Mrs. Ward's Grey can exclaim that for the once orthodox Christian "the parting with the Christian mythology is the rending asunder of bones and marrow," Mark Rutherford can also affirm that the reading of Strauss's *Leben Jesu* has dissolved the figure of the God-man into "mythologic vapour." *The Autobiography of Mark Rutherford, edited by his friend Reuben Shapcott* (1881) and its sequel *Mark Rutherford's Deliverance* (1885) are, in effect, the spiritual diaries of the honest doubter, William Hale White. The first novel shows us the process by which Rutherford lost the simplicity and robust depth of his Calvinistic faith. The second

---

[15] *Ibid.*, Vol. I, p. 196.
[16] *Ibid.*, Vol. II, pp. 74-75. One notes here the partial correspondence of Grey's affirmation with Tennyson's lines: "Our little systems have their day/They have their day and cease to be/They are but broken lights of thee/And Thou, O Lord, are more than they." Grey, however, is a theist, while Tennyson addresses Christ.

records how, by strenuous and agonizing contemplation, he arrived at some "fortifying thoughts" by means of re-interpreting historic Christianity, with the aid of Wordsworth, Spinoza, and Hegel, as a religion of ideas and truths movingly exemplified in Jesus of Nazareth, but a religion, nonetheless, stripped of supernaturalism.

Rutherford reacted strongly against the predestinarian Calvinism of his youth, because of its formalism and its unreality, exhibited in the long sermons which repeated the same formulae: "The minister invariably began with the fall of man, propounded the scheme of redemption, and ended by depicting in the morning the blessedness of the saints, and in the evening the doom of the lost."[17] Equally irrelevant to his condition were the long, meandering, and supposedly extemporaneous prayers in which "our minister seemed to consider that the Almighty, who had the universe to govern, had more leisure at His command than the idlest lounger at a club."[18] The same unreality required that this very circumspect young man should give an account of his "conversion" before being admitted to the full membership of the church, though he was far from being a prodigal. Under parental pressure he was forced to decide on the ministry as his vocation, although his own decided preference was for art. He came up against the demands of Calvinistic orthodoxy in the Dissenting theological college which he attended by preaching a functional doctrine of the Atonement, which was directly related to the fundamental needs of men.

Rutherford finds himself in charge of an Independent church in the eastern counties which includes as representative a group of Philistines as exactly to fit the worst features of the definition of that term by Matthew Arnold. They have none of the Greek graces, and indeed are singularly lacking in the Hebrew qualities that Arnold considered the strength of the Philistines. A narrow-minded, snivelling, sanctimonious company (the caricaturist overcomes the artist in Hale White at this point), they are as unsuited as a congregation for Rutherford as he is to be their minister. Rutherford's doctrine, at this point, is little more than a kindly Stoicism. He preached that Jesus was a solitary and heroic thinker confronted by the enormous double threat of the Jewish hierarchy and the Roman state. In consequence, Jesus "taught the doctrine of the Kingdom of Heaven; He trained Himself to have faith in the absolute monarchy of the human soul."[19] The single humanitarian

---

[17] *The Autobiography of Mark Rutherford*, p. 7.
[18] *Ibid.*   [19] *Ibid.*, p. 35.

he can find in the town is Mardon, the atheist, who is the intelligent artisan equivalent to Mrs. Ward's Wendover and who tries to persuade Rutherford to accept his negative creed.

Rutherford, like Elsmere, undergoes a period of the most intense doubt. Pressed by Mardon's recital of the contradictions in the Gospel narratives, Rutherford is forced to claim that even if Jesus never lived, yet the Christ-idea is a sublime and inspiring conception. Mardon rejects this defence on the ground that a non-existent Jesus makes nonsense of any imitation of Christ. The novel reaches the abyss of despair, with Rutherford's cry of dereliction: "With me the struggle to retain as much of my creed as I could was tremendous. The dissolution of Jesus into mythologic vapour was nothing less than the death of a friend dearer to me than any other friend I knew."[20]

Mardon, the atheist, discourages Rutherford from seeking another pastoral charge until he has a set of suitable beliefs to preach. Nettled, Rutherford claims that he is a theist and that God is the intellect of which the laws of the universe are an expression. But Mardon (who must have been reading Lyell, Chambers, and Darwin) claims that such a Deity is indifferent towards His own creations: "It is an intellect, if it be an intellect at all, which will swallow up a city, and will create the music of Mozart for me when I am weary; an intellect which brings to birth His Majesty King George IV, and the love of an affectionate mother for her child: intellect, which in the person of a tender girl, shows an exquisite conscience, and in the person of one or two religious creatures whom I have known, shows a conscience almost inverted."[21]

Like Elsmere, Rutherford hopes to find the company of Unitarians congenial. His congregation, however, numbers only seventeen souls and, with a single exception, they are living on the negations of the past, on the denial of the orthodox doctrine of the Holy Trinity rather than on a liberating idea of the One God. "Although my congregation had a free thought lineage, I don't think that I ever had anything to do with a more petrified set."[22] They had no sympathy with the great problems then beginning to agitate men. Their whole approach was polemical, not practical. The grey novel ends, after Rutherford has successively tried schoolmastering and assisting a sceptical publisher, with the funeral of Mardon, who had utterly denied the possibility of immortality

[20] *Ibid.*, p. 64.   [21] *Ibid.*, pp. 87-88.   [22] *Ibid.*, p. 100.

by two chilling questions: whether any man desired to continue to exist forever with his present limitations and failings, and whether it was not a miserable egotism which is so anxious for the continuance of the self beyond death.

His deliverance, recounted in the second novel, is accounted for by a new post (as parliamentary correspondent to two papers), a friend who is understanding in religious matters but far from orthodox (M'Kay), and his marriage with Ellen. The two rebels tour the religious assemblies of London and they find a distinguished Anglo-Catholic preacher unconvincing because he regards doubt as devil-inspired, repeats the now discarded argument from prophecy for the Divinity of Christ, and indulges in rhetoric and sentiment instead of honest thought. They are equally dissatisfied by his rationalist opponent who uses the equally mouldering chestnuts of diatribe, such as the immorality of the Old Testament patriarchs and the greed of the Anglican bishops. Rutherford's laconic comment is: "To waste a Sunday morning in ridiculing such stories as that of Jonah was surely as imbecile as to waste it in proving their verbal veracity." Clearly, some third alternative between the credulity of orthodoxy and the iconoclasm of atheism must be found, and it must be a religious way of life which would reconcile faith with intellectual honesty and issue in practical compassion.

He and M'Kay determine to open a room near Drury Lane to alleviate, in a small degree, the intolerable ignorance and misery of the London poor. At the first meeting, M'Kay announced their errand and platform: "He proposed to keep this room open as a place to which those who wished might resort at different times, and find some quietude, instruction, and what fortifying thoughts he could collect to enable them to endure their almost unendurable sufferings. Anything which would be serviceable he would set forth, but in the main he intended to rely on holding up the examples of those who were greater than themselves and were our redeemers. He meant to teach Christ in the proper sense of the word. Christ is now admired probably more than He had ever been. Everybody agrees to admire Him, but where are the people who really do as He did? . . . He would try and get them to see things with the eyes of Christ, to love with His love, to judge with His judgment. . . . He trusted to be able, by means of this little meeting, gradually to attain admittance for himself and his friends into the houses of the poor and do some practical good."[23]

It is clear that here we have another "Company of Jesus" launched in the industrial maelstrom on the frail craft of humanistic goodwill, without the resources of Divine and supernatural Grace. Elsmere's creator, who was an Arnold, had the wit to see that reconstructed rites as well as reconstructed doctrines would be needed, but Rutherford is sanguine enough to believe that a modest philosophy, with Christ as its exemplar, may snatch souls from oblivion.

These attempts at reconstruction were honest and brave, but they proclaim more the noble despair of a Marcus Aurelius than the Gospel of Mark. The new temple of Rutherford's faith was to be constructed from the fortifying thoughts of Spinoza, Hegel, Carlyle, and Emerson. If Jesus Christ was not, as in the Apostolic Church, the Headstone of the corner, His marvellous compassion and friendship for the loveless and friendless was one of the solid foundations, and the two others were the eternal distinction between right and wrong, and the duty of resignation and contentment. If the light in such temples built by honest doubters was not the coruscating radiance of early Christian faith and hope but the grey light of duty and resignation, at least it was better than the midnight black of utter disbelief.

5. The Influence of Science on Religion

It is time to take stock of the impact of the natural, biological, and social sciences on the religion of the age, in however summary a fashion this must be attempted. The most obvious effects were: to increase the number of agnostics and, perhaps, even of atheists; to force the more conservative theologians to a more urgent dogmatism (whether of the Roman Catholic or Protestant literalist types); and to encourage both Liberals of the Arnoldian type and Anglo-Catholics of the Gore variety to make an accommodation of the ancient faith with the new knowledge. In passing, it may be remarked that the Liberal Catholicism of Gore and his companions in Lux Mundi was a new phenomenon, for hitherto the heirs of the Tractarians had regarded theological and political liberalism as of the devil. The theological interpreter and mediator of the century who made such a transition possible was almost certainly F. D. Maurice, who occupied a central place in which he saw both

23 Mark Rutherford's Deliverance, pp. 27-29.

the strength and weakness of the Tractarian, Broad Church, and Evangelical parties.[24]

The victories of science were also shown in other subtly pervasive ways in the theological life of England. Theology was, as befitted its beleagured condition, more hesitant, perhaps more modest in its claims; certainly it was less dogmatic. For this several contributory factors may be discovered.[25] Even some of the orthodox felt that dogmatic and metaphysical definitions (as found, for example, in the Athanasian Creed) had befogged the relative simplicity of a Gospel universal in its import, and did not conceal their suspicion that some theologians and "ritualists" were overconcerned with rationalistic speculation and explanation where the acknowledgment of mystery would have been more in keeping with the nature of the mystery of both Divine revelation and its human appropriation by faith.

There was even an increasing suspicion of metaphysics, which may have been partly due to the influence of Schleiermacher, the defender of feeling in religion, and of Ritschl, who pleaded that the Church was to be conceived as the Community of Reconciliation and that Jesus had the value of God, urging that value-judgments, though not amenable to verification as scientific judgments of fact, were equally important factors in human experience. The Liberals, in particular, wished to eliminate what they considered to be the outworn dogmas and the vestiges of superstition from the Christian Creeds and to "establish an intellectual position that could not be called in question by every advance in historical evidence and physical science."[26]

Many, who found dogma unacceptable, insisted that essential Christianity was, in the famous words of Matthew Arnold, "morality touched with emotion," that is, following the teaching and compassionate example of Jesus, rather than holding any views about His person. All this had the inevitable consequence of restraining the dogmatism of most theologians, so that their work, like that of the scientists, was seen to be of a tentative and provisional character. The day of systems of theology, whether Thomistic or Calvinistic, was felt to be over, and with it the dominance of the

[24] See Chapter XII of *Worship and Theology in England*, Vol. 3, "From Watts and Wesley to Maurice, 1690-1850."

[25] These are carefully analyzed by L. E. Elliott-Binns, *English Thought, 1860-1900, The Theological Aspect*, p. 226, as also by H. G. Wood, *Belief and Unbelief since 1850*, in their consideration of the impact of science on religion during this period.

[26] L. E. Elliott-Binns, *op.cit.*

theologians. As befitting their humiliated estate (though whether modesty or timidity was the dominant motive is unknown), the theologians produced "Essays," not Systems or *Summae*, and as contributors to composite volumes they found safety in numbers.[27]

Not only did the scientific revolution relax the grip of theology on the allegiance of the English people, and even tame the temper of the theologians, but it also affected considerably the emphases and interests of the defenders of theology in their re-statements of doctrine. Already it has been seen that the older, mechanical theory of the inspiration of the Scriptures was giving way to the conception of "progressive revelation,"[28] by which God was believed to be preparing His people under the Old Covenant for the fullest apprehension of His mind and heart in the Mediator of the New Covenant, Jesus Christ, the image of the invisible God, full of grace and truth. This was, indeed, a convenient application of the concept of evolution for Christian apologetics. An equally significant change of emphasis in theology, attributable in part to scientific influence, was the concentration on the Divine immanence. God was no longer conceived as standing apart from His world and, as it were, making occasional miraculous incursions into it, becoming temporarily *Deus revelatus* and rapidly reassuming his characteristic role of *Deus absconditus*.

In a word, as the older theology had emphasized God's transcendence, so the newer theology emphasized His immanence, His in-dwelling. He was believed to be continually active in human affairs as a dynamic Providence and in continuous creation. Despite the dangers of such an emphasis (among them a certain vagueness, a pantheistic tendency, and a failure to do justice to the specifically "saving" acts of God), it led to a greater sense of the Fatherhood and constant care of God, whereas the exclusive emphasis on transcendence had caused God's love to be lost in His sovereignty, and favoured the reception of the Greek theological idea of the Incarnation of Christ as a restoration of man's powers to God's original intention at the Creation. The older English theology had in its emphasis on the individual appropriation of the benefits of the Atonement lost sight of the cosmic implications of

---

[27] It is to the honour of the essayists that they stood by their conclusions and refused to take cover in anonymous or pseudonymous fox-holes, as did some of the iconoclasts, such as Chambers, Seeley, and William Hale White. "George Eliot," as a woman novelist, may be excused for hiding her identity.

[28] This term, unless expanded as "the progressive appropriation of revelation," is dangerously misleading, since it suggests progress in the mind of God.

the Incarnation.[29] Here, again, was a stress less on the discontinuity between Nature and Grace (such as a cross-centered Evangelical theology provides) and more on the continuity between Creation and Incarnation (including Redemption). This emphasis on continuity and immanence was clearly in line with the discoveries of the sciences.

Immanence carried to its logical conclusion would also help to account for the "reduced Christologies" of the period. The Modernists, for example, tended to concentrate on "The Son of Man" to the exclusion of "The Son of God" and to present a purely human Jesus, leading on the one hand to a saccharine religious sentimentality and on the other to some impressive social service in the name of the Carpenter of Nazareth.

It may be that in this rapid survey of theology's indebtedness to science, for its re-statements, we have overstated the subservience of theology and the exclusive influence of science. Undoubtedly, the question of "evidences" and of the nature and authority of religious belief had been raised in the Deistic controversy of the eighteenth century, though hardly focussed with such a blinding glare as in the 1850's. The embryonic stage of the development of literary and historical criticism is to be found in the eighteenth, not the nineteenth century. Unitarian Christologies, offering veneration if not adoration to Jesus, were known in seventeenth and eighteenth century England. It could even be argued, with considerable plausibility, that the Christian revelation contains strong energies of morality and compassion within it, which are released most vigorously when Christianity's doctrinal tenets are under attack, because Christ as Exemplar shines most clearly when attention is withdrawn from Christ, as the Second Person of the Trinity. But even so, science in the Victorian age must at least be given credit for providing the catalyst to release such forces. It can hardly be disputed that the prevailing culture of England since the 1850's has been scientific humanism, so that it would be entirely incredible if theology were to claim to be unaffected by the dominance of science.

It was not, however, an exclusively scientific influence, but, more generally, a secular one. Other aspects of Victorian life and thought were to have their significant impact on the religion of the day. Mill's classic *On Liberty* (1859) certainly paved the way, not only

<hr>

[29] See Chapter IX of *Worship and Theology in England*, Vol. 3, "From Watts and Wesley to Maurice, 1690-1850," for a fuller consideration of the strength and weakness of English Evangelical theology.

for toleration and therefore for the depreciation of dogmatism; but it also helped theologians to realize that a coerced faith is a contradiction in terms, even if this was a discovery that Baptists and Quakers had made in seventeenth century England. Similarly, the political theorists and jurists, in their insistence on the primacy of the remedial element over the vindictive in punishment, helped the theologians to revise or to discard the doctrines of the eternal punishment of the reprobate and the penal substitutionary theory of the work of Christ on the Cross. So, also, the radical reformers and the sociologists, by giving prominence to the governing concept of social justice, help to make the theologians sensitive to the social implications of the Gospel, even if they were anticipated by the seventeenth century "Diggers" and "Levellers."[30]

6. The Person and Work of Christ Re-interpreted

One of the major achievements of the Victorian era was to get behind the "cold Christs and tangled Trinities" of theological orthodoxy to what their successors liked to call "the historic Jesus." Often, indeed, this meant no more than to get behind St. Paul to the Jesus of the Synoptic Gospels. The Tractarians (rejecting much of the Paulinism of the Evangelicals) had begun the process by their frequent sermons on the events and parables of Christ, through which they had exalted Christ as Saviour and Exemplar.

Historical and Literary Criticism by the simple assumption that the earliest is the purest tradition furthered the process, so that Mark, the earliest Gospel, was preferred to John, the latest and supposedly the most complicated, and therefore the one which had a higher proportion of interpretation to fact than the other three. Mark's Gospel, which omitted the highly mythological birth stories included by Matthew and Luke, was believed to portray the essential Jesus, a prophet, a sublime herald of the love of God, and an incomparable teacher, whose life and death on the Cross demonstrated decisively the moral integrity and insight of His teaching. (It was left to later New Testament scholars to show that this, too, was a partial interpretation, and that the eschatological element prominent in all the Gospels had been ignored.)[31] This human and

---

[30] For an over-generous acknowledgment of theology's indebtedness to science, see R. H. Hutton's *Aspects of Religious and Scientific Thought*, pp. 31-32, cited in H. G. Wood, *op.cit.*, pp. 26-27, and judiciously corrected.

[31] For a brilliant discussion of the inadequacy of many liberal portraits of Jesus Christ and a discussion of the basic presuppositions underlying New Testament accounts of Christ, see Edwyn Hoskyns and Noel Davey, *The Riddle of the New Testament*.

194

unhaloed Jesus, however, failed to satisfy the great Cambridge trio of New Testament scholars, Lightfoot, Westcott, and Hort, since it accounted neither for the uniqueness of Christ nor for His continued power in the life of the Church.[32]

It seemed that theologians would have to choose between three theories of the Person of Christ. One important view was the orthodox "two-natures" theory that held Christ was two natures (Divine and human) in one person as was the consentient witness of the Early Church and the formularies of Eastern Orthodoxy, Roman Catholicism, and Anglicanism (in the Niceno-Constantinopolitan Creed and the so-called Athanasian Creed).[33]

Another view was the "Adoptionist" (later to become the favourite view of Liberal Modernism in the twentieth century), which held that God "adopted" Jesus as Messiah at His Baptism, because of His perfect obedience.[34] Its supporters believed that its strength was its denial of the pre-existence of Christ before His birth (as asserted in the Pauline letters and in the Gospel of John), but its opponents asserted that it seemed more like apotheosis, or the divinization of man, than the gracious descent of God in human flesh.

The third view is one that came into increasing favour in late Victorian days, the so-called "Kenotic" theory.[35] This held that, on the basis of the second chapter of the Epistle to the Philippians, the Incarnation was to be interpreted as a genuine *kenosis*,[36] or self-emptying of God, by which in order to become truly man, He became first century man. Thus, necessarily, He gave up the metaphysical attributes of Deity (omniscience, omnipresence, and omnipotence), retaining the perfect moral attributes of holiness and love. Clearly, to become a man is to be in a body and therefore not to be omnipresent. To become a first century man is to be confined by the world-view of a first century man (and therefore to be un-

---

[32] During the last three decades of the century Cambridge University took the lead in New Testament scholarship under the guidance of Lightfoot, Westcott, and Hort. A landmark was the publication of Westcott and Hort's critical edition of the Greek New Testament in 1881. Mauricians in theology, they wrote commentaries that were a model of critical honesty and devotion to the Lord of the Church.

[33] For a most impressive modern defence of the Chalcedonian "Two-Natures" theory of the Person of Christ, see Donald M. Baillie, *God was in Christ: an Essay in Incarnation and Atonement* (1948, revised in 1955).

[34] A perceptive re-statement of the "Adoptionist" position will be found in Frank Lenwood's *Jesus—Lord or Leader?* (1930).

[35] A useful exposition of the "Kenotic" theory, by one who accepted it, is contained in H. R. Mackintosh's historical study, *The Doctrine of the Person of Jesus Christ.*

[36] The Epistle to the Philippians 2:6-7 declares that the Son of God ἐκένωσεν ἑαυτόν (emptied himself), taking the likeness of man; exchanging the form of God for the form of a servant.

aware of the unDavidic authorship of the Psalms). To become human at all is to cease to be omnipotent, and it was asserted that the Gospel narratives indicate that Jesus was hindered by the lack of faith of his auditory from performing mighty works.

This view, although it created new difficulties and did not resolve the *mysterium Christi* (and how can the *unique* ever be explicable in common categories?), was believed to fulfil the two demands of a satisfactory Christology, that it shall present Christ as Saviour, for only One who is holy and Divine can save sinful humanity, and as Exemplar, for only One who is truly man and acquainted with our griefs can be imitated. It is significant that this theory of the Person of Christ, minimizing the metaphysical attributes of God and maximizing the moral attributes, was an attempt to meet the spirit of the age, without surrendering the heart of the Gospel of Grace. It retained the Divine Love, while surrendering omniscience.

The best Victorian re-statement of the orthodox two-natures Christology was Liddon's Bampton Lectures of 1866 on *The Divinity of our Lord and Saviour Jesus Christ*, in which he posed the dilemma: *aut Deus, aut homo non bonus*. Two theologians who proposed the "Kenotic" theory for serious consideration were Charles Gore, the High Anglican and later Bishop of Oxford, and A. M. Fairbairn, the Principal of Mansfield College, Oxford. Gore's exposition was contained in his Bampton Lectures of 1891, entitled *The Incarnation of the Son of God*, and Fairbairn's appeared in *The Place of Christ in Modern Theology* (1893). The first draft of Gore's theory had appeared in *Lux Mundi* (1889).

The new interest in the Incarnation was in part a revulsion from the Western tradition's concentration on the individual appropriation of the work of Christ in the Cross which Evangelicalism had also made central because it was most vividly experienced in the act of conversion. On this view, both Protestant and Catholic, the Cross, with its Atonement, was the Divine remedy for the fall of man and the single hope of the whole human race. Alexandrian theology insisted, however, that the Incarnation was not the result of the Fall of man, but a part of the Divine plan from the very outset and the inevitable consequence of Creation. Man was made in the image of God and the *Logos* or Word of God had been continually active in the world preparing for the supreme revelation of Himself in a historic Person, the Word made flesh, Christ Jesus. In this manner the Incarnation was thought to be the way to Atonement, in fact, *was* the Atonement. This insistence upon the Incarnation as the culmination and climax of a long process of educating the human race was clearly in line with the ideas of immanence and evolution familiarized by the scientists. It was the more readily accepted because of current dissatisfaction with much of the crudeness of popular theories of the Work of Christ, and it indirectly led to their revision.

The second theological revolution of the Victorian age was its provision of new explanations of the significance of the Cross. The older penal, substitutionary theory of the Work of Christ, by which it was thought that the innocent Son of God received the punishment of an angry God instead of sinful humanity, was felt to make Christ "God's whipping boy." It denied the evident unity of the Father and the Son in reconciliation and it exhibited God as a vengeful sadist. R. W. Dale, the Congregationalist, presented a revised defence and exposition of the juridical theory in *The Atonement* (1875), in which he argued that Jesus voluntarily accepted the sacrifice of His life as the Head and Representative of Humanity to satisfy and vindicate God's eternal law of righteousness. J. Scott Lidgett, the distinguished Methodist, in *The Spiritual Principle of the Atonement* (1897) maintained the same view as Dale, but argued that the real basis of penal satisfaction is to be found not in the eternal law of righteousness but in the nature of fatherhood itself.

A new and deeply moving view of the Work of Christ was advanced by the noted Scottish Presbyterian theologian, McLeod Campbell, in *The Nature of Atonement* (1856). He argued that genuine love is always vicarious, suffering for the sins of others, and he saw Christ, the perfectly holy and loving Son of God, performing on the Cross an act of vicarious penance for the entire human race.

In the theories already considered it will be readily seen that two motives are dominant in the re-statements. There is, in the first place, an attempt to humanize, or, rather, to moralize the meaning of the Atonement, and to free it from the crudities that remained in much popular teaching. There is also, in the second place, a recognition that the Atonement is a saving act which has effected a change or, at least, a clarification of the relationship of God to the whole of erring humanity, not merely for penitent individuals. This strongly social emphasis is linked with the growing understanding of the Church as being the very Body and Community of

197

Christ, and R. C. Moberly in his devout yet original *Atonement and Personality* (1901), P. T. Forsyth in *The Work of Christ* (1910), and Henry W. Clark in *The Cross and the Eternal Order* (to pursue the subject into the twentieth century) all claim that the Atonement is an act of cosmic reconciliation.

The new recognition that society's primary concern in punishing offenders against its laws is reformative, not vindictive, changed not only the popular theory of the Atonement, but also the orthodox Protestant notion of Hell,[37] as the place of eternal torment for the impenitent evil-doer. F. D. Maurice was forced to resign from the Chair of Theology in King's College, University of London, in 1853, for casting doubt on the doctrine of eternal punishment, because he had urged that αἰώνιος in the New Testament was incorrectly translated as "everlasting." But the public mind and the immediate future of theology was with Maurice, not his detractors, for not many years later the judgment after an appeal to the Privy Council to require this belief from the holder of an Anglican benefice was reported in a London daily as "Hell dismissed with costs!"[38] While Maurice himself held to conditional immortality as the verdict of the Bible on the future life, there were others who believed in Universalism. This is another significant example of the moralizing of Victorian theology.

7. The Doctrine of the Church

The last fifty years of the nineteenth century are remarkable for increased attention to the doctrine of the Church on the part of theologians, whether Anglican or Free Church. Dr. L. E. Elliott-Binns has rightly observed that the "increasing emphasis on the importance of the Church coincided with a serious decline in its authority and influence during the closing years of the nineteenth century."[39] Many causes may be found for both the increasing interest in and the decline of the authority of the Churches.[40]

---

[37] H. G. Wood, *op.cit.*, p. 33, cites a passage from George Macdonald's *Robert Falconer* to illustrate the perplexity of a godly mother praying for her son lost in Hell. She is caught between the demands of orthodox Calvinism and the impulse of her love. "Gladly would I look down upon his dead face if I could believe that his soul was not among the lost. But oh! the torments of that place and the smoke that goes up for ever and ever, smothering the stars. And my Andrew down in the heart of it, crying! And me not able to get to him. O Lord, I cannot say Thy will be done. But don't lay it to my charge: for if you were a mother yourself, you would not put him there."

[38] *Ibid.*, p. 34.   [39] *English Thought* . . . , p. 264.

[40] Dr. Binns, *ibid.*, suggests that the causes of the decline of the authority of the Church (chiefly, the Church of England) were: Tractarian emphasis on Eras-

Undoubtedly it was the Oxford Movement, itself an *ecclesiastical* revival as well as issuing in an aesthetic revival in religion, which was the major contributory factor in reviving High Churchmanship and in stemming the Erastianism of the Latitudinarian viewpoint. This was achieved by denying that the Church was a mere Department of State, or merely the association of saved individuals (as the Evangelicals had held), and by asserting that it was a supernatural Community, commissioned by the ascended Lord to be the channel of His redemptive work, through the apostles and their successors, the bishops, and perpetuating, by means of its Sacraments, the life of grace among the faithful.[41]

Even where the claims of the Anglo-Catholics were felt to be too high for the institution and too low for Christ, its Head, the very assertion of them provoked Free Church theologians in criticism to develop their own understanding of the authority and function of the Church. In counteracting what they believed to be the nefarious claims of the ritualists and ceremonialists of the High Church party, the Congregationalists subjected the theology behind these practices to a thorough investigation.[42] As a result, says John W. Grant, in his *Free Churchmanship in England, 1870-1940*, "the most striking feature of the Nonconformity of 1870 . . . was the revival of interest in the Church."[43] In that very year many of the leaders of Congregationalism collaborated in the production of a series of essays on the nature of the Church, entitled *Ecclesia*. Such was the excitement engendered by this volume that it elicited further written contributions sufficient in number and quality to justify the publication of a second volume on the same theme.

The influence of Coleridge, and of such a leading Coleridgean as F. D. Maurice, was still pervasive in the Broad Church School. Maurice had indeed criticized the Tractarians for their archaic conception of the Church, affirming that "their error, I think, consists in opposing to the present age the spirit of a former age, instead of the ever-living and acting Spirit of God of which the spirit

---

tianism as the enemy resulted in a lesser national role for the Church to play; the disloyalty of extreme clergymen in the "Ritualistic Controversy" to their bishops and the rules of the Church; and the obscurantism of much preaching and teaching.

41 See Chapter XI on the Oxford Movement in *Worship and Theology in England*, Vol. 3, "From Watts and Wesley to Maurice, 1690-1850."

42 See the following articles appearing in *The Congregationalist* in 1872: in February on Transubstantiation (Vol. I, p. 113); in June on the Baptismal Office (Vol. I, p. 427); in July on the Church Catechism (Vol. I, p. 495); and in December on Confirmation (Vol. I, p. 733).

43 P. 96.

of each age is at once the adversary and the parody,"[44] but he had also taken to heart the aphorism of his teacher that "A Christianity without a Church exercising authority is vanity and dissolution."[45] The Spirit cannot forever wander disconsolately crying through the key-hole of the individual human heart, and must have its responsive corporate instrument, in a word, the Church. In fact, the Holy Spirit has chosen to use the Church.

Moreover, the idea of community, as an organic and interdependent society, was very much in the Victorian air, and this helped to make the claim for the necessity of a Christian society, the Church. This growing sense of community was fostered by the studies of the historians, politicians (notably Gladstone), economists, and sociologists of the day. The very threats to the building of an ordered society, such as the mobility of population, the break-up of family life, and the chasm yawning between the "haves" and "have-nots" (corresponding roughly to Disraeli's "two nations"), accelerated by the rapid industrialization of later Victorian England, made men more acutely aware of the social values imperilled by these developments. Significantly, Westcott wrote in 1886: "Fifty years ago the term 'solidarity' and the idea it conveys were alike strange or unknown."[46]

It is, of course, true that there were strong influences moving in the opposite direction. Sabatier popularized in England a distinction between authoritarian and spiritual religions, thus lending support to the view that there was a serious declension from "the religion of Jesus" to the dogmatism and ecclesiasticism of Paul. Edwin Hatch, author of a splendid hymn on the Holy Spirit ("Breathe on me, Breath of God") and Reader in Ecclesiastical History in Oxford University from 1884, in the Bampton Lectures for 1880 on *The Organization of the Early Christian Churches* asserted boldly that it was Paul, not Jesus, who had established the organized society.

At the very end of this century and at the beginning of the next a further serious anti-ecclesiastical blow was struck by the New Testament critics of the "eschatological" school. They argued that Jesus and his disciples were so convinced of the imminent end of the age that they made no serious plans for the continuity of their

[44] Ed. Sir John Frederick Maurice, *The Life of Frederick Denison Maurice* (2 vols., 1884), Vol. I, p. 217.
[45] *Aids to Reflection*, a note on Aphorism CXII.
[46] *Christus Consummator*, p. 120, cited by Binns, *op.cit.*, p. 264.

society, but merely *interim* arrangements. The more moderate view was taken by A. M. Fairbairn, an Oxford theologian and leading Congregationalist in two books, *The Place of Christ in Modern Theology* (1893) and *Catholicism, Roman and Anglican* (1899). He argued that the "political" and "theological" conceptions of the Church must be distinguished. The "political" conception of the Church was characterised by legalism, sacerdotalism, and ceremonialism. In consequence, the exponents of this view tried to limit the boundaries of the Grace of God, confusing the visible Church with the Kingdom of God, and thus had to regard such extra-ecclesiastical Divine activity as illicit or uncovenanted. They were also guilty of clericalism, forgetting that in the New Testament the Church is the people of God, and that it is there defined in theocratic and ethical, not in sacerdotal and ceremonial terms. He demanded a return to this "theological" conception of the nature of the Church.

Despite these powerful counter-currents, the idea of the Church was steadily gaining ground. In 1870 the idea of the Pope, speaking *ex cathedra*, as the infallible teacher of the Roman Catholic Church, was officially promulgated as a dogma, to the delight of the Ultramontanists. In 1889 Dr. Walter Lock in his essay in *Lux Mundi* had declared that the Church had three essential functions to perform: as a school of virtue, as a guardian of truth, and as a home of worship. English Churchmen were not disposed to doubt the wisdom of this eminently practical approach to ecclesiology. In 1884 R. W. Dale proclaimed the renascence of Churchmanship in Dissent by the publication of his *Manual of Congregational Principles*, in which he declared that the Church is the supernatural creation of Christ Himself, for which he found historical support (long before the existence of Tractarianism) in the Congregational Confession of *The Savoy Declaration* of 1658. Dale had already given a strong hint of his High Churchmanship[47] in the title of his contribution to the *Ecclesia* volume of 1870 which was, "The Doctrine of the Real Presence and of the Lord's Supper."

[47] P. T. Forsyth is the successor of R. W. Dale as a Congregational High Churchman. He wrote: "For the Church is not differentiated from all other societies as these are distinct from each another—by its tradition or its purpose, but by its creative Gospel and indwelling Holy Spirit. It is a body with a personality which they have not; first because it was created by an act of Redemption into which the whole perfect and final personality of its Creator was put; and, second, because it not only wears His stamp but it is inhabited by His personal Holy Spirit, which, and no mere genius, is its life principle." (*The Church and the Sacraments*, 1st edn. 1917, republ. 1947, p. 32.)

201

8. *The Doctrine of the Sacraments*[48]

The same currents and cross-currents in the world of thought that led to a renewal of interest (and criticism of) the doctrine of the Church also served to bring the doctrine of the Sacraments into sympathetic or critical prominence. On the positive side, the Tractarians had taught that spiritual life was essentially sacramental life, and their successors—in the Anglo-Catholic movement—were in even greater danger of teaching an *ex opere operato* doctrine in their objection to receptionist views of the Sacraments that might seem to value the human appropriation by faith more than the Divine initiative and activity in the Sacraments. The so-called "Ritualistic Controversy" accentuated this difference of emphasis between Anglo-Catholic and Evangelical interpretations. If the Anglo-Catholics were accused of turning the Sacraments into magic, they retorted that the Evangelicals made them into empty signs (*signa nuda*) and merely didactic emblems.

Perhaps the most disturbing feature of this controversy, in which there were exaggerations on each side, was that the mystery of the "Real Presence" in the Eucharist was explained or explained away in rationalistic "High Church" or "Low Church" views. This led to an unfortunate concentration on the *moment* of the consecration and on the *species*, with the results that some Anglo-Catholic priests held Eucharists at which only they communicated and the rest of their congregations were non-communicating spectators, not participants. Others practised the reservation of the Host. So divergent and acrimonious were the differences that in 1847 the Bishop of Exeter refused to induct Gorham, the Evangelical, to the living of Brampford Speke, because he would not affirm that there was an immediate regeneration of infants on being baptised in the Triune Name, from which episcopal ruling he successfully appealed to the Privy Council;[49] while, at the other extreme, the year 1870 saw the prosecution of the Rev. W. J. E. Bennett, who openly spoke of the visible presence of the Lord in the Eucharist and of adoration of the consecrated elements.[50] No doubt the many conservative

[48] Some account of the development of Dissenting doctrines of the Lord's Supper is given *supra*, Chapter III, section 5.
[49] See George Cornelius Gorham, *Examination before Admission to a Benefice by the Bishop of Exeter . . .* , and J. C. S. Nias, *Gorham and the Bishop of Exeter.*
[50] See R. C. D. Jasper, *Prayer Book Revision in England*, Chap. VI, for an account of the borrowings from Roman devotional sources for the supplementation of the English Eucharist by Anglo-Catholic priests.

clergy and their congregations were still grateful for the means of grace and accepted the mystery (and its spiritual benefits) without probing too deeply, sharing with Wordsworth the conviction that "we murder to dissect."

On the negative side, there were the more extreme Protestant Liberals who claimed that Jesus had not intended that the Last Supper should be perpetuated in the form of the Eucharist (or, indeed, in any form), and that it was St. Paul who had villainously transformed a simple memorial rite into a secret initiation ceremony on the analogy of the Greek mystery-religions.

Even the argument asserting the uniqueness of the institution of the Sacrament of Holy Communion had little impact on the neophytes of the new discipline of the comparative study of religion, which made great headway during this period.[51]

Then to those for whom the doctrinal test was much less cogent than the moral test of "by your fruits ye shall know them," it was sufficient to point out that the Society of Friends and the Salvation Army (neither of which used the Dominical Sacraments of Baptism and Holy Communion), were unexcelled in their practical Christianity.

It was, then, the Anglo-Catholics, as the successors of the Tractarians, who, as might be expected, preserved most jealously the sacramental heritage of the Church of England. What is surprising, however, is that there were exponents of the doctrine of the "Real Presence" among Free Church ministers. Nor should it be forgotten that the majority of the members in good standing of the Baptists, Congregationalists, Methodists, and English Presbyterians were most faithful in their attendance at the Lord's Supper in their own churches at monthly,[52] and, in some cases, fortnightly, and, very rarely, weekly celebrations.

Certainly Dale and Forsyth among Congregationalist leaders, and Hugh Price Hughes among the Methodists, were exponents of a doctrine far superior to mere memorialism. Forsyth was even to commit himself to the very provocative statement: "It may be surmised that the writer holds a mere memorialism to be a more fatal

---

[51] This type of objection is given special consideration in Charles Gore's *The Body of Christ* and Darwell Stone's *The History of the Doctrine of the Holy Eucharist*.

[52] In 1824, nine years before the Oxford Movement began, J. M. Cramp contended that the majority of Dissenting congregations celebrated Communion monthly. (*An Essay on the Obligation of Christians to Observe the Lord's Supper Every Lord's Day*, pp. 11-12.)

error than the Mass, and a far less lovely."[53] Both Dale and Forsyth protested against the vague immanentalism and the all-too-definite didacticism of the age, which seemed to regard the Lord's Supper as merely an emblem of Christian fellowship, or as a vivid picture-lesson on the love of God. For both the Sacrament is an action of God's holy, redeeming love in His Church, in which Our Lord presents His sacrifice and all its benefits to His people anew.[54] Dale, of course, was far in advance of the rest of his denomination and admitted that his views were not acceptable to the majority.[55] It is significant, however, that even those who retained the Zwinglian Memorialist view were discovering in the Lord's Supper a valuable means for expressing the solidarity and equal dignity of humanity[56] in the Kingdom of God.

What is even more significant was the growing unanimity between the viewpoints of theological leaders, whether of the Anglo-Catholic or Congregational standpoint. They were at one in repudiating memorialism and didacticism, and, positively, in seeing as the central feature of the Holy Communion the redeemed community's offering of its life in conjunction with the offering of Our Lord's Sacrifice to the Father. It is also worthy of consideration that those who hold an objective theory of the Work of Christ, as a Divine action of Sacrifice that opens a new way between God and man, also believe that the Sacrament of Holy Communion is an efficacious means of grace, a "conveying" action; while those who maintain a "moral influence" or Abelardian theory of the Atonement, and see it only as the supreme exhibition of Divine love eliciting love in us, also have a subjective and didactic view of the Sacrament.

8. *The Effects of Theology on Worship, Including Hymnody*

The most noticeable effect of the great Victorian struggle between Faith and Doubt was, of course, to reduce very seriously

---

[53] *The Church and the Sacraments* (1947 edn.), preface, p. xvi.
[54] Dale says of the Lord's Supper: "What He [Christ] gives is His own eternal life as that life was limited and conditioned by the assumption of humanity. He gives us this in giving us the symbol of His broken bread." (*A Manual of Congregational Principles*, p. 152.) Forsyth insisted that we do not sacrifice Christ anew in each re-enactment of the Lord's Supper, but that Christ offers His completed Sacrifice anew in each Communion. (*The Church and the Sacraments*, p. 256.)
[55] *A Manual of Congregational Principles*, p. 158.
[56] See J. Morgan Gibbon's essay-sermon, "The Social Value of the Lord's Supper" in the composite volume, *The Lord's Supper: Eden and Gethsemane*, p. 203, for the Communion seen as the expression of the ideal of social justice, in accordance with the demands of the "Social Gospel."

the attendance at public worship. Criticism inevitably made inroads on Adoration. And the more extreme Liberals were not as wise, as a later Liberal, Dean Inge, who warned: "If you marry the Spirit of your generation, you will be a widow in the next."[57] Many of the Liberal pioneers following the gleaming camp-fires of the Critics found that they were entering, not the Promised Land of Reconciliation where the scientific lion would lie down with the religious lamb, but the howling wilderness of Negation, with fatigued followers trailing behind them, bearing the packs of a vast critical apparatus on their backs and emaciated from the lack of iron-rations. Immanentalism, demythologising, interim-ethics, evolution, and even social justice, and comparable concepts, proved to be—in the absence of a firm rootage in the historic incarnation—marsh-lights, wills-of-the-wisp that led them into the desperate quagmires of uncertainty and into the engulfing sloughs of despond. Only the more careful and most committed learned anew that they must cling, with unyielding grasp, to a supernatural religion; to a Christ, truly Divine as well as human: to an Incarnate, Crucified, Risen, and Reigning Lord of all the centuries, Who would sustain and renew the flagging cohorts of His Church. They, at least, understood as never before the sustenance of holiness to be found in the Scriptures, in the Sacraments and in the Worship and comradeship of the Church, triumphant and militant.

There were others, who would yield the bulwarks of doctrine to the clamant critics, and yet fondly hope that the traditional character of the worship of the Church could be retained. One such was Matthew Arnold (and in this single respect Renan was like him). He championed the Liturgy of the Church of England, and refused to countenance any revisions of its ritual or ceremonial because "Profound sentiments are connected with them; they are aimed at the highest good, however imperfectly apprehended. Their form often gives them beauty, the associations which cluster around them give them always pathos and solemnity. They are to be used as poetry."[58] He even delivered himself of the surprising judgment that "the eternity and universality, which is vainly claimed for Catholic dogma and the ultramontane system, might really be possible for Catholic worship."[59] Religious aesthetics, he failed to realize (forgetting his Platonism) degenerate into sheer relativity unless they are images of a world of Nature, reflecting their

---

[57] W. R. Inge, *The Diary of a Dean*, p. 12.
[58] *Last Essays on Church and Religion*, p. 38.
[59] *Ibid.*, preface, p. xxiv.

Creator or images of Grace reflecting their Redeemer. Liturgy in short has and must have an objective and theological and ontological basis: the Revelation of the Living God, and without that worship is merely a more aesthetic type of Comteism, an impressionist's Paradise, but not the avenue of God and the very gate of Heaven.

Thus, the second half of the century was distinguished for the quiet spirituality of its worship, as befitted Christians engaged in troubled heart-searchings. The trumpets of the pulpits, in most cases, gave forth an uncertain sound. It was only in the realm of praise that the accents of the century are heard with unmistakable clarity, and often with poignancy. The hymns were the spiritual barometer of the period in recording the stormy weather, the grateful lulls in the tempest, and the falling of the gentle rains of mysticism on the aridities of doubt, and the rarer sunshine of Revelation.

Newman's "Lead, kindly Light, amid the encircling gloom" is both the record of a personal crisis and also typical of the epoch in its record of a struggle, its plea for Divine guidance in a darkness that makes men stumble, and in its resignation. The other most famous Victorian hymn, "Abide with me, fast falls the eventide," although written by an Evangelical Anglican, H. F. Lyte, expresses the same mood, uses the inevitable image of light in darkness as it turns from "change and decay in all around I see" to "O Thou who changest not, abide with me." Even the rapturous neophyte of Roman Catholicism, F. W. Faber, a fellow Oratorian of Newman's, writes the typical hymn "Workman of God! O lose not heart" and expresses elsewhere the muted, tender note, as in "O come and mourn with me awhile" with its unforgettable appeal:

> A broken heart, a fount of tears,
> Ask and they will not be denied;
> A broken heart love's cradle is;
> Jesus, our Lord, is crucified.

The unmistakable modern notes of a faith won through conflict and a wistful longing for fuller light are, equally, to be found in Palgrave's "Thou say'st take up thy Cross" and Jean Ingelow's "And didst thou love the race that loved not Thee?" with its repeated interrogation marks. Yet the note of jubilation, especially in conjunction with a sense of the triumph of the Church through the centuries, was not absent. Matthew Bridges in his "Crown Him with many crowns" praises Christ as the Lord of all culture; Bishop

Christopher Wordsworth (the poet's nephew) thanks the "Lord of heaven and earth and sea" for the gifts of Nature as well as of Grace. The victories of the saints, now the Church triumphant, inspire Sabine-Gould's translation in "Through the night of doubt and sorrow," Neale's translation of Joseph the Hymnographer's "O happy band of pilgrims," Faber's "Hark! hark! my soul, angelic songs are swelling," Bishop Heber's great Trinitarian hymn "Holy, Holy, Holy, Lord God Almighty," which re-echoes the triumphant *Sanctus* of the seraphim before the throne of God, and Bishop Wordsworth's "Hark, the sound of holy voices." Yet this was, as it were, a *borrowed* jubilation. It is significant that many of these praises were either translations or imitations of the hymns of the Greek Church of the early centuries. They were not as truly indigenous as the hymns of faith-in-doubt.

Equally indigenous and typical were the hymns of social service, that summoned congregations to hear the call of God in the poverty, sickness, ignorance, and inequalities of the day. Among such hymns were Kingsley's "From Thee all skill and science flow," Thomas Toke Lynch's "Dismiss me not Thy Service, Lord," J. W. Chadwick's "Eternal Ruler of the ceaseless round," Arnold Thomas's "Brother, who on Thy heart didst bear," and Godfrey Thring's "O God of mercy, God of might." Some of these and many of the immanentalist hymns of America, which Garrett Horder popularized in his enterprising compilation *Worship Song*, were products of the influence of either the Christian Socialists in England or the "Social Gospel" movement in America,[60] and they were stronger on the "social" implications than on the "Gospel" imperatives and implementations.

While some recovered the accents of the Old Testament prophets and restored the this-worldly implications of the Christian Gospel, others confused the realization of earthly social goals with the Kingdom of God, unaware that they might be encouraging only an earth-bound religion or a passing mode of thought or sentiment.

[60] Among the many notable American hymns that found their way into English hymnals in the nineteenth century and were expressive of the immanental and social version of the Kingdom of God, were: W. P. Merrill's "Rise up, O men of God"; Whittier's "Immortal Love for ever full," and his "Dear Lord and Father of mankind"; Samuel Johnson's "City of God how broad and far"; and Longfellow's "One Holy Church of God appears" and his "Beneath the shadow of the Cross."

It is also worthy of note that a storm in a teacup, the "Rivulet Controversy," agitated Congregationalists over whether or not to approve the immanental romantic, and occasionally sentimental hymns of T. T. Lynch in his collection, "The Rivulet." Lynch's opponents were the die-hard orthodox Calvinists. (See A. Peel, *These Hundred Years*, p. 221 f., and J. Waddington, *Congregational History, 1850-1880*, pp. 144-47.)

Indeed, not a few of them deserve to be seared with the judgment of Professor Richard Niebuhr: "A God without wrath brought men without sin into a kingdom without judgment through the ministrations of a Christ without a cross."[61] This penetrating criticism does not, however, apply to three great hymns of this genre that appeared at the end of the nineteenth or the beginning of the twentieth century: Dean Liddon's "Judge Eternal, throned in splendour," Robert Bridges' "Rejoice, O Land, in God Thy might," and G. K. Chesterton's "O God of earth and altar" with its marvellously modern litany in the second verse:

> From all that terror teaches,
> From lies of tongue and pen,
> From all the easy speeches
> That comfort cruel men,
>
> From sale and profanation
> Of honour and the sword,
> From sleep and from damnation,
> Deliver us, good Lord!

Another Victorian innovation in hymnody was the composition of children's praises suitable to their age and experience, although it is often assumed that children of that era were supposed to be seen and not heard. To appreciate the achievement it is necessary only to compare the terror of Watts with the tenderness of Christina Rossetti. Watts, who was not consistently fierce, wrote:

> What if His dreadful anger burn
> While I refuse His offered grace,
> And all His love to anger turn,
> And strike me dead upon the place?
> 'Tis dangerous to provoke a God!
> His power and vengeance none can tell:
> One stroke of His almighty rod
> Shall send young sinners quick to Hell![62]

Christina Rossetti understands that the Lord of the Incarnation can stoop to enter in at the low lintel of a child's heart, for she

[61] *The Kingdom of God in America* (2nd edn.), p. 193.
[62] This reference is cited in H. A. L. Jefferson's most perceptive sixth chapter of *Hymns in Christian Worship*. He draws attention to the outstanding qualities of Garrett Horder as an editor of hymns with an interdenominational knowledge and catholicity of spirit.

ends her deceptively simple and charming Christmas carol ("In the bleak mid-winter") with:

> What can I give Him,
> Poor as I am?
> If I were a shepherd,
> I would bring a lamb;
> If I were a wise man,
> I would do my part;
> Yet what I can I give Him—
> Give my heart.

The concreteness of the narrative and the many monosyllables are an inspired accommodation of the doctrine of the Incarnation to childhood's understanding. The pioneer of the newer emphasis on the Divine love attuned to the child's intelligence in praise was Mrs. Cecil Frances Alexander, the author of "Once in royal David's city" and of "There is a green hill far away," who published her *Hymns for Little Children* in 1848. She had many imitators and their hymns were a delight for adults as well as children.[63]

The outstanding difference between eighteenth and nineteenth century worship is that the former was dull, and the latter was lively. This can be attributed to four main factors: instructed teaching in the meaning and the right use of the Prayer Book, the increasing beauty of the interiors and furnishings of the churches, above all, the greatly widened range of themes in the hymn-books and the popularity of hymns over against metrical psalms, and, finally, Harvest Thanksgivings. The Tractarians taught their congregations to say the Responses in the Liturgy (thus doing away with the eighteenth century clerk who was the people's proxy), to revere and understand the doctrines of the Prayer Book and the significance of the ceremonial, as well as to regard the Liturgy as a training of the devotional life. The congregations thus became active participants in the worship.

In the same way, the Tractarian regard for a sacramental religion inevitably led to the aesthetic improvement of the interiors of the churches, however misguided some of the Victorian restorations may have been. Interest could hardly fail to be stirred by the new stained-glass; the newly surpliced choirs now sitting in the

---

[63] Other popular children's hymns of the age were J. D. Burns' "Hushed was the evening hymn," Emily Miller's "I love to hear the story," and Jemima Luke's "I think when I read that sweet story of old." But none could match Christian Rossetti.

chancel[64] (especially when they sang the florid harmonies of Barnby, Stainer, and Sullivan in their anthems);[65] the preacher wearing a surplice in the pulpit instead of the accustomed black gown, and a splendid cope at the celebration of the Eucharist as he adopted the eastward position at the altar; the lighted candles on the altar; the stencillings on the walls; the damask and embroidery on the altar and the hangings; the raised marble steps; and the new gleaming brass lecterns and delicately carved prayer-desks. Clearly, worship had become dramatic again.

Even so, the greatest factor in popularizing Victorian services (for few of the Nonconformist churches adopted the dramatic devices just mentioned as increasingly common in Anglican churches), was the hymnody.[66] Latin and Greek hymns in translations by Caswall and Neale, German hymns in translations by Catherine Winkworth, American hymns introduced by Garrett Horder, and an immense outpouring of new English hymns suited to the modern temper, and fitted to tunes by J. B. Dykes (that prolific and sentimental composer) and his like, gained the enthusiastic approval of the people.

Immanentalism, however, claimed its greatest triumph, not in the "Nature hymns" of the period (such as Bishop How's "Summer suns are glowing"), but in the Harvest Festival, the innovation of R. S. Hawker, the eccentric vicar of Morwenstow in Cornwall.[67] Even if this often degenerated into an exhibition of mere "cupboard love," the red-cheeked farmers, as mystical as the marrows they had produced to competitive and preternatural size, and their sturdy families, crowded to this "festival" with unaccustomed gravity, disguising their zest. Victorian worship was popular wor

---

[64] Dr. Hook, the vicar, first introduced a surpliced choir into Leeds Parish Church in 1841. See Dean S. R. Hole, *More Memories*, pp. 16-19, 21ff. and G. M. Young, *Victorian England, Portrait of an Age*, p. 72 for a contrast between unreformed and reformed Anglican worship.

[65] See E. H. Fellowes, *English Cathedral Music from Edward VI to Edward VII*, p. 192.

[66] In 1811, only after Thomas Cotterill had promised to revise his collection of hymns, some of which he had introduced into the congregation of St. Paul's Sheffield of which he was vicar, and the revision had been sanctioned and its publication paid for by Dr. Vernon Harcourt, the Archbishop of York, was high official approval given to the singing of hymns as a normal part of Divine worship. The first official hymn book for the entire Church in England was *Hymns Ancient and Modern*, which first appeared under that title in 1860 when it included 272 hymns, increased to 386 in the 1868 edition. The music edition first came out in 1861.

[67] J. R. H. Moorman, *A History of the Church in England*, p. 360. The Harvest Festival is credited to P. C. Claughton, G. A. Denison, and Hawker in the *Dictionary of National Biography*. For a description of a service see *Kilvert's Diary: 1870-1879* (ed. and abbrev. by W. Plomer, 1944), p. 75.

ship, even if much of it was sentimental,[68] and the diminishing attendances at Divine Service in the latter part of the century are not to be attributed to dullness, but to the impact of scientific, secular, literary, and historical criticism. Moreover, those who remained loyal Christians found great solace and joy in their adoration of God.

Perhaps the truest verdict on the nineteenth century contribution to worship is the charitable one with which Canon Roger Lloyd begins his study of *The Church of England in the Twentieth Century*: "But most of all it is a story of the revival of churchmanship, the recovery of the arts of worship, and the revaluation of sacraments."[69] If the faithful were fewer, their allegiance to Christ's Church was stronger; if the authority of the Sacraments was challenged by the critics, the communicants were only the more convinced of their efficacy in transformed lives; and if ugly industrialism threw up "dark, Satanic mills" and smoky hovels, crouching beneath them, the houses of God defied it, offering in the architecture, the ceremonial, and the symbolism both an escape and a glimpse of a transformed earth.

[68] Randall Davidson, when Bishop of Winchester, wrote in 1898 of a prevalent danger to the Church in "a weak and sentimental return to emotional rather than intellectual beliefs and forms of devotion." (G. K. A. Bell, *Randall Davidson, Archbishop of Canterbury*, 2nd edn., 1938, p. 331.)

[69] Vol. I (1946), p. 29.

CHAPTER VIII

THE LITURGICAL PIONEERS OF THE OLDER DISSENT: BAPTISTS AND CONGREGATIONALISTS

THE REVALUATION of the nature of worship and its components was in active progress among both Baptists and Congregationalists during the nineteenth century. On the whole, the enterprise was more radically as well as more rigorously pursued by the Congregationalists, and for this difference several reasons may be advanced. The Baptists, like the Methodists, were able to supplement their ordained ministry with the enthusiastic but often theologically unsophisticated labours of local preachers, whose devotional preferences were charismatic rather than formal or liturgical. Baptist deacons were often appointed to lead the praise, and sometimes to assist in the prayers; on some occasions they even deputized for the minister in celebrating the Sacraments.[1] While this was an admirable expression of the Reformation principle of the priesthood of all believers, it was not conducive to dignified worship if the deacon was almost illiterate.

The Reverend J. Collings wrote of two such deacons as late as 1883 who made men scoff who came to pray. One of them in Bristol gave out the hymn "Angels from the realms of glory" in the hectoring voice of a drill sergeant, as if commanding an awkward squad to right-about-turn or shoulder-arms. Collings also knew a deacon who often took part in the public service and once addressed the congregation thus: "The world is full of hintemperance, hinfidelity, and hatheism, what his the remedy, why, send the hitinerant society."[2] Yet another deacon was known to invite the congregation to "taste and see that the *Lard* is gracious."[3] The number of local preachers in the Baptist churches, as well as the encouragement of the praying and preaching gifts of several of their deacons, led to a lower general level of worship, to a con-

---

[1] Unordained deacons celebrated both the Communion and Baptism in St. Mary's Baptist Church, Norwich ca. 1840. See *The Baptist Quarterly*, Vol. IX, 1940-1941, p. 404.

[2] "Conservatism in Religious Worship and Belief"—a paper read by the Rev. J. Collings to the Midland Baptist Union in 1883, p. 5. This pamphlet is to be found in the library of Regent's Park College, Oxford.

[3] *Ibid.*

servatism in the charismatic and pneumatic emphasis in worship; and the power of the local congregation was so great that the preferences in worship of the minister were not allowed to be greatly in advance of the taste of the congregation.

It might be objected that since the Congregational polity is identical with the autonomy of the local congregation in the Baptist form of church government, the results in worship should be the same. In fact, however, there were other important considerations. The Congregationalists had a longer tradition of a learned ministry, going back through the Dissenting Academies to Puritan training in the ancient universities, and they had many more theological colleges in the nineteenth century than the Baptists. They were not able to recruit many local preachers, and this could well be explained as due to the more formal, intellectual, and even occasionally arid character of their worship, which repelled the Baptist eager-hearts.[4]

Furthermore, in the larger London congregations, as well as in some of the leading provincial cities, many of the merchant princes of the Victorian age were more likely to be Congregationalists than Baptists, and they would support such Congregational ministers as wished to provide a decorous Free Church equivalent to the worship of the Established Church. It was not customary for laymen to take leading parts in the worship of the Congregational churches, although they were permitted to engage in the weeknight prayer-meetings.[5]

Even Dr. R. W. Dale's unwillingness to use the title "Reverend" and his insistence upon the right of a layman to celebrate the Lord's Supper once each year at Carr's Lane Church, Birmingham, was thought to be an eccentric concession to the doctrine of the priesthood of all believers. Moreover, Dale's insistence upon this reflects, not the demands of his diaconate or even of his church membership, but rather the extraordinary power of the benevolent spiritual dictator in the Victorian age, when the authority of the Free Church minister was at its peak. The only figure of comparable influence in the same century among the Baptists was C. H. Spurgeon, and no one could ever accuse him of being a

---

[4] A writer in the *Congregational Magazine* of 1843 (p. 639) declares that "the devotional worship of dissenting congregations is, comparatively, so cold," and adds "we do not believe that they possess in the degree that is attainable, the temper and spirit of apostolic piety, or that moral greatness that it would inspire."

[5] But the attendance at these was diminishing so rapidly in 1880 that J. Guinness Rogers devoted an article to the problem in *The Congregationalist*, Vol. IX, 1880, pp. 631 f.

High-Churchman, though they might of being high-handed. Spurgeon was a superb preacher, not a leader of worship.[6]

In Congregationalism, the fight for a richer, more beautiful, and better-ordered worship was carried on by such giants as Newman Hall, Thomas Binney, Henry Allon, John Hunter, and Peter Taylor Forsyth. It was R. W. Dale's distinction to have introduced, not a liturgy, but a profounder conception of the Lord's Supper and to have taught a "real Presence of Christ" instead of the commoner Zwinglian memorialism. The important point to make is that Congregational ministers seemed to have a greater power of leadership over their congregations, and that their metropolitan figures, in particular, were able to experiment liturgically in a way that few Baptist ministers ever dared to try— with the possible exception of Dr. F. B. Meyer, and even he was maintaining (out of conviction, admittedly) the liturgical tradition of his predecessor, Dr. Newman Hall, at Christ Church, Westminster Bridge Road.

1. The Revaluation of Prayers

Despite the greater rapidity of liturgical change within Congregationalism, the critiques of existing worship within the two denominations were remarkably similar. It was commonly felt that the so-called "Long Prayer" was excessively lengthy. As early as 1813, a Cotswold Baptist minister, T. Coles, protests that lengthy prayers are burdensome, "and where weariness begins, devotion ends."[7] He criticizes the tautology, and particularly the excessive didacticism, of Baptist prayers. Addressing himself to his brother ministers, he says: "Remember, also, you come to pray; not to preach; you address yourselves not unto men, but unto God who searcheth the heart."

The same protest was to be more vividly and cogently expressed by the Congregational novelist, William Hale White ("Mark Rutherford"):

"The first, or long prayer, as it was called, was a horrible hypocrisy, and it was a sore tax on the preacher to get through it. Anything more totally unlike the model recommended to us in the New Testament cannot well be imagined. It generally began

---

[6] *C. H. Spurgeon's Prayers* (5th edn., 1906) may be passionate and sincere, but they are too didactic, informal, diffuse, and disordered to count as great prayers.

[7] *Attention to Public Prayer*, the Circular Letter from the Ministers and Messenger of the Baptist Congregational Churches . . . assembled at Fairford, published Chipping Norton, 1813, p. 12.

with a confession that we were all sinners, but no individual sins were ever confessed, and then ensued a kind of dialogue with God, very much resembling the speeches which in later years I have heard in the House of Commons from the movers and seconders of addresses to the Crown at the opening of Parliament. In all the religion of that day nothing was falser than the long prayer. Direct appeal to God can only be justified when it is passionate. To come maundering into His presence when we have nothing particular to say is an insult, upon which we should never presume if we had a petition to offer to any earthly personage. We should not venture to take up his time with commonplaces or platitudes; but our minister seemed to consider that the Almighty, who had the universe to govern, had more leisure at His command than the idlest lounger at a club. Nobody ever listened to this performance."[8]

The very practical suggestion is made by the Reverend C. M. Birrell,[9] a Baptist minister, in 1845, that several short prayers should be substituted for the long or pastoral prayer, in different parts of the service: "one prayer, for example, might be occupied principally with adoration and praise; another with petitions founded on the subject brought to the attention of the assembly." The same learned author adduces St. John Chrysostom as the precedent for several brief prayers.

Two years earlier, a Congregational minister also gave evidence of the impact of the Tractarian Movement upon Dissent in a remarkable essay entitled, "Ministerial Qualification for Public Prayer."[10] He wishes public prayer to be more ardent and affecting and to that end suggests the frequent reading of devotional works. He even suggests that there should be published a series of volumes to be called "The Minister's Devotional Library," comprising "the choicest pieces gleaned from all ages of the Church, and from the whole of Christendom." Sounding the authentic Catholic and Ecumenical note, he insists that "for such an object we should not be afraid of passing over the boundary of Protestantism; and would obtain from Catholic sources, and from the early fathers, whatever would contribute to the treasury of devotional thought."[11]

This, it must be emphasized, is the deliberate judgment of a

8 *The Autobiography of Mark Rutherford*, Chap. 1.
9 "The Worshipping Church, or, Observations on the Manner of Public Worship." The Circular Letter of the Ministers and Messengers of the Lancashire and Cheshire Association of Baptist Churches assembled at Oldham, May 14 and 15, 1845, p. 6.
10 Article in *The Congregational Magazine*, 1843, p. 627 f.
11 *Ibid.*, p. 636.

Congregational minister writing within ten years of the foundation of the Oxford Movement. His list of liturgical *desiderata* includes: the Book of Common Prayer, the Presbyterian Directory of Worship, the Missal and Pontifical of the Church of Rome, King on the Greek Church; Chrysostom's Liturgy, Bingham's Chapters on the Services of the Early Church, the Devotions of Bishop Andrewes, Bishop Wilson's *Sacra Privata*, Jeremy Taylor's Prayers, and the Ancient Latin Hymns.[12] Though not yet prepared to suggest that Congregationalists should employ a liturgy, he recommends "the occasional writing of prayers." In the preparation of his pulpit prayers, the minister would be well advised to steep himself in the devotional classics of the Christian Church. These, he believes, will enrich extemporary prayer with profundity, comprehensiveness and sublimity in style and sentiment, as well as provide it with freshness, power, and beauty; "by such toil, and discipline and tears, the devotions of the sanctuary would become a most interesting and effective part of public worship."[13]

The writer's greatest perceptiveness, however, comes in the recognition that it is not the intellect but the imagination that has to be stirred to provide the passion of adoration, and he offers an analysis of how this need is met by the different denominations of Christians. The Roman Catholic Church supplies the basic need of the imagination through its splendid ceremonial, solemn music, and devotional sentiments. The Anglican Church in her Liturgy makes worship beautiful and impressive to multitudes whose piety is fed upon it. The Methodists are distinguished by a religious experience which is neither erudite nor speculative, nor is it remarkable for its dignified taste; it is rather the religion of the mass of the people, not of the calm temperament of its founder. "The feelings are warmed and gratified by the exciting services of that influential section of the Church. It is not in the pulpit, but in the prayer-meeting and the class-room, that its power chiefly resides. These are its scenes of fervid feeling, and of attractive sympathy; and from them its disciples come forth refreshed, strengthened, and happy."[14] By contrast, Congregational worship lives in the intellect rather than in the heart. Its sobriety and calm make it inevitably passionless. It is a type of worship for the sturdy intelligentsia, not for the multitudes who are unreflective, or trembling in spirit; nor indeed is it suitable even for those who feel deeply as well as reason profoundly.

12 *Ibid.*, pp. 636-37.   13 *Ibid.*   14 *Ibid.*

The same issue of *The Congregational Magazine* confirms the truth of the analysis in an article by Dr. Edward Payson, who charges that "our devotional performances are too often in the language of the understanding, rather than of the heart." Theoretically the prayers are extemporary, but actually they are made up almost entirely of Scripture passages and commonplace phrases transmitted from one generation of ministers to another, "so that we may more properly be said to *make a prayer* than to *pray.*"[15] He also feels that the general prayers want particularity and definiteness.

The languishing of the life of devotion in the Baptist and Congregational Churches in this period must be attributed in part to the over-emphasis on the importance of the sermon, so that the rest of the service was regarded as merely preparatory and even preliminary. Coles, the Baptist minister in Chipping Campden, noted that only his fellow ministers were to blame if too many of their church members thought it "enough to be present in the house of God by the commencement of the sermon."[16] There was too much truth in Charles Kingsley's gibe that "Dissenters go to chapel chiefly to hear sermons."[17] As late as 1867 the same complaint is heard from the lips of a Baptist pastor: "Do we not sometimes make prayer and praise, which should be of the first importance, incidental to our services, so that people are said to go to the house of God to hear the preacher?"[18] It is even possible that this represents on the part of the minister a sacerdotalism which is all the more powerful for being entirely unconscious.

The same anonymous writer argues that a union of voices as well as of hearts should offer prayer to God, and, in consequence, "Why may not the congregation take some audible part in public prayer, thus meeting in some measure the wishes of those who are ready to ask for a modified liturgy?"[19] Charles Stanford, a Baptist leader, felt it incumbent upon him to raise the question of how to improve Baptist public worship at the Annual Session of the Baptist Union in London in 1870.[20] He, too, excoriated its didacticism and its subjectivity: "It is a reproach frequently urged against the type of religious life supposed to prevail in our com-

[15] "Faults in Public Prayer"—an article in *ibid.*, pp. 484 f.
[16] T. Coles, *op.cit.*, 1813, p. 7.
[17] *The Good News of God*, p. 53.
[18] "On Things relating to Public Worship"—circular letter, published Cirencester, 1867.
[19] *Ibid.*
[20] "On Improvement in the Mode of Public Worship," London, 1870.

217

munion, that it is not sufficiently adorative; that it is too eager towards man, too careless towards God; that it thinks too much of subjective profit, and too little of Divine praise; that it makes us too apt to call ourselves hearers rather than worshippers."[21]

He does not think that a liturgy is a way out of these difficulties; he wants, not so much a prepared composition, as a prepared man. Positively, however, he suggests dividing the Long Prayer by a hymn, the regular use of the Lord's Prayer in divine worship, and, with the greatest diffidence, recommends "the occasional use of an old metrical creed, more especially the devout and stately *Te Deum*."[22] He also suggests the use of a lectionary so that the selection of lessons may not be purely arbitrary. But his policy, in his own words, is the desire for "re-*animation*, not re-*formation*."[23]

There is also general agreement that an improved posture in public prayer is necessary. One writer, who remains anonymous, deplores the common habit in Congregationalism of sitting during prayer: "we think that the habit of sitting during prayer,—so general in our places of worship,—indicates the absence of deep devotional feeling. Such a practice we consider indecorous and irrelevant."[24] The editor of the magazine to which the article had been contributed dissents from the generalization in a footnote, though admitting that many do sit. Another writer, however, supports the editor, and maintains that the most frequent posture for prayer among Congregationalists is in the standing one.[25] Birrell, the Baptist minister, pleads for kneeling in prayer as a suitable exterior indication of an inner obedience to God, and as a uniform posture in place of either sitting or standing.[26]

The debate was to continue throughout the century and it was generally believed that merely minor modifications of the Puritan tradition would bring an appreciable improvement in worship. Against this excessively utopian view, however, there were factors working in the other direction: the sheer dead weight of custom prevented the timorous from reformation; the fear of superstition became itself a superstition; the ignorance that prefers the easy, complacent, charismatic way; a lethargy about worship so long as the preaching remained vigorous; and the growing suspicion of

21 P. 8. 22 *Ibid.*, p. 13. 23 *Ibid.*
24 "On Ministerial Qualification for Public Prayer," *The Congregational Magazine*, 1843, p. 627.
25 *Ibid.*, p. 731.
26 *The Worshipping Church, or, Observations on the Manner of Public Worship*, pp. 5-6.

the liturgical revolution attempted by the High-Churchmen of the Oxford Movement, all played their part.

On the other hand, it would be to do a gross injustice to the worship of nineteenth century English Dissent to imply that all the practitioners of free prayer were complacent charismatics or windy tautologists. Since the Baptists were more fervent protagonists of the excellence of extemporary prayer during this century than the Congregationalists, it is only fair to their reputation to point out that at least one of their ministers, the unhappily named S. A. Tipple of South Norwood, could prepare prayers of the most felicitous diction, in which there are occasionally flashes of the pure diamond of poetry. They set the thought of God in the vastness of His universe, and combine with a sense of wonder a pity for man's misery and temptations, and a conviction of the reality of his aspirations and his victories. Too lengthy, abounding in too many quests and too few discoveries, they yet have the occasional concise phrase, happy image, or pictorial epithet, and the true insight of the mystic.

Two examples of his prayers may be cited: the first on the purpose of prayer, and the second on the power to see God in all events. The first reads: "Lord, restore and revive us with moments of prayer, of going forth from the dust and din of the actual to the calmness of the ideal in uplands of holy contemplation. Bring us to those heights where we are humbled for due enlargement, where we are chastened and cleansed with the vision of our faults and errors, where our souls become ours in being subdued to Thine, and we see the transient in the light of the everlasting, Nature and man and the world in the light of the throne of God."[27]

The second prayer reads thus:

"Lord of all, since all happenings may be gates of divine access to us, if we will but allow Thy coming, come to us in storms no less than in calms, in demons that harry us no less than in angels that soothe, that all of whatever kind may be to us for wisdom and righteousness, for sanctification and redemption . . .

"Lord of all, let us not deem Thee absent from any part of the universe, or from anything we suffer, lest we lose the use and service of it, or from any error we assail, lest we lose the little germ of truth it may enfold. Help us to find Thee in every temple,

[27] Tipple wrote *Sunday Mornings at Norwood* in 1883, as an anthology of his sermons with appropriate prayers. In 1912 he produced *Spoken Words of Prayer and Praise*. The first citation is from the latter, p. 27.

however pagan, in every creed, however false or defective, in the Arab sheikh as in the Hebrew patriarch, in the lore of the Greek as in the conscience of the Jew."[28]

These are not great prayers, but they are important in indicating how one Baptist minister, though refusing to use a liturgical type of service, gave his prayers as much preparation as his sermons.

There were also Congregational ministers who excelled in the gift of free prayer. One of the old stalwarts was the Reverend John Angell James, the distinguished predecessor of Dr. R. W. Dale in Birmingham. An account of his poignant prayers for particular mourners at the funeral of the Reverend John Ely of Leeds is reported by a minister of the Methodist New Connexion who was present:

". . . and the Rev. J. A. James offered a prayer the most touching I have *ever heard*. He first expressed how sorrowful they all felt to meet on so sad an occasion, but thankful it was not to mourn over a lost reputation . . . 'What has the West Riding done' he said, 'oh God, that Thy hand should have fallen so heavily upon it? Sanctify the event, oh God, to the good of all. Make it a warning and a blessing to this congregation, to this Church, and his brethren in the ministry.'

"The feeling in the congregation has now become very excited. He now went on to pray for the aged and pious mother who sat at the feet of her beloved son, who had long been expecting to hear a sweet voice from heaven saying, 'Come away to the skies.' Next he prayed for the brother, who, I believe, was a doctor in the West of England. Next he tenderly asked God to sustain and comfort the widow, till she and her sainted husband should meet again. Then oh, how touchingly, he begged God's fatherly care, guidance, protection, and blessing for the now fatherless child."[29]

For those who read this account in cold print over a century after the event took place, and who cannot hear the low, urgent pleading of the minister's voice, much of the effect will be lost; but even they must surely recognize that no written prayer with its generalities could pierce the heart like these deeply personal and particular lamentations. The real difficulty about Dissenting free prayer was not that its aims were too low, but that they were too high. They presupposed that every gathering of the community of Christ would be a Pentecost, directed by the Holy Spirit; but where

[28] S. A. Tipple, *op.cit.*, pp. 224-25.
[29] From a record of 1847 included in John Waddington, *Congregational History: 1800-1850*, p. 594.

the Holy Spirit was impeded by the dullness, lack of preparation, and spiritual deadness of the minister, the experience was a tragic disappointment. The pioneers of liturgical forms in the English Free Churches were determined that the disappointments should be fewer.

2. The Earliest Pioneers in Liturgical Forms

The great names in this field were, of course, Thomas Binney and John Hunter, who will receive detailed consideration, but they did not break the ice of Nonconformity's congealed adherence to extemporary prayers. The anonymous authors of *A New Directory* in 1812 were the first in the century to insist that free prayers should be supplemented with written forms. Until this momentous step had been proposed and taken, the way would not be open for the provision of a Free Church liturgy. This volume, then, is as significant in the history of Dissenting worship as the decision of Isaac Watts to make the transition from a free paraphrase of the Psalms to hymns of Christian faith and experience.

One of the earliest, if not the earliest, Congregational liturgy was compiled by the Reverend Mr. Thomas, minister of Stockwell Congregational Chapel, with the title of *The Biblical Liturgy*.[30] It consists of twenty orders of worship, each illustrating one facet of Christian truth, and all consisting entirely of Scripture. The form of each order comprises: the statement of the truth selected, illustrations of different aspects of it, devout meditations upon it, a prayer, a hymn, the Lord's Prayer, and a doxology. It is a pre-composed form of worship, but not strictly a liturgy, since the words are to be read by the minister in their entirety. It is defective not only in the lack of responsive sections but also in its excessive didacticism. It can never be right to restrict the prayers of the worshippers to one theme; yet it at least avoided the besetting weakness of extemporary prayer, its disorder and diffuseness.

In the 1860's Newman Hall, the minister of Christ Church, Westminster-Bridge Road Church, London, took courage in both hands and produced his *Free Church Service Book* of which the fourth edition appeared in 1867. Two years later there appeared anonymously another Congregational liturgy of similar composition, entitled *A Form of Morning and Evening Services for the*

---

[30] It was produced prior to 1856 since it is referred to on pp. xix and xx of Binney's preface to Charles W. Baird's *A Chapter of Liturgies: Historical Sketches*.

Use of Free Churches.[31] Although it was published in London and Manchester, it was first used in the Congregational Church at Cheetham Hill in the latter city. If *The Biblical Liturgy* was excessively cautious in its refusal to depart from the very words of Scripture, the two subsequent attempts at liturgy erred on the side of a slavish dependence upon the Book of Common Prayer, of which they were all too patently mere anthologies. Their importance was that, after a break of two centuries, they laid claim to the devotional heritage of the Christian centuries as they were mediated by the Anglican Prayer Book.

Similar compilations continued to be produced to the end of the century,[32] of which one notable example was another Anglican imitation named *Devotional Services for use in Mill Hill School Chapel* (1895). Though it is not strictly within the scope of the present chapter, it might be mentioned that the most creative early attempt to produce a liturgy in which the new wine was poured into the old liturgical wine-skins was a Unitarian compilation by Sadler and Martineau, *Common Prayer for Christian Worship* (1861). All these early attempts at a liturgy for the Free Churches made possible the finest liturgy of all, John Hunter's *Devotional Services for Public Worship* (1886). Dr. F. B. Meyer appears to be the only Baptist minister of distinction who was prepared to experiment with liturgical forms during this century.[33]

3. *Thomas Binney*

If Hunter was Congregationalism's greatest liturgist in the nineteenth century, Thomas Binney was its greatest early exponent of the theory of worship. It was greatly to his advantage that his liturgical views could hardly be accused of emanating from Canterbury, so confirmed a believer was he in the disestablishment of

---

[31] It abbreviated the Prayer Book services, included the Litany as part of Evening Prayer, and allowed a place for free prayers in each order of worship.

[32] Another interesting example is that arranged by C. Silvester Horne and T. Herbert Darlow entitled "Let Us Pray": *a Handbook of selected Collects and Forms of Prayer for the use of Free Churches.* Its vigorous preface includes the statement that "there is a subtle irony in the situation that the element in her [the Church of England's] services most generally rejected by Free Churchmen should be the unpriestly and congregational element of common prayer," p. 4. I owe this reference to the courtesy of the Reverend Robert H. Smith, Minister of Bebington Congregational Church, Cheshire.

[33] However, H. W. Stembridge, Baptist minister of Hatch Beauchamp produced *A Ritual of Marriage and Burial Services designed for the use of Dissenting Ministers.* It is an abridgement of the Prayer Book offices.

religion.[34] In three respects Binney was a pioneer: he changed the face of preaching, prayer, and praise in Congregationalism. Until his time Nonconformity was under a double disadvantage: it was so conscious of the dangers of Anglicanism (to which, indeed, its Puritan predecessors of 1662 owed their ejection from the National Church) as to forget the qualities of its worship, so that Dissenting worship was excessively bleak and bare; furthermore, it so glorified the duty of preaching that "the worship of prayer and praise had degenerated into mere introductory exercises of a preaching service."[35]

Binney's contributions were made in theory and practice. He edited and published in England a notable American work on liturgies by Dr. Charles Baird of New York, a Presbyterian minister of New York City, who recalled the Reformed Churches, now the proponents of free prayer, to their earlier heritage of liturgies. Binney wrote an important introduction to the work, and a most relevant appendix, entitled "Touching the Question, 'Are Dissenters to have a liturgy?'" His approach may be conveniently set forth in summary fashion in his own words. Maintaining that numerous publications and current discussions "indicate dissatisfaction with the state of worship amongst us—worship properly so-called; they show a yearning for something deeper and richer than we have, deeper devotion and richer song; something, too, in which the people shall take a prominent and active part, not in psalmody only, but in supplication; in which they shall be called vocally to utter some portions of the Church's *common prayer*, so that by audible repetitions and appropriate response, they shall feel that they positively *do* pray, as well as listen to another praying. . . . It may induce Presbyterian and Nonconformist ministers to pay more attention than many of them have hitherto done to the *worship* of the Church; to cultivate, if I may say so, devotional taste; to use in prayer modes of speech, and even tones and gestures more simple, natural, becoming and devout; in speaking to 'the Father' to speak more from the heart than from the head; to be more

---

[34] It is unfortunate that no full-length biography of Binney exists, since he was undoubtedly the most distinguished London Congregational minister of his day, the founder of the Colonial Missionary Society, twice elected the Chairman of the Congregational Union of England and Wales, an inspired hymn-writer, and a man who changed the style of preaching and worship in Dissent. An important short biographical sketch of him appears in *Sermons Preached in the King's Weigh House Chapel, London, 1829-1869 by T. Binney, LL.D.*, edited by Henry Allon, D.D.

[35] Allon's introduction, *op.cit.*, p. xl.

religious and less theological; to think more of the wants that are to be made known to God, than of points and systems which are to be taught to men. And, in addition to these things, to encourage, for the joy and solace of the Church, as means alike of edification and grace, better and higher forms of praise than those with which many have hitherto been content. The people, too, may be led . . . to a deeper sense of the solemnity of worship than is often felt, and to a more becoming behaviour in the House of God than is sometimes seen; to more reverence, great stillness, less noise, more punctuality, everything, in short, that shall make it manifest that they come themselves to engage in the Service; . . ."[36]

Aware, as Binney is, of the earlier liturgical traditions of the Reformed Churches, and conscious of the help of a partial dependence upon liturgical forms, he is "strongly against the principle of *confining* worship to the provisions of a strictly imposed ritual, a thing admitting of no variation, and forbidding free prayer."

Binney's advocacy of the combination of liturgical forms with free prayers was strengthened by the undoubted fact that he was greatly gifted in the exercise of spontaneous prayer. He had a style fecund in images, a mind that identified itself with the varied needs of mankind in their sin and sorrow and their doubt and struggles, and the pathos and sincerity of his prayers made many attend his church for the devotion rather than for the doctrine.[37] Moreover, no man knew better than he that both free prayer and forms of prayer were as insubstantial as shadows unless they were used by men who had assiduously cultivated the discipline of the spiritual life. This, indeed, was the burden of his great sermon addressed to his fellow ministers of the Congregational Union in *The Closet and the Church* (1849). It was characteristic of his wisdom that he felt that both free prayer and liturgical forms had their own right to exist within the framework of the same service. He believed that ample provision should be made in each service of worship for the expression in free prayer of the individual and immediate necessities of members of his congregation whose inmost thoughts, fears, and temptations he knew by pastoral visitation; he

---

[36] Binney's preface to C. W. Baird's *A Chapter on Liturgies*, pp. xxv-xxvi.

[37] E. Paxton Hood in an excessively anecdotal and homiletical account of Binney, *Thomas Binney, His Mind, Life and Opinions*, records two impressions of his public prayers. "I think one of the finest estimates I ever heard of Mr. Binney was in the impression I heard of him as produced upon an intelligent hearer, that 'he was a devotional man talking intelligently'" (p. 159). "I believe before he made a great impression as a preacher, his prayers in public took people by surprise." (*ibid.*) Cf. Allon, *op.cit.*, p. xliv.

was also convinced that a place ought to be found in the same diet of worship for the liturgical expression of the common and permanent religious needs of mankind.[38]

In the interesting appendix he contributed to Baird's *A Chapter on Liturgies*, he made some positive suggestions by which a liturgical modicum (no more) might be added to existing Dissenting worship. This would make provision for the responsive reading of the Psalms, a vocal confession of sins, the Lord's Prayer, and the recitation of the Apostles' Creed.[39] His modernity is shown in a strong preference for a distinctive dress for both minister and choir, and for the kneeling posture in prayer, as well as for the provision of a prayer-desk, so that the minister need not pray from the pulpit and thus less easily fall prey to the temptation to preach in his prayers. "I confess," he writes, "I don't like to see a man go into a pulpit as an auctioneer goes into his rostrum, or as a lecturer ascends his platform, and comes before an audience. But Dissenters have no idea of a congregation being anything else *but* an audience. Hearing with them is everything. In fact, they have very little else to do."[40]

In sum, Binney believed that worship was the offering of the Church, not of the minister alone, and that this required the use of some liturgical forms to express the common needs and faith of Christians and of some free prayers to channel the peculiar wants of the particular congregation. His whole aim was so to prepare the worship of his services that, without undervaluing preaching, the congregation "would as much regret the loss of the worship, as of any sermon however eloquent, or even spiritual."[41]

Binney's contribution to the development of praise in English Dissenting worship was not less significant than his recommendation of the partial use of liturgical forms of prayer. It is scarcely possible to imagine how dreary was the incessant metrical psalmody in Dissent. E. P. Hood says of the bad old days that "Old Walker and the pitch-pipe were the sons of Korah in our services; indeed, it is a very curious priesthood of melody to look back upon —that which officiated with fife and fiddle, giving such effect as we may suppose to most of the services of our temple."[42] In those days, "inasmuch as Romanism had made beautiful things to be an

38 Ed. Henry Allon, *op.cit.*, pp. xliv-xlv.
39 Appendix to C. W. Baird, *op.cit.*, pp. 320 f.
40 *Ibid.*, p. 291.
41 Binney's preface to C. W. Baird, *op.cit.*, p. xxvi.
42 *Thomas Binney: His Mind, Life and Opinions* . . . , p. 167.

abomination in religious service, it was thought that a barn-like architecture, and a music where all chords were only used for discordance, were most fitted for the production of Divine impressions."[43]

Allon describes the situation when Binney commenced his ministry, in 1823, in less flamboyant but equally grave terms: "There was probably not a Nonconformist congregation in the kingdom who would not have deemed it almost a compromise of principle to sing the rhythmical Psalms of the Old Testament. Within the Established Church, Tate and Brady, and without it, Dr. Watts, must render these into iambic verses before it was lawful to sing them."[44] Binney made his revolutionary views known in the celebrated lectures which he gave to the congregation of the King's Weigh-House Church, and he presented these in summary form in his famous sermon, *The Service of Song in the House of the Lord*.

His greatest single achievement in praise was to introduce into Dissenting worship the singing or chanting of the Psalms and Canticles. Though not himself a musician, he sought the advice of experts in preparing a new book of psalmody, and he was joined in this task by Dr. William Cooke, a deacon of his church, and by Dr. Lowell Mason of New York. Binney was not a small-minded man; he was, unlike so many Dissenters of his age, prepared to recognize the dignity and beauty of Anglican worship. In reference to Binney's attitude towards the Church of England's worship, Stoughton rightly declares that "he had a taste for its architecture, for its liturgy (with amendments), and for its music."[45]

The quality of his devotional sentiment and its expression can be grasped in the first three verses of his great hymn, "Eternal Light":

Eternal Light! Eternal Light!
How pure the soul must be,
When, placed within Thy searching sight,
It shrinks not, but with calm delight,
Can live and look on Thee.

The spirits that surround Thy throne
May bear the burning bliss;
But that is surely theirs alone,
Since they have never, never known
A fallen world like this.

[43] *Ibid.*, p. 159.   [44] Ed. Henry Allon, *op.cit.*, pp. xxxix and xl.
[45] Ed. John Stoughton, *A Memorial of the late Rev. Thomas Binney, LL.D.*, (2nd edn., 1874), pp. 122-23.

O how shall I, whose native sphere
Is dark, whose mind is dim,
Before the Ineffable appear,
And on my naked spirit bear
The uncreated beam?[46]

This sense of the transcendent majesty of God, which only makes more marvellous His amazing mercy to our race of rebels, underlies and motivates Binney's life-long dedication to the task of bringing back the dimension of reverence into Dissenting worship, and makes it reasonable to link his name with that of the other great pioneer of Congregational worship, Isaac Watts.[47]

Unlike so many liturgiologists, Binney avoided the Scylla of an exclusive dependence upon liturgy and the Charybdis of a depreciation of preaching. Indeed, he was a pioneer in the modern mode of preaching, which is practical and colloquial, rather than theological and rhetorical. Here, again, to understand the revolution that he began, we must know what preceded him. The Georgian sermon was "Johnsonese without Johnson's vigour and point."[48] Far from avoiding the obvious, the Georgian ministers seemed to cut across country in search of it. Samuel Palmer (1741-1813), the editor of *The Nonconformists' Memorial*, preached, as everyone in his century did, on Tillotson's favourite text, "For His commandments are not grievous." Palmer commends the commandments because they are not unreasonable, not impracticable, not dishonourable, not dangerous, not unpleasant, nor are they unprofitable.[49] One sympathizes with Principal Caird's judgment that Georgian sermons were constructed expressly to ensure that human beings would not listen to them!

Binney's theology could not be fitted into the Procrustean bed of the older Calvinism and its double predestination; in fact, he rejected speculative doctrine altogether. His preaching was concrete in form, and rarely argumentative. It was essentially "a ministry of divine things to human necessities."[50] It was the application of the Gospel of God to the great variety of human needs: to men in their ignorance and temptation, their struggles and fears, their sorrows and sins, their joys and hopes. (Its closest eighteenth century parallel is Doddridge's *The Rise and Progress of Religion*

[46] *Congregational Praise*, No. 21.   [47] *Ibid.*, p. 32.
[48] John Brown, *Puritan Preaching in England*, p. 205.
[49] *Ibid.*, pp. 205-06.
[50] Ed. Henry Allon, *op.cit.*, p. lv.

227

in the Soul.) His own practice is shown in the advice he gave in a lecture to Divinity students: "As you walk through the streets, having prayed in the study, keep your eyes open there. Look at the things, prices and people, how they buy and how they sell, the sellers and the purchasers, the hours of labour and the hours of rest. Try to look at all; try to know the whole tariff of trade, and do not be afraid to find in it matter for your sermons. You are to be teachers—try to commend yourselves to every man's conscience in the sight of God. Know the world's thoughts and the world's ways, that you may be the world's masters and ministers."[51]

Like a famous earlier Puritan, Binney did not counsel "a fugitive and cloistered virtue." He sallied forth into the world that he might commend the good news to men, not as discarnate souls, but in the warp and woof of their commercial and industrial contexts, as workers and citizens.

If his thought was concrete, so was his style. He disliked the rhetoric of the older manner of preaching which moved from stately paragraphs to a florid peroration like a procession and which shouted in denunciation and whispered in pathos and pleading. He preached quietly and in colloquial speech, spiced with wit, and illustrated from practical observation and experience. This, it must be emphasized, was a radical change from the religious platitudes of the Established Church and the desiccated theological expositions of the Nonconformist pulpit of his day. His sermons, planned but never written out in full, were, above all, like inspired conversation. In manner and matter they were modern. One may consider, for example, the witty way in which he took leave of his first congregation at Newport, in the Isle of Wight: "I cannot but know that some of my impressions with reference to the final awards of a future state have been a great trouble and grief to some of you; well, now I am leaving you, I have done with you, and you will be able to have it your own way; and all that I have to say is, that those of you who *want* to have everlasting punishment may *have* everlasting punishment."[52]

Another modern trait is his gift for choosing a striking text for a topical sermon.[53] Preaching on honesty, he embroidered the incident of a banker, reputed to be pious, who had been tried and convicted of fraudulence at the Central Criminal Court, and his arresting text was: "The hand of him that betrayeth me is with me

[51] John Brown, *op.cit.*, pp. 213-14.
[52] E. P. Hood, *op.cit.*, p. 6.
[53] John Stoughton, *op.cit.*, pp. 34-35.

on the table."[54] He preached on the Divine justice, exemplifying it in the notorious case of an assassin who had been apprehended in America after his flight across the Atlantic and was brought back to England to be tried and condemned; on this occasion Binney's text was: "No doubt this man was a murderer, whom, though he hath escaped the sea, yet vengeance suffereth not to live."[55] In liturgy, praise, and preaching Thomas Binney was a trail-blazer, and theological students flocked to hear him and imitated him when they were called to their own churches as ministers.

4. John Hunter

John Hunter (1848-1917) was not as colourful a personality as Binney, but Congregationalism and the Free Churches generally are greatly in his debt as a liturgist.[56] Only James Martineau, among Nonconformists, is worthy to be compared to him as a writer of prayers that are shaped in the traditional moulds of the collect and the litany, but are also the expressions of the religious and social demands of the nineteenth century. Hunter's theory and practice of worship are concentrated in three publications: *Devotional Services for Public Worship*[57] (first edition, 1882); *Hymns of Faith and Hope* (first edition, 1889); and the treatise, *A Worshipful Church* (1903). Since the second of these volumes is not to be considered, it is only just to recognize that Hunter, like Binney, was a religious poet. A sublime short hymn can reveal to us the beating heart of Hunter's devotional concern:

> Dear Master, in whose life I see
> All that I would, but fail to be,
> Let Thy clear light for ever shine
> To shame and guide this life of mine.
>
> Though what I dream and what I do
> In my weak days are always two,
> Help me oppressed by things undone,
> O Thou, whose deeds and dreams are one.[58]

---

[54] Luke 22:21.   [55] Acts of the Apostles 22:20.

[56] An admirable biography of Hunter exists, written by his son, the present Bishop of Sheffield: Leslie S. Hunter, *John Hunter, D.D., A Life*. John Hunter was minister of the following Congregational churches: York (1871-1882); Hull (1882-1886); Trinity, Glasgow (1887-1901 and 1904-1911); and King's Weigh-House, London (1901-1904).

[57] The first edition of 1882 contained 28 pages; the edition of 1901, which represents the final form, contained 327 pages.

[58] No. 462 in *Congregational Praise*.

This has been described by an eminent contemporary hymnologist as "a perfect example of the Christian lyric-epigram."[59]

Hunter shared Binney's conviction that "the ideal of public worship is the union in one service of free and liturgical prayer."[60] For this reason he did not propose that his *Devotional Services* should establish a fixed form of worship, but its purpose was "rather to afford the means of variety in public prayer, and to save it from becoming a one-man utterance, and not a general and congregational worship."[61] His advance on Binney was two-fold: he provided several new liturgical expressions of worship for the Free Churches, and he set his prayers firmly within the commercial and industrial context of nineteenth century society. The emphasis of many of his prayers is not unlike that of the great American exponent of the "Social Gospel," Walter Rauschenbusch, in the latter's *For God and The People: Prayers of the Social Awakening* (1910).

Hunter's great gift was that he combined with the newer theological emphasis on the social implications of the Gospel, a mastery of the traditional Christian faith and of its hallowed liturgical forms of expression. The mystic was also the crusader for social justice. On the one hand, the mystic is inspired by the Communion of Saints and writes as a traditionalist: "Almighty and everlasting God, in communion with Thy saints in all ages, with patriarchs and prophets, apostles and martyrs, with our beloved dead who have fallen asleep in Thy peace; we, who are striving to do and bear Thy blessed will on earth, adore Thee and offer to Thee our praises and supplications."[62]

On the other hand, the social reformer could pen these incisive and prophetic words of prayer: "From all inordinate cares and ambitions; from maxims of cunning and greed; from the godless pursuit of pleasure and gain; from wronging the poor and from envying and flattering the rich; from keeping back the price of labour and from rendering eye-service; Good Lord, deliver us."[63]

What is it that makes Hunter's *Devotional Services* so outstanding? It is not merely that it is the first dignified Congregational liturgy in English, nor even that its language is as aspiring as it is chaste, nor even again that the people are given their responsive rights in worship. The secret of its success does not even lie in the

---

[59] Erik Routley, *Hymns and Human Life*, p. 154.
[60] *Devotional Services*, preface.   [61] *Ibid.*
[62] Cited from the Fourth Order of Service in *Devotional Services*.
[63] *Ibid.*

princely ruthlessness with which he raids the devotional treasures of all branches of the Christian Church. It lies in the unusual combination of the traditional and the modern in Hunter. Stylistically he is a traditionalist, using the techniques of monumental concision in the collect, or of accumulating impact in the Litany form, and he is steeped in the thoughts and phraseology of our common Catholic heritage in worship. Equally he is a nineteenth century theologian, expressing the Divine immanentalism and the emphasis on the historic Jesus as mankind's greatest exemplar, and expounding the Kingdom of God as the realization of social justice in the political and industrial order.[64] His historicism saves him from being merely ephemeral, while his sense of the relevance of the Gospel to the variegated life of his own day delivers him from the liturgist's temptation to mere antiquarianism.

No English composer of forms of worship has ever expressed the "Social Gospel" with such compassion, incisiveness, and liturgical felicity. Worship was never, for Hunter, an escape from the agonies of contemporary life, nor the sanctification of the *status quo ante*. At one moment he is commending the dignity of honest labour:

MINISTER: For those that work with their own hands, that they may serve Thee in all things; and for those that buy and sell and get gain, that they may be rich toward God:

PEOPLE: We beseech Thee to hear us, O Lord.[65]

At another he remembers before God the inhumanity of man to man:

MINISTER: For our fretful sufferance of wrong; for the vindictive passions we have cherished; for our intolerance, injustice and uncharitableness; for our readiness to blame and our want of thoughtfulness, patience, kindness, and sympathy in our social relations:

PEOPLE: Have mercy upon us, O God.[66]

At yet another moment he recalls, like Amos, the fearful responsibilities of the rich:

MINISTER: For the rich and the great, that they may not be high-minded, nor trust in any outward prosperity, but only

---

[64] He was an admirer of the theology of F. D. Maurice.
[65] Taken from the Second Order of Service.
[66] Taken from the admirable Service of Confession.

231

in Thee, remembering that they are but stewards of Thy bounty, and that at last they shall be called to render their account:

PEOPLE: We beseech Thee to hear us, O Lord.[67]

In a phrase of his own composing, his aim is that "all work shall be worship," and every vocation worthy of the children of God. His sense of the great variety of human callings is admirably expressed in the Ninth Order of Service, in which he includes special intercessions for the Sovereign and the Royal Family, judges and magistrates, members of Parliament and local councillors, parents and children, men of wealth and poor men, physicians and nurses, all in need of compassion, our friends and our enemies.

Hunter had the true liturgist's gift for literary architectonic, for rhythmical and balanced phrasing, as in the opening of a prayer recalling the unity of the Church militant on earth with the Church triumphant in heaven: "O Lord God, the Life and Light of the faithful, the Strength and Hope of those who labour and suffer, the Everlasting Refuge and Rest of the dead; . . ."[68]

His imagination was dowered with a rich concreteness which makes his prayers vivid, as in the Prayer for Easter Sunday Evening: "We rejoice in His finished work, and in His victory over the world. The sword and the spear and the sceptre lie broken before His cross, and in His submission and humiliation we see the power of God and the wisdom of God."

Most of all, he had the liturgist's gift for the monumental and unforgettable phrase. Some of these phrases have become the prayer currency of the English Free Churches: "the sacred and tender ties that bind us to the unseen world"; "for the tasks and trials by which we are trained to patience"; "for the order and constancy of nature, for the beauty and bounty of the world"; "the secret and blessed fellowship of the Cross"; "the sweet and solemn hopes that cluster round the new-born"; "forgotten to us, but dear to Thee"; "Thine the light that shineth in the eyes of holy prophets"; "May wisdom and knowledge be the stability of our times"; and, perhaps, the profoundest of them all, "the strength to do and bear the blessed will of God."

His greatest single liturgical invention is the moving invitation to the Holy Communion. It is so admirable that it might almost be

[67] Taken from the Second Order of Service.
[68] From the Tenth Order of Service.

inserted as it stands before the Prayer of Humble Access in the Anglican Prayer Book. "Come to this sacred Table, not because you must, but because you may . . ." it begins, and it ends, "Come, not to express an opinion, but to seek a Presence and pray for a Spirit."

It is no filial exaggeration on behalf of the influence of his father's *Devotional Services* that Dr. Leslie Hunter makes, when he claims: "It has proved one of the most influential contributions . . . to pastoral theology in the non-episcopal churches. Ministers who would dislike to read or to be seen to read prayers from a book in their pulpits, have sought inspiration and suggestion from its pages; many men, too, who have made little use of it in the ordinary services of the Church, have made regular use of its special orders of services . . . and the occasional prayers which it contains."[69]

In attempting to evaluate Hunter's contribution to the practice of worship, one must not forget the immensity of his task in attempting, as it were, to compete with the Book of Common Prayer. His gifts lie in parallelisms and antitheses of phrases, in the occasional phrase that stabs the conscience awake, in the wedding of ancient prayer form and modern language, and in the wide range of interests expressed. This mystic was also gifted with sufficient realism to be relevant as can be seen in the inclusion of "A Prayer for the Doubting" and "A Prayer in a time of Religious Declension." Nonetheless, there are weaknesses in his *Devotional Services*. There is the occasional reference to God in the third person, when He should be directly addressed in prayer. There is an associated weakness—the tendency to didacticism, as in the following phrases from a prayer in the Burial Service: "We learn by living. Thou art training us by labour, quickening us through trial. . . ." Even his Collects are too loose in form and their continuity and concision is broken. Sometimes, too, he takes the liberty of altering masterpieces, and this is inevitably for the worse, as when, in the interests of intelligibility, he rewrites the Anglican Collect beginning "Prevent us, O Lord," so that it becomes the much weaker "Direct us, O Lord. . . ." On the whole, however, these are spots on the sun. It is arguable that Hunter's *Devotional Services* has raised the standards of the worship of the English Free Churches more than any other book, with the single exception of Wesley's *A Collection of Hymns for the use of the People called Methodists*.

His chief contribution to the theory of worship was set forth in

69 Leslie S. Hunter, *John Hunter, D.D., A Life*, pp. 211 f.

his treatise, *A Worshipful Church* (1903). Hunter was unusual in his century in thinking that the best test of the worth of a Church to humanity was neither its humanitarian zeal nor its helpful teaching, but its worship, which should inspire and hallow all life. The adoration of God was man's chief privilege, and Christianity's distinctive contribution to the worship of mankind was "the filial idea and the filial spirit."[70] He conceived that the Protestant reaction against form and symbolism had gone too far, both because it had robbed public worship for many generations of helpful and lovely prayers and because it had made the intellectual element suffocate the aesthetic. In consequence, the Puritan Churches all alike suffered from "poverty and prosaic stupor of the imagination both in their teaching and ritual."[71] Citing Bacon's remark to the effect that there is a superstition against superstition, he wrote trenchantly: "It is time the Free Churches of England had outgrown their fear of everything Roman or Anglican. The darkness is not all in one place, nor the light."[72] The Free Churches of England ought to have the best ritual of worship, and "it is part of our Christian liberty to rise superior to tradition and custom, even to our own tradition and customs."[73]

In a remarkable defence of Christian symbolism, Hunter reminded his readers that the mind may be addressed through the eye as well as through the ear. He argued that the Nonconformist fathers who would not add the silent parables, allegories, and Biblical characters of stained-glass windows, mural decorations and statuary to the exhortations of the living preacher, yet "had their own undivine decorations, and were not slow in erecting marble slabs to the honour and glory of departed pastors and elders."[74] He maintained that the abuse of a symbol is not sufficient reason for its abandonment; otherwise, the Sacrament and the Bible itself would have to be relinquished. "Without a parable or picture Jesus spake not to His disciples, and without a universe of symbols or pictures God is still unknown and unknowable."[75]

He wished to distinguish the two functions of the minister as a representative of the people pleading their cause before God, and as a representative of God proclaiming His Word to the congregation. In the first capacity the minister should pray from a prayer-desk, for "when leading in prayer he ought to be near the people and almost on their level—as becometh a fellow-worshipper."[76]

---

[70] *The Worshipful Church*, p. 6.   [71] *Ibid.*, p. 14.   [72] *Ibid.*, p. 15.
[73] *Ibid.*, p. 17.   [74] *Ibid.*, p. 28.   [75] *Ibid.*, p. 30.   [76] *Ibid.*, p. 31.

The pulpit should be kept exclusively for preaching, and the lessons should be read from a lectern. The Communion Table, he believed, should be central. Hunter also approved of suitable ministerial dress, remarking that "it is a good sign that the black gown is coming back into use in the Free Churches of England. A secular dress in reading-desk and pulpit detracts from the dignity of worship, and to the eye of many it gives a common, if not contemptible, aspect to our religious ritual."[77]

Hunter had important caveats to utter against hymns and church music. Hymns were, in his mind, of outstanding importance as the shapers of popular belief, and he believed that they would outlast the creeds. For this reason it was essential to avoid hymns that were unreal, exaggerated, artificial, sensuous, or morbid in their sentiments, or those written to express scholastic or sectarian interpretations of the Christian faith and life. "The hymns most suitable for common worship," he wrote, "are those which give expression to the fundamental experiences and persuasions of the religious soul. . . ."[78] Holding that there was no basic antagonism between choral and congregational singing, he yet felt that many churches in his own day had gone music-mad and that congregations were in more danger of being "choir-ridden than priest-ridden." Consequently, "everything has to be jealously guarded that has a tendency to foster the fatal notion of substitution in worship, or the idea that the people are spectators or hearers of worship, and not the worshippers."[79]

Hunter was also a pioneer in claiming the use of the Christian Year for the Free Churches. Soon after he went to Scotland he began to observe in Trinity Congregational Church, Glasgow, the festivals of the Christian Year and the seasons of Advent and Lent. In 1890 he held daily services in Holy Week. In his first year in Glasgow, 1887, his church was "one of the few, if not the only non-episcopal church, where Christmas Day and Good Friday and All Saints' Day were observed."[80] In *The Worshipful Church*, he insists that the Christian Year belongs to the whole of Christendom and claims it for his own denomination. It has, to his way of thinking, a double value: first, as giving a centre to the teaching and life

---

77 *Ibid.*, pp. 40-41. From about 1890 onwards his son informs us that Dr. Hunter, who had hitherto been studiously anti-clerical in dress, wearing a white shirt, gold studs, a black necktie, a silk hat, frockcoat and waistcoat, always wore a gown, cassock and bands. Cf. Leslie Hunter, *op.cit.*, pp. 66-67.

78 *Ibid.*, p. 43.

79 *Ibid.*, p. 44.

80 *Ibid.*, p. 93.

of Christ, and, second, as providing an opportunity for the systematic discipline and culture of the devout life.[81]

The sermon he values highly as the "Sacrament of the Word." He finds three types of sermon current in his own day. One is the apologetical or explanatory sermon, of which he remarks that "it is the fate, not the fault, of the modern pulpit that it has so much explanatory and controversial work." The second type of discourse he excoriates as "the vulgarity of sensational preaching." He dislikes stunts and excessively topical themes, but he is interested in the correlation of religion and culture in the sermons of Dr. George Macdonald, who used the poems and plays of Shakespeare, Dante, Burns, Wordsworth, and Tennyson for religious object-lessons. His preference is for the third type of sermon: that expressing a genuine spiritual authority based upon experimental and practical mastery of the secrets of the life hid with Christ in God.[82]

His chief importance in this treatise, however, is his insistence that the fullest diet of worship should combine forms of prayer, free prayer and silent prayer. He argues that in his own exciting and noisy world, the need for silent prayer is greater than it has ever been, and maintains that "in silent, quiet waiting and communion the holiest and deepest aspirations of the soul may find expression."[83] In his judgment liturgical and free prayer have each earned the right to exist, and he insists that they should exist side by side. "Opportunity ought to be given in every service for the introduction of free prayer when the minister is moved thereto; but it is good that the larger part of the prayers should be before the eyes and in the hands of the people, that they may be able directly to participate in the worship, and that their worship may be saved from the unregulated and unchastened individualism of one man."[84]

Few men, in his view, are qualified to lead in the freer type of prayer and even they are not always at their best; moreover, these spontaneous expressions of prayer rarely meet the common needs and circumstances of the people. Furthermore, free prayers mean that the worshippers are hearing prayers, rather than praying themselves. Yet he could not believe that modern worshippers should be tied down to the ancient expressions of piety as in the

[81] *Ibid.*, p. 63.

[82] *A Worshipful Church*, p. 46. It is worth noting that Hunter was a superb preacher. Principal P. T. Forsyth, a close friend, called him "the greatest master we had of manuscript preaching." Leslie Hunter, *op.cit.*, p. 175. There is no more truth in his case than in Binney's in the common charge that it is only those who cannot preach who are liturgically-minded.

[83] *A Worshipful Church*, p. 51.   [84] *Ibid.*, p. 52.

Roman Breviary and Missal or in the Anglican Prayer-Book. The admirable balance of his mind is revealed in the following statement: "There is something vastly better than either the Puritan or Episcopalian order of worship, and that is an order that blends the truth and good of both orders. The ideal of public worship is the union in one service of free and liturgical prayer, I like form, but I like freedom also. The present has its claims as well as the past, and it is not so poor and barren that it cannot supply any more of the material out of which the ancient liturgies were formed. I am unwilling to believe that liturgies saturated with mediaevalism are the only ones which our religion can produce. . . . The fatal risk of insincerity is incurred in worship when words because of dear and venerable associations are becoming more and more sacred to us than ideas."[85]

Hunter's vast influence on the theory and practice of Free Church worship can be seen in the single fact that the non-liturgical Churches bought up ten editions of his liturgical compilation *Devotional Services* between 1882 and 1920, and the volume is still in print.[86] Recalling that Binney, Hunter, and W. E. Orchard (author of *Divine Service*) were all ministers of the King's Weigh-House Congregational Church in the West End of London, one is tempted to conclude that this church was the most significant liturgical laboratory of the English Free Churches in the nineteenth and twentieth centuries.

5. The Sacraments

The Baptists, as might be expected, laid a heavier emphasis than the Congregationalists upon the Sacrament of initiation, which they restricted to believers, as contrasted with the more frequent paedo-baptism practised by the Congregationalists. As the century developed, however, the Baptists felt some need for a place in their public worship in which the rights of children within the Christian community could be recognized. In the first two decades of the century it was common for infants to be brought to the Baptist churches for the ministers to give them a Christian "name." For example, the Register Book of the Baptist Church at Capel-y-ffin

[85] *Ibid.*, pp. 52-53.
[86] He founded in 1893 and was for many years the secretary of The Congregational Church Service Society, the aims of which were: "to promote the regular and systematic culture of the devout life, the revival of worship and reverent observance of Christian ordinances in families and congregations of Christ's Church." Leslie Hunter, *op.cit.*, p. 92.

in Breconshire, Wales, records the following items: "William and Daniel and Mary and Sarah. The two sons and two daughters of Wm. Jones by Sarah his wife were named (as above) before many witnesses 6th of January 1812." "John the son of John Nichols by Blanche Williams his intended wife was Named before witnesses. Feb. 19, 1813."[87]

In some churches this was felt to be insufficient, for we learn that in the General Baptist Church at Outwood near Shepphards, on the borders of Surrey and Sussex, the records of the church read: "It is agreed that if any person shall bring or apply to the Church to dedicate a Child to the Lord, that it be adopted, according to Christ receiving Children, but to use no name."[88]

This custom of the dedication of infants in Baptist churches could claim a mid-eighteenth century precedent, for it was employed by the "Barton Preachers"—a group of evangelical Christians in Leicestershire which had adopted the Baptist way in 1755. Their practice is thus described: "They brought their infants, in the time of public service, to the minister; who, taking them in his arms, pronounced an affectionate benediction on them, using on this occasion the words in which Aaron and his sons were instructed to bless the children of Israel: 'The Lord bless thee and keep thee,' etc. (Numbers 6, 24-27). Suitable admonitions to the parents, and earnest and affectionate prayer for them and their offspring, concluded the solemn and interesting transaction."[89]

The desuetude into which this custom had fallen is probably to be attributed to the rapidly diminishing strength of the General Baptists during the latter eighteenth and early nineteenth centuries. Its widespread renewal was probably due chiefly to the influence of John Clifford, a renowned metropolitan Baptist preacher and minister in Victorian days. His reason for introducing the practice, first in the homes of parents of new-born children and later in the church, was to meet the desire of so many of his congregation to associate their children formally with the Church and to seek a Divine blessing upon their infants.[90]

[87] Register Book as cited in *The Baptist Quarterly*, Vol. III (1926-1927), pp. 186-87.

[88] As cited in *The Baptist Quarterly*, Vol. IV (1928-1929), p. 75.

[89] Adam Taylor, *History of the English General Baptists*, Vol. II, pp. 29 f. I owe this reference to the courtesy of the Reverend Robert L. Child, Principal-Emeritus of Regent's Park College, Oxford. It appears in his pamphlet *The Blessing of Infants and the Dedication of Parents.*

[90] R. L. Child, *op.cit.*, pp. 3-4. The increasing growth and popularity of Sunday Schools would also make some such custom desirable.

While there was this evidence that the Baptists, although insisting that the Sacrament of initiation be restricted to believers, were approximating to the practice of the Congregationalists (and, in this respect, of Christendom) in the dedication of infants, some Congregationalists were approximating to Baptist practice in preferring a service of Dedication to the traditional "christening." The characteristic immanental theology of the age, not to mention the strong objection in some Dissenting quarters to the *ex opere operato* insistence of the Tractarians on Baptismal regeneration, was responsible for the change. It is significant that the Congregationalist Hunter included in his Baptismal Service in *Devotional Services* both the traditional formula for Baptism and an alternative form which read: "In the faith and fellowship of the Church of Christ, I dedicate thee to God, our Father in heaven." The meaning of this ordinance for Hunter is made explicit in the Exhortation which teaches that the Baptism of children is a thanksgiving; a testimony that all children are God's and that their Divine Father claims them as His own; a dedication of the child to the will of God; and a consecration of the parents "to new and holier fidelities."

Not all services for the dedication of infants were as insistent upon the Divine initiative in salvation, nor upon the fact that the child was now entering upon a corporate spiritual life in the Church of Christ. More often the subjective and individualistic emphases so predominated that the Sacrament of Baptism degenerated into an affirmation of the faith of the parents and of their good intentions in dedicating the child to God, as if their protestations were of more moment than what God had done for the salvation of the human race in Christ, the benefits of which were available for appropriation by the children of the covenanted community of Christ, His Church. A clear, vigorous, yet unmagical interpretation of Christian Baptism for children, with equal emphasis upon its objective and corporate nature, had to wait until 1917, when Dissent's greatest twentieth century theologian, a "Barth before Karl Barth," P. T. Forsyth, had completed his work, *The Church and the Sacraments*.

The same subjective and individualistic emphases distorted the Lord's Supper.[91] Although Robert Hall among the Baptists and

---

[91] The subject of Eucharistic interpretation in the Free Churches is treated more fully in Chapter III, section 5, *supra* and so can be dismissed more summarily here. Further research is necessary before more confident conclusions can be arrived at that are valid for all the denominations. The Reverend John K. Gregory has prepared a perceptive study of the theory and practice of the Lord's

239

R. W. Dale among the Congregationalists taught the high Calvinist dynamic and receptionist doctrine of the Sacrament, in which the agent was the Holy Spirit conveying the benefits of Christ's atonement and resurrection to the Church, they were in the minority. The eviscerated Zwinglianism of the official Sacramental theology of Congregationalism was only too nakedly apparent in the *Declaration of the Faith, Church Order and Discipline of the Congregational or Independent Dissenters, as adopted at the Third General Meeting of the Congregational Union of England and Wales* in 1833. The pygmy successors of the stalwart fathers of *The Savoy Declaration* of 1658 declared: "They believe in the perpetual obligation of Baptism and the Lord's Supper: the former to be administered to all converts to Christianity and their children, by the application of water to the subject, 'in the name of the Father, and of the Son, and of the Holy Ghost'; and the latter to be celebrated by Christian Churches as a token of faith in the Saviour, and of brotherly love."[92]

As to terms of admission to Communion, they affirmed: "They believe that the fellowship of every Christian Church should be so liberal as to admit to Communion in the Lord's Supper, all whose faith and godliness are, on the whole undoubted, though conscientiously differing in points of minor importance; and that this outward sign of fraternity in Christ should be co-extensive with the fraternity itself, though without involving any compliances which conscience would deem to be sinful."[93]

When such views as these were held within both the Congregational and Baptist Communions, it is not surprising to learn that attendance at the Lord's Supper was poor, particularly in the early years of the century.[94] The marvel is rather that the power of the Sacrament itself, with its numinous overtones and hallowed associations, was able to prevail in the popular mind over the implied depreciation of it by the theologians and by the enthusiasts for total abstinence and hygiene who substituted grape-juice for the wine and individual communion cups for the chalice.[95]

Supper in nineteenth century Congregationalism in England as an Oxford University doctoral dissertation, which can, with his permission, be consulted in the Bodleian Library, Oxford. No comparable study, however, exists for the Baptists, Methodists, Presbyterians, or Unitarians, in the period under review.

[92] Published London, 1833. Article XVIII.   [93] Article XIII.

[94] John Waddington in *Congregational History, 1800-1850*, p. 138, tells of a Peckham church were there was an attendance of 500 at worship, of whom only 15 remained to the Communion. The date is 1801.

[95] Unfermented wine was introduced into Congregationalism in 1878, as recorded in Albert Peel, *These Hundred Years*, p. 283. For a Baptist defence of this custom

One looks back longingly beyond the tiers of electro-plated trays bearing their diminutive glass cups in modern Nonconformist Communion services to the earlier nineteenth century celebrations in which the gleaming silver chalices, flagons (or servers), and patens stood upon the spotless linen of the Holy Table, and a dignified simplicity and reverence marked the ordinance. At least, one imagines, there was then no cult of gaucherie and informality. This can be an illusion. The picture presented by the Communion vessels in the Bow Baptist Church in the eighteen-twenties is a rather different one:

". . . a man named Parnell pictured the congregation in walled-in pews, shivering in great-coats and cloaks before the heating-stove was installed. The preacher was in a high three-decker pulpit, the precentor below sounding a note on the syringe-like wooden pitch-pipe, the servant-maids on the back forms and the children in the gallery.

"They sat to sing their slow chants, droning two lines after the words had been read and stood with their backs to the minister during the prayer.

"Most had large-type Bibles at their side in the pews and had Watts' and Rippon's Praise selections. On the seats rested horn lanterns and beneath them ringed pattens.

"At the communion service, amidst the pewter stood black bottles containing so rare a vintage from the cellars of brother Henry Tippen that fellow officers never failed to take for use at home."[96]

Yet the other side of the coin can be inferred from the splendid communion-plate which was the special pride of so many Dissenting churches in the eighteenth and nineteenth centuries. It is known, for example, that the Baptist Church in Eagle Street, London, had by the year 1756 no less than twelve silver communion cups, two silver tankards, and two silver dishes (to serve as patens), and to these were added later two silver candlesticks, making a most resplendent Communion service.[97]

---

see Dawson Burns, *Communion Wine: a lecture given at the Chelmsford Institute on Monday, April 18, 1887, under the auspices of the Chelmsford Temperance Society.* Burns writes: "Of all places in the world, the safest place for any human soul ought to be the Lord's Table; but if you have intoxicating wine there . . . it is a place of possibly great temptation" (p. 17).

[96] *The Baptist Quarterly,* Vol. VI (1932-1933), pp. 32-33.

[97] Joseph Ivimey, *A History of the English Baptists,* Vol. IV, pp. 578, 594-95, 612-13. Ivimey was minister of this very church.

All in all, the greatest progress in worship was made in Dissent in the areas of prayer and praise, rather than in the more devout and deepened understanding of the Sacramental life. That was left for the ensuing century to recover in greater fulness. With the immanental theology of the day, and the necessarily reduced Christology which was its consequence and which saw Jesus as a great prophet and social reformer rather than as the Incarnate Lord and as inspirer of individuals instead of the Head of the Church, it was inevitable that the religion of such liturgical pioneers as John Hunter, the Congregationalist, and James Martineau,[98] the Unitarian, exceeded their theological explication of the faith; otherwise their influence could not have been as profound as it undoubtedly was in the Free Churches.

The liturgical revival could not arrive in all its fulness until there would come into being a theology that would be distinctively Biblical in its understanding of the depths and ramifications of sin in social structures as well as in individuals and also in the realization of the integrating and transforming grace of God which creates a new community in the people of God, whose central service is the Eucharist in which Word and Sacrament are the supreme means of grace. That theology, profoundly Biblical, deeply Patristic, ecumenical in scope and relevance, corporately expressed in the worshipping and witnessing Church, was to be the task of the next century to explicate amid the stresses and anxieties of problems deeper than the many the Victorians faced. Among Free Churchmen only Peter Taylor Forsyth[99] was its prophet in seeing its Biblical realism, its demand for social justice, its ecumenical impact, and its aesthetic implications, and he was largely a voice crying in the wilderness to be heard with eager acceptance by a generation born when he was dying. Only such a theology (a neo-orthodoxy with a consciousness of strong social obligations inherent in the Gospel of God), bringing back into the vocabulary of Christians the forgotten word and power of "Grace," could restore to its primacy the adoration of the living God by a living Church. On the Anglican side Stewart Headlam and Charles Gore were to combine, though in less passionate and incisive terms, a theology of grace and a sociology of charity and justice.

In the meantime, the Free Churches were fortunate to have had

98 See Chapter IX, *infra*.
99 See the admirable expositions and evaluations of Forsyth's theology by two American scholars, Robert McAfee Brown of Stanford University and William Bradley of Hartford Theological Seminary, detailed in the Bibliography.

the examples of Binney, Hugh Price Hughes,[100] John Hunter, and James Martineau[101] to call them in a time of intellectual doubt, doctrinal dilution, social perturbation, and ethical relativism, to the chief end of man, the adoration and service of God renewed in corporate worship and utilizing the resources of the centuries.

[100] See the life of this distinguished Methodist "Catholic" and Socialist by his daughter, Dorothea Price Hughes (1905).
[101] See Chapter IX, *infra*.

CHAPTER IX
THE NEWER DISSENT: METHODISM
AND UNITARIANISM

THE TITLE OF THIS CHAPTER may seem to imply an un-likely alliance of Methodists and Unitarians in worship; the intention, however, is rather to suggest that both denominations, though different in theological outlook (pietism characterizing the Methodists and rationalism the Unitarians) and in social composition and culture (Methodism being the community of the lower and lower middle classes and Unitarianism the association of the intellectuals and the affluent middle classes), were yet alike in two respects as newcomers to English Nonconformity.

They were, in the first place, both denominations that had sought to remain within the Establishment and had been reluctantly forced into the company of the English Dissenting denominations.

In the second place, they still retained, though to a decreasing degree as the century progressed, some elements of the liturgical heritage of the Establishment. The Methodists, for example, continued to use the Anglican Communion Service, whether in the full form of the Book of Common Prayer or in Wesley's Abridgement originally prepared for the Methodists of North America. Their inventiveness was also seen in their popular architecture.

The Unitarians, whose rationalism was opposed to the enthusiasm represented by the more charismatic character of extemporary prayer, continued with remarkable fecundity to produce their own revisions of the Anglican liturgy throughout the century, although successive waves of revision departed farther from the Anglican shore. At the same time their very freedom to experiment was a proof that the new denominations had joined the ranks of Dissent, whose views on worship they gradually came to approximate as the century proceeded, as, for example, in the occasional and sometimes frequent use of free prayers, whether prepared or unprepared.

I. THE METHODISTS

1. Two Liturgical Camps

The death of their great founder in 1791 left the Wesleyan Methodists in two opposed liturgical camps. On the one hand, there were the conservative laymen and the ministers who had been closely associated with Wesley as loyal followers who valued the attachment to the National Church in the highest degree, of whom the most influential was Dr. Jabez Bunting, the Secretary of the Conference for a long period. On the other hand, there was a much larger group consisting of most of the preachers and the general body of the people who valued the distinctive ordinances of Methodist piety and had been too often rebuffed by unsympathetic Anglican clergymen to feel any sense of loyalty to the Established Church or to its incomparable Liturgy.

This state of divided loyalties was clearly revealed in the permissive nature of the directives on worship issued by the Conference immediately after Wesley's death, and it continued until the year 1834.[1] The very need for "The Plan of Pacification" of 1795 implied the existence of a state of war. Clearly the conservatives could claim that their venerable founder under God was on their side, for had he not declared, "I live and die a member of the Church of England; and none who regard my judgment will ever separate from it"?[2] At the same time the fact that John Wesley had ordained ministers made it increasingly difficult to maintain that the Methodists were societies within the Church of England. Moreover, many members of these societies had come from the ranks of the Dissenters or had no ecclesiastical connection whatever. Besides, even those who owed their baptism to the Church of England often had only the most formal and reluctant association with the Established Church, while their vital allegiance lay with the preachers who had converted them and with their fellow-members of the societies with whom they had shared their testimonies in bands and classes.

Thus a vast number of Methodists, both preachers and lay folk, were eager that their own preachers should administer the Sacraments to them. In these circumstances the circumspect plan was a compromise intended to satisfy both the loyalist conservatives and the popular desire for separate services. The cautious words of the "Plan of Pacification" tell their own story:

"The Sacrament of the Lord's Supper shall not be administered in any chapel, except a majority of the trustees of that chapel . . . and of the stewards and leaders belonging to that chapel (as the

---

[1] There was also a considerable group that held a middle position of neutrality between the armed camps of the Church and Dissent. See the speeches of Warren and Ward in the 1834 Conference, as reported in Benjamin Gregory *Sidelights on the Conflicts of Methodism, 1827 to 1852*, pp. 158, 161.

[2] *The Arminian Magazine*, issue of April 1790.

best qualified to give the sense of the people) allow of it. Nevertheless, in all cases, the consent of the Conference shall be first obtained. . . . Provided that, *in all chapels where the Lord's Supper has been already peaceably administered, the administration of it shall continue in future.* . . . We agree that the Lord's Supper be administered among us, on Sunday evenings only; except where the majority of stewards and leaders desire it in Church hours. . . . Nevertheless, it shall never be administered on those Sundays on which it is administered in the parish church. The Lord's Supper shall always be administered in England, *according to the form of the Established Church*: but the person who administers shall have liberty to give out hymns, to use exhortation, and extemporary prayer. Wherever Divine Service is performed in England on the Lord's day, in Church hours, the officiating preacher shall read either the service of the Church, our venerable father's abridgement, or at least the lessons appointed by the calendar. But we recommend either the full service or the abridgement."[3]

The Conference might consist of the hundred ministers in whom the authority of the Connexion was invested, yet the power of the people was already manifesting itself in the separatist tendency. Considering the numbers of the Connexion, and the aggressive Sacramentarianism of the Tractarian wing of the Church of England,[4] it is remarkable that Methodism was able to retain its Anglican liturgical heritage as long as it did in the nineteenth century. That this tradition lived on was due to the vigorous sponsorship of the Methodist patriarchs of the period, including Adam Clarke, Jabez Bunting, Robert Newton, Richard Watson, and Thomas Jackson.

T. P. Bunting, in his account of his father's liturgical practices, indicates that Jabez Bunting and Adam Clarke both preferred to use the service of the Book of Common Prayer rather than Wesley's abridgement of it.[5] In general, Bunting thought "that where a congregation could be induced to concur in a mode of worship which united the advantages of a liturgy and extemporaneous address to God, the case of the people and the general purposes of worship would be better served than by an adherence to one of these plans only. So, therefore, the Liturgy was used in the

---

[3] *Documents of the Christian Church*, selected and edited by Henry Bettenson, pp. 359-60.
[4] The loyalist Bunting declared in 1841, "Unless the Church of England will protest against Puseyism in some intelligible form, it will be the duty of the Methodists to protest against the Church of England." Gregory, *op.cit.*, p. 317.
[5] T. P. Bunting, *The Life of Dr. Bunting*, Vol. I, p. 138.

earlier service of the Sabbath, though not even then to the exclusion of free prayer, while extempore prayers only were used at the later services."[6]

When the Rev. Joseph Entwistle had asked the advice of Dr. Adam Clarke as to whether to introduce an organ and the Anglican Liturgy into Brunswick Chapel in Liverpool, he received the following loyalist reply: "With respect to the introduction of the Liturgy of the Church of England—this book I reverence next to the Book of God. Next to the Bible it has been the depository of the pure religion of Christ; and had it not been laid up there, and established by Acts of Parliament, I fear that religion would, long ere this, have been driven to the wilderness. Most devoutly do I wish that, wherever we have service on the forenoon of the Lord's Day, we may have the prayers read. This service contains that form of sound words to which, in succeeding ages, an appeal may be successfully made for the establishment of the truth professed by preceding generations. Had it not been, under God, for this blessed book, the Liturgy of the English Church, I verily believe Methodism had never existed. I see plainly that, where we read these prayers, our congregations become better settled, better edified, and put farther out of the reach of false doctrine. Introduce the Church Service in God's name, not in any *abridgement*, but in the genuine original."[7]

It is clear that the two great leaders of Methodism after Wesley's death maintained Wesley's own contention that the most edifying type of worship for Methodists was a union of the formal and the free, using Christian tradition and the guidance of the Holy Spirit.

Some who had been used to extemporary prayer also came to appreciate the value of the Anglican Liturgy. Such a one was Dr. R. Newton, who had ministered in circuits in Scotland and the north of England before coming to the London West circuit in 1812. He found that Liturgy was in use in most of the London Methodist chapels. His biographer, Thomas Jackson,[8] declares of Newton that, at this period ". . . he contracted such a love for the Liturgy that in future life it afforded him a sincere satisfaction to

---

[6] *Ibid.*, pp. 381 f.

[7] *Ibid.*, p. 386.

[8] Jackson's own view may be gathered from the following sentence from his anonymously issued pamphlet, *Answer to the Question, Why Are You a Wesleyan Methodist?* which is cited on p. 46 of Gordon Rupp's *Thomas Jackson Methodist Patriarch*: "Some of the best hours in my life have been spent in the use of her [the Church of England's] truly sublime and evangelical liturgy."

be appointed to circuits where the people were accustomed to the use of it. The Liturgy recommended itself to his ear and taste by the rhythm of its periods and the form of its diction, and to his heart by the evangelical sentiments which it embodies and the spirit of pure and elevated devotion by which it is pervaded. The comprehensiveness of its petitions for all classes of the human race gave expression to the expansive charity of his sanctified heart and in the use of this 'form of sacred words' he felt himself able to worship in spirit and in truth."[9]

If there is more of Jackson than of Newton in this eulogy of the Anglican Liturgy, its value as a witness to the ongoing respect for the Book of Common Prayer in mid-century Methodism is all the greater, for Jackson had the authority of a President of the Conference in the year of its Centennial celebration of the founding of the first Methodist societies, as well as of being the manager of its official bookroom and editor of its chief publications and the first professor of church history in the institution that became known as Richmond Theological College, London.[10] In the memorial volume which he wrote, *The Centenary of Wesleyan Methodism* (1839), he claimed that the Liturgy was still widely used: "The incomparable Liturgy is regularly used in many of the Chapels of England and in all the Mission Chapels of the West Indies. Translations of it have been made by Wesleyan missionaries into various languages for the use of their congregations especially in the East. It is also always used in the administration of the Lord's Supper both at home and abroad."[11]

It is particularly significant that Methodism's early nineteenth century theologian, Richard Watson, whose authority was displaced only by the much later and more perceptive, systematic work of W. B. Pope in his *Compendium of Christian Theology*, would have neither of the extreme views which would limit Christian worship to liturgical forms alone or exclusively to free prayers. His judicious conclusion was: "The whole, we think, comes to this,—that there are advantages in each mode of worship; and that, when combined prudently, the public service of the sanctuary has its most perfect constitution. Much, however, in the practice of Churches is to be regulated by due respect to differences of opinion, and even to prejudice, on a point upon which we are left at liberty by the Scriptures, and which must therefore be ranked

[9] Thomas Jackson, *Life of R. Newton, D.D.*, p. 76.
[10] See Gordon Rupp's stimulating appreciation, *Thomas Jackson Methodist Patriarch*. [11] Pp. 281-82.

among things prudential. Here, as in many other things, Christians must give place to each other, and do all things 'in charity.' "[12]

We may safely conclude that by the middle of the century a considerable number of Methodist churches in the metropolis and in the larger provincial cities continued to use the Anglican Order for Matins in their morning worship, or the abridgement of it prepared by John Wesley. On the other hand, we may also suppose that in the country churches, which were often without the help of an ordained minister, only the lessons of the Anglican calendar survived, and that, apart from the praises, the services were an exact counterpart of the Free Church tradition. It should also be remembered that in the city evening services the Free Church tradition of worship was followed. In fact, it was only in the Sacrament of the Lord's Supper that the Methodists universally followed the Prayer Book, and, even here, their exhortations, hymns, and interjected extemporary prayers provided a charismatic supplement to a hallowed form.

How is the waning of the Prayer Book heritage, with the exception of the Sacramental services, and occasional ordinances such as marriages and burials, to be accounted for? In part, as we have suggested, by the popular demand for a charismatic type of service, as contrasted with the demand on the part of leading and ageing ministers for loyalty to Wesley's own wishes. An equally significant factor, however, was the impact of the Oxford Movement, which forced the Methodists out of their middle position between the Establishment and Dissent and into the arms of Nonconformity in order to rebut the charge of being Romanist.[13] The divisions within Methodism, leading to the foundation of other Methodist Communions with a more democratic type of polity, such as the Primitive Methodists,[14] also led in the direction of the worship of the older Dissent. Moreover, by the middle of the century there was hardly a minister left who could remember the days when Methodists were societies within the Establishment, and, even if they could, they were more interested in adding to the general Non-

[12] The original edition of Richard Watson's *Theological Institutes* appeared in London from 1823-1829. The citation is from p. 394 of the one-volume edition issued in New York in 1830.

[13] Cf. Gordon Rupp, *Thomas Jackson Methodist Patriarch*, p. 22: "[The Oxford Movement] was soon to turn its attack with special vehemence upon the Methodists, doing more than any other single fact to provoke the alliance of Methodism with the Free Churches, and driving later Methodism, in its own self-defence and in its apprehensions of renascent Popery, from its old middle position."

[14] See the Chapter VI, section 2, *supra*, for an account of Primitive Methodists and their worship.

conformist pressure to disestablish the Church of England and thus to maintain a genuine religious pluralism in England where effectiveness and strength of denominational allegiance, rather than a dependence upon the crutches of the state or the prestige of tradition, would be the hallmarks of public acceptance.

On a lower level there was a determination on the part of a common Nonconformist front to be rid of the political and educational disabilities from which the Free Churches would continue to suffer until the Church of England were to be disestablished.[15] The difficulties that the "Plan of Pacification" had attempted to gloss over in 1795 had not been overcome by 1834, as Gregory's account of the Conference meeting in that year had shown. Dr. Jabez Bunting might indeed insist that "When we give our people the Sacraments in our chapels we publicly guard against its being taken as a sign of separation" and cite a letter of Charles Wesley to the effect that they were the best Methodists when they were first for the Church of England and then for the Methodists; but the realistic answer was given by Dr. Beaumont, who retorted: "Mr. Wesley, like a strong and skilful rower, looked one way while every stroke of his oar took him in the apposite direction." Beaumont concluded that Wesley had never declared that he would go no further from the Church and pleaded that breathing room was necessary for Methodism, confessing, "I do not like to be tacked on to the Established Church."[16] It was Beaumont who spoke for the future, as Bunting's vision was dimmed by nostalgia.

2. Free Prayers

The victory of free prayer over set forms in Methodism was never complete, however. To this day there are several Methodist churches which rejoice in using the Anglican Form of Morning Prayer,[17] and most still use the Anglican Order for Holy Communion, even if in a slightly abridged form. The existence of the Methodist Sacramental Fellowship is a proof that the loyalists like Adam Clarke and Bunting, Richard Watson and Thomas Jackson, were never without successors, one of whom was a superb preacher, namely, Hugh Price Hughes, who was already an enthusiast for a "dignified and choral liturgical choral service" in

---

[15] See the present author's *The English Free Churches*, pp. 143-82.
[16] Benjamin Gregory, *Sidelights on the Conflicts of Methodism*, pp. 155-56.
[17] Cf. Townsend, Workman and Eayrs, *A New History of Methodism*, Vol. II, p. 493, and J. Bishop, *Methodist Worship in Relation to Free Church Worship*, p. 47.

1873 while in the Dover circuit as a comparatively young man.[18] His daughter writes of Hugh Price Hughes that "with all his sympathy for unconventional methods he disliked extremes, and would speak of them with distaste. The method of morning worship that was personally preferable to him was always that of the Liturgy, and it was a desire to profit by its discipline that led him to adopt the experiment of a liturgical service. . . ."[19] It is significant, however, that at this period Hughes's traditionalism was regarded as an unfortunate innovation by many members of his congregation, only because the tradition was more honoured in the breach than in the observance.

The proof that the Oxford Movement exposed any Methodist who wished to combine the Anglican and Free Church traditions of worship, as Wesley himself did, to the charge of "ritualism" is to be found in a rare volume written between the years 1881 and 1885 and entitled *Methodist Ritualism or a Few Thoughts on the Methodism of Today.*[20] The burden of this jeremiad is that Methodism at this period is in a low spiritual condition. The diagnosis is that Methodism is more conscious of its human founder, Wesley, than of its divine Founder, Christ. Furthermore, it is too eager to mimic the High Church party in the Establishment. As evidence for this charge the author cites a description taken from *The Methodist* of a service at the Wesleyan Chapel in Blackheath: "It was the full evening service, the 'Amens' were all sung, the Creed and Lord's Prayer were intoned to a full organ accompaniment, and even the General Thanksgiving was intoned."[21] He further notes that Tallis' Responses, the *Cantata* [*sic*] *Domino*, and the *Deus Misereatur*, were all chorally rendered, arguing that this is incontrovertible proof that Methodism is "fast departing from the simplicity of the Gospel."[22] This particular church contains only black heathens, it seems. He also attributes the low spiritual temperature in Methodism in general to a failure to teach justification by faith and sanctification as the work of the Holy Spirit.

The real gravamen of his objections is lodged against a formal-

[18] Dorothea Price Hughes, *The Life of Hugh Price Hughes by His Daughter*, pp. 103-04.

[19] *Ibid.*, p. 241.

[20] The booklet bears the anonymous description "By an old-fashioned Methodist." It was printed in London without a date. It appeared on the accession list of the Bodleian Library, Oxford, on 21 January, 1886, yet it must have been written after 1881 since p. 5 refers to that date. Its author was apparently a George Walker of Eaglescliffe, Durham.

[21] *Ibid.*, p. 10.

[22] *Ibid.*

ism and ceremonialism that creep in only when vital devotion has expired. "We must get into ornamental art and embellish our worship," he writes. "Behold Methodism a factory for tinsel, and her ministers up to the latest fashion in Church millinery."[23] His soul is bared in the desperate cry:

"Oh for the out-pourings of the heart in earnest prayer, which we used to hear from old Methodist ministers when they took hold of God and heaven,

> When heaven came down our souls to greet,
> And glory crowned the mercy's seat.

Under such pleadings everyone present both saint and sinner felt the power and influence. . . ."[24]

Such criticism not only betrayed prejudice and insensitivity to the earliest Methodist tradition of worship, but it also revealed the depth of the attachment to the simple spontaneity and sincerity of the experience of a holy man praying freely. It is as well to be reminded of the minor Mountains of Transfiguration to which unliturgical prayer can transport its saintly devotees. Nor should it be forgotten that some ministers and lay preachers took the greatest of care in the preparation of their pulpit prayers. Leslie Church rightly draws attention to one such prayer that combines spiritual penetration with felicity of style, and is an index of the thorough devotional preparation of soul and mind that one Methodist minister exemplified. Elizabeth Rhodes, a devout Methodist church member, committed a prayer of her minister's to memory and wrote it down in her journal. It reads thus: "Lord, let me be obedient without arguing, humble without feigning, patient without grudging, pure without corruption, merry without lightness, sad without mistrust, sober without dulness, true without duplicity; fearing Thee without desperation, and trusting Thee without presumption. Let me be joyful for nothing but that which pleaseth Thee, and sorrowful for nothing but what displeaseth Thee: that labour be my delight which is for Thee, and let all weary me that is not in Thee. Give me a waking spirit, and a diligent soul, that I may seek to know Thy will, and when I know it may I perform it faithfully to the honour and glory of Thy ever blessed Name."[25] It is by an accident that this prayer was preserved, and we may

23 *Ibid.*, p. 31.
24 *Methodist Ritualism*, p. 26.
25 L. F. Church cites the prayer in his *More About the Early Methodist People*, pp. 223-24 from *Memoir of Elizabeth Rhodes by Herself*, pp. 53-55.

assume that many such had a moving effect upon the congregations that heard them but were otherwise no sooner uttered than lost to posterity.

3. Methodist Services in General

We are fortunate in possessing an extremely reliable as well as moderate account of Methodist services in England during the second decade of the nineteenth century by the hand of Jonathan Crowther. His work is entitled *A True and Complete Portraiture of Methodism.*[26] It is sufficient to say of it that it almost lives up to its pretentious title, so accurate and authoritative is its information.

The most valuable section, for our purposes, is that entitled, "The General Mode of Public Worship,"[27] from which it is possible to abstract a typical Methodist Order of Worship during the first decade of the nineteenth century. The Morning Order of Worship would consist of the following items: hymn, prayer (extemporary or liturgical), hymn, short lesson, sermon, hymn, short extemporary prayer, benediction (II Cor. 13:14).

Apparently the Order of Evening Worship is almost identical, apart from two changes. The sermon would be much longer than in the morning, and if the morning service had been non-liturgical (that is, if it had used neither the Book of Common Prayer nor Wesley's abridgement of it), then the appropriate Epistle and Gospel had to be included in the evening worship. If, however, the Book of Common Prayer or the abridgement were used in the morning service, extemporary prayer was to be included. Crowther adds, however, "they seldom pray long, as Mr. Wesley advised them never to pray more than five or eight minutes at one time; he likewise cautioned them against long singing, as well as long and loud preaching. In these respects he was himself a pattern, seldom detaining the congregation more than an hour."[28]

Crowther also indicates that great stress is to be laid on the importance of the hymnody and of the preaching. He rightly observes that "Singing makes a more considerable part of the worship of the Methodists than perhaps of that of any other denomination of Christians; hardly any exercise so powerfully affects and raises the soul to heavenly things, as that of singing psalms, hymns, and

[26] All references will be to the American edition of 1813.
[27] Pp. 221-26.
[28] P. 221. In 1836 Dr. Bunting told the Conference: "Sing, pray, or preach, or do as you please; but two hours in the morning and two hours in the evening—we cannot feed our people with less." (Benj. Gregory, *op.cit.*, p. 228.)

spiritual songs."[29] The sermon, he insists, is of a moderate length; neither is it too long, nor do the Methodist preachers "wrap up their sermons in a mumbling whisper, in about twelve or fifteen minutes."[30] The Methodists were renowned for their sermons delivered without the benefit of manuscript. Although this gives their ministers great freedom of address, Crowther insists that they are neither rhapsodical nor incoherent because by premeditation "they study the order and substance of their discourses."[31] Each Methodist preacher tries to remember Wesley's advice to preach both the Law and the Gospel, to expound plain texts, adapting the subjects to the comprehension of the congregation, and to beware of affected or awkward gestures, phrases or pronunciation.

Perhaps most interesting of all is Crowther's sensitivity to outside criticism on the score of the charismatic interruptions of the Methodist services by the interjections and ejaculations of the enthusiastic members. His reply to the charge is to assert that some persons cannot restrain themselves on the occasion of extraordinary outpourings of the Spirit of God, and he would rather risk the danger of an excessive vitality than of a dead formality. He even suggests that ejaculations are entirely appropriate expressions of the liberation which the experience of conviction and conversion bring.

He maintains that Methodist services are orderly and uniform in character, except in the extreme variety of times at which they are held. "In some of our chapels, the preaching is at seven in the morning, and six in the evening; in some at nine in the morning, half past one, and six; and in others at half past ten, at two and at six. And in some few instances there are still other variations: this is regulated by circumstances, and those times are fixed upon, which are judged to be the best."[32]

Crowther also offers a full explanation of why the Methodists found it impossible to maintain, according to John Wesley's wish, "a strict union with the Church of England." Its importance deserves citation:

"As far as circumstances would admit, Mr. Wesley and his followers have laboured to maintain a strict union with the Church of England. But as they had no other bond of union than that of piety, some joined them who had been brought up dissenters; and in consequence of this, the ministers to whose congregations they

29 Jonathan Crowther, *op.cit.*, p. 222.
30 *Ibid.*, p. 221.   31 *Ibid.*   32 *Ibid.*, pp. 223-24.

had formerly belonged refused to let them partake of the Lord's supper with them, and also to baptize their children. Some ministers of the established church behaved in a similar way; others of these were so miserably deficient in point of religion, that many of them could not in conscience receive the sacrament at their hands. There were others whose preaching was so contrary to the articles and homilies of the church, or so full of bitter railing against the Methodists, that many could not think it to be their duty to attend their ministry.

"In some places also, our chapels were at a great distance from any church; and in others the churches were too small. In consequence of these circumstances, our service was allowed in church hours in sundry places. This was strongly opposed by some of the preachers, and by many of the people. But where a large majority was in favour of it, and no division of the society was likely to take place, the conference soon found themselves under the necessity of conceding the point. Where a majority of the trustees, the stewards, and leaders, signify to the conference their desire to have service in those hours, their desire is complied with.

"The case is the same respecting the Lord's supper, the baptizing of children by our preachers, and burying the dead in burying grounds belonging to our chapels; where the majority of the trustees, stewards, and leaders are against these, nothing of the kind takes place.

"Meantime, the preachers are neither to do nor say anything to influence the people either the one way or the other. And no preacher is *required* to read the Common Prayer, or to baptize, or to administer the Lord's supper, or bury the dead, contrary to his own judgement. As to the people, where we have these privileges, some join their brethren in them, and some do not, but go to the church, receive the sacrament, have their children baptized, and bury their dead there. To this we make no objections, but let every man do as he is persuaded in his own mind."[33]

This citation gives us one important clue as to why the Methodists tended increasingly to prefer the Free Church, rather than the Anglican liturgical tradition. It was simply that the wishes of the majority of the people could not be overruled by the most loyalist of the old-school Methodist ministers. Soon a generation would arise which had never experienced even a part-time or Sacramental affiliation with the Church of England. Even in the

[33] *Ibid.*, pp. 225-26.

period under consideration we notice that extemporary prayer, preaching that was virtually extemporary, and the joyful singing of hymns, not to mention the interruptions of praise and prayers by spontaneous ejaculations on the part of individuals—all elements in worship for which no exact equivalent could be found in the Anglican tradition—laid a far greater stress on the charismatic than the formal and traditional elements in worship. This preference would inexorably cause the Methodists to throw in their lot in worship with the other English Free Churches, the Baptists, Congregationalists, and Presbyterians, with a consequent diminution of the Anglican heritage in Methodist worship.

4. Hymnody

"The Singing Methodists" continued to live up to their name, although "the generation that followed the Wesleys was practically barren of Methodist hymn-writers."[34] Nevertheless, during a period when Methodism was still uncertain as to whether it was affiliated to the Church of England or a separate Dissenting denomination, and when it was troubled by dissensions within, the unity of Methodist doctrine and piety was kept alive among the faithful at least as much by the Methodist Hymnbook as by Wesley's Sermons and Notes on the New Testament. They were as efficacious in the new century as they had been in the old as a theological primer, an expression of lyrical adoration, a pre-eminent channel of private piety, and a democratic contribution to Methodist public worship.[35] Methodism in this century indeed had its four commentators, of whom Dr. Adam Clarke was chief, but "it was not the commentary on the shelf, but the song in the heart which inspired and continually instructed the first Methodists"[36] and, we might add, their immediate successors.

The hymnody of the Methodists still continued to be appreciated as experimental divinity. In terms echoing John Wesley's own description[37] of it, Jonathan Crowther recalls how it expresses every mood and condition of the Christian: "The hymns used by the Methodists are adapted to the various states and exercises of the mind of the pious person, and to all the different circumstances of life.

[34] Townsend, Workman, and Eayrs, *A New History of Methodism*, Vol. II, p. 253.
[35] See Chapter V, section 8, *supra*.
[36] Leslie F. Church, *More About the Early Methodist People*, p. 229.
[37] Wesley's words were: ". . . this book is in effect a little body of experimental and practical divinity."

Our large hymn-book contains a body of experimental and practical divinity, and is variously calculated to assist and quicken men to walk in the fear of the Lord, and in the comforts of the Holy Ghost."[38]

Crowther is not less emphatic in regard to the aesthetic quality and style of the hymns, but his chief concern is to commend "the spirit of piety, which the reader will find breathing through the whole collection."[39] As the theological foundations and the lyrical enthusiasm of these hymns had preserved the religion of the heart in a day of rationalism, so were they to shape a warm piety in a period when the winds of doubt and the zephyrs of material success were to buffet or allure the ark of Methodism. These hymns were, indeed, the real Liturgy or "Use" of the Methodist people. The leaders, however, had to be on their guard lest the revivalists introduce sentimental jingles. Dr. Jabez Bunting, for example, cautioned in 1836, "Instead of 'Come to Jesus' and ranting tunes, we should have 'God of all grace and majesty.'"[40]

5. Baptisms, Marriages, Burials

The anomalous position of Methodism in the early decades of the nineteenth century, as a self-styled "Body," which was neither in the bosom of the Church of England nor in the arms of Dissent, was reflected in the reluctance with which many Methodists, both preachers and laity, administered or received Methodist occasional ordinances in worship.[41] Thirty years were to pass after the "Plan of Pacification" before the travelling preachers, even when exercising every function of the ministry, were to call themselves ministers. During these years the members of each society, either at their own wish or by the request of their relatives, were regularly buried in the parish graveyard by the clergyman of the parish. Moreover, they were often attended by their preachers simply in the capacity of mourners. The large majority of weddings were

[38] *A True and Complete Portraiture of Methodism*, p. 223. Thomas Jackson makes the same point in declaring: "There is scarcely a feeling of the heart, from the first dawn of divine light upon the understanding and desire after God, till the believer's triumphant flight to the celestial paradise which is not here expressed in language beautifully forcible and appropriate." Cited p. 22 of Gordon Rupp, *op.cit.*
[39] Crowther, *ibid.*   [40] Gregory, *op.cit.*, p. 247.
[41] See Townsend, Workman, and Eayrs, *op.cit.*, Vol. I, p. 386, footnote 1, where it is stated: "There were several cases in which no service was held in church hours, and some where the Sacraments were not administered as late as 1870, probably later." It should also be noted that it was only in 1836 that the Conference approved of public ordination by the laying on of hands.

solemnized in the churches of the Establishment, including even the weddings of the preachers themselves.[42] A considerable number of baptisms continued to be administered in the parish church.[43]

In these circumstances it was inevitable that when Methodism in the local societies took official cognizance of its separation from the Church of England, and the majority of the officials voted to have their own ordinances, that these should closely approximate to the forms of the Book of Common Prayer. Although Wesley had approved the enlivening of the Order for Holy Communion in the Prayer Book with the singing of Methodist hymns and the inclusion of extemporary prayers and exhortations, it was not until 1869 that the Order for Holy Baptism was allowed to receive similar treatment.[44] On the other hand, it was permissible in burial services to include an exhortation.[45]

One distinctive custom of the Methodists in their burials became widely known as "singing funerals." This custom had originated at least as early as 1774 at the funeral of John Nelson, a Yorkshire stone-mason and one of Wesley's most trusted lay preachers. When the funeral procession arrived at Birstal, where the interment was to take place, the throng was a solid mass of human beings stretching for half a mile. Then "William Shent of Leeds, a local preacher, and a personal friend of the deceased, gave out appropriate hymns as the people passed along."[46] In this way the Methodists, with luminous rather than the conventional lugubrious faces, gave a convincing demonstration of their Resurrection faith.

6. Sacramental Theory and Practice

The nineteenth century was hardly propitious for the development of sacramental devotion in any of the Free Churches, nor did the Methodists prove the exception to the rule.[47] The latent Non-Juror tradition in Wesley may have been appreciated by a few of the metropolitan preachers who were Wesley's juniors, but it never gained a strong foothold in the Connexion as a whole. For this state of affairs many reasons may be found. The formal and

---

[42] In the Methodist Conference of 1840 Dr. Bunting said: "Marriages may be quietly introduced. But I must maintain that Conference has expressed its judgment that marriages in our chapels should not be encouraged." (Gregory, *op.cit.*, p. 298.)

[43] Townsend, Workman, and Eayrs, *op.cit.*, Vol. I, pp. 388-89.

[44] J. Bishop, *op.cit.*, pp. 114-20 for a discussion of the nineteenth century Methodist theory and practice of Baptism.

[45] J. Crowther, *op.cit.*, p. 226.

[46] Thomas Jackson, *The Centenary of Wesleyan Methodism*, p. 95.

[47] Cf. J. Bishop, *op.cit.*, pp. 121 ff.

liturgical tradition in worship was fused with the charismatic and spontaneous in Wesley himself, but for thousands of his simple followers the Prayer Book rites, with their musty, archaic language and dignified ceremonies, seemed artificial compared with the simple freshness of their love-feasts and covenant services. The four years (1791-1795) when the Methodists were prohibited from having their own Sacraments began a bad tradition, with the result that many must have thought of the preaching services as the staple diet of worship and the Sacraments as optional extras. Furthermore, since the right to administer the Sacraments was given to all preachers in full Connexion, though many were unordained, this break with the will of the Wesleys must have been offensive to many conservatives. Also, since Sacramentarianism was the mark of the Oxford Movement, the Methodist reaction against it tended to a serious disparagement of the Sacraments and their place in the Christian life. In addition, the love-feasts and the class-meetings (especially the former) would supply many of the spiritual needs of the people to which the Holy Communion ministered.

Then, again, rugged individualism was increasingly the order of the day in Victorian England, with little sense of the social and communal nature of man, and the increasing expansion of British imperial influence during the century caused men to fix their eyes on the horizons of the future. In short, there was neither time nor inclination for the retrospective look at history and tradition. Finally, the attachment of a greater importance to preaching than to Communion was also part of Methodism's approximation to its sister Dissenting denominations. "Methodism," says Rattenbury, "was hardening down into a separate denomination, and there would be a tendency perhaps to emphasize services which were sectarian and separatist in character rather than those which were Catholic and continuous with other Church life."[48]

Perhaps the most curious feature of Methodist worship in this period is the conflict between the high official expositions of the significance of the Sacraments and the comparatively low appreciation of them on the part of the majority, at least as far as the latter is indicated by the level of Eucharistic practice. To be sure, there were exceptions on both sides. Hugh Price Hughes of West London Circuit is said to have been "so far a sacramentarian as to hold that

---

[48] J. E. Rattenbury, *Wesley's Legacy to the World*, p. 192. See debates of 1843 Conference in Gregory, *op.cit.*, pp. 351 f. for the approximation to Nonconformity.

the partaking of bread and wine in the Eucharist was an appointed symbol of mystic participation in the life of Christ, bringing a special blessing to the communicant."[49] On the other hand, J. H. Rigg,[50] a convinced anti-Anglican who was influential in the last two decades of the century, must have had a significant impact on Methodist practice, for only thus can be explained the omission of the sacred manual acts of fraction and libation of the elements in the Communion service in the *Book of Offices* of 1882.

The official teaching about the meaning of the Sacraments never degenerated into mere infant dedication (in expounding Baptism) or into mere memorialism (in explaining the Lord's Supper). On the contrary, a high Calvinistic doctrine of the Sacraments as signs and seals of God's covenant with His people, authenticated by the Holy Spirit, is as plainly taught in Watson's *Theological Institutes* as in W. B. Pope's *A Compendium of Christian Theology*. Watson wrote: "As, therefore, the sacraments, when considered as *signs*, contain a declaration of the same doctrines and promises which the written word of God exhibits, but addressed by a significant emblem to the senses; so also as *seals*, or pledges, they confirm the same promises which are assured to us by God's own truth and faithfulness in his word (which is the main ground of all affiance in his mercy), and by his indwelling Spirit by which we are 'sealed,' and have in our hearts 'the earnest' of our heavenly inheritance."[51]

W. B. Pope's admirably expounded teaching reveals its unmistakable Genevan origin. Of the Sacraments he says: "These have been instituted for the perpetual observance of the Christian Church, and placed among its means of grace. As means of grace they have elements of difference, and elements in common with the other means. Their difference is that they are Federal Transactions: signs and seals of the covenant of redemption. As signs, they represent in action and by symbols the great blessings of the covenant; as seals they are standing pledges of the Divine fidelity in bestowing them on certain conditions, being the Spirit's instrument in aiding and strengthening the faith which they require, and in assuring to that faith the present bestowment of its object. Thus they are, on the one hand, objective institutions which assure the continu-

---

[49] Townsend, Workman, and Eayrs, *op.cit.*, Vol. I, p. 460.
[50] See his *Oxford High Anglicanism*.
[51] Watson, *Theological Institutes*, p. 429. We may note that Watson also says, "We have called baptism a federal transaction; an initiation into acceptance of the covenant of grace . . ." (p. 430).

ance of the Spirit's administration of redemption in the Church, and, on the other, subjective confirmations to each believing recipient of his own present interest in the covenant."[52]

It is an ironical turn in the history of Christian doctrine that the Arminian Methodists should have better preserved the Calvinistic doctrine of the Sacraments in the English Free Churches of the nineteenth century than the Calvinistic Congregationalists, Baptists, and Presbyterians.

It would, however, be a mistake to conceive the Methodist administration of the Sacraments as an authentic continuation of Puritan practice, even if of Puritan theory; for Methodism had its own distinctive emphases in rites that were of Anglican rather than Puritan ancestry. The Communion rail in Methodist churches was itself a reminder of Anglicanism, rather than of Puritanism, as was the kneeling posture for the reception of the elements from the hand of the minister. Nonetheless, a distinctive Methodist feature was the fact that groups, rather than single individuals, approached the Communion rail. According to Bishop, this is Methodism's corporate expression of its belief in the Communion of Saints.[53] The Puritan tradition, however, is continued in the linking of the preaching of the Word to the Holy Communion. A further distinctive mark of the Methodist Communion was the conception that this was not only a confirming ordinance but also a converting one. For this reason the invitation to participate was not restricted to members or believers. This may, indeed, be the origin of the so-called "open invitations" at present common among the other Free Churches, but a departure from their traditions. Certainly, this was a distinctively Methodist innovation. Dr. Adam Clarke may be cited as confirmation for the continuance of a practice that Wesley himself had encouraged,[54] when he says: "Every minister of Christ is bound to administer to every man who is seeking the salvation of his soul, as well as to believers."[55]

7. Distinctive Methodist Services

The love-feasts, watch-night services, and covenant services had been originally established by Wesley as supplements to the services and Sacraments of the Established Church. Such was their popularity and their meeting of the need for a simple, spontaneous,

---

[52] *A Compendium of Christian Theology* (2nd edn., 1880), Vol. III, pp. 299-300.
[53] J. Bishop, *op.cit.*, p. 137.   [54] John Wesley, *Works*, Vol. I, p. 262.
[55] Cited J. Bishop, *op.cit.*, p. 138.

sincere, warm type of piety that they continued to be appreciated by Methodists long after Methodism had its own preaching and communion-services.

The love-feasts were held quarterly and they consisted of a meeting of two hours in which prayer and praise were mingled with testimonies to the goodness of God. The assembly fed on bread and water and sold the uneaten bread to provide financial assistance for the poorer members. Jonathan Crowther describes them thus: "The Methodists think, that love-feasts were of apostolic institution. They are mentioned in the 12th verse of the epistle of Jude. . . . In modern times, the Moravians and Methodists are the only Christians, at least in this part of the globe, who hold love-feasts. Among the Moravians, the general refreshment made use of by them, at love-feasts, is tea. And upon these occasions they read the accounts of the success of their missions in the different parts of the world. The Methodists, at these meetings, take only bread and water. The love-feast is both begun and ended by singing and prayer; a travelling preacher presiding. The time is chiefly taken up in relating Christian experience. Any person may speak who chooses. They are generally very agreeable, edifying, and refreshing seasons. They tend to promote piety, mutual affection, and zeal. A collection is made, the first object of which is to pay for the bread used on the occasion; and the surplus is divided among the poor members of the society where the love-feast is held."[56]

These feasts were held more frequently in the larger societies, but in the smaller ones they were held only once or twice a year.[57] They did not, for all their earlier popularity, survive into the twentieth century. Perhaps, as the societies came increasingly to provide their own Communion services the need of the love-feasts was met in this way. Another possible explanation of their demise may be that as the Methodists grew in social respectability and status, they became less attracted to the more charismatic type of ordinance, which put a premium on relating personal experiences of the grace of God. As Methodism established itself as one of the most vigorous of the Free Church denominations, it was inevitable that it should be characterized more by dignity and decorum than by ardour. A still further possibility is that the breaking away

[56] J. Crowther, *Portraiture of Methodism*, p. 243; also Crowther, *Methodist Manual*, pp. 147-48.
[57] Crowther, *Portraiture of Methodism*, p. 243.

from the Wesleyan Body of the Independent Methodists and of the Primitive Methodists who stressed the charismatic characteristics in worship made the truncated Wesleyans less enamoured of such practices.

The watch-night services also flourished for a time only to disappear entirely, no doubt for the same reasons as the love-feasts. Crowther is also our informant on the nature of these gatherings. He writes: "When these are kept according to their original design, and the practice of Mr. Wesley, they do not conclude until the clock strikes twelve at midnight. In many places, however, latterly, something that has been so-called has begun and concluded earlier. A watch-night that is held till midnight usually begins at half past eight o'clock. . . . Originally the service at a watch-night consisted of a short suitable sermon, and then the rest of the time was occupied in alternate singing and prayer. For this service we have an appropriate set of hymns. Now, however, it is not uncommon, but rather very common, in addition to the sermon at the beginning, for some other preacher or preachers to give a word of exhortation at intervals. These seasons are generally very solemn and impressive."[58] The watch-night services continued only as annual occasions, marking the transition from the old year to the new.

Another distinctively Methodist service, the covenant service, has, however, endured to the present time. What better time could have been chosen for the renewal of the Methodist people's covenant with God than the first Sunday of the New Year, when the members of the congregation were reminded by nature herself of the mutability of life, and the inexorability of time, and by the Gospel that their life was a stewardship for which they must give account at the judgment seat of Christ? What better opportunity for making a clean break with the past than the commencement of another year? What better form could it take than the communal renewal of an engagement of the affections and of the will to serve God in the imitation of Christ in the power of the Holy Spirit, such as the covenant service supplied, and the Holy Communion that followed it as the completion of the evening service? What was more fortifying to faith than the impressive scene of the entire local Methodist family in Christ solemnly renewing its vows together?

Here was a service in which the acceptance of the Christian's

[58] J. Crowther, *Methodist Manual*, p. 148; and his *Portraiture of Methodism*, pp. 243-44.

vows were more than the recital of a creed, for it included old penitents "with thoughts too deep for tears," and young aspirants with ideals that were largely inarticulate. This service endured as an unique amalgam of Puritanism and Pietism. Puritanism alone might have reduced the covenant into a narrow legalism; Pietism alone might have dissolved the covenant into subjectivism; together Puritanism and Pietism stressed both the objective element, the Divine promises manifest in the Incarnate and Crucified Christ, and the subjective element, the adoring love and fealty of the fellowship, responding in faith. Ever since its first establishment on August 6, 1755, the covenant service has proved to be an annual means of grace, and it is in no danger of devaluation among the English Methodists of today.

II. *UNITARIANISM*

As the Presbyterians had hoped for comprehension within an enlarged Establishment first in 1660 and later in 1689 and had ultimately accepted a position within English Dissent, the Unitarians of the succeeding century experienced the same succession of exaltation and depression. The consolation of the English Presbyterians might be that the *elect* of God are few; the cold comfort of the English Unitarians (who rejected the doctrines of original sin, pre-destination, and election) had to be that the culturally and socially *select* also are few. Each aspired to comprehension but dwindled to a denomination.

Even the most rationalistic among the Unitarians prove how conservative are the ways of men in worship, and what an unconscionable time old sentiments and habits are in dying. Their essential conservatism in worship is admirably demonstrated by the retention of the Established Church's type of formulary of worship (even if the old bottles were at first filled with heady new wine), and by the persistence throughout the Enlightenment and after of that Biblical Unitarianism which derived its authority and inspiration from the Scriptures, as seen in the writings of Lindsey and Priestley, and their nineteenth century successors.

1. *Tradition and Reaction*

Just as the Transcendentalists in New England were to revolt from the negations and the cold rationalism of the ex-Congregational churches that had become Unitarian ice-boxes, so in England there was a reaction against the ex-Presbyterian Unitarian heterodoxy that time had made into a chilly, customary, conventional religion. Emerson was the chief liberator in America, Martineau in England. In each country, customary Unitarianism was indeed in the House of Bondage, imprisoned by the rusting rationalistic and iconoclastic bars of the previous century. William Hale White's novels are critical enough of the mechanical repetitiveness of Calvinistic orthodoxy in Victorian Congregationalism, but he is even more caustic in his criticism of Victorian Unitarianism, especially in the smaller towns. Its spiritual deadness was symbolized for him by Mark Rutherford's finding of a funeral sermon in the pulpit of the Unitarian country church to which he was called as minister, which indicated that it had been used, with only the alteration of the personal pronouns and adjectives to fit the burial of persons of either sex and presumably all ages.[59] In the small congregation he found only one woman whose practical, generous, and pious heart was not paralyzed by the negations of her head: the feelings of the rest were utterly desiccated.

John Stoughton, the Congregational historian, who honours intelligence but respects the Gospel more, in his evaluation of Victorian Unitarianism is perceptive as well as partizan when he writes: "with all the ability of its ministers, all the respectability of its congregations, all the culture of its society, and all the services which it rendered to science, literature and liberty, it did not advance in numbers or power. So far from it, its history for fifty years is one of decline. The causes are obvious. A dry, hard cold method of preaching generally marked the pulpit; warm, vigorous spiritual life, appeared not in the pews. No greater contrast can be imagined, than between the Methodist and the Presbyterian [Unitarian] preacher, the Methodists and the Presbyterian people. The unction, the fire, the moral force so visible in the one case, is absent in the other. Methodism laid hold on the conscience of England; Presbyterianism did not. The sympathy elicited there, is found wanting here; and no culture, no intellectual power, no respecta-

---

[59] *The Autobiography of Mark Rutherford*, chap. VII, p. 100, reads: "Although my congregation had a free thought lineage, I do not think I ever had anything to do with a more petrified set . . . so far as I could make out the only topics they delighted in were demonstrations of the unity of God from texts in the Bible, and polemics against tri-theism. Sympathy with the great problems then beginning to agitate men, they had none." White is recalling events of a generation before 1881.

bility of position could make up for the lack of earnest gospel preaching and warm-hearted spiritual life."[60]

In similar vein, "Onesimus," the anonymous editor of three volumes of early nineteenth century accounts of preachers, singles out the distinguished divine, Robert Aspland, minister of the Unitarian Meeting, Paradise Field, Hackney, as typical of the Unitarian spirit. While acknowledging that Aspland's prayers are written out, studied with care, well organized, possess stylistic splendour, and are solemnly delivered, yet he insists that "they exhibit not that ardour of soul, that holy zeal, which indicates an evangelical mind, led by the Spirit of truth into the presence of the majesty on high."[61] "Onesimus" further contends that the Unitarian's preaching is "studious, ratiocinative, and acute—with a polished style, good voice and manliness of mien; he is yet tied to his manuscript as by fetters." But, "all is headwork and nothing more."[62] A religion of revolutionary red had turned to cerebral grey.

It is clear that the dead hand of tradition had descended even upon the former theological innovators, even if we discount much of the criticism of orthodox Dissenters as partizanship, poisoned by the sense of social and intellectual inferiority and embittered by the disappointment felt because the Unitarians had legally taken possession in Britain of 178 places of worship which had originally belonged to the orthodox Presbyterians. (This number represented four-fifths of their 253 places of worship in 1834.) Whether or not the judgment of orthodox Dissenters was jaundiced, there was serious inquiry if Unitarianism, being a diminishing movement, was not also a dying one. Waddington reported in 1834 that in the 40 places of Unitarian worship in Lancashire and Derbyshire "the average number of hearers is under twenty-five."[63] Almost exactly a century before, the Deists and the Socinians seemed to be the party of the future; in 1834 they seemed to be the party of the past.

Not all Unitarians, however, were committed to the fetters of a rationalism uninfluenced by the emotions. Priestley himself, superb scientist that he was, was a sufficient humanitarian and propagan-

---

[60] *Religion in England under Queen Anne and the Georges*, ii, p. 229.

[61] *The Pulpit, Or, A Biographical and Literary Account of Eminent Popular Preachers, interspersed with occasional clerical criticism, By Onesimus*, iii, pp. 329, 331.

[62] *Ibid.*

[63] *Congregational History: 1800-1850*, p. 312. Though the Unitarians were strong in Liverpool and Manchester in Lancashire, the Derbyshire figures (since there was only one industrial city, Derby, included) would not have told as impressive a story as, for example, the Norwich, Birmingham, or London attendances at worship.

dist of liberty to know that men cannot live by reason alone. It is of interest that Mrs. Barbauld, a Unitarian blue-stocking, should have joined forces with Priestley in his battle against a restrictive rationalism as expressed in Gilbert Wakefield's *Inquiry into the Expediency and Propriety of Public or Social Worship.* Her *Thoughts on Devotional Taste*[64] claimed that the emotional element was basic in Christian piety, vindicated faith as well as reason, and warned that mere intellectual inquisitiveness in religion would reduce ardour to frigid and inconclusive speculation. In this concern she was a precursor of the Martineau who wanted to combine intellectual honesty and outgoing concern for his brother men with a profound obeisance before the Living God and the ethical imitation of Jesus.

The liturgical watershed for nineteenth century Unitarianism is the year 1862, when first appeared *Common Prayer for Christian Worship*, a formulary which combined the best of the older tradition in the first eight forms of service and in the orders for the two Sacraments, and which also expressed in the preface and in the remarkable ninth and tenth orders the genius of Martineau and the new Unitarian spirit and ethos which he exemplified with such distinction.[65] This important formulary, which was often re-issued and often imitated, will be considered in detail later in this chapter. Here it will suffice to give some brief indication of the "modern temper" of Martineau's Unitarianism. The source of the older Unitarian inspiration was undoubtedly the Bible and however these beliefs might be tinctured by rationalism it was a rationalism that always appealed for confirmation to the Bible against the testimony of the historic Creeds. It is, therefore, properly called Biblical Unitarianism, because it asserted, along with the unity of the infinite and eternal God, the pre-eminence of Christ among men, His authority as exemplar and teacher, and even, in many cases, His Resurrection and Second Coming. Its source was an older conception of revelation, ratified in the sacred oracles of the Scriptures.

The newer Unitarianism of Martineau refused in any sense to

---

[64] See Mrs. Anne Laetitia Barbauld's *Works* (ed. Lucy Aikin), Vol. II, pp. 413 f.

[65] In the second part of this chapter I am greatly indebted to the researches of the Rev. A. Elliott Peaston, the historian of Unitarian forms of worship in England, which are contained in his Oxford dissertation *The Prayer Book Reform Movement in the XVIIIth Century* and in two important articles, respectively, "Nineteenth Century Liturgies" in *Transactions of the Unitarian Historical Society*, Vol. VII, No. 3, pp. 215 f. and "Dr Martineau and the 'Ten Services,'" Vol. VII, No. 4. The seventh volume of the *Transactions* covers the years 1939-1942.

regard the work of Christ as Mediatorial for He was viewed as a rare and compassionate leader rather than the Lord of the Church, as one who was imitable precisely because as man he shared the human lot of all men. These negations of Martineau were matched with the most positive affirmation of devotion to Jesus, which in its delicacy and depth is equalled only by the tenderness of the English mediaeval mystics and surpassed only by Thomas à Kempis' *Imitatio Christi* or Loyola's *Exercitia Spiritualia*.

The newer spirit was akin to Transcendentalism in its German and American forms, rather than to the older Biblical Unitarianism, despite the saturation of Martineau's prayers with Biblical diction, imagery, and insight. It was a philosophical rather than a theological inspiration in the precise and traditional sense of the latter term. It was the fruit of meditation on man's role in the universe, in its moral, aesthetic, and intellectual aspects rather than a response to the Divine self-disclosure of the Biblical revelation speaking with its own interior authority by the power of the Holy Spirit, as the authentic judging and saving Word of God. Martineau's understanding of religion has strong Kantian overtones in its emphasis on God, freedom, duty, and immortality, but the Pietism which was in Kant's background displays itself in the foreground of Martineau's concern. Aware of the importance of honest faith that can commend itself to reason, Martineau had the sensitivity of the artist and the poet, and his religion no less than Schleiermacher's is marked by a profound sense of dependence upon God, and of the importance of experience in renewing man's relationship to God and his fellows.

Other influences that can be detected in his prayers are the Presbyterian sense of the majesty of God and of man's duty to glorify Him (but with a complete rejection of the doctrines of original sin, predestination, and election)[66] and an Anglican sense of the art of worship requiring a common formulary of prayer, with a chaste and carefully chosen diction, balanced cadences, and responses which alone make the worship truly corporate. His rationalism is seen in his insistence upon integrity of thought and life, in his concern for all humanity, in his insistence upon that freedom which is man's greatest privilege (and which the Augustinian tradition in Catholicism and Protestantism interprets as license), and in his refusal to limit the Divine Providence to ecclesiastical channels. But it is a rationalism that is chastened by

[66] As the name might suggest, Martineau was of Huguenot ancestry.

a sense of actual sin. The uniqueness of Martineau lies, however, one might suggest, in the fact that he is a Pietist in the Rationalist Tradition.

2. *Old Wine in Old Bottles*

While Martineau changed the direction of Unitarian thought and feeling from 1862 onward, both before and after Martineau the older tradition of a Biblical Unitarianism expressing itself in successive revisions of the Book of Common Prayer, after the fashion of Lindsey, lived on. It was quite characteristic of the period that equally significant examples of worship-books of this type for the expression of the devotions of Biblical Unitarians were produced before and after 1862.[67] In 1826 Robert Wallace published his *Forms of Prayer for Unitarian Congregations* in Chesterfield. In 1847 G. B. Brock produced for his Swansea congregation a further Prayer Book revision after the manner of Lindsey. In 1859 Goodwyn Barmby issued his *Special Services of Public Worship for Use in the Churches of Christ* at Wakefield. Two years later Robert Ainslie printed *The Church Book for the Use of the Congregation of Christ Church, Brighton.*

These four forms of corporate worship have several common characteristics and together may be regarded as typical of Biblical Unitarianism. The belief in miracles and supremely in the miracle of the Resurrection of Jesus is dominant (in Wallace of Chesterfield and in Barmby of Wakefield). There is even an eager expectation of the Second Coming of the Messiah and of the Day of Judgment. Another strong characteristic is the revision of the Creeds and traditional Canticles (such as the *Te Deum*) and ecclesiastical prayers (like St. John Chrysostom's) in terms of a greater conformity to the Scriptures, as exemplified by Barmby of Wakefield and Ainslie of Brighton. Further, there is a complete rejection of sacerdotalism whether explicit or implicit. For Wallace of Chesterfield the Lord's Supper is simply a commemoration, not a Communion, and he is typical also in rejecting any suggestion of original sin in the Baptismal order and therefore of any hint of a priestly miracle. Brock of Swansea makes it unnecessarily clear in the Absolution following the eviscerated General Confession that it is God, not the minister, who grants remission of sins. (The Book of Common Prayer, however, is equally clear that the minister

[67] A. E. Peaston, "Nineteenth Century Liturgies," Vol. VII (1939-1942), No. 3, pp. 215 f. of *Transactions of the Unitarian Historical Society*, London.

is only God's deputy and servant in giving absolution in His name.)

Even after the liturgical revolution represented by Martineau (and Sadler his elder co-compiler of *Common Prayer for Christian Worship*) in 1862, admirable service-books modelled directly on the Book of Common Prayer continued to appear. The most influential of them was the work of the distinguished literary critic and chaplain to Queen Victoria, Stopford Brooke, which he had prepared for the use of his Bloomsbury congregation in 1891. Directly dependent on this revision were two others: Copeland Bowie's *Seven Services* of 1900 and a liturgical order compiled for Sheffield Unitarians in 1906. More independent in character were two other revisions of the Book of Common Prayer, one being published in Birmingham, entitled *A Book of Prayer in Ten Orders of Public Worship* (1904) and the other in Halifax, for the use of the Northgate End Chapel in 1913.

The Birmingham revision of the Liturgy was designed to permit the congregation to engage more directly and actively in worship, and sung responses from the Bible and the Book of Common Prayer were provided. The unusual feature of the Halifax Liturgy was its inclusion in a sixth order of service, which is a poetical paean of Divine praise, of George Eliot's "O may I join the choir invisible," and Stopford Brooke's "Slow comes the evening o'er the hill." Even these additions would not have been possible but for the place Martineau had found for the feelings, and the poem of George Eliot must have seemed congenial in its expression of the Commemoration of the faithful departed, because this had been a characteristic of Martineau's orders of worship. Thus, even when Biblical Unitarianism and the maintenance of the Anglican forms seem generally to ignore the modern spirit in Martineau, they are also seen in part to be imitating him.

The single *outré* and exotic volume of orders of Unitarian worship during the period was Peter Dean's *Prayers and Ministries for Public Worship in Six Services* which he prepared for his Walsall congregation in 1878. This exceptional volume consisted of a collection of devotions drawn from all the major religions of the world. Its dependence upon the Book of Common Prayer and the Bible was slight, since the Lord's Prayer and the Beatitudes represent the only distinctively Christian elements in the book. Its comprehensiveness was equalled only by its didacticism, which is evidenced in the selection of a single theme or mood for each separate order of worship. But even this unusual, original, and

270

bizarre volume had its precursor in the manual of worship produced by David Williams in 1776, which he named *A Liturgy on the Universal Principles of Religion and Morality*.[68] On the whole, however, the corporate forms of worship which have been referred to were remarkable for their consistently and even monotonously eighteenth century theology and for their use of the Anglican techniques of worship. They serve only to show the need for the pioneering work of Sadler and Martineau, which owes its fame to the hoarding and scattering of treasures old and new.

3. The New Wine of James Martineau (1805-1900)

From 1862 to the present time at least forty different English Unitarian formularies of worship have been prepared, but easily the most distinguished of them was *Common Prayer for Christian Worship* which became the pattern for many others. Peaston claims, with justice, that it was as much of an archetype for Unitarian worship in the nineteenth century as Samuel Clarke's revision of the Prayer Book had been for the eighteenth century. In short, "it marks a new era in Unitarian liturgy," and it is "historic because for the first time Nonconformists produced a liturgical editor of rare genius."[69] That editor was Martineau.[70]

His life was an admirably balanced combination of ministerial and academic duties, for along with his influential Liverpool and London pastorates he was for forty-five years professor of mental and moral philosophy and political economy in Manchester New College, which was removed to London in 1853, Martineau following four years later.[71] He was principal of the college from 1869 to 1885. He was minister of the following Unitarian congregations: Paradise Street Chapel, Liverpool (1832-1848); Hope Street Church, Liverpool (1849-1857); and Little Portland Street Chapel, London (1859-1872).[72] This combination of duties enabled him to cultivate the mind and spirit together to the advantage of both, and to the great benefit of his students and his congregations. His pastoral preparation was incorporated in four volumes of sermons, *Endeavours after a Christian Life* (1st series

[68] See Chapter VII, section 4, *supra*, for a brief discussion of this work.
[69] Peaston art., "Nineteenth Century Liturgies," Vol. VII, No. 3, p. 219 of *Transactions of the Unitarian Historical Society*.
[70] The work is analyzed in the fourth and fifth sections of this chapter, *infra*.
[71] Subsequently the College moved to Oxford, where it is now designated Manchester College, and has included some of Oxford's most famous names as its Principals, notably J. Estlin Carpenter and L. P. Jacks.
[72] See Preface, *Prayers in the Congregation and in the College*.

271

1843; 2nd 1847) and *Hours of Thought on Sacred Things* (1st series 1876; 2nd 1879), in various hymnbooks, and in the *Home Prayers* of 1891. His ethical and philosophical preparation is harvested in *The Rationale of Religious Enquiry* (1836), *The Types of Ethical Theory* (1885), *A Study of Religion* (1888), and *The Seat of Authority in Religion* (1890).

To attempt to understand this complex and sensitive mind and heart, it is necessary to know what he greatly cared for and what he disliked. His two chief dislikes were a "sacrosanct priesthood and an enforced uniformity."[73] Correlatively, he valued as life itself the priesthood of all believers and freedom for enquiry and commitment in religion. He had the secularist's distrust of the Church and the saint's trust in God.

His views on worship are of particular importance. He disliked the sacerdotal religion of the English Prayer Book[74] and found its opening confessions exaggerated: "Surely, we none of us believe, and Christ did not mean to teach that human persons in general, and his disciples everywhere and always, are in the case of the prodigal son?"[75] He felt equally averse to the reiterated appeals to God to remember His promises, as if God were only a feudal overlord who had to be reminded of his duties because of the service men had rendered to Him. As his biographer J. Estlin Carpenter remarks, this Anglican type of devotion "stood in sharp contrast with the Puritan type, which placed the essence of devotion in the free outpouring of affection, begotten by realizing the relations in which he has deigned to draw us to himself."[76] Penitence was important for Martineau, but he felt that it should not drown the chorus of praise, and that it was evoked most meaningfully by the Christian's prior sense of gratitude.[77] He gave an absolute primacy to worship over all instruction in his services, successful preacher though he was. He wrote: " I cannot conceive of a Church without the worship of a Living and Personal God. With this I think a Church must begin, and not end: and short of this we can have . . . only clubs or associations for particular objects, not any fusion into a common spiritual life."[78]

73 See article on James Martineau in *Encyclopaedia Britannica* (printing of 1957), Vol. 14, p. 989 b.
74 For his dislike of sacerdotal religion see J. Drummond and C. B. Upton, *The Life and Letters of James Martineau*, Vol. 1, pp. 381-84.
75 *Op.cit.*, Vol. 1, p. 386.
76 *James Martineau, Theologian and Teacher*, pp. 414-15.
77 A view supported by the 1928 Revision of the Prayer Book.
78 Longmans published the Ninth and Tenth Orders of the composite 1862 volume separately under this title.

It was with convictions such as these that Martineau set out to produce the two services (the Ninth and Tenth) of *Common Prayer for Christian Worship*. His own emphases in worship can be found most clearly expressed in the content of the prayers of his own devising. For this purpose the *Prayers in the Congregation and College* (posthumously published in 1911) are particularly valuable because they provide often relatively unpolished specimens of his work from 1844 to 1882, as contrasted with the carefully revised and stylistically polished prayers of the *Two Services*.[79]

The profoundest impression they leave is of a man awed and abased in the presence of the mystery, the majesty, and the holiness of God, who is also merciful. As for Gerard Manley Hopkins, so for Martineau God was, "lightning and love." Otto might have taken the following prayer as a modern expression of the *mysterium tremendum et fascinans*, written by a man of scrupulous honesty and delicate sensitivity:

"O Thou who art our Refuge and our Help! we enter now thy secret place, Most High, and seek rest within the shadow of the Almighty. O Lord, why do we so trust in thee, for thou art very terrible? Thou hangest the world upon nothing, yet we dwell thereon in peace. Thou barest thine arm in the lightning, yet we work in the fields which thou smitest, and own it as thy messenger. There is no blackness and darkness and tempest where thou art not; yet we believe thine infinite light behind the cloud. Yea, Lord, though the storms of death break us in pieces we are not afraid; for with much mercy wilt thou gather us and take us where there is great calm.

"But, O God most just! let not our security be as the confidence of fools. . . . We would look up to Thee, O thou Holiest, we ask no recompense of our obedience, lest we receive only the wages of sin, and die; but leave ourselves to thine infinite pity in the hope that to them who loved much, and repented with many tears, thou wilt say, 'Your sins are forgiven; depart in peace.' "[80]

Second only to this numinous sense of "sacred dread" is the emphasis on sacrifice. "Amid the profusion of thy gifts," beseeches Martineau, "may we remember that we are disciples of one who had not where to lay his head; make us ashamed of sloth and indulgence, and teach us for his sake to deny ourselves and offer ourselves up a living sacrifice to thee."[81]

[79] *Prayers in the Congregation and College*, pp. 11-12.
[80] *Ibid.*, p. 43.   [81] *Ibid.*, pp. 13-14.

There is also a profound respect for and deep attachment to the historic Jesus as the first Christian, if not as the Mediator; as the exemplar of sacrifice, if not himself the uniquely acceptable Sacrifice. The imitation of Jesus is frequently assumed to be the norm for every Christian.[82] The dependence upon the Christology of Schleiermacher is most clearly manfested in a prayer of 1850 written in lyrical apostrophes: "O Fount of everlasting Wisdom! Light of our life! Soul of our souls! with whom prophets have communed in every age, but whom the Man of Sorrows hath chiefly known, let thy blessed traces still be found. Thou renewest the youth of devout souls: we dedicate ourselves afresh to the simplicity of Christ, and aspire again to do and bear thy perfect will."[83] Elsewhere Martineau begs that God will "fill us with the divine humility of Christ."[84]

Again, the silver hope of immortality, if not the golden assurance of the resurrection, irradiates these prayers. Moreover, there is a strong sense of the communion of noble spirits unsevered by the shears of death. The first prayer in the volume concludes with the words: ". . . and bear us into thy communion of saints by which pure and open souls, in earth or heaven, are knit together and to thee."[85]

His generous spirit is expressed in the comprehensive concern for all sorts and conditions of men and women, especially the poor, the anxious, the careless, the afflicted, young and the aged, which is expressed in words that are always pertinent and sympathetic, yet never sentimental or trite.[86]

Finally, as we are impressed by the Augustinian-Calvinist sense of the sovereignty of the Holy God of grace, so do we recognise the ethical strenuousness of the Puritan tradition in his prayers. It is piercingly expressed in two short petitions. The first reads: "Wake in us a soul to obey thee, not with the weariness of servile spirits, but with the alacrity of holy angels";[87] and the second: "May we dread above all the poisoned sweetness of sin, and choose rather the

---

[82] *Ibid.*, p. 36, provides an example in its conclusion: "And may all draw nearer this day to the likeness of Jesus Christ, in whom thou wert well pleased," as also *ibid.*, pp. 13-14, cited in the previous penultimate paragraph. The most vigorous example of the *imitatio Christi* is found in the concluding affirmation of another prayer: "For life and death we trust ourselves to thee as disciples of Jesus Christ" (p. 38).

[83] *Ibid.*, p. 40.

[84] *Ibid.*, p. 13.

[85] *Ibid.*, p. 6. See also pp. 18 and 24.

[86] *Ibid.*, pp. 23-24. There is, however, little sense of social justice.

[87] *Ibid.*, pp. 17-18.

bitterest draught of healthful duty."[88] Theoretically the rationalist tradition had rejected Calvinism, but, like Pascal, Martineau was to discover that the heart has its reasons that reason knows not.

4. The Origin and Aim of the "Common Prayers for Christian Worship" (1862)[89]

The remarkable Preface of this work explains how it came to be compiled, at the wish of a group of London Unitarian ministers under the leadership of Dr. Sadler[90] of Hampstead, and how the more revolutionary spirit of Martineau expressed itself in the Ninth and Tenth Services, and ultimately in the revision of the whole in accord with the modern spirit. It should, however, be made clear that the Preface appeared anonymously, but that it was common knowledge among the London Unitarian ministers, whose advice had been sought, what was in fact composed by each of the two major contributors.

The Preface begins by observing that the freest of Free Churches are aware of the advantages of having a Book of Common Prayer. While many will still prefer the outpouring of extempore prayer, either from habit or because they associate genuine fervour with free prayer, others will care more for "the fitness than the newness of the language" and will value the sacred associations and the sense of communion with Christian assemblies far and near which such a formulary evokes.

A historical excursus follows which is designed to show that while the Reformation generally favoured the practice of free prayers, an exception was made in the National English Church, which the less extreme Puritans, the Presbyterians, were content to follow (abating a few objections) in order to secure comprehension within a wider Established Church. Of such were Baxter and Calamy, and their liturgical mantle has descended upon the Unitarians. This explains why Unitarians prefer a formulary

[88] *Ibid.*, p. 29.

[89] The first edition of *Common Prayer for Christian Worship* appeared in London in 1862. Owing to the kindness of Professor James Luther Adams of the Harvard Divinity School I have had access to the rare Boston first edition of 1863 which is substantially the same as the 1862 edition and from which all citations are taken. The publisher's note indicates that "the only alterations made are such as were required to adapt the book to the use of churches in this country. A few brief prayers—those for the Royal family, and a few others—have been omitted." The Preface appears unchanged. The citation is from pp. 1-2.

[90] Sadler was deeply read in such seventeenth century devotional divines as Jeremy Taylor and Richard Baxter.

for corporate prayer and maintain the older Presbyterian concern for integrity of belief, untrammelled by the historic creeds, and re-echo their "longing for a worship that unites."[91]

The original design of the London ministers was for "a new Liturgical compilation, to be gathered, in a Catholic spirit, from the devotional writings of every Christian age." It was found impossible of attainment, partly because of the need "of adapting the parts to the whole" and partly because "of the requirements of theological honesty." A party of the ministers was anxious that new treasures should be added to the old, in order "to reach more effectively some chords of modern feeling."[92] The duties of producing the new treasures and of revising the entire work were undertaken by Martineau.

5. *An Analysis of Its Contents*

Common Prayer for Christian Worship consists of a Preface (of 12 pages); Ten Services consisting of five forms for weekday use and five for Sunday use (pp. 19-172); a collection of Collects for the Christian Year, aptly titled (pp. 173-94) and of Prayers and Thanksgivings (pp. 195-222); five pages of Collects suitable for use before or after the Sermon; and Special Services for the Communion, the Baptism of Infants (and those of Riper Years), Confirmation, Matrimony, Visitation of the Sick, Burial, and Prayers to be used at sea (pp. 228-87).

Martineau's contribution to the volume now demands consideration. The Ninth and Tenth Services demonstrate his inventiveness in technique as well as in content. He is adept at producing new Canticles[93] by collating Scriptural passages, as he is at providing new responses to prayers. For example, after the prayers of contrition, petition, and the remembrance of the communion of saints, he supplies the congregation with the Dominical *pax*, as recorded in John 14:27, as their response.[94]

His real genius, however, is to be found in the freshness of an authentic first-hand experience of God felicitously phrased, and in the range of his moods of prayer ranging from the awed humility of his prayer of contrition and the mystical sense of the Communion of Saints to the prophetic insight of his Intercession for the Nation. "Thy praise is only our abasement, and the greatness

91 Preface, pp. 2-3.   92 *Op.cit.*, p. 3.
93 For example, "Lo! at length the True Light . . ." in the Ninth Service.
94 Ninth Service.

of thy mercy is the measure of our guilt" has the genuine ring of the Bible and the Prayer Book. The Prayer for the Spirit of Christ is authentically prophetic, as it pleads with God: "Send forth his spirit speedily into the dark places of our guilt and woe, and arm it with the piercing power of thy grace. May it reach the heart of every oppression, and make arrogancy dumb before thee."[95]

Martineau sounds like a latter-day Amos, as he cries, "Make us equal to our high trusts; reverent in the use of freedom, just in the exercise of power, generous in the protection of weakness. . . . Let it be known among us how thou hatest robbery for burnt-offering; that the gains of industry may be all upright, and the use of wealth considerate."[96]

The tenth Service also abounds in prayers that are modern classics of devotional expression. There is, for instance, the moving prayer of confession: "O God ever-blessed and holy; none but the Angels and thy Redeemed can serve thee with perfect joy. On us, as we look up to the light of thy countenance, the shadows of shameful remembrance fall: and to all thy mercies we still must answer with a cry for more."

How admirable that the prayer for divine guidance should lead to the responsive promise of the congregation: "Even as he said to all, 'If any man comes after me, let him deny himself, and take up his cross daily and follow me.' "[97] Mysticism has no escape from morality, but rather adoration is the incentive to obedience.

Who would guess that an English Unitarian had composed the following catholic prayer for the Church, if he did not know that the author was James Martineau? "O God, who didst send thy word to speak in the prophets and live in thy Son; and appoint thy Church to be the witness of divine things in the world; revive the purity and deepen the power of its testimony: and through the din of earthly interests and the storm of human passions, let it make the still small voice of thy Spirit inly felt. Nearer and nearer may thy kingdom come from age to age; meeting the face of the young as a rising dawn, and brightening the face of the old, 'Lord, now lettest thou thy servant depart in peace.' Already let its light abash our guilty negligence, and touch with hope each secret sorrow of the earth. By the cleansing power of thy Son, make this world a fitting forecourt to that sanctuary not made with hands, where our life is hid with Christ in God.[98]"

Of these two services taken together, it may be remarked that

[95] *Ibid.*   [96] *Ibid.*   [97] Tenth Service.   [98] *Ibid.*

they reach the highest pinnacle of Free Church worship in their expression of the holy and mysterious transcendence of God ("the free winds of thine invisible Providence"), in the humility, contrition, and resolve that His grace evokes, and in their reverence for the sacrificial life and passion of Jesus, the undaunted Pioneer and Exemplar of our faith. The diction and arrangement show a combination of Biblical words, images and insights, a classical gift for clarity, concision, and mellifluous cadence. The influence of the Bible and the impact of a study and imitation of the collects is paramount. Martineau also had the common-sense of the true liturgist in the varying moods, types, and lengths of his prayers, in the judicious intermingling of praise, readings, and prayers, and, above all, in the comparative brevity of each service (half the length of Matins or Evensong in the Book of Common Prayer) and in the memorable and profound succinctness of his prayers which no repetition would exhaust or make stale. Whether acknowledged or unacknowledged, Martineau's prayers have become a notable part of the currency of prayer in English devotional life. Their only defect is that, an irritating didacticism although usually submerged, occasionally emerges to deflect the attention from God to man.

6. The Special Services

The Orders for the Lord's Supper and Baptism are inevitably an anti-climax after the services for which Martineau alone was responsible. Yet, if Martineau had not penned the Ninth and Tenth Services, they might well have been considered the climax of the entire book. For, although employing a "reduced Christology," they attempt to express, consonant with Unitarian belief, the modern meanings of the ancient and traditional Eucharistic and Baptismal services.[99]

The Lord's Supper is particularly interesting if conceived in this light. It can then be seen that the meaning of the ordinance is, according to the first exhortation, to render gratitude for "the word and work of Jesus Christ" who died on the Cross to make us "in spirit children of God" and instituted this Supper "that we may remember his exceeding love, and by cherishing a holy fellowship with him be partakers of his joy, and bring forth the fruits of

---

99 It should be noted that Martineau himself favoured the use of language less conducive to a Mediatorial interpretation of the work of Christ, than these prayers and exhortations express. One judges that there is more of Sadler than Martineau in the Special Services.

278

righteousness." The alternative exhortation supplies a modern equivalent for the *Sursum Corda*: "And now to this end, lift up your minds and hearts on high, where Jesus abideth in the glory of his Father," which is immediately spoiled by clumsy didacticism of the admonitory type.

A revised prayer of Humble Access and an alternative petition for acceptance follows the exhortation. Then the Scriptural authority for the rite (I Corinthians 11:23-26) follows, according to Presbyterian usage, and the minister communicates first and then the people. The words of delivery have three alternative forms: one is Scriptural and memorialist in intention; the second is a testimony to the faith of the congregation in Christ; the third is simply a declaration that the bread and wine are emblems of the broken body and shed blood of Christ. The congregation then makes an affirmation of its loyalty to Christ by repeating either John 17:24-26 or a declaration that "Under the veil of earthly things, we now have communion with Jesus Christ: but with unveiled faces we shall soon behold him; and by him all his true disciples will be presented before the presence of his Father's glory with exceeding joy." These all too slight affirmations appear to take the place of the historic creeds in the Holy Eucharist of the Roman Catholic, Orthodox, and Anglican Churches, or that of the Covenant in the Puritan tradition.

The usual position of the *Sursum Corda* and the Prayer of Intercession in the Western rites is immediately before the Fraction, Libation, Consecration, and Delivery of the sacred Elements; in this order for the Lord's Supper they follow the Communion. Martineau or his colleague must, however, had some good reason for this and it may be that they were following Eastern precedent. The supposition is given greater probability from the immense public interest in the Eastern Rites elicited by the Oxford Movement and the Cambridge Ecclesiologists and their successors, and by the hint of an *epiclesis* which appears in the prayer immediately preceded by the explicit *Sursum Corda* and the *Gloria*, and which begins: "Father of our spirits; mindful of Christ's life and teachings, his death upon the cross, his resurrection and ascension, and his seat at thy right hand, we have partaken of this bread and this wine in remembrance of him. We beseech thee to sanctify them and us; and may we who eat of one bread and drink of one cup be made one with each other in the fellowship of the same Holy Spirit, and one with thee and thy dear Son." The rest of the prayer in its range of intercession for many classes of people and simple conciseness is also reminiscent of the Eastern Liturgies.

Certainly this Lord's Supper was a great advance over any other English Unitarian Order that had appeared, and it was richer by far than most of the deplorably Zwinglian Lord's Suppers celebrated in English Dissent during this time. Its whole approach, however, seems to render it so historical and traditional as to take it far beyond the bounds of the most generous Unitarianism in doctrine. But this very criticism may be only one further tribute to the revolution that Martineau had in mind when he helped Sadler to edit *Common Prayer for Christian Worship.*

The Order for Ministration of Baptism to Infants calls for little explanation. It begins in a convincingly traditional way, after the Exhortation, with a prayer to "admit this infant, we beseech thee, into the bosom of thy Church, into the service of Christ, in the arms of thy mercy, and into the communion of saints." The interrogations require a promise to instruct the child in the Gospel and to "keep God's holy will and commandments." After the parents have named the child, the minister declares, "This water is an emblem of the purity which Christ desired in the soul of all who come to him." The child may then be baptized either in the traditional Triune formula or "in the name of Jesus Christ." If the parents so desire, the child may be dedicated instead, one formula being: "In the name of Jesus Christ, I dedicate thee to God our Father in heaven." Then after a new-style Benediction of the child, an address to the parents is followed by the prayers for them and for their child, the Lord's Prayer, and the Blessing. In this Order, too, there is some conflict between the objectivity implied in the traditional language and the subjectivity by which it is later explicated.

When a liturgical genius like Martineau writes modern classics of prayer his influence is bound to be profound. This can be seen most immediately in the work of his son-in-law, who compiled *Orders of Public Worship for use in the Chapel of Manchester College, Oxford,* and became the leader of the English Unitarians of his day. The impact of Martineau's ideas of worship on his denomination in England is proven by the demand for a second though unrevised edition of the *Common Prayer* in 1875 and for a revised edition in 1879, which was retitled *Ten Services of Public Prayer.* In 1899 *The Order for Morning and Evening Prayer* issued in Liverpool, which was discussed but not adopted by the Ullet Road Church, was greatly in Martineau's debt; *The Services for*

the Use of the Congregation worshipping at Chapel Lane Chapel,
Bradford (1905) were partly based on *Common Prayer*, as were
the eighth, ninth, and tenth services in *Services for Divine Worship*
prepared for Upper Chapel, Sheffield.[100] The American Unitarians
required other editions of the work after the first Boston edition
of 1863.

The widest influence, however, was felt in the ranks of the other
Free Churches in England. Martineau's prayers influenced John
Hunter's *Devotional Services*, and many of them were included in
Euchologion, in W. E. Orchard's *Divine Service* and in *The Free*
Church Book of Common Prayer, to mention a few of the more im-
portant compilations, two of them from the present century. Many
of Martineau's prayers warrant ecumenical usage.

[100] See A. E. Peaston's article on "Nineteenth Century Liturgies." *Transactions*
of the Unitarian Historical Society, Vol. VII (1939-1942), No. 3, pp. 215 f.

CHAPTER X

THE POWER OF THE VICTORIAN PULPIT

THE NINETEENTH CENTURY, like the seventeenth, was a great age of the pulpit. Both were ages of enthusiasm, of transition, of national self-consciousness. In such times, as the older stabilities are giving way, men seek guidance from their religious mentors and, if this is forthcoming, the churches and chapels will be crowded. While the Victorians could not boast preachers of devout erudition like Lancelot Andrewes, nor of brilliant imagination and stylistic verve like John Donne, nor even of ethical insight equal to Jeremy Taylor's, they too had their pulpit giants. They were perhaps men of greater solidity than brilliance, though Newman's gem-like flame could have borne comparison with any seventeenth century candle. But, parallels apart, how can the extraordinary magnetism and drawing-power of the Victorian pulpit be accounted for, particularly since, to twentieth century taste, the sermons of that time seem inordinately prolix, tediously repetitive, rarely original, and frequently pompous?

1. The Magnetism of Victorian Preaching

It is commonplace to explain the power of the Victorian pulpit by the tedium of a Victorian Sabbath in which no competing attractions were permitted. F. W. Robertson denied this roundly and insisted that the preacher's task was newly circumscribed because other agencies had taken away many of the functions of the preacher and prophet in former times. Robertson averred: "By the change of times the pulpit has lost its place. It does only part of that whole which used to be done by it alone. Once it was newspaper, schoolmaster, theological treatise, a stimulant to good works, historical lecture, metaphysics, etc., all in one. Now they are partitioned out to different officers, and the pulpit is no more the pulpit of three centuries back, than the authority of a master of a household is that of Abraham, who was soldier, butcher, sacrificer, shepherd and emir in one person."[1]

[1] Ed. Stopford A. Brooke, *The Life and Letters of Frederick W. Robertson*, Vol. II, pp. 59-60.

Moreover, moral duties (and in some cases theological doctrines) were also proclaimed by the poets, novelists, and essayists of the day with notable success, as in the cases of Tennyson and Browning, George Eliot and Mrs. Humphry Ward, Carlyle, Ruskin, and Matthew Arnold.[2] Furthermore, in the latter part of the century it became common for city art-galleries to be opened to the public on Sunday afternoons. Clearly, then, the Victorian preacher was far from being immune from competition. Even so, the competition was not as acute as it has become in our own time, with television, radio, and the theatre and moving pictures drawing considerable numbers away from the churches. More to the point, however, is the consideration that the motor-car had not been invented in the nineteenth century and consequently people lived in more stable communities. Contemporary mobility and social rootlessness, not to mention suburbia, are ugly developments of our own time, made possible by cheap, popular, and speedier transport. Even when the new factors are given their full weight, they do not explain why the eighteenth century pulpit was dull and the nineteenth century pulpit relatively exciting, for each was without the rival social activities of the twentieth century.

The fact remains that to many Victorians sermon-tasting was both a duty and a delight. As moderns are attracted to particular actors, musicians, and film stars, so Victorians flocked to the various popular preachers of their choice. The education of a Victorian connoisseur of sermons could be a lengthy and arduous apprenticeship, as in the case of one Edward Clodd of that period. When he came up to London in 1855, he changed the rather restrictive atmosphere of his Baptist home in Norfolk for the liberal and ampler air of several notable divines. Each time he went to hear one of them, he found the church or chapel thronged. For a dozen years, while he laboured as a bank clerk, his absorbing interest was to listen to Sunday sermons or weekday lectures on the subjects of the day. He heard Thomas Binney thundering in his Dissenting broadsides at the Established Church from the pulpit of the King's Weigh-House,[3] the romantic and literary sermons of Alexander Raleigh,[4] and Newman Hall's coercive-eloquence at Rowland Hill's

[2] Rashdall insisted that Tennyson and Browning were the greatest theological teachers of the day. (P. E. Matheson, *Life of Hastings Rashdall*, p. 177.) See also W. R. Inge (in the *Studies of English Mysticism*, p. 35), who said: "The poets have been our most influential prophets and preachers in the nineteenth century."
[3] E. Paxton Hood, *Thomas Binney, His Mind, Life, and Opinions*, provides a lively portrait.
[4] See ed. Mary Raleigh, *Alexander Raleigh; Records of His Life.*

old chapel in the Blackfriars Road. He was, however, by no means denominationally bigoted, for, in addition to these three Congregational ministers, he listened to the philosophical and ethical sermons of the eminent Unitarian divine, Dr. James Martineau, in the Great Portland Street Chapel, and his attendance at Anglican churches was marked by the same catholicity, for he heard F. D. Maurice at Lincoln's Inn Chapel, Dean Stanley at Westminster Abbey, and Canon Liddon at St. Paul's Cathedral.[5] Using this and other sources for her judgment, Amy Cruse rightly concluded in her book, *The Victorians and their Books* (1935), that "no right-minded Victorian thought his Sunday properly spent unless he had heard at least one sermon."[6] Some regularly attended twice and a few enthusiasts went to a third service each Sunday. Clearly, sermon-tasting was a favourite diversion that also counted as a duty and was thus doubly attractive to the Victorians.

Undoubtedly part of the attraction may be attributed to the variety of personalities, with strongly marked views, which the Victorian pulpits afforded. Prolix as most of these preachers were, they were rarely mealy-mouthed. Joseph Parker, whose unruly locks were the index of an untamed and untameable personality, electrified the congregation of the City Temple once by a series of admonitions addressed on the occasion of the New Year to Queen Victoria, and another time, preaching on the Armenian atrocities, concluded his peroration with a fervent, "God damn the Sultan."[7] Not all the Victorian preachers were as ebullient as he, or Spurgeon, or their prototype, Rowland Hill; but there was a great variety of approach as well as of personality in the Victorian pulpit. Some preachers were Biblical expositors, some teachers of doctrine, some apologists, some ethicists, and several polemicists; this variety was accounted for partly by the changing theologies of the day and partly by the great social issues that forced men to take sides. Charles Kingsley and James Baldwin Brown were available for those who wished to liberate theology from the cast-iron decrees of Calvinism or for others who were interested in the social implications of the Christian message and community. Equally, those who sought for the solid reassurance of orthodoxy in its Patristic or Calvinistic forms could count on getting it from Newman and Spurgeon. For those who preferred theism to Christianity in the traditional mould, there were always the philosophical and ethical

5 Edward Clodd, *Memories.*   6 *Op.cit.*, p. 108.
7 A. L. Drummond, *The Churches pictured by "Punch,"* pp. 43 f.

discourses of Martineau which provided food for mind and heart. Those with developed literary tastes could revel in the polished sermons of Stopford Brooke and Alexander Raleigh. The lovers of drama would turn to the leonine Parker, and the admirers of a quiet devotional approach found help in Robertson and F. D. Maurice. In short, here was God's plenty.

In addition to variety, Victorian sermons catered to the deep need of a changing age for firm standards of belief and conduct. The Biblical faith was to fight for its life as in the Deistic controversy of the previous century, and there was a desperate need for apologists. During this period the historic Christian faith sustained a triple onslaught from the natural, biological, and social sciences. Its attackers were Lyell the geologist, Chambers the encyclopedist and amateur astronomer, Charles Darwin the biologist, and Herbert Spencer the sociologist. Those who stood by the ancient landmarks and refused to come to terms with modern knowledge found solace in the sermons of Newman, Liddon, Church, Dale, and Spurgeon. The inquiring spirits, looking for an accommodation between Genesis and Geology, faith and fact, Christianity and Socialism, flocked to hear such liberal preachers as F. D. Maurice, A. P. Stanley, F. W. Robertson, and Charles Kingsley. The significant fact is that much distinguished Victorian preaching was a defence of the Christian faith and of its relevance to nineteenth century conditions. On the whole, the men of the pulpit bore their responsibilities well and chose to answer difficulties rather than to play the fatally easy role of iconoclasts. They seemed to accept the task assigned to them by Goethe, who had declared: "Give us your certainties; we have doubts enough of our own."

If the primary task was to awaken or confirm faith, the secondary one was to maintain in all their integrity the validity of the Christian ethical imperatives. This was necessary in a period of moral relativism. Both Anglican and Dissenting ministers in the major pulpits provided their congregations with ethical guidance in the economic and industrial problems of the day. The Anglicans, F. D. Maurice, Charles Kingsley, and F. W. Robertson, proclaimed the need for social justice if Socialism were not to supplant Christianity. This was extremely unpopular doctrine in many quarters, for it was still believed by many that the Church of England consisted of the Tory party on its knees. R. W. Dale, the Free Churchman, taught Birmingham the meaning of civic righteousness as the responsibility alike of captains of industry and the most humble employee. Thus

THE DRIVE TOWARDS INNOVATION

the very relevance of the doctrinal and ethical issues dealt with in the Victorian pulpits was one of the major reasons for the magnetism of the preachers in this period.

Finally, it must be appreciated that the Victorian age was the last to appreciate and practise great oratory, whether in Parliament, on the platform, or in the pulpit. The leading preachers were the counterparts of the politicians, public lecturers, and actors of the day. As Gladstone, Disraeli and Bright, Bradlaugh and Henry Irving, had their "fans," who sought every opportunity to hear their heroes, chuckled at their quips and sallies, relished their purple patches, bridled with them in righteous indignation, and wept at their pathos, so the sermon-tasters had their favourite preachers whose superior points they widely advertised. What we might account their chief defect—namely, their leisurely prolixity—members of a Victorian congregation would applaud as evidence of their favourite preacher's staying-power and of his comprehensive treatment of a topic that could be lovingly savoured in print during undisturbed Sabbath afternoons, so that none of the finer points might be lost. During the middle years of the century, sermons were the most popular form of reading. Spurgeon's sermons, for example, were carried in full by American and Australian daily newspapers, and Parker claimed that the back row of the City Temple reached to the Rocky Mountains.

The annual sermons preached in May at the assembly of a denomination or at the yearly gathering of the supporters of a missionary or charitable organization were regarded as preaching marathons—a test of the endurance of ministers and their auditories alike. When Edward Irving preached the Annual Sermon of the London Missionary Society in 1824, he had to pause twice—for hymns to be sung—while he recovered his strength, for the sermon lasted three and a half hours![8] John Angell James, Dale's predecessor at Carr's Lane Independent Meeting House in Birmingham, preached on a similar occasion at almost equal length, and was revived by the oranges which his friends threw into the pulpit to sustain him.[9] That sermon, incidentally, was preached *memoriter*, and his brother, who sat in the capacious pulpit, prompted him from the manuscript when he seemed to falter. *Punch* seemed to be out of step with the public demand in describing a lengthy

[8] Margaret Oliphant, *The Life of Edward Irving, Minister of the National Scotch Church, London, illustrated by his Journals and Correspondence*, p. 146.
[9] *The Congregationalist*, Vol. VII (1877), pp. 448 f.

sermon as a "clerical error," when it depicted a "Patent Pulpit" equipped with a clock and a mechanical Gothic canopy which, at a pre-determined moment, could act as a parson-snuffer.[10]

Even though the example of the conversational preaching of Thomas Binney (described as "inspired talk") was beginning a pulpit revolution,[11] the older, oratorical style of preaching was slow in dying. Parker and Spurgeon, the best known of the Dissenting preachers, used it to the end, and unashamedly employed the devices of pathos and humour, as well as a structure that imprinted "headings" on the retina of the memory. In its Victorian hey-day the form of the sermon was as artificial as an epic; it was constructed on a conventional model and elaborated into grand rhetorical sentences and paragraphs, so that it "moved like a procession and came to an end like a tragedy."[12] The plan of the oratorical sermon of the day was clearly borrowed from contemporary books on rhetoric.

The skeleton outline is provided by Dr. Alexander Raleigh in a lecture on "The Plan and Growth of a Sermon" which he delivered to theological students in a London College. It comprised four parts: first, a brief exordium; second, a proposition which is to be as clear as language can make it; third, a proof, "which should be very intelligible, perfectly fair, and based as far as possible on unchallengeable truths of general experience"; and, finally, a conclusion "which should be personal and practical."[13] On the whole, the Victorians greatly preferred the formal rhetorical sermon to any casual, unpremeditated utterance, and found the plan of a sermon, with its several sub-divisions, its variety of illustrations, its breadth and aptness of citations, and its culminating peroration, the proof that their minister had been soundly occupied in his study.

2. The General Characteristics of Victorian Sermons

Victorian preachers were greatly addicted to producing topical sermons. This is their first and most obvious characteristic. In an age where there was acute conflict between the old faith and the

---

[10] A. L. Drummond, *The Churches pictured by "Punch,"* pp. 39 f.

[11] *Sermons preached in the King's Weigh-House Chapel, London, 1829-1869 by T. Binney, LL.D., Second Series,* ed. with a critical and biographical sketch by Henry Allon, D.D., London, 1875, pp. liv-lv.

[12] *Ibid.,* p. lvi. Evidently Cardinal Manning agreed with Binney about the need for a revolution in preaching, for the three maladies of piety in his view were "pulpit oratory, theatrical music, and fancy devotions." (Shane Leslie, *Henry Edward Manning,* p. 329.)

[13] Ed. Mary Raleigh, *op.cit.*

new science, and between the older classical and theological virtues and the newer ethics of utilitarianism and social Darwinism, the devout turned to their preachers, hoping that they could save the older values now in jeopardy or at least snatch what they could from oblivion. The preachers, for their part, if they believed orthodoxy to be irretrievable, reconstructed their theology on a firmer historical, experiential, and rational foundation. Two options were open to them, orthodoxy or liberalism, and each had its dangers. Orthodoxy safeguards its truth at the risk of obscurantism and apparent irrelevance; liberalism grasps at relevance often at the cost of rationalizing or diminishing revelation. Of the four major Victorian preachers, Newman and Spurgeon took the first alternative and Dale and Robertson the second.

Disraeli had warned the liberal Dean of Westminster, Dr. Stanley, in the celebrated words, "Mr. Dean, no dogmas, no deans."[14] His reply is not recorded, but he might well have retorted, "Prime Minister, unpopular preaching, empty pews." The fact of the matter is, that from the middle of the century onward, the tides of human knowledge were fast eroding the cliffs of Christian dogma. Lyell showed from his study of fossils and rocks that Creation, far from being a matter of days, was the product of millennia; Chambers, popularizing Laplace's nebular hypothesis for the origin of the universe, seemed to superannuate even a Deistic God; Darwin's *Origin of Species* relegated man from angelic to ape-like status; the comparative study of religions[15] seemed to dissolve Christianity's uniqueness by classifying it as one of the higher moral religions; and Strauss and Renan between them made of the incarnate, atoning, and risen Saviour of historic Christianity a gentle Galilean teacher unfortunately liquidated by the collusion of Jewish and Roman authorities. Not since the third decade of the eighteenth century had Christianity to face such an attack. Inevitably, then, the battle for the minds of men was fought in the pulpits and the lecture-rooms. Only a supremely confident dogmatism or a lily-livered cowardice would have evaded the central intellectual issues of the day. That is why topical sermons were so common.

14 L. E. Elliott-Binns, *English Thought, 1860-1900: The Theological Aspect*, p. 223.

15 This new discipline was intensively studied from 1860 onwards, years during which Edward Caird produced *The Evolution of Religion*, F. B. Jevons, *Introduction to the History of Religion*; Max Müller, *The Origin and Growth of Religion*; Grant Allen, *The Evolution of the Idea of God*; and Andrew Lang, *Myth, Literature and Religion* and *The Making of Religion*.

Some of these showed extreme ingenuity in the selection of appropriate texts, though these were often mere pretexts. Thomas Binney had a genius for relevant topics and recondite texts. In 1851, the year of the Great Exhibition, he preached on "The Royal Exchange and the Palace of Industry." The Crimean War elicited a sermon entitled "The Terribleness of God's Doings towards Men and Nations." His most ingenious selection of text and topic was of Acts 28:4 to illustrate the inexorable justice of God. The text read: "No doubt this man was a murderer, whom, though he hath escaped the sea, yet vengeance suffereth not to live." The occasion that prompted the sermon was the execution of an infamous assassin, after his flight across the Atlantic, his apprehension in America, and his trial and condemnation in England. When Josiah Conder, the hymn-writer died, Binney preached an eulogy from the text: "The songs of David, the son of Jesse, are ended."[16] Binney's gift was shared by Thomas Raffles, minister of Great George Street Congregational Church, Liverpool, from 1812 to 1861. On the Sunday immediately after the burning of his church, his text was, "our holy and beautiful church where our fathers praised Thee is burned up with fire."[17] Spurgeon, too, was adept at picking the apt text. In 1858 he preached two sermons from the Grand-stand of Epsom Race-course. In the afternoon his text was, "So run that ye may obtain," and in the evening, "Yea, come, buy wine and milk, without money and without price."[18]

In other cases the passages of Scripture selected for exposition excite admiration less for their ingenuity than for their relevance to the larger issues of the times. For example, F. W. Robertson chose to expound the relations between Nabal the man of wealth and David the man of work in a remarkable sermon entitled "The Message of the Church to Men of Wealth." He summed up his introduction thus: "In modern language, The Rights of Labour were in conflict with the Rights of Wealth."[19] Spurgeon also knew how to select striking texts, such as the following from Job 35:10: "But none saith, Where is my God, my Maker, who giveth songs in the night?" R. W. Dale, too, shows a rare touch of imagination in choosing to discourse on the sovereignty of Christ over society

[16] J. Stoughton, *A Memoir of the late Rev. Thomas Binney, LL.D.* (2nd edn., 1874), pp. 34-35.

[17] Article by G. S. Veitch: "Raffles of Liverpool" in *Transactions of the Congregational Historical Society*, Vol. IX (1924-1926), pp. 100 f.

[18] C. H. Spurgeon's *Autobiography* (4 vols.), Vol. II, p. 339.

[19] First Series of Sermons, No. XVII, p. 185.

and culture on the basis of Revelation 19:12: "Upon His head were many crowns."[20] Newman, although he preached the enduring verities of the Christian faith, certainly related his sermons to the crisis of the times. In his *Discourses to Mixed Congregations* (1849), the first fruits of his Roman Catholic preaching, he preaches on "Faith and Doubt" and on "The Neglect of Divine Calls and Warnings," and his apologetical concern is evident in every sermon.

It is, of course, one of the supreme virtues of the sermons of F. W. Robertson, the father of psychological preaching, that they were relevant to the varied moods of the day. He discoursed on the scepticism of Pilate,[21] on Thomas as the type of the doubter,[22] on Elijah as the victim of despondency,[23] on Christ as the supreme image of heroic loneliness,[24] on religious depression,[25] on the faith of the centurion,[26] on the victory of faith,[27] and on how to attain rest.[28] Undoubtedly this was a telling way to speak to the conditions of his hearers.[29]

Alexander Raleigh's view was typical of the way the more balanced Victorian preachers envisaged their duties: "I hold tenaciously to the old faith—I desire to possess as much as possible of the new culture. . . . But while holding and defending the old truth, which modern innovation and temerity would explain or steal away, I am persuaded that it may be held and preached so as to be consonant and congenial with every element and aspect of a true human progress."[30]

A second trait of Victorian preaching was the frequent and unashamed appeal to the emotions, especially to pity and fear, in ways that today would be regarded as sentimental and sadistic. E. Paxton Hood, perhaps the most indefatigable chronicler of the Victorian preachers, maintained that the use of pity and fear as inducements to conviction was the dominant characteristic of the sermons of the nineteenth century.[31] The Victorian appeal to fear was, however, rarely an invoking of the inexorable doom that awaited sinners in the sulphurous flames of Hell, as it was employed in the

---

[20] Sermon XVI of *The Laws of Christ for Common Life.*
[21] Series I, Sermon XXI. [22] Series II, Sermon XX. [23] Series II, Sermon V.
[24] Series I, Sermon XV. [25] Series II, Sermon VIII. [26] Series II, Sermon IX.
[27] Series III, Sermon II. [28] Series IV, Sermon XXV.
[29] Canon Charles Smyth described Robertson as "the first and greatest of the psychological preachers of the Church of England" in *The Art of Preaching*, p. 229.
[30] Ed. Mary Raleigh, *op.cit.*, pp. 227-28.
[31] *The Throne of Eloquence*, p. 444.

previous century by Jonathan Edwards in his famous sermon, "Sinners in the hands of an angry God."

This was no longer possible in the liberal climate of the later Victorian age, when so orthodox a theologian as F. D. Maurice lost his theological chair at King's College, London, because he had been bold enough to interpret "everlasting punishment" as being only "for an age." As men became less dogmatic about the doctrines of the last things, and as tolerance and universalism increased their hold, it became almost impossible to preach what Whitefield had called "the terrors of the Lord." The appeal to fear now took the form of stressing the frustration, futility, and waste of an unChristian life (what might be termed an utilitarian eschatology), or of stern denunciations of those who neglected the second commandment.

Newman is the supreme exemplar of the first approach to fear in his *Dream of Gerontius*, as well as in his sermons, as F. W. Robertson is of the second approach. Newman imagines the Divine Judgment with the utmost vividness: "O what a moment, when, breathless with the journey, and dizzy with the brightness, and overcome with the strangeness of what is happening to him, and unable to realise where he is, the sinner hears the voice of the accusing spirit bringing up all the sins of his past life. . . ."[32] Newman's narrative continues by exposing the shabby shifts of the soiled soul at self-justification and showing the utter waste of spirit such a life entails. Robertson interiorizes Hell. "Hell," he says, "is the infinite terror of the soul whatever that may be. To one man it is pain. . . . To another it is public shame. . . . To others . . . it is the hell of having done wrong . . . the hell of having quenched a light brighter than the sun—infinite maddening remorse."[33]

Each of these distinguished preachers knew how to sound the solemn knell of judgment. Sometimes it took the form of biting irony for Newman, as when, now a Roman Catholic, he excoriates the Established Church of England as "an appendage, whether weapon or decoration, of the sovereign power; it is the religion, not even of a race, but of the ruling portion of a race"; or when he describes the Pharisee as the reluctant witness of Mary Magdalene's tribute of tears for her Lord: "And he, the proud Pharisee, suffered her to come so that she touched him not; let her come, as we might

[32] *Discourses addressed to Mixed Congregations*, p. 40.
[33] Series I, Sermon VIII, "Pharisees and Sadducees at John's Baptism."

suffer inferior animals to enter our apartments without caring for them; suffered her as a necessary embellishment of the entertainment."[34] Such quiet irony strikes like cold steel. Robertson's sternest denunciations are kept for the prosperous who are also callous. In his renowned sermon, "Christ's Judgment respecting Inheritance," he insists that covetousness is at the root of England's "squalid pauperism and the worse than heathen degradation of masses of our population." He warns the rich in the terrible accent of truth: "The price which the man in authority has paid for power is the temptation to be insolent. The price which the rich man pays for his wealth is the temptation to be selfish. They have paid in spirituals what they have gained in temporals."[35]

C. H. Spurgeon produced the same shock of moral awareness by an anecdote, as he demonstrated that salvation is by faith and not by social standing. He imagined the over-polished lady enquiring, "I want to know if there are two places in heaven, because I could not bear to hear that Betsy in the kitchen should be in heaven along with me, she is so unrefined."[36] Occasionally, however, Spurgeon uses the direct attack of fear: "If there be no hereafter, live as you like; if there be no heaven, if there be no hell, laugh at me! But if these things be true, and you believe them, I charge you as I shall face you at the judgment bar of the Lord Jesus in the day of judgment—I charge you by your own eternal welfare, lay these things to heart."[37] (Jonathan Edwards could ignore the conditional "if"—it is a sign of Spurgeon's century that he could not, even when making a positive appeal.) A contemporary caricature paid tribute to Spurgeon's old-fashioned directness. It was called "Brimstone and Treacle."[38] "Treacle" was the average minister of the day, depicted as a meek, bespectacled cleric reading his sermon from a manuscript. Spurgeon was "Brimstone"; his arms flung apart and his face the image of vivacity, he typified daring and directness.

Dale, too, was forthright when the occasion called for it. He particularly despised the sentimentality of so many Victorian hymns which, by implication, denied the sovereignty of Christ. "Why," he once exclaimed from the pulpit, "people who talk to Christ in that way forget that Christ is King, that He is not to be

[34] *Op.cit.*, pp. 80-81.   [35] Series I, Sermon XVII.
[36] Series I, pp. 300-01.   [37] Series IV, p. 208.
[38] A chapter entitled "Charles Haddon Spurgeon" by F. C. Spurr in ed. R. S. Forman, *Great Christians*, p. 523.

fondled, but to be reverenced."[39] He concluded, "Let us serve Him. He has served us." Dale acknowledged a legitimate Biblical ground for using fear as a means of dislodging the complacent and impenitent, declaring it to be a principal object of a preacher to discover how he can awaken the sense of guilt.[40]

If the Victorian preachers were noted for their use of fear as a dissuasive, they were even more expert in the use of pathos. The nineteenth century English gentleman was perhaps less given to the Stoicism of the stiff upper lip than his present counterpart. Certainly, the use of pathos, and even of bathos, by Charles Dickens cannot be interpreted as an indication that his novels were read only by women and children. Two reasons may be found for the Victorian use of pathos in the pulpit, the one practical, the other theological. The practical problem of the preachers was to turn a formal or nominal profession of faith into an existential and living dependence upon God, and this could be done only by awakening the religious affections—by melting them in tenderness. In this way a top-of-the-mind religion could be converted into a bottom-of-the-heart faith. The key for the preacher was St. Paul's: "The love of Christ constraineth us."

The practical need was strongly reinforced by the theological revolution of the day, which emphasised the humanity of the Saviour, at one with man in His temptations, loneliness, difficulties, and sufferings. The liberal preachers, therefore, did away with "cold Christs and tangled Trinities," preferring to evoke tenderness towards the Son of Man. Fairbairn rightly said that "the most distinctive and determinative element in modern theology is what we may term a new feeling for Christ."[41] Its most popular expression, denuded of miracle and mystery, but not of tenderness, was Seeley's *Ecce Homo*, which appeared in 1865.

Probably F. W. Robertson was the greatest Victorian pulpit artist of the feelings, a master at eliciting tenderness and pathos. He saw most clearly that a divine yet profoundly human Jesus alone could evoke the passionate allegiance of men of his time. In season and out of season Robertson proclaimed that the Gospel was essentially one of sympathy. In a sermon based on the story of Zacchaeus, the despised tax-collector who was welcomed by Our Lord, he said: "Salvation that day came to Zacchaeus's house.

[39] *The Laws of Christ for Common Life*, p. 276.
[40] Nine *Lectures on Preaching* (3rd edn.), p. 211.
[41] *The Place of Christ in Modern Theology*, p. 116.

What brought it? What touched him? Of course, 'the Gospel.' Yes; but what is the Gospel? What was his Gospel? Speculations or revelations concerning the Divine Nature?—the scheme of the Atonement?—or of the Incarnation?—or Baptismal Regeneration? Nay, but the Divine sympathy of the Divinest Man. The love of God manifested in the face of Jesus Christ."[42]

No other preacher of the time so immersed himself in the tragic aspects of life and entered into sympathetic rapport with those stricken by suffering, paralysed by doubt, and driven desperate by poverty. He never failed to present salvation as a sharing in the fellowship of Christ's sufferings. Robertson was well aware that the belief in the Divinity of Christ was fading away in his time, and that the only realistic approach was to lead men *per Jesum ad Christum*, not as orthodoxy was continuing to do, *per Christum ad Jesum*.[43] The important thing in his judgment was to "lay the foundations of a higher faith deeply in a belief of His Humanity."[44] It was Robertson's conviction that only through the visible life of the Divinest in the flesh that God could become intelligible to man, and that Christ was God's idea of our nature realized. In short, as his biographer says, "the Incarnation was to him the centre of all history, the blossoming of humanity"[45] and the ultimate proof that perfection was attainable. Robertson himself said: "It is not the Redeemer's sinlessness, nor His unconquerable fidelity to duty, nor His superhuman nobleness that win our desire to imitate. Rather His tears at the grave of friendship, His shrinking from the sharpness of death, and the feeling of human doubt which swept across his soul like a desolation. These make Him one of us, and therefore our example."[46]

Dale shared Robertson's view, and believed that it was essential for Christian faith to recall that Christ was self-sustained in His supreme conflict with evil. Such a faith is encouraging, for "As He has shared our frailty, suffering, and conflict, we are to share His eternal triumph and blessedness."[47] Newman, like Dale, always insisted upon the Divinity of Christ, but—for all his reticence in the presence of mystery—has a most moving sermon on "The

[42] Series I, Sermon V, pp. 77-78.
[43] An excellent example of a modern life of Christ using the same method is Karl Adam's *Jesus, Son of God*.
[44] A. Stopford Brooke, *The Life and Letters of Frederick W. Robertson*, Vol. II, p. 169.
[45] *Ibid.*, p. 176.
[46] Series I, Sermon IV, p. 59.
[47] *Christian Doctrine, A Series of Discourses*, p. 73.

Mental Sufferings of Our Lord in His Passion."[48] This begins by pointing out that it is man's acute memory of suffering which makes pain more bitter for him than for the beasts; then Newman goes on to remind us that Christ refused the anodyne of wine, so that His full and undistracted consciousness was given over to agony, and He bore the crushing moral burden of all the world's sins so that, kneeling in Gethsemane, He was "putting off the defences of His divinity." Thus Newman's Christology, for all its adamantine Athanasian orthodoxy, had more of the Epistle to the Hebrews and of nineteenth century humanitarianism in it than, for example, the Tome of Leo.

One of the most famous examples of admirably controlled pathos is Newman's farewell sermon as an Anglican, at Littlemore, delivered to the parishioners and to his personal friends, with its conclusion stated in a tensely impersonal way:

"And O, my brethren, O kind and affectionate hearts, O loving friends, should you know anyone whose lot it has been, by writing or by word of mouth, in some degree to help you thus to act; if he has ever told you what you know about yourselves, or what you did not know; has read to you your wants or feelings, and comforted you by the very reading, has made you feel that there was a higher life than this daily one, and a brighter world than that you see; or encouraged you, or sobered you, or opened a way to the inquiring, or soothed the perplexed; if what he has ever said or done has ever made you take interest in him, and feel well inclined towards him; remember such a one in time to come, though you hear him not, and pray for him that in all things he may know God's will, and at all times be ready to fulfil it."[49]

It was only a master preacher like Newman who could make the Magdalen's piercing of the incognito of her Lord an object-lesson in faith, an instance of visualizing the numinous, and the meeting of the impure but aspiring human love with the Divine descent of grace a mirror of the drama of our salvation. "She looks and she recognizes the Ancient of Days, the Lord of life and death, her Judge; and again she looks, and sees in His face and in His mien a beauty, and a sweetness, awful, serene, majestic, more than that of the sons of men, which paled all the splendour of that festive room. Again she looks, timidly yet eagerly, and she discerns in His eye and in His smile the loving kindness, the tenderness, the

[48] *Discourses addressed to Mixed Congregations*, No. XVI.
[49] *Sermons of the Day*, pp. 463-64.

compassion, the mercy of the Saviour of man."[50] In that single cameo is cut the heart of the Gospel, so that the simplest may discern the mystery of judging, forgiving, and transforming grace.

In robustness of approach Spurgeon was unequalled, but his attempts at tenderness seem maudlin beside Newman's. One unfortunate failure in pathos must stand for many. In this instance he wished to caution parents against treating infant piety with suspicion, so he told the story of a minister who was convinced of the reality of a young girl's piety, yet refused to admit her to church membership. Spurgeon's sepulchral *basso* provides the lugubrious tone for his conclusion: "When the child heard that, a strange gloom passed over her face, and the next morning when her mother went to her little bed, she lay with a pearly tear or two on each eye, dead for very grief."[51] The artificiality of the anecdote, its palpitating sentimental adjectives, are enough to induce tears of wrath in the modern reader's eye: it is so obviously the crude effect of a "tear-jerker."

Where the appeal to the emotions was used rarely and with restraint, it undoubtedly enabled the Victorian preacher to pierce the arteries encrusted with sophistication and complacency, and to allow the religious affections of trust, adoration, and obedience to flow freely again. Those who denied the Divinity of Christ as a dogma often came, by the evocation of the courage, tenderness, and faith of a humanized Jesus, to follow Him as Leader. Thus by the thunders of fear and denunciation, the Victorian preacher tried to reach consciences unmelted by the sunshine of grace.

"Solemn" and "portentous" are the epithets that naturally spring to mind in describing the demeanour of Victorian divines. But this is to forget that wit and even humour were weapons employed by some of the leading pulpit personalities. The use of wit and humour is, indeed, the third distinguishing characteristic of Victorian preaching. One might venture the view that popular preachers in the Established Church were notable for wit, and the Free Church pulpit giants for humour. Newman, as well as Sydney Smith, are typical of the former group, as Binney and Spurgeon are of the latter, and the difference may be explained in part by the different social levels of their congregations.

Dale felt it necessary to tell theological students at Yale: "Gentle-

[50] *Discourses addressed to Mixed Congregations*, p. 81.
[51] Series II, Sermon XXII, p. 348.

men, I decline to believe that dulness is necessary to dignity."[52] Binney needed no encouragement in deflating pomposity as a failure in the basic Christian virtue of humility. He once described the "Angels"—the officers of the Irvingite Catholic and Apostolic Church—as "full grown boys of five foot four playing at priests."[53] Spurgeon was, of course, the most humorous of Free Church ministers. He would readily use a quip, an epigram, an amusing anecdote, or even a pun, like his mentor, George Whitefield. For example he told flagging Christians, "The cordial you need is *lacrymae Christi!*" He shocked his pietistical congregation by declaring it was his firm intention to smoke cigars to the glory of God. He warned his people, "Lay not election as a pillow for you to sleep on. . . . God forbid that I should be sewing pillows under armholes that you may rest comfortable in your sins."[54] Ever a critic of pomposity, he cautioned his theological students against using artificial intonations in the pulpit. Whimsically he declared that there were three to be avoided like the plague: the *ore rotundo* ("that dignified, doctoral, inflated, bombastic style"); the "steeple-in-the-throat grandeur" (Anglican affectation); and the "mincing" ("servant-girlified, dawdling, Dundrearyish").[55] He has a fund of amusing anecdotes and employs one of them to remind students of preaching never to have lengthy introductions to their sermons. He tells of an excellent Christian woman who once went to hear John Howe, and, as he had taken up an hour for his introduction, she observed that "the dear good man was so long a time in laying the cloth, that she lost her appetite."[56]

Newman's sermons lack the racy humour of Spurgeon's, but there are occasional flashes of wit, usually in the form of word-play or irony. An example of the former is provided in a sermon on "Intellect the Instrument of Religious Training," in which he said of St. Augustine that "if he has been a luminary for all ages in the Church since, many thanks do we owe to his mother, who, having borne him in the flesh, travailed for him in the spirit."[57] It was certainly a metaphysical wit like Donne's that framed the imaginative sermon, "Omnipotence in Bonds," with its subtle variations on the theme of Divinity circumscribed in the Incarnation.

---

[52] *Nine Lectures on Preaching* (3rd edition), p. 35.
[53] E. Paxton Hood, *Thomas Binney, His Mind, Life and Opinions*, p. 278.
[54] Sermons, Series II, p. 82.
[55] *Lectures to My Students* (a selection from the three original volumes), p. 112.
[56] *Ibid.*, p. 133.
[57] *Sermons preached on Various Occasions*, Sermon I, p. 3.

His irony could have a humorous twist to it, as when, admitting the past sins and crimes of the Roman Catholic Church, he argues that they have been few considering its long history and great temporal power, and turns the rapier of his ridicule to the Free Churches: "If there are passages in our history, the like of which do not occur in the annals of Wesleyanism or Independency, or the other religions of the day, there have been no Anabaptist pontiffs, no Methodist kings, no Congregational monasteries, no Quaker populations."[58] Even the most self-confident antagonist who entered the lists against Newman fell a victim of that irony that could not be parried, as Kingsley learned to his cost. Even so, it is a cruel weapon, at odds with the otherwise spiritual armoury of one who had spared others but not himself. Spurgeon's humour, by comparison, was the expression of his *bonhomie*, for he laughed with men, not at them, unless they were hardened Pharisees. Cardinal Manning was also a great exemplar of the use of wit in the pulpit, with a gift for the incisive definition. Divorce, for example, he defined as "successive polygamy," and guilt as "our sins multiplied by our mercies." His most famous pun was on the three stages in the life of a lawyer: "He gets on, gets honour, gets honest."[59] Whimsy, humour, or irony, congenial or cruel, were the spices with which the strong meat of the Gospel was flavoured by Victorian preachers and no doubt it helped in the digestion of wholesome doctrine.

A fourth characteristic of Victorian preaching was the delight in scenic grandeur—in Nature in her most dramatic or restful moods. This was doubtless caught from the enthusiasm of the Romantic poets whom the preachers cited with such delight. It was, in part, an aspect of the immanental conception of God during this period; in part, a revulsion from the factories and hovels of the industrial revolution, and a confession with Cowper that "God made the country and man made the town"; and, in part, it was also a desire to provide imaginative colour in their discourses, even if that colour was only a purple patch. But either by direct description or by citation, Nature (not in the Tennysonian form, "red in tooth and claw" but in either Wordsworthian tranquillity or Byronic storm hues) made her inevitable appearance. Robertson, Raleigh, and Spurgeon are entirely representative preachers in this respect. Spurgeon had the countryman's observation of and delight

---

[58] *Ibid.*, Sermon, "Christ upon the Waters," p. 146.
[59] Shane Leslie, *Henry Edward Manning, His Life and Labours*, p. 330.

in Nature and he often looked no farther than his own garden for an illustration. This stern determinist was probably more of a Pantheist (or Panentheist) than he realised, as in the following illustration of the thoroughness of Divine Providence: "I believe that every particle of dust that dances in the sunbeam does not move an atom more or less than God wishes—that every particle of spray that dashes against the steamboat has its orbit as well as the sun in the heavens—that the chaff from the hand of the win-nower is steered as the stars in their courses. The creeping of an aphis over the rosebud is as much fixed as the march of the devastating pestilence—the fall of the sere leaves from the poplar is as fully ordained as the tumbling of an avalanche."[60]

When Spurgeon looked for an image with which to liken the peaceful mind resting in God, he turned to submarine caves: "The only comparison I can find is in that unbroken tranquillity which seems to reign in the deep caverns and grottoes of the sea—far down where the sailor's body lies, where the sea-shells rest un-disturbed, where there is nought but darkness, and where nothing can break the spell, for there are no currents there, and all is still—that is somewhat like the Christian's soul when God speaks to him."[61] Similarly, E. Paxton Hood records that one of Alexander Raleigh's most memorable sermons was a parable drawn from his observation of nature: "And some of the Kensington people still speak of Dr. Raleigh's bird whose broken song, heard in Holland Lane as he passed to chapel one Christmas morning, seemed to him like the promise we have here, in our wintry life, of the Eternal Spring."[62]

F. W. Robertson was renowned for his strongly aesthetic bent which found sermonic expression in his love of nature, of art, and of poetry, as the material of his illustrations.[63] He showed that the law of vicarious sacrifice is written into the universe as well as in man: "The mountain-rock must have its surface rusted with putrescence and become dead soil before the herb can grow. The destruction of the mineral is the life of the vegetable. . . . Further still: have we never pondered over that mystery of nature—the

[60] Series II, p. 201.

[61] Series IV, p. 68.

[62] *The Throne of Eloquence*, p. 225. The Venerable Bede, we may note, records in his *Ecclesiastical History*, that the flight of a bird, as an emblem of the after-life, was used by one of the thanes of King Edwin of Northumbria to persuade him to adopt Christianity because the missionaries had certain knowledge of life after death.

[63] Stopford A. Brooke, *The Life and Letters of Frederick W. Robertson*, Vol. I, pp. 184 f.

dove struck down by the hawk—the deer trambling beneath the stroke of the lion—the winged fish falling into the jaws of the dolphin. It is the solemn law of vicarious sacrifice again."[64]

Robertson's observation of nature provided him with two superbly contrasted images of repose in his sermon on "Rest": "It is not the land locked in ice which suggests repose, but the river moving on calmly and rapidly in silent majesty and strength. It is not the cattle lying in the sun, but the eagle cleaving the air with fixed pinions, that gives you the idea of repose combined with strength and motion. In creation, the rest of God is exhibited as a sense of power which nothing wearies. When chaos burst into harmony, so to speak, God had rest."[65]

It is significant that the reader will have to search long in the sermons of Newman and Dale to find any evocations of the beauty of Nature. Strongly theological minds (unless of the Platonic and Alexandrian cast), with an overwhelming concern for ethics, do not readily lend themselves to the allurements of aesthetics in a fallen world. They turn to the pageantry of Grace rather than to Nature; or if to Nature as to a veil behind which stands God. Such were the cases of Newman and Dale. That they had some measure of truth on their side would be admitted even by Robertson, who warned that "Feeling is given to lead into action; if feeling be suffered to awaken without passing into duty, the character becomes untrue."[66]

For all its dangers, the use of Nature passages in Victorian sermons brought an element of the sublime and the beautiful into even the dingiest industrial chapels and a sense, if not always of the numinous, at least of the Creator as the Divine Artist. Finally, they provided a temporary relief from the heavy doctrinal expositions or stern denunciations of the preacher which were, no doubt, all the better received because their mentors had allowed the hearers to take a country walk during the interval of the illustration.

On the whole, then, the leading characteristics of Victorian preaching were: a practical and relevant discussion of religion in relation to living intellectual and social issues; a deliberate appeal to the emotions of pity and fear; a flavouring with the spices of humour and wit; and a fondness for illustrations drawn from Nature or from the Romantic poets.

From these generalizations it will be easier to appreciate the

---

[64] Series I, Sermon IX, pp. 114-15.
[65] Series IV, Sermon XXV, p. 810.
[66] Series I, Sermon XX, p. 224.

distinctive contributions made by four princes among Victorian preachers.

3. John Henry Newman (1801-1890)

It has been suggested that Newman's fame as a preacher was adventitious, owing to two accidents of history. The first was that as vicar of the university church of St. Mary-the-Virgin in Oxford he became the focus of the revolutionary Tractarian Movement in which many minds shared but in which Newman took all the credit. The second accident, so it is alleged, is that his sermons were bought and read as an Anglican expiation for a long and unwarrantable aspersion from which he was cleared only by the appearance of the *Apologia pro vita sua*.[67] This is, indeed, a cynical judgment on Newman's contemporaries, not to mention a superficial estimate of the abiding qualities in the sermons themselves, which are now acclaimed as literary and theological classics. Men of many denominations still turn to them (a few perhaps in mere curiosity) chiefly for their penetrating understanding of human nature and destiny and for their moral guidance and spiritual illumination, which are admirably expressed in the economy of nervous and subtle English prose. The interior drama of his life, in which he ever followed the "kindly Light" in complete fidelity "amid the encircling gloom" has an existential attraction which has caused an enthusiastic modern Roman Catholic writer to name Newman "the Augustine of our calamitous era."[68]

It was as a preacher that Newman first attracted attention and his pulpit life owes much of its interest to the three very different congregations to which he ministered in Oxford, Littlemore, and Birmingham. St. Mary's in Oxford was a congregation made up chiefly of dons and university undergraduates, with a sprinkling of professional and trade families added. In Littlemore, by contrast, he had a typically small, conservative, and rather unimaginative rural congregation. The congregations which the Oratorians in Birmingham served were mainly representative of the toiling industrial masses, and, of course, included many Irish immigrants with mercurial tempers and magnificent loyalties. To all of them he preached the doctrines of the Church of Christ, the reality of the unseen world, and saintliness as the end of human life. But the style of his approach naturally varied with the type of the congre-

---

67 W. C. Wilkinson, *Modern Masters of Pulpit Discourse*, p. 176.

68 J. H. Newman, *Sermons and Discourses* (2 vols.), ed. C. F. Harrold, Vol. I, p. xii. See A. Whyte, *Newman: An Appreciation*, p. 37.

gation he was addressing, as may be seen by a study of his printed sermons.

The *Parochial and Plain Sermons*, which appeared in eight volumes, were preached between 1835 and 1841 to his congregations at Oxford and Littlemore, and are distinguished from his later work by great reserve in the expression of feeling: by a decided preference for moral as compared with doctrinal topics; by each being founded upon a text the central idea of which, looked at from many viewpoints, is the thread of the discourse; and—it should be noted—they were read to the congregation.[69] One of the greatest adaptations Newman had to make on becoming a Roman Catholic was to preach without dependence upon his manuscript. Thus his Catholic sermons, at least those preached on ordinary occasions, are marked by greater simplicity, freedom and directness of expression, more deliberate effects of contrast, greater certitude and finality in belief, more tender perorations in the form of direct addresses to God the Father, Our Lord, or to the Virgin, and, above all, a confidence in expounding distinctively Roman Catholic teaching and usages,[70] and in the polemical use of irony against Protestantism.

The *Discourses addressed to Mixed Congregations* appeared in 1849 and immediately demonstrated an abandonment and freedom and a use of rhetoric which Newman's Anglican reserve had not permitted. The greatest of them were: "On the Neglect of Divine Calls and Warnings" with its ruthless probing of human motives and its sudden projection of the dazed sinner into Judgment; "The Mental Sufferings of Our Lord in His Passion," a burning analysis of the cost of our Redemption; "Men not Angels, the Priests of the Gospel," with its vivid miniatures of the saints; and "Faith and Doubt" with its concise and clear definitions.

The *Sermons preached on Various Occasions*, which were published in 1857 and presuppose an intelligent auditory, resemble the Anglican sermons because many of them were preached to the University Church in Dublin, some to his Brothers in the Birmingham Oratory, and still others were delivered on important Catholic occasions. In this collection appears the finest sermon Newman

---

[69] C. Stephen Dessain in the intro. to *Faith and Prejudice and other Unpublished Sermons of Cardinal Newman*, p. 11, writes: "As an Anglican he had read his sermons. Now, anxious to avoid all singularity, he conformed to the Catholic custom."

[70] Alexander Whyte, *op.cit.*, pp. 110-11, says: "At best he was a tethered eagle in St. Mary's pulpit; he is now the untrammelled sovereign of the whole spiritual sky."

ever wrote, "Omnipotence in Bonds." It is an astonishing exploration of the paradox of Divine Grace, strongest when apparently weakest. It is, in effect, one sublimely sustained image, of the humiliation of the Son of God in the Incarnation, buttressed with Scriptural citations from beginning to end. It is also a summary of the life of Christ from the bondage in the Virgin's womb, in the confines of the swaddling clothes of infancy, in the chains of parental authority, under the restraints of temptation, beneath servitude to men's needs, manacled on the Cross, to the ultimate cramping of the shroud in the tomb. When we are prepared for the glorious liberty of the Resurrection by Newman's forceful phrase, "He tore open the solid rock," the sermon surprises us by the reminder that the omnipotent Christ is ever in the bonds of the Eucharist by which He made provision "for perpetuating his captivity to the end of the world." The practical purpose of this moving representation of God's mightiest act is "to teach us our place in His wide universe and to make us ambitious only of that grace here and glory hereafter, which He has purchased for us by His own humiliation."[71]

The volume also allows Newman to exercise his historical imagination to the full, as when he contrasts the brief success of the reformer Savonarola in Florence with the quieter but more enduring triumph of St. Philip Neri, Apostle to Rome, in "The Mission of St. Philip Neri"; or when he tells the story of Catholicism in England up to "The Second Spring"; or relates the proud endurance of the Roman Church through varied vicissitudes, as in "Christ upon the Waters."

The varied styles of these three sets of sermons have been aptly described as Doric in the *Parochial and Plain Sermons*, Corinthian in the *Mixed Congregations*, and Ionic in the *Various Occasions*.[72] Even if the second volume reveals the enthusiasm of the neophyte as compared with the calmer judgment of the third volume, they both differ from the first series by the fact that they are exhortatory and polemical, and are addressed as much to those external to the Catholic Church as to those who heard them; this may account for the severity and the scorn revealed in these two Catholic volumes of sermons.

While the Catholic sermons undoubtedly gain in the greater range of effects that Newman allows himself—in their directness and challenge, inexorable pursuit of worldliness, deeper pathos,

---

[71] P. 90.
[72] J. J. Reilly, *Newman as a Man of Letters*, pp. 74 f.

boldness of imaginative flights, and searing irony—there is also a considerable loss. The refinement and delicacy of feeling, the reserve and carefulness of statement, the humility of the earliest sermons, combined with the absence of criticism of other branches of Christ's Church, command the enduring respect of readers from every Christian communion. The more theatrical effects and the polemical thrusts in the Catholic sermons make capital for the Roman fold at the cost of a wider appreciation.

It is possible to understand Newman's decision to change his style of preaching by giving full weight to two considerations. Newman, as an ex-Anglican, was bound to be an object of suspicion and it was imperative for him to prove the genuineness of his new loyalty by an adoption of its customs in preaching as in devotion. In the latter matter, Newman had been persuaded against his better judgment to adopt the Italian and more ardently sentimental mode of prayer at the insistence of Father Faber. This he came to regret, as can be seen in a letter which he wrote to his former Tractarian colleague, Dr. Pusey, in 1866: "I prefer English habits of belief and devotion to foreign . . . and in this line of conduct I am but availing myself of the teaching I fell in with on becoming a Catholic."[73] It may also be true that he regretted the theatrical and polemical approach of his first Catholic sermons. It is significant that several of the sermons in the second Catholic volume (notably, "Purity and Love," "Faith and Doubt," and "God's Will the End of Life") represent a return to Anglican topics and style.

The second factor to be considered is the drabness of the Birmingham environment itself and the need of his Catholic parishioners for a livelier and more dramatic style to sustain their interest—one abounding in images, pathos, irony, and enthusiasm. (Oxford undergraduates, after all, were used to concentrating on abstruse lectures of an hour's duration, and did not require such concessions.) Certainly Newman's sensitive spirit was acutely aware of the depressing industrial context of life in Birmingham: this even finds repeated expression in his sermons. In the first sermon of *Discourses addressed to Mixed Congregations* he confesses that it is only a concern to win souls from the grip of the world that "prompts us to settle down in a district so destitute of temporal recommendations, but so overrun with religious error and so populous in souls."[74]

[73] *The Difficulties felt by Anglicans in Catholic Teaching considered* (4th edn.), pp. 20-22.
[74] P. 6.

Years later, in the *Sermons preached on Various Occasions*, he again refers to the unprepossessing surroundings: "We have not chosen for ourselves any scene of exertion where we might make a noise, but have willingly taken that place of humble service which our Superiors chose for us. . . . We have deliberately set ourselves down in a populous district, unknown to the great world, and have commenced as St. Philip did, by ministering chiefly to the poor and lowly. We have gone where we could get no reward from society for our deeds, nor admiration from the acute or learned for our words."[75] So sensitive a man must immediately have felt that his sermon style must accommodate itself to the needs of "the poor and lowly." The harshness of his earlier Catholic style must then be attributed to the excessive enthusiasm of a convert to do as Rome does, and to a genuine wish to accommodate himself to the needs, capacities, limitations, and interests of his humbler parishioners.

Though Newman's sermons have their abiding qualities as spiritual literature, their impact cannot be understood apart from the appearance, voice, manner, and personality of Newman himself. Fortunately the written accounts of many eye-witnesses are extant and they help to evoke Newman's pulpit magic. They all emphasize two commanding characteristics as clues to his magnetism: the sheer spirituality of this man and his uncanny psychological penetration. Matthew Arnold's description marvellously suggests his unearthly appearance and the heavenly direction of his life: "Who could resist the charm of that spiritual apparition, gliding in the dim afternoon light through the aisles of St. Mary's, rising into the pulpit, and then in the most entrancing of voices, breaking the silence with words and thoughts which were religious music— subtle, sweet, mournful? I seem to hear him still saying, 'After the fever of life, after weariness and sickness, fightings and despondings, languor and fretfulness, struggling and succeeding; after all the changes and chances of this troubled unhealthy state at length comes death, at length the white throne of God, at length the beatific vision.' "[76]

Dean Lake and J. A. Froude are deeply impressed by his exploration into the recesses of the human conscience. Lake remarks

[75] P. 241. His dislike of Birmingham is even less disguised on p. 113 of the *Discourses*, where he says: "You find the whole groundstead covered with the large buildings, planted thickly up and down, the homes of the mechanical arts. The air is filled below with a ceaseless, importunate, monotonous din . . . ; and overhead a canopy of smoke, shrouding God's day from the realms of obstinate, sullen 'toil.' "
[76] *Discourses in America*, pp. 139-40.

that "as he entered into the subject more fully, the preacher seemed to enter into the very minds of his hearers, and, as it were, to reveal them to themselves, and tell them their very innermost thoughts."[77] Froude is more vivid: "He seemed to be addressing the most secret consciousness of each of us, as the eyes of a portrait appear to look at every person in a room."[78]

These accounts tell much of Newman's power but little of his manner. This is probably because he had no mannerisms worthy of attention. An anonymous reporter fills in the background: "Action in the common sense there was none. His hands were literally not seen from the beginning to the end. The sermon began in a calm musical voice, the key slightly rising as it went on; by and by the preacher warmed with his subject, till it seemed as if his very soul and body glowed with suppressed emotion. The very tones of his voice seemed as if they were not his own. There are those who to this day, in reading many of his sermons, have the whole scene brought back before them. The great church, the congregation all breathless with expectant attention, the gaslight just at the left hand of the pulpit, lowered that the preacher might not be dazzled: themselves, perhaps, standing in the half-darkness under the gallery, and then the pause before those words in *The Ventures of Faith* thrilled through them, 'They say unto Him, "We are able."'"[79]

Froude, too, remarked on Newman's dramatic pauses before some crucial observation (dramatic because he used no other theatrical device or rhetorical technique in his Anglican days). In particular, he recalled a pause in the midst of his sermon on "The Incarnate Son, a Sufferer and a Sacrifice": "Newman had described closely some of the incidents of our Lord's Passion; he then paused. For a few moments there was a breathless silence. Then in a cold clear voice, of which the faintest vibration was audible in the farthest corner of St. Mary's, he said, 'Now I bid you recollect that He to whom these things were done was Almighty God.' It was as if an electric stroke had gone through the church, as if every person present understood for the first time the meaning of what he had all his life been saying. I suppose it was an epoch in the mental history of more than one of my contemporaries."

Others remarked on the deliberate plainness and economy of

[77] Ed. K. Lake, *Memorials of William Charles Lake* . . . , pp. 41-42.
[78] *Short Studies on Great Subjects*, Vol. IV, p. 278 f.
[79] Froude, *op.cit.*, Vol. IV, p. 286.

the language,[80] and a sense that Newman's imaginative temperament was severely held back in the reins of a classical style. The effect was that of pent-up power, as of the restraining wall of a hydro-electric dam, or like the lithe, nervous leashed-in energy and speed of a greyhound. Sir Francis Doyle wrote: "It seemed to me as if I could trace behind his will, and pressing, so to speak, against it, a rush of thoughts and feelings, which he kept struggling to hold back, but in the end they were too strong for him, and poured themselves out in a torrent of eloquence all the more impetuous for being so long repressed."[81] Dean Lake insisted that the style was "simple, refined, and unpretending, and without a touch of anything that could be called rhetoric" and referred "to a suppressed vein of the poets which was so strong a feature of Newman's mind." He summed up the quality of Newman's diction thus: "His language had the perfect grace which comes from uttering deep and affecting truths in the most natural and appropriate words."[82]

All who heard Newman were convinced that they had come under the spell of a peerless preacher. Froude, who later became an agnostic, said that each of Newman's sermons was "fascinating by its subtlety, welcome—how welcome!—from its sincerity, interesting from its originality, even to those who were careless of religion: and to others who wished to be religious but had found religion dry and wearisome, it was like the springing of a fountain out of the rock."[83] Lake asked: "Is it too much to say of such addresses that they were unlike anything we had ever heard before, and that we have never heard or read anything similar to them in our after-life?"[84] It is clear that for his fifteen years at St. Mary's Newman held a commanding influence over the religious life of the University of Oxford which the subsequent experience of the undergraduates was never able to efface.

What were his preaching aims and the doctrines that he taught? In the titles of two of his Catholic sermons, his endeavour through-

---

[80] The following lines of Newman from the *Lyra Apostolica*, p. 85, disclose Newman's stylistic ideal:

> Prune then thy words, the thoughts control
> That o'er thee swell and throng;
> They will condense within thy soul,
> And change to purpose strong.

[81] *Reminiscences and Opinions* (p. 145), cited in "The Vicar of St. Mary's" a chapter written by R. D. Middleton in ed. Henry Tristram, *John Henry Newman: Centenary Essays*, pp. 127-28.

[82] *Op.cit.*, pp. 41-42.

[83] *Op.cit.*, Vol. IV, pp. 283-84.

[84] *Op.cit.*, p. 41.

out his life was to prove "Saintliness, the Standard of Christian Principle," or "God's Will the End of Life." His aim was to bring the mind so easily distracted by doubt, the heart so facilely attracted by idols, and the will wounded by original sin, into the integrity and control of Christ, which is both captivity and liberation. Holiness, so he believed with all his soul, is what the human personality in time and eternity is meant for in the providence of God. It was his task to demonstrate in the Incarnation, the Cross and the Resurrection, God's loving claims to man's allegiance and His remedy for worldliness, and to bring to mind those exemplars of the life of holiness, the saints. In his Catholic days he dwelt even more in the company of the saints, especially with the Blessed Virgin, stressed the nature of the Church as the only ark of salvation in the storm-tossed sea of this world, and emphasized the perpetual presence of Christ in the Sacrament.

He deserves to be known as the finest preacher of the Incarnation in the nineteenth century. No one had such a gift of making ancient dogma take on living relevance. The truth he taught was the fruit of his Patristic researches into the Christology of Athanasius, Basil, and Cyril, where he learned that only an adamantine orthodoxy could stand up to heresies ancient or modern. The sixth volume of the *Parochial and Plain Sermons*, with the discourses on "Christ the Son of God made Man," and "The Incarnate Son, a Sufferer and a Sacrifice" as well as the majestic "Omnipotence in Bonds" of the *Sermons preached on Various Occasions*, are theological preaching in the grand manner. Dr. Alexander Whyte, himself one of the most eminent preachers of the Church of Scotland, pays generous, but also just, tribute to them in these words: "Newman delivers all his readers ever after from a cold, dry, notional, technical, catechetical mind, he so makes every article of the Creed a very fountain of life and power and beauty. He so lifts up his superb imagination to its noblest use, that he makes, first himself, and then makes us to see, the Divine Persons and their Divine relations and operations as never before. . . ."[85]

It was Newman's supreme achievement not only to make orthodoxy enchanting, but to invest abstract and complex philosophical theology with movement and life, and to make the realities of the invisible world seem so vivid that the material world seemed a mere shadow. Only a profoundly devout and mystical soul, gifted with imagination and a scholarly mind, could achieve such an evocation

[85] *Op.cit.*, pp. 126-27.

of the numinous; moreover, Newman was almost unique in his time in swimming so strongly against the naturalistic tides.

A belief of almost equal importance for Newman was the Communion of Saints. Nature herself was for Newman the almost transparent veil that manifested the power and mercy of God and his ministering angels, as his sermon "The Powers of Nature"[86] so finely demonstrates. If Newman meditated on the angels, he sought the company of the saints. "They are to us who see them," he observed, "what wealth, notoriety, rank and name are to the multitude who live in darkness—objects of veneration and worship." They are also a source of guidance and encouragement, for "they are always our standard of right and truth; they are raised up to be monuments and lessons, they remind us of God, they teach us what Christ loves, they track out for us the way that leads heavenward."[87] The atmosphere of that empyrean in which he lived is finely suggested in the prayer that ends his sermon, "Waiting for Christ": "God in mercy rouse our sluggish spirits, and inflame our earthly hearts, that we may cease to be an exception in His great family, which is ever adoring, praising and loving Him."

Newman was ever conscious of the spiritual might of the Church with its vast contingents of triumphant saints inciting the Church Militant on earth to doughtier combat, and he saw that the glory of the Church was its Catholicity—its universal and charitable embrace of all sorts and conditions of men. Most movingly he expressed this thought: "She is the solace of the forlorn, the chastener of the prosperous, and the guide of the wayward. She keeps a mother eye for the innocent, bears with a heavy hand upon the wanton, and has a voice of majesty for the proud. She opens the mind of the ignorant, and she prostrates the intellect of the most gifted."[88] In a superb image Newman shows that the Church holds the conscience of the nations and therefore the well-being of civilisation in her hands: "When the greatest of the Romans was in an open boat on the Adriatic, and the sea rose, he said to the terrified boatmen, *Caesarem vehis et fortunam Caesaris*, 'Caesar is your freight and Caesar's fortune.' What he said in presumption,

---

[86] *Parochial and Plain Sermons*, Vol. II, Sermon XXIX.

[87] *Discourses to Mixed Congregations*, "Saintliness the Standard of Christian Principle," p. 109. He had written, as early as on p. 27 of the first volume of the *Parochial and Plain Sermons*: "What a blessed discovery it is to those who make it, that this world is but vanity and without substance: and that really they are ever in their Saviour's presence."

[88] *Discourses to Mixed Congregations*, p. 268, from the sermon, "Prospects of the Catholic Missioner."

we, my dear brethren, can repeat in the faith of that boat, in which Christ once sat and preached."[89]

He insisted as much on the institutional nature of the Church as upon its devotional and interior life. It was for him a visible society founded by Our Lord and continuing to his own day, with the government vested "in the very dynasty which His Apostles began," who themselves were appointed by Christ as His vice-gerents. This dynasty was the episcopate, which links the primitive Church with the contemporary Church.[90]

He was firmly convinced of the Real Presence of Christ in the Eucharist and wrote of it with great feeling in his novel, *Loss and Gain*. In one sermon he said: "We *know* we eat His Body and Blood. The Lord began His ministry with a miracle, the turning of the Water into Wine. He closed it by a greater, the gift of His Body and Blood in the Holy Communion."[91]

Though a great doctrinal and ecclesiastical preacher, Newman was also an admirable expositor of Christian duty, though this aspect of his ministry predominated in the Oxford days. His sermons on "Secret Faults," "Profession without Practice," "The Danger of Accomplishments," "Moral Consequences of Single Sins," "Religious Cowardice," and "Unreal Worlds" were sharp arrows driven home to the conscience. Even in his Catholic days, when his themes are largely doctrinal, this "beagle of the Invisible Hunter" (as François Mauriac has styled the Catholic priest) pursued men into the caves of complacency or the thickets of illusion in which they tried to hide and dragged them out into the noonday light of revealing holiness, that Christ might capture them.

No brief study such as this can do justice to the excellences of Newman's sermons, but their outstanding qualities have been listed. These are: their profound spirituality, their integrity, their probings into the evasions of the human reason and conscience, their adamantine orthodoxy and fidelity to Divine Revelation, and their astonishing capacity for visualizing the abstract and the invisible. Their technique is an art that conceals art (except in the more contrived effects of the earlier Catholic sermons) in the limpidity and lucidity of the language, in the quiet inevitability of the impact—like snow on snow—and in the pithiness of his definitions. When he uses rhetoric, there is a great variety in his

[89] *Discourses to Mixed Congregations*, pp. 259-60.
[90] *Parochial and Plain Sermons*, Vol. ii, p. 273 and Vol. ii, p. 210.
[91] *Sermons on Subjects of the Day*, p. 43.

effects: the massed clauses, the concise epigram, the felicity of the few illustrations always subordinated to the theme, the contrasts of characters or of times, the tenderness of his pathos and the scorn of his irony, the topic that develops as naturally as a bud into blossom, and, above all, the suiting of his sermons to the needs and capacities of his three very different congregations.

Even with these many and admirable qualities, there are also weaknesses. In all his ethical teaching there is not a hint that social justice is a Divine as well as a human demand and little sense that the structures of society, as well as individuals, are in rebellion against God. (Maurice, Kingsley, and Robertson were truer prophets than Newman in this respect.) Some of his sermons are clouded with that bigotry which sees only the mote in the eye of the neighbouring denomination. Even his sincere admirer, Alexander Whyte, is forced to say that "the very best of the sermons are tainted with some impertinent aside at Evangelical truth, or at some real or imaginary, or greatly exaggerated, defects in the doctrine or in the life of the Evangelical preachers of his day."[92] Some have objected to the apparent lack of a plan in his sermons,[93] but others may think the natural progression of the thought an advantage. It could, however, be counted a weakness in him that his illustrations are singularly few, however admirable they are. More disturbing, however, is Newman's occasional selection of a text as a pretext, using Scripture as a convenient aerodrome from which to take off on his doctrinal, moral, and even speculative flights. However these defects are to be weighed, they seem inconsiderable in comparison with the integrity of his transparent spirituality and consecration, and with the most impressive sermon of them all—his life.

4. F. W. Robertson of Brighton (1816-1853)[94]

Even a Victorian monumental mason was not on oath when incising tributes to the dead; all the more remarkable, then, is the honesty of the marble eulogy of Robertson in Brighton. "He awakened," it declares, "the holiest feelings in poor and in rich,

[92] Op.cit., pp. 90-91. Whyte believes that the bigotry abated in his Catholic days, but I believe it is stronger, rather than weaker. For evidence, see Discourses to Mixed Congregations, pp. 174, 218, 265-66.

[93] Notably E. C. Dargan in A History of Preaching, Vol. II, pp. 517-18, and W. C. Wilkinson, Modern Masters of Pulpit Discourse, pp. 175-76.

[94] See H. Hensley Henson, Robertson of Brighton and Charles Smyth, Art of Preaching 747-1939, pp. 225 ff.

in ignorant and learned. Therefore is he lamented as their guide and comforter." It rightly emphasized the mediatorial character of Robertson's ministry, in which he had warned members of each class of the peculiar temptations of their status, reminded them of their complementary contribution to society, and insisted that their spiritual standing was of far greater importance than their social status. The tribute is also significant in reminding us that his great gifts of mind[95] were joined to a magnanimous and deeply sympathetic heart, and that no one ever thought this cleric a snob.

After taking his degree at Oxford, his brief ministerial life (he died in his thirty-seventh year) was spent inconspicuously in the service of the Church of England. From 1840 to 1842 he was an assistant curate in Winchester; for the next seven years, in Cheltenham. After a few months in Oxford, he went as incumbent of Holy Trinity Chapel in Brighton. There from 1849 to 1853 he was accorded the fullest measure of appreciation by a loyal congregation (and local fame), disturbed only by unpleasantness from his rector and defamation from the mouths of bitter Evangelicals who disliked his liberal theology. He died from a brain tumour, having spent the last six months of his life in unremitting agony in a shuttered room.

His national fame was entirely posthumous. It resulted from the publication of his sermons, hardly any of them having before been published, and none of them received the literary revision of this consummate stylist, because he preached extemporaneously from notes and jottings, only troubling to clarify the divisions of his sermons and to write out the introductions in full. That such unfinished sermons should have gained the acclaim they did is explicable only on the assumption that they were masterpieces of apologetical and prophetical preaching, which in a day of acute social change brought home to the Victorian public the relevance of the Biblical revelation. It is possible that their condensed form even recommended them, so rarely practised a virtue was brevity in this period. But a wide circle of readers put a higher estimate on the substantial qualities of intellectual and spiritual insight, great candour, breadth of culture, intense feeling, imaginative power, and lucidity of thought, structure, and expression.

Robertson's total output was small. In addition to a series of

[95] Henry Crabb Robinson reports Wordsworth as saying that Robertson's sermons were "the most satisfactory religious teaching which has been offered to this generation." (*Diary, Reminiscences and Correspondence*, Vol. II, p. 385.)

five volumes of sermons posthumously published,[96] there appeared two volumes of theological lectures (the first on Genesis in relation to the new cosmology, and the second on Corinthians), an analysis of *In Memoriam*, and a volume of miscellaneous addresses. It was, of course, the sermons that made Robertson a household name in England, so that his literary congregation far outnumbered his living hearers.

As a loyal minister of the Church of England, with considerable independence of mind and spirit, Robertson would have considered any "party" affiliation on his part as a constriction—like the wearing of a strait-jacket. His catholicity allowed no place for partisanship, for he had learned from men as theologically distant from each other as Newman and Channing. This spirit is splendidly expressed in a sermon on the judgment of God on a materialistic England which was worthy of F. D. Maurice at his best, and much more pithily phrased. Should God's judgments fall on England, says Robertson, it will be, "Because we are selfish men: and because we prefer pleasure to duty, and traffic to honour; and because we love our party more than our Church, and our Church more than our Christianity; and our Christianity more than the truth, and ourselves more than all."[97] Such a man refused to belong to either Tractarians or Evangelicals.

The Evangelicals, though he was brought up among them, repelled him by their insistence upon speculative doctrines (such as predestination), their atomistic ideas of the Church, and their worldliness and vindictiveness.[98] He felt nearer in spirit to the Tractarians, for he admired their sacrificial work in poor and forgotten parishes, applauded their aesthetic sensitivity,[99] and even appreciated their understanding of the importance of forms and symbols. He was an appreciative reader of Keble's *Christian Year* and of Newman's sermons. He differed from the Tractarians only in emphasis: they seemed to him to suggest that forms produced life, whereas they merely sustained life. His own illustration of the difference was that as bread will not create but will maintain life, so will forms of belief and worship. In his correlation of Divine Revelation with the new cultural developments of man, as in his concern for social justice, his closest affiliation would have been

---

[96] Consisting of just over a hundred sermons in all.
[97] Series II, Sermon XIII, p. 352. Note the verbal echoes of Coleridge in this passage. Cf. Shedd, *Complete Works of Coleridge*, Vol. I, p. 273.
[98] Ed. Brooke, *Life and Letters*, Vol. I, pp. 105-07.
[99] He was one of the first to recognise the talents of the Pre-Raphaelites, *ibid.*, p. 185.

with the Broad Church of Arnold, Whately, Maurice, Kingsley, and Tennyson.

His was essentially a mediating and apologetical theology, looking for the truth that lay beneath the exaggerations of partisanship, and believing that no truth in science, history, or art could contradict the Christian faith, since the Master of souls was also the Logos or Wisdom of God in the flesh. His percipient synthesis sought even for a measure of good in evil. He described his theological method in the following, rather summary form: "The principles on which I have taught: First, the establishment of positive truth, instead of the negative destruction of error. Secondly, that truth is made up of two contrary propositions, and not found in a *via media* between the two. Thirdly, that spiritual truth is discerned by the spirit instead of intellectually in propositions; and, therefore, that truth should be taught suggestively, not dogmatically. Fourth, that belief in the Human character of Christ's Humanity must be antecedent to belief in His Divine origin. Fifthly, that Christianity, as its teachers should, works from the inward to the outward, and not *vice versa*. Sixthly, the soul of goodness in things evil."[100]

So radical in its methodology, yet so orthodox in its conclusions, Robertson's apologetical approach owed a good deal to Coleridge, especially to his *Aids to Reflection*, itself an amalgam of the religious idealism of Schleiermacher and the ethical idealism of Kant. The chief ideas that he borrowed and exploited to the full in new ways were the following: the conviction that religious truth is felt, not reasoned out; a sense of the immanence of God in the universe, humanity, and the individual human soul; ethical obedience and a hatred of sham as the tests of human character (perceptions which owed even more to Carlyle than to Coleridge); a broader understanding of the nature of Biblical inspiration; a recognition of the centrality of the Incarnation, and a consequent dismissal of the arguments from prophecy and miracle as merely rationalistic proofs.[101] It is his firm grasp of theological method, his ethical emphasis, and his aesthetic sensitivity (the latter fed by Coleridge, Wordsworth, and Tennyson), and his reading in science, history (including military history) and letters, that impart such breadth and interest to his sermons.

Above all, his distinctive quality is the burning conviction that

[100] *Ibid.*, Vol. II, pp. 160-61.
[101] Dr. Samuel Johnson happily termed such arguments "Old Bailey theology."

Christianity alone explains the tasks and problems of life and thought. Barstow perceives this when he says, "Other preachers have brought human life to the interpretation of Christianity. He would bring Christianity to the interpretation of life."[102] The point is that Robertson was a gifted Biblical expositor combining an understanding of the historical context of the Scriptures with a profound sense of their suggestiveness in providing principles for practical guidance. Primarily a student of the Christian Revelation (he learned the whole New Testament by heart in Greek and English) he concentrated on ideal humanity as it existed in Christ. This had for him a double relevance: the historical fact of the Incarnation was proof that a life of perfection was possible for human flesh and an abiding incentive to all followers of the Christian Way.

Each of his theological principles deserves fuller exposition and illustration because Robertson made such remarkable use of them in demonstrating the relevance of Christian truth to all human problems and situations, intellectual, moral, social, political, economic, and ecclesiastical. Only two are here selected for treatment. First, we shall attempt an understanding of the important but difficult statement that truth lies in the acceptance of two contradictory propositions. This is exemplified in his discussion of current doctrines of the Holy Communion: "In opposition to the Dissenting view, it *is* Christ's body and blood received; in opposition to the Romanists' view, it is *not* Christ's body and blood to those who receive it unworthily. We do not go between the two. Each of these opposite statements of the Dissenter or the Roman Catholic are truths and we retain them."[103] In explanation, Robertson would have argued that the sacrifice of Christ was offered only once and no more, but that the truth contained in Transubstantiation which the ultra-Protestant misses is that the sacrifice is daily repeated, in a spiritual manner, in the hearts of all faithful Christians.

The other principle to be illustrated is the belief that an age in which men cannot be persuaded directly of Christ's Divinity must be approached through the humanity of Jesus. "Those who hold it," wrote Robertson, "have petrified it into a theological dogma without life or warmth. . . . How then are we to get back to this belief in the Son of God?—by authority or by the old way of persecu-

[102] See the second chapter of Lewis O. Barstow's *Representative Modern Preachers* for a perceptive study of Robertson.
[103] Ed. Brooke, *op.cit.*, Vol. II, pp. 161-62.

tion?. . . The other way is to begin at the beginning. Begin as the Bible begins, with Christ the Son of Man. Begin with Him as God's character revealed under the limitations of humanity." Robertson then calls for an imaginative identification with the Son of Man, until His spirit is caught:

"Feel with Him when He looked round about Him in anger, when He vindicated the crushed woman from the powerless venom of her ferocious accusers; when He stood alone in the solitary Majesty of Truth in Pilate's judgment-hall; when the light of the Roman soldiers' torches flashed on Kedron, in the dark night, and He knew that watching was too late; when His heart-strings gave way upon the Cross. Walk with Him through the Marriage Feast. See how the sick and weary come to Him instinctively; how men, when they saw Him, felt their sin, they knew not why, and fell at His feet; how guilt unconsciously revealed itself, and all that was good in men was drawn out and they became higher than themselves in His presence. Realise this. Live with Him until He becomes a living thought,—ever present—and you will find a reverence growing up which compares with nothing else in human feeling."[104]

Robertson's central concern was to insist, not on the Divinity of Christ, but on the Humanity of God in the Incarnation. This was, he believed, essential to assure men of God's sympathy with their problems. Thus, the very limitations of the Son of Man were a proof of His genuine humanity, making Him an authentic exemplar of our race. "We are shocked," he wrote, "at the partial ignorance of Christ, as if it were irreverence to think of it; we shrink from believing that He really felt the force of temptation, or that the forsakenness of the Cross and the momentary doubt have parallels in our human life. In other words, we make that Divine life a mere mimic representation of griefs that were real and surprises that were feigned, and sorrows that were theatrical." The consequence is serious: "But thus we lose the Saviour. For it is well to know that He was Divine; but if we lose that truth we should still have a God in heaven. But if there has been on this earth no real, perfect human life, no love that never cooled, no faith that never failed, which may shine as a lodestar across the darkness of our experience, a light to light amidst all convictions of our own meanness and all suspicions of others' littleness, why, we may have a religion, but we have not a Christianity. For if we lose Him as Brother, we cannot

[104] From an unpublished sermon in *ibid.*, pp. 169-70.

316

feel Him as a Saviour."[105] No preacher of the day can equal Robertson for his entering into the fellowship of Christ and His sufferings.

Second only to the Incarnation was his emphasis on the Resurrection. Quite typical, also, was his Johannine stress on eternal life as a new dimension of life in Christ here and now, rather than the mere continuity of life beyond the grave. This, too, was something to be experienced as a reality, not to be dogmatically asserted. "There are men," he claims, "in whom the resurrection begun makes the resurrection credible." Such men have a buoyancy, shown in the fact that "their step is as free as if the clay of the sepulchre had been shaken off: and their hearts are lighter than those of other men, and there is in them an unearthly triumph."[106] Keeping Christian doctrine as close to experience and as far away as possible from mere speculation of theorizing, he ranged far and wide in search of analogies for faith. For example, he believed that physical nature itself manifested the universal principle or law of vicarious sacrifice.[107] Similarly, he maintained that there is a relation between man's triad in discord (body, soul, spirit) and the Divine Trinity in Unity, and the discord is resolved by the act of sanctification.

The principle of faith as trust he found rooted deep in human experience: "When, in reliance upon your promise, your child gives up the half hour's idleness of today for the holiday of tomorrow, he lives by faith; a future supersedes the present pleasure. When he abstains from over-indulgence of the appetite, in reliance upon your word that the result will be pain and sickness, sacrificing the present pleasure for the fear of future punishment, he acts in faith: I do not say that this is a high exercise of faith—it is a very low one —but it is faith."[108]

Robertson's constant emphasis on experience, on faith speaking to the heart, had its apologetical advantages and also its religious dangers. The advantages were that once Christianity ceased to be defined in propositional and doctrinal terms, it was removed from the area of rationalistic controversy. "No science," he claimed, "can sweep away the ever-lasting love which the intellect does not even pretend to judge or recognise."[109] Faith is thus immune from the

105 Series II, Sermon IX, "The Faith of the Centurion." Robertson was also anxious to insist that Christ has taken up His humanity into the Godhead, and that "the Redeemer not only was but is man." In the Incarnation and its experience we are therefore assured of "the truth of the human heart of God." (Series I, Sermon VII.)

106 Series II, Sermon XX, "The Doubt of Thomas."

107 Series I, Sermon IX, "Caiaphas's View of Vicarious Sacrifice."

108 Series III, Sermon II, p. 45.   109 Series I, p. 157.

insidious attacks of the intellect. The humility of faith cleanses men from the arrogance of the intellect which in its pride is capable of excluding God by its myopic concern for specialized interests. The astronomer, concentrating on the laws of motion, might forget the First Cause, just as the surgeon in his concentration on flesh, muscle, and bone might forget that matter cannot organize itself in ordered beauty, or the metaphysician concentrating on the laws of mind might forget that these very laws may be produced by spiritual influences. Thus men "look at Nature, but do not look through it to Nature's God."[110]

The chief peril of an emphasis on experience is sheer subjectivity, which can take the extreme form of an idiosyncratic religion or of an utterly aesthetic shower bath—a luxuriating in the emotions—a "feeling for feeling's sake." Robertson was safeguarded from these possibilities by his historical rootage in the Incarnation, and by his invariable practice of Biblical exposition in the pulpit. His strong ethical emphasis protected him from mere aestheticism. He recognised that, while beauty might be the handmaiden of religion, she might also be a seductress: "Refinement—melting imagery—dim religious light; all the witchery of form and colour—music—architecture; all these, even coloured with the hues of religion, producing feelings religious or quasi-religious, may yet do the world's work."[111] In season and out of season he insisted that "obedience is the organ of spiritual knowledge."[112] His repeated admonition was: "Feel God, do His will, till the absolute Imperative within you speaks, as with a living voice, Thou shalt and Thou shalt not, and then you do not think, you *know* there is a God."[113]

Concentration on Robertson's fine apologetical sermons must not lead to any neglect of his importance as a social ethicist, for, apart from the small band of Christian Socialists, there were few who dared to speak like an Amos on the political and economic issues of the day. Of the ninety-three printed in the first four series of sermons, two deal specifically with social justice, and six others are concerned with social issues.[114] The two most important sermons in this group are, respectively, "The Message of the Church to Men of Wealth" and "Christ's Judgment respecting Inheritance."

The first of them deals with the laws of property in conflict

[110] Series III, Sermon XVIII, p. 594.
[111] Series I, p. 135. Advent Lecture on "The Grecian."
[112] The title of Sermon VII, Series II, p. 300.
[113] Series II, Sermon VII, p. 304.
[114] These are: Series II, Sermon XIII; Series III, Sermon XIV; Series IV, Sermons XII, XXIII, and XXVI.

with rights of labour, the embarrassing but central problem of the century. With great candour, Robertson declares it to be "a social falsehood that wealth constitutes superiority, and has a right to the subordination of inferiors." He brushes aside the complaint of the wealthy that there is no longer any respect of inferiors for superiors, by reminding the affluent that in the old days servants were protected by their master. They are now protected by law, so the old bond of loyalty has been dissolved. Firmly, he says, "No. That patriarchal system has passed forever." He affirms that the Gospel can fortify the human spirit in the most difficult of social conditions, but he also confesses that "there are some in the world to whom, speaking humanly, social injustice and social inequalities have made goodness impossible."[115] He maintains that political economy and the social teaching of the Church alike preach love, rather than selfishness. The only difference is that political economy arrives at this result not as the Church does— through the spiritual impulses of charity—but by the terrible lessons of revolutions, wars and famines. The principles which cement a society are three: the spiritual dignity of man, the law of sacrifice, and the matter of rightful influence. The first principle is revealed by Scripture, for Israel's model king is to be a shepherd, and Christ the Regenerator of our human race is humbly born as the poor woman's child. With eloquent indignation he asserts: "Whoever helps to keep alive that ancient lie of upper and lower, resting the distinction not on official authority or personal worth, but on wealth or title, is doing his part to hinder the establishment of the Redeemer's Kingdom."

His second principle is an entirely practical one, for "the largest charity is the best economy" and "concessions extracted by fear only provoke reaction further."[116] In support of his third principle, he points to the primitive Church, where "they had all things in common," and he claims that the coming state of society will be one where "unselfish services and personal qualities will command, by Divine right, gratitude and admiration and secure a true and spiritual leadership" and where the old fixities of class differentiation will be overwhelmed.[117] He ends this truly prophetic utterance by a indictment of the clergy of the Established Church: "We have produced folios of slavish flattery on the Divine right of power. Shame on us! We have not denounced the wrongs done to weakness . . . and woe to us in the great day of God if we have been the

[115] Series I, Sermon XVII, pp. 189-92. [116] Op.cit., p. 194. [117] Ibid., p. 197.

sycophants of the rich instead of the redressers of the poor man's wrongs."[118] These were brave words for 1851!

The second major social sermon took its departure from Luke 12:13-15, where the incident is described in which Our Lord refuses to settle the quarrel of two brothers about their inheritance. This narrative, said Robertson, had been interpreted as a mandate for a refusal to mix religion and politics. This is unacceptable, he suggests, because how without such a mixture can the kingdoms of this world become the kingdoms of our God and of His Christ? He admits that Christ's religion cannot be tied to a radical or socialist political program, but neither can it be appealed to as the sanction for the sanctification for the *status quo ante*. Robertson refutes the gibe that the Church of England is merely the Tory party on its knees. Christianity commits itself to eternal principles that it may "establish a charity, and a moderation, and a sense of duty, and a love of right, which will modify human life according to any circumstances that can possibly arise."[119] "The cause of the inequalities in the economic order is acquisitiveness on both sides, for the cry, 'Divide' has its roots in covetousness just as truly as 'I will not.'"[120] Robertson perceptively argues that the price of wealth is the temptation to selfishness and insolence. He tells the rich men that they have paid for temporals with spirituals, and he warns the poor men: "Blame their sins if you will, or despise their advantages; but do not think you can covet their advantages, and keep clear of their temptations."[121] The magnificent impartiality of Robertson's treatment of this acute social problem is one further proof of his great mediatorial ministry.

While the development of Robertson's religious thought has been of chief interest hitherto, his admirable homiletical technique also warrants consideration. His sermons are remarkable as profound expositions in particular of the historical and biographical sections of Holy Writ, and the lessons he teaches are easily remembered from the sub-divisions of his discourses. His most common division is two-fold and this enables him to make an effective use of contrasts: describing the man of God and the man of the world, the rich and the poor, the Divine and the human, time and eternity. All his sermons disclose his intellectual vigour and penetrating spirituality.

His illustrations are drawn from a wide range of scientific,

118 *Ibid.*, p. 198.   119 Series I, Sermon XVIII, p. 202.
120 *Ibid.*, p. 205.   121 *Ibid.*, p. 208.

military, historical, and literary sources. Robertson was deeply disappointed when his indifferent health seemed to point away from a career in the army, and he often illustrated the obedience of faith from the valour of soldiers or sailors.[122] As the Incarnation was the principal illustration of God's love in action, making an imitation of God possible for the least cerebral of men, so Robertson incarnated his abstract principles in illustrations that were apt and illuminating. For example, when his problem was to make concrete the abstract truth that sin is a *privatio boni*, merely the absence of any ordering principle for the will, the solution is provided by the image of a pilotless ship: "what we mean when we say the natural man must sin inevitably, is this, that he has strong natural appetites, and that he has no bias from above to counteract these appetites: exactly as if a ship were deserted by the crew, and left on the bosom of the Atlantic with every sail set and the wind blowing. No one forces her to destruction, yet on the rocks she will surely go, just because there is no pilot at the helm."[123] He illustrates the loneliness of death from the last look of an emigrant leaving the fatherland.[124] The power of symbols to express an invisible idea yet a real one, is illustrated from "a flag which at one level is only a bit of torn and blackened rag, hanging from a fortress" but at a higher level is for the soldiers defending it "their regiment, their country, their honour, their life."[125]

The diction of his sermons is always natural and clear, the almost transparent medium of his personality. He can crowd large thoughts into a small compass, "infinite riches into a little room," and provide definitions as deft as they are illuminating. The extraordinary sympathy of the man is revealed gradually, for the sermons begin quietly but end with overmastering moral and religious passion, and the syntax accordingly changes from lengthy, leisurely sentences to the concentrated energy of feeling that demands expression in short, staccato sentences, with the repetition of stress words. In one essential respect his style is like Newman's: his art conceals art.

Robertson's qualities as a preacher are many: deep expositor, and apologist, always pertinent to the problems of society and culture; social prophet, yet fairer than most; a teacher of ethics

---

[122] Series I, Sermon XVI, p. 184, for example, has an admiring reference to Nelson's magnificent message as proving that to trust men is to make them trustworthy.
[123] Series I, Sermon VIII, pp. 91-92.
[124] Series III, Sermon XVII, p. 579.
[125] Series I, pp. 282-83.

whose life adorned his teachings; a personality in which mind and heart accorded well; a man of dedication and of the most absolute honesty; never professional in his sympathy; above all, one who never used the pulpit as a coward's castle. Yet even he—saint and preacher of social reform—lacked in his personal life the radiance and confidence of faith. His singular, pronounced, and increasing morbidity, for which his ill-health and his cruel final sickness of mind must bear the chief blame, was so contrary to the Resurrection outlook of the Christian man as Robertson himself had described it that it made him unable to accept the sincerely expressed gratitude of his congregation as genuine. A minor defect, which he shared with many subjects of the Queen and Empress Victoria (and natural enough in a period of imperial expansion), was a chauvinism that boasted of a nation "whose sons can die at their posts silently without thinking that forty centuries are looking down on them."[126] In partial exoneration, it may be recalled that he had hoped for a military career, in the tradition of his family, so that his admiration of men of action is understandable; moreover, he was himself a most valiant defender of new views of Christian truth.

So brilliant, honest, and sympathetic a preacher of the Gospel, he also had the gift of humility, for he saw his task as being "to bring the soul face-to-face with God, and to supersede ourselves"[127] and he recognised that "ministerial success lies in altered lives and obedient, humble hearts; unseen work recognised in the judgment day."[128] Only a very humble man, with rich homiletical gifts such as Robertson possessed, could say and mean, "Sermons are crutches—I believe often the worst things for spiritual health that ever were invented."[129]

5. R. W. Dale of Birmingham (1829-1895)

Dale was probably the most impressive pulpit personage of the Free Churches in the nineteenth century, which is far from implying that he was handsome. Indeed, so swarthy was his face, from which lustrous eyes shone, that an old lady who for many years had refused to contribute to foreign missions became a regular supporter on hearing him preach in Surrey Chapel. She gave as her

---

[126] Cited p. 54 of L. O. Barstow, *op.cit.*
[127] Series IV, Sermon I, p. 634.
[128] Series II, Sermon V, p. 293.
[129] Ed. Brooke, *op.cit.*, Vol. I, p. 332.

reason that, having seen what God could do for "that poor Hindoo" she could refuse no longer.[130] Dale's impressiveness is to be found rather in the range of his mind and the breadth of his cultural interests, which enabled him to preach with singular freshness for forty-two years to the same important congregation in England's second largest city, Birmingham; in the crusade that he led for a new ethical revival to complement the earlier evangelical and aesthetic revivals; in his public service for education, which included membership of a Royal Commission investigating the nation's elementary education and the chairmanship of the Birmingham School Board and of the governing bodies of Mansfield College, Oxford, and of the King Edward Grammar Schools, Birmingham; and in his reputation as a preacher, which led to his being called to the chairmanship of the Congregational Union of England and Wales in 1869 and to his delivery of the Lyman Beecher lectures on preaching at Yale University in 1877.[131] He was, moreover, a distinguished theologian[132] and historian.[133]

Such was his influence in Birmingham as the leader of "Christian Civics" that a London newspaper declared of the election of Joseph Chamberlain as a Liberal Member of Parliament for the city that "Mr. Dale has nominated Mr. Chamberlain, and the will of Mr. Dale is the will of Birmingham." When this was reported to Chamberlain, he courteously replied, "If that be so, there is not a member of the House of Commons who will have a better, wiser, or nobler constituency."[134] He was rightly called "an unworldly man of the world"[135] and it was a description he would have liked, for he conceived it to be his duty to expound the imperatives of a this-worldly Christian ethic, or, in his own words, "Christian Worldliness."

Dale stood firmly, but not uncritically, in the Evangelical tradition. To the doctrines of orthodox Christianity, such as the Holy Trinity, the Incarnation, the Atonement, and the Resurrection, he gave unqualified adherence, but he regarded the more speculative elements of Calvinism, such as its tenets of total depravity and

---

[130] A. W. W. Dale, *The Life of R. W. Dale of Birmingham*, p. 202.
[131] These were published in 1877 as *Nine Lectures on Preaching*.
[132] For his defence of the objective view of the *Atonement*, in a book of that title, he won the approval of Cardinal Newman for its orthodoxy.
[133] He wrote the classic *History of English Congregationalism* for which he had gathered a remarkable collection of documents, now the Dale Collection in Mansfield College Library, Oxford.
[134] A. W. W. Dale, *op.cit.*, p. 421.
[135] The tribute is that of his friend, Dr. Guinness Rogers, cited in ed. R. S. Forman, *Great Christians*, p. 173.

double predestination, as unacceptable. In his opposition to pietism, which allowed God to rule in the individual soul but not in social, political, and economic life, he manifested his Puritan and theocratic heritage. His criticisms of the Evangelical Revival were directed to its atomistic doctrine of the Church, its comparative neglect of the Sacraments, and its disregard of the duties of corporate Christian action.[136] He was also disturbed by the pietist's concentration on his own salvation and his utter disregard for the weightier matters of the Christian Law. This conviction is revealed in an anecdote about him. After a meeting of the Birmingham School Board, Canon O'Sullivan, a Roman Catholic priest, remarked, a little acidly: "Dale, when do you mean to quit politics and look after your own soul?" The substance of the reply was: "I have given my soul to Christ to look after; my duty is to do His will and leave the rest to Him."[137] The province of preaching in which he excelled was the ethical, and no nineteenth century divine can compare with him in the application of Christian ethical principles (originally conceived in an agrarian context) to the changed environment of a modern commercial and industrial society.

Dale held that there were three basic types of sermons: the first was doctrinal; the second, moral; and the third, to strengthen the religious affections.[138] Dale was a master of the first two of this trio, but he lacked the sustained imagination (and perhaps the sympathy) to make a success of the third category. He was weakest in the area where Robertson was strongest. His lecturing technique was suited to the first two categories.

In the first part of his pulpit ministry at Carr's Lane Chapel, he thought it his duty to re-affirm, to expound, and to defend the historic and orthodox Christian doctrines. This was rare in a day of iconoclasm and theological change, as may be gathered from the preface to his *Christian Doctrine, a Series of Discourses.*[139] There he tells how, only three years out of his theological college, he met a Birmingham minister who remarked, "I hear you are preaching doctrinal sermons to the congregation at Carr's Lane; they will not stand it." Dale's immediate reply was, "They will have to stand it." The congregation must obviously have appreciated the solid confirmation and deepening of their faith that Dale provided in his doctrinal sermons, for they were soundly based on the

---

136 These criticisms are detailed in *The Evangelical Revival and Other Sermons.*
137 A. W. W. Dale, *op.cit.*, p. 174.
138 *Nine Lectures on Preaching*, p. 23.
139 P. v.

Bible, illuminated by Patristic learning, and developed in a cogent and relevant way. These eight meaty discourses are concerned with the great central themes: the existence of God (two sermons), the Humanity of Christ, the Divinity of Christ (two sermons), the Holy Spirit, the Holy Trinity, Man, Sin, and the Atonement (three sermons).

Though Dale was prepared to use the arguments for the existence of God from design, beauty, and conscience, he was unconvinced of the power of natural theology as a *praeparatio evangelica*. According to him, the God of so many theists seemed so remote as to make the Incarnation inconceivable.[140] He was convinced it is by way of experience that men come to know God, an experience open to them in many different ways if they live in a Christian land. A moral failure may learn of Christ's liberation from the tyranny of evil habits; another saddened by the sense of finitude may learn of the infinite horizons of Christian hope; a third, burdened with a guilty conscience, receives the relief of Divine forgiveness; yet another, being friendless, learns of the wonder of Christ's eternal companionship; and the last finds his aesthetic longings satisfied by the wonder of Christian worship. Thus Dale shows that many avenues lead to God, and, by implication, rejects the ultra-Protestant stereotype of "conversion."[141]

Like Robertson, he finds it necessary to begin with the real humanity of Christ, for not only the earliest but also contemporary heresies are Docetic in character, denying the genuineness of the Lord's humanity and thus the effectiveness of His role as exemplar of the human race, quite contrary to the witness of the New Testament. Dale points out that many, including James and Jude, His brothers, could speak of Our Lord's childhood; the disciples knew that He had physical wants like other men and that He showed surprise on learning of Lazarus' death and ignorance of the time of the Second Advent, and manifested a genuine humanity in His friendships, as shown by His weeping at the grave of Lazarus. Christ had expressed indignation against the Pharisees, experienced temptation before and during His public ministry, and even doubt during His supreme conflict. The end of all was, "As He has shared in our frailty, suffering and conflict, we are to share His eternal triumph, glory and blessedness."[142]

140 Dale is convinced of the truth of Pascal's observation that there is a complete disjunction between "The God of Abraham, Isaac and Jacob" and "le dieu des philosophes."
141 From the second discourse.   142 P. 73.

Such an approach might be thought to persuade men of Christ's humanity, but only at the cost of making it more difficult to establish His Divinity. Dale, however, shows that the New Testament records also witness to the distinctiveness of Christ in four respects: His freedom from any consciousness of sin; His complete authority over men; His assumption that He has power to save men from their sins, and its acceptance by men; and His constant declaration that He had come to give men Eternal Life, a personal gift deriving from His sacrificial death.[143] Dale's admirable summary shows that he had studied the principles of historical criticism to good effect, and was able to answer some of the doubts which that very discipline had raised.

In his treatment of sin, Dale defines it broadly as "a violation of the Divine order in human life," stressing its corporate origin and its pervasiveness throughout the social relationships of life. While insisting on the reality of human freedom, he acknowledges that it has limits. He accepts the Biblical assumption of the universality of human sin, but, far from accepting the traditional doctrine of original sin, he maintains that only one New Testament passage supports it. Sharing in the sin of the human race, Christians also share in its corporate redemption in Christ, who is the propitiation for the sins of the world.

Dale's exposition of the Atonement discusses the subjective or moral theory which asserts that it is by Christ's revelation of God's love to us on the Cross we are redeemed, and the objective view that Christ revealed the Divine love by dying for mankind. Only the latter theory, Dale feels, is adequate to the fact that the death of Christ is the ground of the forgiveness of our sins by God, and to the manifestation of God's holiness and wrath, as well as His mercy. The second discourse on Atonement raises and answers objections to the objective theory, while the third discourse on the theme explains its enduring truth: as a declaration that Christ's solidarity with men in their sins is deeper than their solidarity with themselves; as proof that God's holiness is maintained—for being righteous He cannot share our sins, but in Christ the Incarnate Son shares our life—; and, finally, as incontrovertible evidence that Christ is the way to the Father, because He has not only confessed our sins but suffered for them, and by thus accepting God's judgment on sin, He releases us from its penalty.

Dale's gift of asking the central question is seen in the seventh

143 From the fifth discourse.

discourse—that on the Holy Trinity. There he demands: "Whether in the Incarnation of Our Lord and in the 'coming' of the Spirit and His permanent activity in the Church and in the world, there is an inner and eternal life of God?" His answer is: "From eternity to eternity—this is the Trinitarian doctrine—God is Father, Son, and Holy Spirit."[144] Dale further argues that the doctrine of the Trinity meets man's need for a God both immanent and transcendent: thus the transcendent Father is revealed in Christ His Son and this knowledge and power are mediated to each succeeding generation by the Holy Spirit.[145]

Christianity, says Dale, has a subtle doctrine of man, as made in the image of God and "this is the ultimate secret of his moral responsibility and of his moral inability." Dale warns against a false spirituality which would deny the legitimate rights of the flesh as a revived Manichaeanism and lead by reaction either to a "gloomy and cruel asceticism" or to "flagrant and reckless immorality."[146]

All this is solid and substantial orthodox divinity and by his teaching Dale performed a needed service for the heirs of the Evangelical Revival in the Free Churches and farther afield. But these sermons, for all their Biblical fidelity, clarity, and acumen, lack the imaginative fire that lights up the doctrines from within, as in Newman's incandescent doctrinal sermons. Dale, although he advised theological students to preach some sermons of this type in each year of their ministries, began to feel that it was not enough to preach doctrine. He was convinced that Christianity's and therefore the preacher's task was less to inform the mind than to transform the will. A letter he wrote in 1860 stated: "To assist the intellect is much; to quicken the conscience and confirm the righteous will is more."[147] It was in following this conviction that he made his distinctive contribution to the English pulpit.

The cream of his ethical sermons was skimmed off in the volume, *The Laws of Christ for Common Life*.[148] His originality is seen in his contemptuous dismissal of the customary distinctions between sacred and secular occupations, and between professions and trades. Making the point that everyday business life, commonly called "secular," is a Divine calling, he startles us with the remark that "God Himself has done and is always doing, a great deal of

[144] *Christian Doctrine*, p. 152.
[145] *Ibid.*, pp. 161-62.
[146] *Ibid.*, pp. 177-93.
[147] A. W. W. Dale, *op.cit.*, p. 143.
[148] Published in 1884.

work that we must call secular."[149] He insists that Creation and Providence are secular work. Thus "it is as secular a work to create the sun to give light in the day-time, as to make a lamp, or to build gas-works, or to manufacture gas to give light at night." In consequence, "our secular work is just of the same kind as a great part of God's work."[150] Here was a conception of Christian vocation to thrill engineers and industrialists in the vast Midlands city.

He brought similar cheer to the commercial members of his congregation suffering from an inferiority complex because they were engaged in trade and looked down upon by the supposedly altruistic professions. Dale derided the view that "in a profession a man has to place his duties to others first and his own interests last, and in a trade he has a right to care only for his own interests, and may leave others to look after themselves."[151] The professional theory is undoubtedly the Christian theory, but it is equally applicable to trade. Vocations are complementary and cooperative, and men in all callings should think of themselves "as comrades in a great army, fighting side by side, under the high command of God, against want, ignorance, disorder, and sin."[152] Many individuals, of course, will have no choice of occupation open to them and they must continue to serve God where they are. Where they have a choice, the first question ought not to be, Where can we earn most for least labour, but, Where can we use our abilities best for the glory of God and the welfare of man?[153] Furthermore, to accept one's daily work as a Divine calling will transform one's conduct in the direction of greater industry and integrity and everything will be done "as in the eye of God."[154]

In addition to Dale's originality, the breadth and variety of his ethical themes are admirable. He treats the relations between employer and employee, wealth and property as stewardship, the privileges and strains of family life, the importance of justice preponderating over sentiment in writing testimonials, the different Protestant and Catholic conceptions of sainthood, the due sovereignty of Christ over culture and society, and the municipal duties of Christians. Nor does he forget the greatly neglected virtue of Christian courtesy. On this wide variety of themes, his judgments are profoundly Christian, practical, and full of common sense irradiated by grace.

[149] *The Laws of Christ for Common Life*, p. 4.
[150] *Ibid.*, pp. 4-5. [151] *Ibid.*, p. 12. [152] *Ibid.*, p. 15. [153] *Ibid.*, p. 10.
[154] Here one is reminded of Dale's saturation in Puritan ethics and especially of Milton's insistence upon work being done as under the Great Taskmaster's eye.

He shows that Socialism is no recent phenomenon: in primitive Christianity it was the voluntary expression of the spirit of brotherhood; it underlay monasticism, although it had no application to family and social life in general; it has continued to inspire many noble community dreams. Yet Dale recognized that for Socialism to succeed, a great transformation of human nature would be necessary. He cites with approval the epigram: "Socialism says, 'What is thine, is mine'; Christianity says, 'what is mine, is thine'; the difference is infinite." But Dale added his own emendation: "Christianity really teaches us to say, 'What seems thine is not thine; what seems mine is not mine; whatever thou hast belongs to God; you and I must use what we have according to God's will.' "[155] His belief is that a true concern for the stewardship of wealth and property will protect men from the disposition to get them unjustly, and will relieve them from the cares of riches. By a single operation it will remove the cancers of cupidity and envy.[156]

Justice is interpreted as the expression of love toward others. His ethics are saved from the imputation of legalism by an appreciation of the sheer generosity of grace, and the extras of courtesy and sympathy. He remarks, a little acidly, that burning evangelists are so busy laying the foundations of character that one sees too many "rows of half-finished Christians."[157] In a noble sermon on "The Grace of Christ the Law of Conduct," he says that grace exceeds love, passes beyond all claims, and confers benefits which the law would not allow. He insists that true grace is to seek uncongenial company and to embrace that noble poverty "which comes upon men as the result of the free and voluntary service which they have rendered to the ignorant, the suffering and the wretched."[158]

His sound Christian realism and his humour are apparent in a sermon on Family Life. Charity, of course, begins at home, and, in Keble's words, the home provides us "room to deny ourselves." Dale comments: "No doubt. But I should be very sorry for the people that I live with to discharge their home duties in the spirit of martyrs. God preserve us all from wives, husbands, children, brothers and sisters, who go about the house with an air of celestial resignation!"[159] This most unsentimental of men then lists the basic requirements for a successful marriage in their order of

155 *Laws of Christ for Common Life*, p. 35.
156 *Ibid.*, p. 25.   157 *Ibid.*, p. 109.
158 *Ibid.*, p. 154.   159 *Ibid.*, p. 178.

importance: good sound health, perfect truthfulness, temperance, industry, courage, fortitude ("the power to bear pain and trouble without whining"), unselfishness, good sense ("to save you from the misery of having to live with a fool"), and, most importantly, loyalty to Christ ("for blending in perfect unity").[160]

The most striking and characteristic part of his ethical teaching is what has been called "Christian Civics"—that is, the municipal political responsibility of Christians. He told the Yale students that the idea that the discharge of political duty is inconsistent with maintaining spirituality is a flagrant hypocrisy, adding, "the men who urge it are not too spiritual to make a *coup* in cotton or coffee."[161] He is convinced that it is a narrowing of the impact of Christ's teaching to limit it to individual souls and not to extend it to the social ordering of human life. Christ's intentions were, nonetheless, thwarted in the history of the Christian Church. The family and the political forum were soon believed to be too worldly for those who sought Christian perfection in the flight from the family and the world in a monastery. St. Paul, however, describes the levying and collecting of taxes as a divinely appointed function of the civil magistrate. This, as Dale remarks, throws a new light on the vocation of income-tax inspectors and customs officers. It is, therefore, a civic duty to pay all taxes honestly.

This, however, is far from exhausting civic responsibilities. "We have no military conscription in England," says Dale, "but our constitution requires that very large numbers of men should give a considerable proportion of their time to certain national and municipal duties" and "the system would break down apart from the work of those . . . who pay a voluntary tax levied on personal service."[162] Dale's conclusion is that a man may have as clear a Divine call to become a member of Parliament or a municipal councillor as to go as a missionary to the heathen.[163] A country without such excellent volunteers for municipal government, or one run by place-seekers, would ruin the life of its cities: education would deteriorate; the unswept streets and the imperfectly drained sewers would destroy the public health; inefficient organization of the police would lead to the increase of crime; and public servants and finances would be unreliable. For these reasons it is a "dereliction of Christian duty" for competent Christians to refuse to stand for municipal office. It is also a civic duty for all Christian citizens

160 *Ibid.*, pp. 182-83.   161 *Nine Lectures on Preaching*, p. 256.
162 *Laws of Christ for Common Life*, pp. 195-96.   163 *Ibid.*, p. 198.

to use their votes with discrimination. Not to vote is irresponsibility; "to vote corruptly is felony; it is to appropriate to our own purposes what we have received as trustees for the town or nation."[164]

A final topic in discussing Dale's ethical teaching must be the impressive sermon on "Christian Worldliness."[165] He begins by contrasting Christian other-worldliness with Christian worldliness. The former view regards nature, literature, science, and politics with indifference or contempt. The latter view, Dale's, is to characterize other-worldliness as ingratitude to the Creator and Preserver of the world. Dale believes the first view to be Catholic, the second Protestant. The Catholic saint is commonly envisaged with a "thin, pale face, the eyes red with tears, or weary with watching, the transparent hands, the wasted form," and this is the product of a noble despair. The Protestant ideal of a worldly Christianity is marked by a sense of justification by faith, of forgiveness granted, and of the adequacy of Divine power for every need. Dale becomes almost enraptured as he eulogizes an ideal Protestantism, finding victory in the world: "Protestantism, with its clear, strong, happy consciousness of alliance with God, gave men courage to fight the world—to fight its evils instead of flying from them. It believed in the great idea of the noble prayer—'Thy will be done'— not in the Church merely—but 'Thy will be done on earth'—in the family, on the farm, in the counting-house, in the courts of kings, in the painting-room, in the college, in the school—'Thy will be done on earth as it is in heaven.' "[166]

It seems appropriate after citing a rare example of Dale's use of rhetoric to consider his preaching technique, although his sermons owed almost everything to the matter and almost nothing to the manner of their arrangement and delivery. It is, of course, true that the lucidity of his diction (clear index of a clear brain) helped his expositions. But no man made fewer concessions to his hearers. He appealed almost exclusively to intelligent and practical people: civic leaders, professional people, captains of industry and commerce, and educationalists made up the bulk of his congregation, to whom he poured out the well-digested contents of a thoughtful, comprehensive, and well-stored mind. But he employed few illustrations and hardly a single anecdote, and he was never given to pathos or to descriptive writing. His sermons are like lectures, apart from the occasional use of indignation and irony and the

[164] *Ibid.*, p. 201.   [165] Fourteenth discourse.
[166] *Laws of Christ for Common Life*, p. 233.

emphasis on the practical usefulness of his teaching. Occasionally he lightens a sermon with quotations[167] or wit.[168] Although he knew that all the popular arguments favoured extemporary preaching, he took a full manuscript with him into the pulpit. In defence of this practice he observed, "I do not accept the superstition which implies that the spirit of God is with us in the pulpit and not in the study."[169]

It was in the study that Dale's real mastery of his themes emerged. It is significant that two of his *Nine Lectures on Preaching* were devoted to "Reading." The breadth and depth of his own reading must have seemed formidable, even depressing, to his young hearers, for, in addition to reading the New Testament (for texts and contexts!), he urged them to study theological controversies; the sermons of English[170] and French divines; famous orations; history (especially of one's country) and biographies of statesmen, religious leaders, literary men, and artists; treatises on political economy and science; and the European classics. Moreover, this reading was to be disciplined by careful note-taking. This would supply them with sermon-material as it had him for so many years. As a final encouragement he noted, "Half an hour's reading will often give you the substance of three sermons."[171] One suspects that Dale, in order to cover all the ground his sermons touched on, had emulated the practice of those eminent Puritan divines, Baxter, Owen, and Howe, whom he mentions approvingly, who spent between nine and thirteen hours a day in their studies. Dale himself was an admirable example of a godly and learned Puritan minister.

Solidly Biblical, soundly orthodox, radically ethical, his preaching yet lacked a certain quality which makes him look like a shire horse in shafts compared with Newman's lithe and winged Pegasus. That missing quality was imagination, which would have furnished him with a fecundity of illustration[172] and a deeper psychological

---

[167] *Ibid.*, The ninth discourse has citations from Pope, Tennyson, Browning, Burke, and Gibbon.

[168] *Ibid.*, p. 104. Here he says of the writers of anonymous letters: "Such persons may have discovered a 'mote' in their brother's eye, but they show they have a 'beam' in their own eye big enough to support—not merely the roof of a house but the roof of a gaol."

[169] *Nine Lectures on Preaching*, p. 158.

[170] The preachers mentioned here are: Irving, Chalmers, Guthrie, Hall, Maclaren, Spurgeon, Binney, Parsons, Newman, Pusey, Manning, Robertson, and Liddon.

[171] *Ibid.*, p. 119.

[172] Yet the opening illustration of Sermon XVI in the *Laws of Christ* taken from Egyptology, shows that Dale had the capacity, but apparently not the inclination to indulge it.

understanding of his hearers, for whom he would have supplied some of the devices of rhetoric to keep their interest with greater facility. Dale himself was sufficiently honest and humble to admit the defect, and perhaps even to exaggerate it: "But I fear that the truth occupies too large a place in my thought, and that I have been too much occupied with the instrument—the Divine instrument—for effecting the ends of the ministry, too little with the actual persons to be restored to God." Even so, in a period of acute spiritual doubt he held his people to the Christian allegiance for forty-two years.

6. *C. H. Spurgeon (1834-1892)*

Like Newman, but without his profundity or scholarship, Spurgeon swam strongly against the tide of the age. In fact, he even felt uncomfortable among the most conservative of the Evangelical Dissenters, the Baptists, whom he accused of modernistic tendencies in the famous "Down Grade" controversy that threatened to disrupt the denomination. A preacher of evangelical common-places, he owes his widespread fame to his manner, rather than to the matter of his sermons.[173] As a result, his preaching technique has been widely studied, and the three volumes of his *Lectures to My Students* continue to have a large sale.[174]

The "boy preacher of Cambridgeshire" was a prodigy, who was not expected by critics to have staying power in his maturity. The critics had remembered only that he was self-educated, but they had forgotten the Calvinist tradition in which he was reared, with its high evaluation of expository preaching, and they had not reckoned with the determination, discipline, and ingenuity of the young Spurgeon. Born of Huguenot stock, son and grandson of Congregational ministers, he was particularly influenced by his grandfather. The latter taught him to value the devotional treatises of the Puritan divines and he found most help in Bunyan, Doddridge's *The Rise and Progress of Religion in the Soul*, Baxter's *Call to the Unconverted*, Alleine's *Alarm to Sinners*, and J. A. James's *Anxious Enquirer*.[175] It was ironical that the future unbending Calvinist was to be converted by a local preacher in the

---

[173] A view shared by F. C. Spurr in ed. R. S. Forman, *op.cit.*, p. 523.

[174] See the new one-volume edition of Zondervan, Grand Rapids, Michigan, 1955.

[175] C. H. Spurgeon's *Autobiography compiled from his Diary, Letters and Records by his Wife and his Private Secretary* (4 vols.), Vol. I, p. 104.

neighbouring Primitive Methodist chapel, who took as his text, "Look unto Me, and be ye saved, all the ends of the earth."[176] Like a true Calvinist, Spurgeon then bound himself to the service of God by a covenant, in the following terms:

"O great and unsearchable God, who knowest my heart, and triest all my ways; with a humble dependence upon the support of Thy Holy Spirit, I return to Thee Thine own. I would be for ever, unreservedly, perpetually Thine; Whilst I am on earth I would serve Thee; and may I enjoy Thee and praise Thee for ever.

"Feb. 1, 1850. Charles Haddon Spurgeon."[177]

Though a Congregationalist, with typical independence and thorough honesty, Spurgeon searched the Scriptures to come to a conclusion on the issue of infant or believers' Baptism. Deciding that the New Testament favoured the Baptists, he joined them. He threw himself immediately into the tasks of a Sunday School teacher and a local preacher in the Cambridgeshire villages, where he was an instant success. At the age of seventeen he was invited to the pastorate of the Waterbeach Baptist Church and in two years he had doubled the numbers by conversions.

News of this prodigy of a preacher reached as far as the metropolis, where the deacons of the once famous but now rapidly deteriorating Park Street Baptist Church resolved to invite Spurgeon to preach to the congregation with a view to accepting the pastorate. Though he was only nineteen when he began his ministry in South London, his was an immediate and almost embarrassing success. It was clear that his distinguished predecessors, Keach, Gill, Rippon, and Angus, had an even more distinguished successor in Spurgeon. Two years after his arrival the church was too small to accommodate all who wished to hear him, and while the enlargements to the edifice were being completed he preached to a crowded Exeter Hall. Soon even the enlarged church proved too small and it was decided to build the Metropolitan Tabernacle (soon to be known as "Spurgeon's Tabernacle") large enough to accommodate 5,000 sittings and to provide standing room for another thousand. In the interim Spurgeon preached to the famous few and the forgotten thousands who flocked to hear him in the Surrey Gardens Music Hall. In his new "Tabernacle" he preached (including morning and evening services) to 10,000 persons every Sunday from

[176] *Ibid.*   [177] *Autobiography*, Vol. I, p. 129.

its opening in 1861 to his death in 1892. By 1877 the membership of the church had grown to 5,152.[178] He published 2,500 different sermons and his collected sermons amounted to nearly forty volumes. Thus he conclusively refuted those who denied that he had staying-power.

Though he was now minister of probably the largest congregation in Protestantism, and a pulpit celebrity whom the common people came to hear, as the intellectuals flocked to Liddon at St. Paul's, or the professional and commercial families to Parker at City Temple, he had other irons in the fire. During the week days he was in great demand as a church anniversary preacher throughout the English Free Churches. And, as if this were not enough, this stalwart founded and maintained Pastors' College[179] (now Spurgeon's Theological College) in 1854, the Stockwell Orphanage, the Colportage Society, and the Book Fund in 1866, and only the previous year he began to edit a monthly magazine, *Sword and Trowel*.

If we look for a parallel to Spurgeon's pulpit success with the masses, we are not likely to find a closer one than George Whitefield.[180] He, if anyone, was Spurgeon's hero and model. It is significant that Spurgeon not only cited numerous anecdotes of the great popular preacher but wrote a book about Whitefield filled with an almost filial gratitude. Both made their names as enthusiastic preachers. Both were unyielding Calvinists in doctrine. Both had remarkably sonorous voices. (Spurgeon was heard by over 25,000 people at Crystal Palace and Whitefield was heard by two companies of two adjacent ships when he preached from the central one while crossing the Atlantic in convoy.) Both found it easy to arouse tears and smiles. Both were dramatic in utterance and gesture. Each was an inveterate punster. Both used simple, racy, colloquial Anglo-Saxon speech. Both revelled in telling anecdotes in the pulpit. Both preached with great effect in the open air. Both had sympathetic and congenial personalities. Both were great money-raisers and founders of orphanages. But there the likeness ends. Spurgeon's sermons were much more orderly in construction than Whitefield's and Spurgeon was far the better organiser. Spurgeon was a Dissenting minister, but Whitefield had the prestige of

---

[178] W. C. Wilkinson, *Modern Masters of Pulpit Discourse*, p. 206.

[179] By 1874 the college had sent 500 men into the ministry. (*Autobiography*, Vol. III, p. 164.)

[180] Spurgeon wrote, "My own model, if I may have such a thing in due subordination to my Lord, is George Whitefield. . . ." (*Autobiography*, Vol. II, p. 66.)

an Anglican clergyman who succeeded equally well with rich and poor alike. Spurgeon was successful with the lower middle classes and with artisans.

Spurgeon's was emphatically a theology of grace, in the evangelical succession of Paul, Augustine, Luther, Calvin, and the English Puritan divines. "I preach," he said, with characteristic defiance, "the doctrines of grace because I believe them to be true; because I see them in the Scriptures; because my experience endears them to me; and because I see the holy result of them in the lives of believers. I confess they are none the less dear to me because the advanced school despises them: their censures are to me a recommendation."[181] The trouble lay not in the doctrines of grace, but in his often legalistic interpretation of them, and in his stereotyped view that there was one and only one way to conversion. This rigidity is manifest in the final sermon he preached in the Surrey Gardens Music Hall on December 11, 1859, which was a digest of his doctrinal views: "I question whether we have preached all the counsel of God unless predestination, with all its solemnity and sureness, be continually declared—unless election be boldly and nakedly taught as one of the truths revealed of God. It is the minister's duty, beginning from the fountain-head, to trace all the other streams; dwelling on effectual calling, maintaining justification by faith, insisting upon the certain perseverance of the believer, and delighting to proclaim the gracious covenant in which all these things are contained, and which is sure to all the chosen, blood-bought seed. . . ."[182]

To the "three R's" of Puritanism ("Ruin, Redemption, and Regeneration")[183] he added predestination, election, a substitutionary Atonement,[184] eternal punishment for the unregenerate, and the inerrancy of the Scriptures. In common with many Evangelicals of his time he was utterly opposed to Biblical and historical criticism and so was unable to distinguish with sufficient clarity between the primary authority of the Word-made-flesh and the words of Scripture. This accounted for a greater emphasis on the Atonement than on the Incarnation, on the death of Christ rather than His life, and also for a disjunction between Creation and Regeneration so that if his Christ was the Lord of individual souls, He was not

181 *Ibid.*, p. 87.
182 *Ibid.*, pp. 228-29.
183 *Ibid.*, Vol. I, p. 37, and Vol. II, p. 359.
184 See Series IV, Sermon XIII, p. 218.

conceived as the Head of the Church (with Newman), nor as the Lord of culture and the world (with Robertson and Dale). Moreover, for one who so insisted on the literal inerrancy of the Scriptures his exegesis could be capricious, idiosyncratic, and even grotesque. His expository preaching is neither systematically doctrinal nor comprehensively ethical. It has been acutely described thus: "He deals with Scripture in such a way that it catches the fancy, stirs an emotional interest, and doubtless secures practical results, but conveys to the mind no clear and connected knowledge of Biblical truth."[185] His expository preaching, for all its subjectivity, lacks the audacious penetration of a Robertson. It might be termed Biblical docility, though Spurgeon would have preferred to call it Biblical fidelity. Without the mould of a Calvinistic theology, his exegesis would have been ineffective in its total impact. But the dogma and the authority of conviction with which Spurgeon preached proved satisfactory to the unquestioning and unsophisticated thousands who heard him.

It is, however, Spurgeon's sermon technique that calls for serious consideration. It was a compound of many qualities. Among these must be included naturalness of manner and diction, an orderly structure with sub-divisions that could easily be remembered, striking beginnings to arrest and lively anecdotes and illustrations to hold the attention, a deep sympathy and a disarming directness of approach, and a mastery of humour. These are the very skills that Dale lacked.

His diction and syntax were simple, natural, familiar, and colloquial. "I wish," he once said, "to lay the formalities of the pulpit aside and talk to you as if you were in your own houses."[186] On another occasion he observed, "Ye are all my witnesses, that if there be a Saxon word, or a homely phrase, a sentence that is tough and market-like, that will tell you the truth, I always use that first."[187] His sermons abounded with colloquialisms. Illustrating the inability of a distracted man to attend to God's Word, he said: "When I have cows and dogs and horses in the pulpit, I cannot hear the Gospel preached. When I have got a whole week's business and a ledger on my heart, I can not hear then."[188] To liberal, accommodating theologians, he says: "Gentlemen, pull the velvet out of your mouths; speak God's Word; we don't want any of your

185 L. O. Barstow, *Representative Modern Preachers*, p. 396.
186 Sermons, Series IV, p. 208; see also I, p. 9.
187 Sermons, Series IV, p. 244.
188 Sermons, Series IV, p. 408.

alterations."[189] Deriding the religious formalist, he observes: "Here up in the dark attic of the head, his religion has taken its abode; he has a best parlour down in his heart, but his religion never goes there—it is shut against it."[190] Metaphysical or recondite preachers, he declares, seem to think that Christ said to His disciples not, "Feed my sheep," but "Feed my giraffes."[191] Such vigorous concrete terms were the steel points of his well-aimed darts.

His approach was never subtle, flanking, or devious, like Newman's, whose effects are achieved as unobtrusively as snowflakes; it was direct, manly, even defiant. Such candour and masculinity were especially attractive to the humbler members of his congregation. The pulpit was the place for decision and commitment. A little grandiloquently, Spurgeon said: "The pulpit is the Thermophylae of Christendom; it is here that the battle must be fought between right and wrong."[192] An anonymous journalist gave his impressions of Spurgeon in "The Evening Star" of November 5, 1856: "When he has read his text, he does not fasten his eyes on a manuscript and his hands to a cushion. As soon as he begins to speak, he begins to act,—and that, not as if declaiming on the stage, but as if conversing with you on the street. He seems to shake hands with all around, and put everyone at their ease."[193]

With great ingenuity, he made his sermons easily memorable by their orderly sequence and their headings, each of which was the summary of a lesson. When he preaches on the text: "And as he was yet a coming, the devil threw him down and tare him. And Jesus rebuked the unclean spirit and healed the child and delivered him to his father," Spurgeon devises the following mnemonic: "the devil's doings, designs, discovery and defeat."[194] Using the striking text from Job 35:10, he preaches on "Songs in the Night, their source, their matter, their excellence, their uses."[195] His admirable divisions of a sermon on "Foretastes of Heavenly Life" enable him to expound an abstract theme with great concreteness. Here he conceives heaven as a place of security, of perfect rest, of complete victory and glorious triumph, of complete acceptance with God, and the idea of our most hallowed and blissful communion.[196] Equally, he can extract the last drop of meaning from a Scriptural metaphor, as when expounding Galatians 3:10 he divides his

189 *Ibid.*, I, p. 31.   190 *Ibid.*, I, p. 95.
191 *Lectures to My Students.*   192 *Autobiography*, Vol. III, p. 157.
193 *Ibid.*, Vol. II, pp. 242-43, is where the account is cited.
194 Sermons, Series II, p. 297.
195 *Ibid.*, Sermon XI.   196 Series III, Sermon IX.

subject into three headings: to try the prisoner, declare the sentence, and proclaim his deliverance.[197] Spurgeon warned his theological students of the importance of good arrangement in sermons, cautioning them that their future congregations would not like "muddled-up sermons in which you cannot tell head from tail, because they have neither, but are like Mr. Bright's Skye terrier, whose head and tail were both alike."[198]

Spurgeon was also a master of the art of startling the attention of his congregation right at the beginning of a sermon. Preaching on Jonah's words, "Salvation is of the Lord," he begins: "Jonah learned this sentence of good theology in a strange college. He learned it in the whale's belly, at the bottom of the mountains, with the weeds wrapped about his head, when he supposed that the earth with her bars was about him for ever."[199] Another sermon begins: "I will show you three fools."[200] In thus plunging in medias res, Spurgeon's diving into the ocean of his theme can be contrasted with the conventional clergyman of his day who shiveringly lingered on the sands of the sea of truth.

He knew also how to sustain the attention he had so dramatically aroused; he learned it from the Puritan preachers. "The reason why the old Puritan preachers could get their congregations was this— they did not give their hearers dry theology; they illustrated it; they had an anecdote from this and a quaint passage from that classic author; here a verse of poetry; here or there a quip or a pun— a thing which nowadays is a sin above all sins, but which was constantly committed by those preachers I have ever esteemed as the patterns of pulpit eloquence."[201] Variety is the spice of sermons, as well as of life. Spurgeon set a high value on illustrations as both illuminating doctrines or duties and providing relief and contrast from the high seriousness of a sermon. He quoted with approval the epigram of Thomas Fuller: "Reasons are the pillars in the fabric of a sermon; but similitudes are the windows which give the best lights."[202]

It is of some interest to analyse the 73 citations contained in Spurgeon's four series of sermons. The largest single group, consisting of 21, come from the English Evangelical preachers. Of these, as we might expect, there are 7 references to Whitefield and 5 to his successor, Rowland Hill. Sixteen citations come from

[197] Series IV, Sermon XV.
[198] Lectures to My Students (abridged edn.), p. 131.
[199] Series III, p. 194.   [200] Series III, p. 283.
[201] Autobiography, Vol. III, p. 153.   [202] Lectures to My Students, p. 349.

the English Puritans, with Bunyan accounting for 11 of them. The poets comprise the third largest group, with 13 citations; they include Shakespeare, Dante, Virgil, Byron, Cowper, Herbert, Hood, and Walter Scott. The fourth group, to whom 9 references are made, are the Reformers; Luther's 6 and Calvin's 2 imply no theological preference but only how much more quotable Luther is! There are also several miscellaneous classical and historical references. It is plain that although Spurgeon had received no higher education, he continued to educate himself by disciplined, if restricted, reading.

His illustrations are derived from many sources: historical anecdotes, proverbs, pictures, personal experience, and natural observation. They are on rare occasions the product of a sustained imagination. A typical illustration of his earlier, self-conscious mode, demonstrates the importance of small things: "There is a spider on the wall, but he taketh hold on king's palaces and spinneth his web to rid the world of noxious flies. . . . There is an insect under water, but it builds a rock . . . but here is a man that God made and gave him nothing at all to do! I do not believe it! God never makes useless things."[203]

From this rather stilted illustration, with its naively expressed conclusion, Spurgeon rapidly progressed to the natural and concise comparison of cowardly Christians to the fair-weather nautilus: "What a multitude of fair-weather Christians we have in this age! Many Christians resemble the nautilus, which, in fine, smooth weather swims on the surface of the sea, in a splendid little squadron, like the mighty ships; but, the moment the first breath of the wind rustles the waves, they take in their sails, and sink into the depths."[204] Later, Spurgeon will find illustrations in remoter areas of experience, as in the snaring of wild ducks in Lincolnshire or in a portrait in the National Gallery.[205]

A naturally sympathetic and humorous man, Spurgeon knew how to evoke tears and laughter from his congregation. We may be sure that his frequent references to the plight of the poor were warmly received by a congregation of small shopkeepers, clerks, and artisans, with their families.[206] Occasionally Spurgeon attempts a moving mystical strain in which he is very successful. In one sermon he addresses our Lord directly, and in as felicitous a manner

---

[203] Sermons, Series I, pp. 142-43.   [204] Series I, p. 378.
[205] See Series III, p. 44, and Series II, p. 39.
[206] See Sermons, Series III, Sermon X; Series II, Sermon XI; Series I, pp. 18-19; 300-01.

as Newman: "If, when the nail was in Thine hand, O Jesus, Thou didst rout all hell, canst Thou be defeated now that Thou hast grasped the sceptre?"[207] On another occasion, musing on the Passion, he says: "Each of the thorns becomes a brilliant in His crown of glory; the nails are forged into His sceptre, and His wounds do clothe Him with the purple of empire."[208]

In general, however, his attempts at humour exceed his essays in pathos. He had a racy mother wit, constant cheerfulness, and a cordially congenial personality. His gift of mimicry made it always a pleasure for him to tell a humorous anecdote, of which the following is quite typical, since it poked fun at a distinguished atheist: "I recall a story of Mr. Hume, who so constantly affirmed that the light of reason is abundantly sufficient. Being at a good minister's house one evening . . . on leaving, the minister offered to hold him a candle to light him down the steps. He said, 'No; the light of nature would be enough; the moon would do.' It so happened that the moon was covered with a cloud, and he fell down the steps. 'Ah!' said the minister, 'you had better have a little light from above, after all, Mr. Hume.' "[209]

To come to a final estimate of Spurgeon's contribution to the Victorian pulpit, it must be recalled that he preached to larger congregations than any other man in England, and that, apart from the Calvinistic certainties welcomed by his unsophisticated and conservative hearers, it was the enthusiasm, the manly directness, the racy vigour of his phrasing, the clarity and order of his planning, and the variety and aptness of his illustrations and references, that accounted for his widespread appeal. On the debit side, however, must be set cultural and even theological Philistinism (which makes him a boor beside Newman, Robertson, and Dale), a frequently eccentric exposition of Holy Writ,[210] and a maudlin sentimentality. His sermons lack profundity, erudition and elegance, but, as compensations, they have vigour, relevance, and interest.

[207] Series IV, p. 378.
[208] Series II, p. 144.   [209] Sermons, Series I, p. 32.
[210] As an example, consider Series IV, Sermon I, "The Parable of the Ark." The allegory runs as wild as ever it did in the mediaeval pulpit. Taking the Ark as a type of the Church, Spurgeon declares that the single window in it means that all Christians need the ministry of the Holy Spirit. The rooms he interprets as the denominations of the Church; the single door stands for Christ the only way to salvation. The storeys of the Ark represent the different levels of attainment, and the clean and unclean animals represent the variety of sinners accepted in the Gospel. (The clean surely would more naturally represent the Pharisee? But it is all too subjective—a meaning imposed on rather than found in Scripture.)

7. Four Pulpit Masters

The selection of Newman, Robertson, Dale, and Spurgeon as the four masters of the pulpit in the Victorian era requires justification. They were chosen on the basis of three criteria: as eminent representatives of different denominational traditions in preaching; as varied personalities in a day of pulpit personalities; and, finally, as exemplars of very different homiletical styles.

Newman demanded inclusion both because his sermons are regarded as literary classics in the art of persuasion, and because his career provides an illuminating commentary on the different requirements of the Anglo-Catholic and Roman Catholic pulpits. Newman was not, however, a lone star in the Roman Catholic sky; the urbane and polished Cardinal Wiseman and the vigorous and witty popular apologist, Cardinal Manning, were bright lights in their day. Canon Liddon and Dean Church could also make strong claims for inclusion as representatives of the Anglican High Church pulpit.

Robertson was included as the most sensitive and thoughtful preacher of the Broad Church Movement in the Church of England, whose sermons had an astonishing posthumous reception. In the same school other claimants for distinction include F. D. Maurice, Charles Kingsley, Thomas Arnold, and Dean Stanley.

Among the Congregationalists R. W. Dale was not the only stellar preacher, though his combination of doctrinal and ethical preaching made him probably the most solid and substantial Free Church preacher of the period.[211] Binney (who changed the style of preaching from the oratorical to the intimate) has claims as an innovator, Baldwin Brown as a thinker, Raleigh as a literary preacher, and, not least, Joseph Parker, the lion-maned orator of City Temple.

Charles Haddon Spurgeon shares the claim to be the most significant Baptist preacher of the century with two others. Robert Hall was indisputably the greater and more thoughtful orator, but he belongs to the early part of the century; Alexander Maclaren was a much more sensitive and faithful Biblical expositor than Spurgeon. What is certain, however, is that Spurgeon's congregations, in the Metropolitan Tabernacle, the Surrey Gardens Music Hall, Exeter Hall, and the Crystal Palace, were the largest of the period. He

[211] J. K. Mozley, an Anglican theologian, says of the Congregationalist Dale: "a great Christian teacher and a great Christian man, one of the greatest of the century . . . a light of the Church Universal." See ed. R. S. Forman, *Great Christians*, p. 172.

was the George Whitefield of the nineteenth century. Methodism could have made an excellent claim for the inclusion of Hugh Price Hughes,[212] but his evangelical emphasis was represented by Spurgeon and his social passion by Robertson. Furthermore, considerable attention was given to the greatest of all Methodist preachers, John Wesley himself, in the previous volume.

These four ministers were selected also as representing different denominations and as preaching to divergent types of congregations. Newman's pulpit ministry spanned the Church of England and the Church of Rome. With equal acceptance he preached to the intellectual élite of Oxford at St. Mary's, to the simpler rustics at Littlemore, and to the sons of toil in the great industrial city of Birmingham. Robertson, with similar imaginative identification, gained and held the interest of the professional classes and the labouring folk of a southern coastal resort at Brighton, in the Anglican proprietary chapel of the Trinity. Dale's Congregational church in Birmingham, Carr's Lane, included civic and professional leaders, captains of industry, and working people, all welded into a unity because he refused to accept the distinction between "sacred" and "secular" callings, or between "professional" and "trade" occupations. Spurgeon's mighty Metropolitan Tabernacle on the southern side of the Thames was filled both morning and evening with between five and six thousand souls, many of them the underprivileged who flocked there for new hope in the grinding struggle against poverty and temptation to hear a man of the people who was also a man of God.

The homiletical techniques of the four preachers were as various as their types of congregations and provide a further reason for their selection. Newman was the scholar-saint. His quiet sermons made vivid the invisible world in a day of aggressive materialism; yet this otherworldly preacher had an astonishing insight into the remoter recesses of the rationalizing human personality. The scholar brought before the eyes of his congregations the vast panoramas of human history as, like a second Augustine of Hippo, he showed the providential interpretation of history and contrasted the empty pomp of passing empires with the enduring Church which baptized new nations and cultures into Christian truth and obedience. His was great *ecclesiastical* preaching, which made the central doctrines of the Christian faith come alive with relevance and power. His favourite themes were the paradoxes of Grace, as exemplified in

212 See Dorothy Price Hughes, *The Life of Hugh Price Hughes.*

the Son of God incarnate stooping to conquer the human race, or in the sinless Sufferer on the Cross atoning for the sins of the callous and careless. His "Omnipotence in Bonds" is perhaps the finest theological and artistic sermon of the century. He called the stragglers of the Church Militant to renew their zeal as he brought before them the pageant of the Church Triumphant with its saints and martyrs as the trophies of grace. As a saint, he made the wonders of the invisible world seem inevitable and God near. His sincerity was transparent, and the integrity of his ascetical character and the conception he had of his calling made it unthinkable for him to play to the gallery. His art was, therefore, concealed. It consisted only of a variation in tempo or a significant breathless pause in the silvery voice to prepare for unusual emphasis. Only in his Roman Catholic days did he dispense with the habit of reading his sermons. Serene and elevated in his manner, as befitted one who never forgot that he was God's spokesman, he surprised his hearers with his psychological penetration—his words struck like poniards to the very quick of their consciences as he exposed their shabby temptations and soiling doubts. As one who, by Divine grace, had conquered both, he would show his congregations how to gain the victory.

Robertson of Brighton had the same kind of personality: holy, absolutely honest, intense and sympathetic, translucent in his sincerity. As a sensitive and even original interpreter of the Scriptures, with a passion for intellectual integrity and social justice, however, he had no equal during the period as an *apologetical* preacher. The "two nations" represented in his congregation counted him as a peculiarly approachable saint. His sermons radiated candour and consecration, and his congregation knew that he had grappled with every doubt and temptation that he described and for which he supplied such practical prescriptions. He was, like Keats, one "for whom the miseries of the world are miseries and will not let them rest." His mysticism owed more to Nature than did Newman's and his preaching was more Biblically grounded.[213] Robertson also shared Newman's psychological insight, but he was prepared to apply Biblical principles to the social problems of the day. Here the difference is marked: Robertson

---

[213] Newman often took a Biblical text as the starting-point of a sermon, and his imagery, illustrations, and diction were Biblically saturated. He preferred doctrinal or practical sermons whereas Robertson's sermons were always expositions of a Biblical passage. Barstow in *Representative Modern Preachers*, p. 79, draws attention to this in Robertson.

showed a clear affinity with the Christian Socialists, Newman none. Robertson's was a Gospel for society and the world; Newman's was for individuals and for the Church, but not for the world.

R. W. Dale, like Spurgeon, was a stocky, stolid man, without the physical graces of Newman and Robertson. Nor do his sermons share the memorable structure, the unforgettable passages, and the incisive insights and epigrams that mark the true classics of preaching. In a day of religious scepticism and ethical relativism, Dale felt compelled to proclaim the enduring Christian doctrines and the abiding imperatives of Christian ethics. He deplored the "valetudinarian spirituality" of those Christians who so readily accepted the benefits of state and municipal protection, sanitation, and education, but who regarded politics as unworthy of their interest. He was a great *ethical* preacher, as his volume *The Laws of Christ for Common Life* so amply demonstrates. "Civic Righteousness" was his predominant pulpit theme, an appropriate one for the leading Free Church minister in England's second largest city. Dale believed that a genuine Christian vocation was possible even in the midst of the industrial maelstrom and he practised what he taught by active electioneering and by serving on a Royal Commission appointed to examine the nation's elementary education. He recognised that social justice was the legislative expression of love for one's remote neighbour. He might have assented to the bold dictum of a younger Congregational minister who became a member of Parliament and declared: "The ballot-box is the sacrament of brotherhood."[214]

C. H. Spurgeon, by contrast, took the pietistical view that preachers should keep politics out of the pulpit and should influence others. His preaching was directed towards conversion: it was *exhortatory* in character. Based upon the examples of the seventeenth century Puritans and the eighteenth century evangelist George Whitefield (his hero), he preached the three "R's" of Calvinism: Ruin by the Fall, Redemption by Christ, and Regeneration by the Holy Ghost. A self-educated man, he compensated for his paucity of themes by his avaricious reading and fertility of illustration. Indeed, it was the power of personal conviction, the vivid and pawky stories that he told, the pathos and humour of his moods, and the fellow-feeling that he conveyed, that together

[214] A saying of the Rev. Silvester Horne, M.P.

commended his old-fashioned Gospel to the thousands who heard him every week of his crowded life.

Newman's, then, was doctrinal and ecclesiastical preaching, Robertson's expository and apologetical, Dale's doctrinal and ethical, and Spurgeon's exhortatory. Each preacher in his own way attained success (except Robertson, whose fame was posthumous). Together they illustrate the vigour and variety of the Victorian pulpit.

8. *The Effect of Preaching on Worship*

A final question remains: What effect, if any, did popular preaching have upon the worship of the period? If we may accept M. Will's classification of three major types of worship, as developed in his monumental study of the philosophy and psychology of worship, *Le Culte*, the Oracle, the Mystery, or the Sacrifice will predominate in any tradition of worship. It is clear that popular preachers speak as interpreters of the "oracles of God" (Calvin's name for sermons), and that, unless they are mystics or otherwise extremely sensitive to aesthetic values, and unless they belong to a Church which safeguards the centrality of the Eucharist, they will undervalue the Sacrament of Sacrifice. In the case of Newman, his preaching is subtle and suggestive, instead of philosophical and rational, and the sense of the numinous and the invisible was strong in him. So for him the sermons, far from being a substitute for worship, were a preparation for the Holy Communion which God has with men. In the case of F. W. Robertson, a keen aesthetic sense, a genuine appreciation of forms and symbols, a deep and natural Christ-mysticism, and ordination in the Church of England gave him a balanced sense of the need for both Word and Sacrament. Dale, being a strongly doctrinal and ethical preacher, and a Nonconformist too, might be expected to neglect the Lord's Supper. But the expectation would be wrong; so high was the sacramentalism in a handbook of Congregational doctrine that he prepared for the denomination that he was forced to withdraw the sacramental section of the work. It is surely significant that Canon J. K. Mozley regards Dale's sacramental doctrine as providing the main lines of the late Canon O. C. Quick's important treatise on *The Christian Sacraments*—a compliment rarely paid by an Anglican to a Free Churchman on this of all subjects.

When we come to Spurgeon, however, it is clear that his didactic tendency was unwarrantably carried over from his sermons to his prayers, which were rambling and declaratory in character. It is, it must be confessed, all too common for popular preachers to seem to treat Almighty God as if He were a member of their congregations and neither omniscient nor omnipotent. For such (and especially for any with tendencies to demagoguery) T. S. Eliot's reminder would be salutory:

> You are not here to verify,
> Instruct yourself, or inform curiosity
> Or carry report. You are here to kneel
> Where prayer has been valid.[215]

Where this is forgotten, and there is no objectivity of a Liturgy to complement the necessary subjectivity of a sermon, idiosyncrasies creep into the prayers and even the Sacrament becomes of value, not as a means of grace so much as a badge of our faith and affiliation to a religious community in the barest Zwinglian fashion. It is to be feared that this was all too often the case in Victorian England and it was symbolized in Dissenting edifices by the flattening out of the pulpit into an all-dominating platform.

The necessary recourse to the defence of the beleagured Christian faith by the use of the weapons of reason and experience, as well as the need to reach the uncommitted thousands by providing them with "popular services," inevitably lowered the quality of worship. Where brief and bright services were held for the benefit of the masses, worship became merely the extension of evangelism, or, as with the solos of Sankey, a preparation for the sermons of Moody. As a result chiefly of the Great Exhibition of 1851, an interdenominational attempt was made to relate Christian worship and preaching to the capacities of the outsiders. Spurgeon made his attempt in Exeter Hall (which he took for four months in 1855) and later in the Surrey Gardens Music Hall. These successes caused a number of ardent Evangelicals to reopen Exeter Hall in the Strand as a centre for worship and preaching, where a shortened form of Evensong was used. The St. James Hall in Piccadilly was opened for the same purpose. From 1853 onwards Dean Milman started a series of special evening services at St. Paul's Cathedral, as did Dean Trench in Westminster Abbey during the summer months from 1856 to 1864. More zealous than acute were the enthusiasts who engaged theatres for evangelical crusades. "The

[215] *Little Gidding* (*The Four Quartets*), lines 45-48, *The Complete Poems and Plays, 1909-1950* (New York: Harcourt, Brace and Company, 1952), p. 139.

stage became a pulpit," a contemporary journalist informs us, "and a crowd of the lower class might be seen in the pit and the gallery; whilst other persons, some as critics and spectators, occupied the boxes. Some of the former indeed made noisy demonstrations, and tore papers in pieces—amusing themselves with the eddying fragments."[216] These circumstances might be thought more conducive to a *saturnalia* than to sacred worship, and preaching removed from the context of a sacred sanctuary and a dedicated people of God and isolated from its necessary connection with the Sacrament was bound to degenerate into the cultivation of tricks and stunts to keep the shallow interested.

Such preaching was more likely than ever to become a substitute for worship. This was an ever present danger in Victorian England even in the conventional sanctuaries, where the titillation of the sermon compensated for the formality and dullness of much Anglican worship and the disordered extemporaneity of some Free Church worship. The greater the preacher's popular appeal, the greater the danger. Three of our four pulpit giants resisted the perilous temptation, giving equal place to prayers and preaching, to Sacrament and Sermon.

[216] Cited John Stoughton, *Religion in England from 1800 to 1850*, Vol. II, p. 426.

BIBLIOGRAPHY

1. Liturgical Texts
2. Periodicals
3. Sources in English Literature
4. Books

1. SELECTED LITURGICAL TEXTS
(Arranged Chronologically by Denomination)

ANGLICAN

Arnold, John Henry (ed.), *Anglican Liturgies* (Alcuin Club, London, 1939), containing the English Rite of 1662 and 1928, the Scottish Liturgy, the American and South African Rites, and the Liturgies of India and Ceylon

CATHOLIC APOSTOLIC CHURCH

The Liturgy and Other Divine Offices of the Church (London, 1847; New York, 1851)

The Order for the Daily Services of the Church and for administration of the Sacraments, as the same are to be conducted at Albury (n.d., but pre-1858)

FREE CHURCH (chiefly Congregational in editorship)

A New Directory for Nonconformist Churches, containing Remarks on their Mode of Public Worship, and a Plan for the Improvement of it (1812)

A Form of Morning and Evening Services for the Use of Free Churches (London and Manchester, 1869)

Newman Hall, *Free Church Service Book* (4th edn., 1867)

John Hunter, *Devotional Services for Public Worship* (1st edn., 1882; 10th revised edn., 1920)

Devotional Services for use in Mill Hill School Chapel (1895)

C. Silvester Horne and T. H. Darlow. *"Let us Pray:" a Handbook of selected Collects and Forms of Prayer for the use of Free Churches* (1897)

METHODIST

(Primitive Methodist)

Forms for the Administration of Baptism; the Solemnization of Matrimony; Administration of the Lord's Supper; Renewing our Covenant with God; and, For the Burial of the Deed . . . drawn up by Order of the Primitive Methodist Conference Assembled at Newcastle-on-Tyne, June 1859, for the use of such Primitive Methodist Ministers as may require them, and sanctioned by the Conference held at Tunstall, June 1860 (1861)

(Wesleyan Methodist)

Order of Administration of the Lord's Supper and Baptism . . . as used by the Wesleyan Methodists (1848)

PRESBYTERIAN

(English)

Directory of Public Worship (1898)

351

(Scottish)
Euchologion (published by the Church Service Society of the Church
of Scotland, Edinburgh, 1867; important annotated edn. by
G. W. Sprott, 1905)
Presbyterian Forms of Service (published by the Devotional Associa-
tion of the United Presbyterian Church, Edinburgh, edns. of 1891,
1894)
A New Directory for Public Worship (published by the Free Church
Public Worship Association in 1898)
H. J. Wotherspoon. *The Divine Service, A Eucharistic Office Ac-
cording to the Forms of the Primitive Church* (1893)

ROMAN CATHOLIC

Missale Romanum. Editio II juxta typicam Vaticanam amplificata I.
(New York, 1942)
Rituale Romanum. Desclée ed. (Romae, Typis Soc. S. Joannis
Evangelistae, 1914)

UNITARIAN

James Martineau and Thomas Sadler. *Common Prayer for Christian
Worship* (1862; 1875; revised edn., 1879 with new title, "Ten
Services of Public Prayer")

2. PERIODICALS

DENOMINATIONAL

ANGLICAN

The Church Quarterly Review
The Ecclesiologist
Theology

BAPTIST

Circular Letters of various county Baptist Associations (of which
there is a substantial collection in the Angus Library of Regent's
Park College, Oxford)
The Baptist Quarterly
Transactions of the Baptist Historical Society

CONGREGATIONAL

The Congregationalist
The Congregational Magazine
The Congregational Quarterly
Transactions of the Congregational Historical Society
The Yearbooks of the Congregational Union of England and Wales

METHODIST

The Arminian Magazine
The London and Holborn Quarterly Review
The Watchman
Transactions of the Wesley Historical Society

PRESBYTERIAN

The Catholic Presbyterian
The Church Service Society Annuals
The Scottish Journal of Theology

ROMAN CATHOLIC

The Dublin Magazine
The Month
The Tablet

UNITARIAN

The Hibbert Journal (interdenominational liberal quarterly)
Transactions of the Unitarian Historical Society

INTERDENOMINATIONAL

Church History (Chicago)

SECULAR

Journal of the Royal Institute of British Architects
Macmillan's Magazine
The Listener (organ of the British Broadcasting Corporation)

3. SOURCES IN ENGLISH LITERATURE

(While occasional references are made to the writings of Wordsworth, Coleridge, Scott, Byron, Keats, Browning, Carlyle, Dickens, Hazlitt, Kingsley, Charlotte M. Yonge, Clough, James Thomson, Christina Rossetti, George Macdonald, "George Eliot," Thomas Hardy, W. H. Hudson, Compton Mackenzie, Emerson, O. W. Holmes, and many others, the ensuing list concentrates on the sources of which fuller use was made.)

ESSAYS AND CRITICISM

Matthew Arnold, *St. Paul and Protestantism* (1871); *Literature and Dogma: an Essay towards a better Apprehension of the Bible* (1873); *Last Essays on Church and Religion* (1877); *Discourses in America* (1885). (These were used for their insight into the attempt to liberalize traditional religion on a moral and cultural basis and for Arnold's conservative attitude towards the Anglican Liturgy.)

John Ruskin, *The Stones of Venice* (1851-1853). (This was used to illuminate Ruskin's success in popularizing Gothic architecture and art among Low Church and Dissenting circles in which Pugin was anathema.)

NOVELS

John Henry Newman, *Loss and Gain* (1848). (This didactic and unequal novel supplements the *Apologia* and is written much nearer the time of Newman's submission to Rome, while it supplies vivid accounts of the Church "parties" of the day and of some of the wilder forms of sectarianism.)

Elizabeth Cleghorn Gaskell, *Ruth* (1852). (This novel was used for its charming evocation of a Presbyterian-Unitarian Meeting House in the eighteenth and nineteenth centuries.)

Margaret Oliphant, *Salem Chapel* (1862) (A lively account of Dissenting religious mores and architecture)

William Hale White, *The Autobiography of Mark Rutherford* (1881) and *Mark Rutherford's Deliverance* (1885)

Mrs. Humphry Ward, *Robert Elsmere* (1888). ("Mark Rutherford" and Mrs. Humphry Ward probe the agony of honest doubt and of liberal theological reconstruction, respectively, in Dissent and Anglicanism. In addition, "Mark Rutherford" provides vignettes of small town Dissent, Congregational and Unitarian, in the days when the Calvinistic decrees and Puritan ways of worship began to be challenged.)

Samuel Butler, *The Way of All Flesh* (1903). (This novel was used for its shrewdly ironical account of Victorian religion, and particularly for its devastating criticism of Evangelical family prayers.)

Peter De Vries, *The Mackerel Plaza* (Boston, 1958). (The author, a minor latter-day Butler, satirizes the liberal, culture-accommodating suburban Christianity of today and the incantation type of religious revivalism.)

DRAMA

George Bernard Shaw, *Major Barbara* (1905). (This gives a reluctantly admiring analysis of the attractions of the Salvation Army.)

POETRY

John Betjeman, *Bats and Belfries* (1945) and *Mount Zion, or, In Tune with the Infinite* (n.d.). (These were employed for their half-satrical, half-nostalgic evocations of Victorian ecclesiastical architecture by an architect-poet.)

Alfred, Lord Tennyson, *In Memoriam* (1850) (This great poem and *cri du cœur* [of the heart fighting the head] typifies the struggle of faith with honest scientific doubt.)

4. BOOKS

(Except where otherwise stated, all books were published in London)

Abbey, C. J. *The English Church and its Bishops* (2 vols., 1887)

Abercrombie, Nigel. *The Life and Work of Edmund Bishop* (1960)

Addleshaw, G. W. O. and Etchells, F. *The Architectural Setting of Anglican Worship* (1950)

Alexander, H. L. *Life of Joseph Addison Alexander* (Vol. 1, 1870)

Allchin, A. M. *The Silent Rebellion, Anglican Religious Communities 1845-1900* (1958)

Allon, Henry (ed.). *Sermons preached in the King's Weigh-House Chapel, London, 1829-1869, by T. Binney, LL.D.*, Second Series (1875)

———. *et alii The Ecclesia* (1870)

[Anonymous] *A New Directory for Nonconformist Churches Containing Remarks on their Mode of Public Worship, and a Plan for the Improvement of it* (1812)

[Anonymous] *Plymouth Brethrenism: its Ecclesiastical and Doctrinal Teachings; with a Sketch of its History* (2nd edn., 1874)

Anson, Peter F. *The Call of the Cloister* (1955)

———. *Fashions in Church Furnishings, 1840-1940* (1960)

Arnold, J. H. and Wyatt, E. C. P. (eds.). *Walter Howard Frere: a Collection of papers on liturgical and historical subjects* (1940)

Baillie, D. M. *God was in Christ: an Essay in Incarnation and Atonement* (1948, revised edn. 1955)

Baird, C. W. *Eutaxia, or a Chapter on Liturgies* (1856)

Baker, Augustine. *Holy Wisdom, Or, Directions for the Prayer of Contemplation extracted out of more than forty treatises* (ed. Sweeney, New York, n.d.)

Baker, J. E. *The Novel and the Oxford Movement* (Princeton, 1932)

Balleine, G. R. *A History of the Evangelical Party in the Church of England* (1908, revised edns. 1933, 1951)

Bannerman, D. D. *The Worship of the Presbyterian Church with Special Reference to the Question of Liturgies* (Edinburgh, 1884)

Barbauld, Anne Laetitia. *Works* (ed. Lucy Aikin, 1825)

Barstow, L. O. *Representative Modern Preachers* (1904)

Bass, Clarence B. *Backgrounds to Dispensationalism* (Grand Rapids, Michigan, 1960)

Baumstark, Anton. *Comparative Liturgy* (revised by B. Botte, ed. by F. L. Cross, 1958)

Baxter, Robert. *Irvingism . . .* (1836)

Beck, G. A. (ed.) *The English Catholics: 1850-1950* (1950)

Bell, G. K. A. *Randall Davidson, Archbishop of Canterbury* (2nd edn., 1938)

Benham, T. W. and Davidson, R. T. *Life of Archibald Campbell Tait, Archbishop of Canterbury* (3rd edn., 2 vols., 1891)

Bennett, Frank. *Chester Cathedral* (1925)

Bennett, James. *History of Dissenters in the Last Thirty Years, 1808-1838* (1839)

Benson, A. C. *Life of Edward White Benson* (1899)

Benson, E. W. *The Cathedral: Its Necessary Place in the Life and Work of the Church* (1878)

Benson, Louis F. *The Hymnody of the Christian Church* (New York, 1927, reissued Richmond, Virginia, 1956)

Betjeman, John (ed.). *Collins Guide to English Parish Churches* (1958)

———. *Complete Poems* (1959)

Betjeman, John. *First and Last Loves* (1952)

Bett, Henry. *The Hymns of Methodism* (1913)

Bettenson, Henry (ed.). *Documents of the Christian Church* (1943)

Bevan, Edwyn. *Symbolism and Belief* (1938)

Binney, Thomas. *The Closet and the Church* (1849). (See also Allon, Baird, Hood, Search, and Stoughton)

Birrell, C. M. *The Worshipping Church, or, Observations on the Manner of Public Worship* (Rochdale, 1845)

Bishop, John. *Methodist Worship in relation to Free Church Worship* (1950)

[Bonar, Andrew A.] *Presbyterian Liturgies with Specimens of Forms of Prayer for Worship as Used in the Continental Reformed and American Churches; with the Directory for the Public Worship of God Agreed upon by the Assembly of Divines at Westminster; and Forms of Prayer for Ordinary and Communion Sabbaths, and for other Services of the Church* (Edinburgh, 1858)

Booth, Bramwell. Article, "The Salvation Army" in Hastings' *Encyclopedia of Religion and Ethics*, Vol. XI

Bourne, Hugh. *History of the Primitive Methodists, Giving an Account of Their Rise and Progress to the Year 1823* (1823)

Bouyer, Louis. *Newman, His Life and Spirituality* (New York, 1958)

Boyd, Malcolm. *Crisis in Communication: A Christian Examination of the Mass Media* (New York, 1957)

Bradley, William L. *P. T. Forsyth, the Man and His Work* (1952)

Brémond, H. *The Mystery of Newman* (1907)

Briggs, Martin S. *Puritan Architecture and Its Future* (1946)

Brilioth, Yngve. *Eucharistic Faith and Practice, Evangelical and Catholic* (1930)

Brinton, Howard H. *Creative Worship* (1931)

———. *Friends for 300 Years* (New York, 1953)

Brooke, Stopford A. (ed.). *The Life and Letters of Frederick W. Robertson* (2 vols. in one, Boston, 1870)

Brown, C. K. F. *A History of the English Clergy, 1800-1900* (London and New York, 1953)

Brown, John. *Puritan Preaching in England* (1900)

Brown, Robert McAfee. *P. T. Forsyth: Prophet for Today* (Philadelphia, 1952)

Bullock, F. W. B. *Evangelical Conversion in Great Britain, 1696-1845* (St. Leonard's-on-Sea, 1959)

Bunting, T. P. *The Life of Dr. Bunting* (2 vols., 1859)

Burgon, J. W. *Lives of Twelve Good Men* (2 vols., 3rd edn., 1889)

Burnet, George B. *Holy Communion in the Reformed Church of Scotland 1560-1960* (Edinburgh and London, 1960)

Burns, Dawson. *Communion Wine . . .* (1887)

Burton, Edwin H. *The Life and Times of Bishop Challenor, 1691-1781* (2 vols., 1909)

Butler, A. J. *The Life and Letters of J. W. Butler* (1897)

Campbell, J. McLeod. *The Nature of Atonement* (1856)

Cardale, John Bate. *A Discourse delivered in the Catholic Apostolic Church, Gordon Square, on the occasion of consecrating the Altar, and opening the Church for Public Worship, Christmas Eve, 1853* (1854)

———. *Readings upon the Liturgy and other Divine Offices* (2 vols., 1874)

Carlile, J. C. *C. H. Spurgeon* (1933)

Carpenter, J. Estlin. *James Martineau, Theologian and Teacher* (1905)

Carson, R. H. *The Lord's Supper* (Belfast, 1867)

Challenor, Richard. *A Manual of Prayers and other Christian Devotions* (1758)

———. *A Short Treatise on the Method and Advantage of withdrawing the Soul from being employed on Creatures in order to occupy it on God alone* (transl. from Fr. John Chrysostom, 1765)

———. *God Everywhere Present* (transl. from Bondon, 1765)

———. *Meditations for Every Day in the Year* (1754)

———. *Memoirs of the Missionary Priests* (2 vols., 1741)

———. *The Garden of the Soul; a Manual of Spiritual Exercises* (1st edn., 1740; greatly revised edn. Westminster, Maryland, 1945)

Chew, J. Sanders. *The Lord's Supper and the Lord's Day: One as Often as the Other* (Birmingham, 1858)

Child, R. L. *The Blessing of Infants and the Dedication of Parents* (1946)

Church, Leslie F. *More About the Early Methodist People* (1949)

Church, R. W. *Occasional Papers* (2 vols., 1897)

Clark, Henry W. *History of English Nonconformity* (2 vols., 1911-1913)

———. *The Cross and the Eternal Order* (1943)

Clark, Sir Kenneth. *The Gothic Revival: An Essay in the History of Taste* (1928; 2nd edn., 1950)

Clarke, B. F. L. *Church Buildings of the Nineteenth Century* (1938)

Clodd, Edward. *Memories* (1883)

Coleridge, S. T. *Notes on English Divines* (vol. 4 of *Works*, ed. H. N. Coleridge, 1853)

Coles, T. *Attention to Public Prayer* (Chipping Norton, 1813)

Collings, J. *Conservatism in Religious Worship and Belief* (1883)

Cope, Gilbert. *Symbolism in the Bible and the Church* (1959)

Cornish F. Warre. *A History of the English Church in the Nineteenth Century* (2 vols., 1910)

Cramp, J. M. *An Essay on the Obligation of Christians to Observe the Lord's Supper Every Lord's Day* (1824)

Cross, F. L. *Darwell Stone, Churchman and Counsellor* (1943)

Cross, F. L. (ed.). *The Oxford Dictionary of the Christian Church* (1957, corrected 1958)

Crowther, Jonathan. *A True and Complete Portraiture of Methodism* (New York, 1813)

Crowther, Jonathan. *The Methodist Manual* . . . (Halifax, 1810)

Dale, A. W. W. *The Life of R. W. Dale of Birmingham* (1898)

Dale, R. W. *A Manual of Congregational Principles* (1884)

―――. *Christian Doctrine, A Series of Discourses* (New York, 1895)

―――. *Discourses Delivered on Special Occasions* (1866)

―――. *History of English Congregationalism* (1907)

―――. *Nine Lectures on Preaching* (3rd edn., 1878)

―――. *The Atonement* (1875)

―――. *The Evangelical Revival and Other Sermons* (1880)

―――. *The Laws of Christ for Common Life* (1884)

Darby, J. N. *On Worship* (Bristol, 1852)

―――. The *Works* of (ed. W. Kelly, 33 vols., 1867-1883)

Dargan, E. C. *A History of Preaching* (Vol. ii, New York, 1912)

Davies, Horton. *A Mirror of the Ministry in Modern Novels* (New York, 1959)

―――. *The English Free Churches* (1952)

―――. *The Worship of the English Puritans* (1948)

―――. *Worship and Theology in England, From Watts and Wesley to Maurice, 1690-1850* (Princeton, 1961)

Davies, Walford and Grace, Harvey. *Music and Worship* (1937)

Declaration of the Faith, Church Order and Discipline of the Congregational or Independent Dissenters, as adopted at the Third General Meeting of the Congregational Union of England and Wales (1833)

The Dictionary of National Biography (63 vols., 1885-1900)

Dillistone, F. W. *Christianity and Symbolism* (1955)

Dix, Gregory. *A Detection of Aumbries* (1942)

―――. *The Shape of the Liturgy* (1945)

Drummond, A. L. *Edward Irving and his Circle* (1938)

―――. *The Church Architecture of Protestantism* (Edinburgh, 1934)

―――. *The Churches in English Fiction* (Leicester, 1950)

―――. *The Churches pictured by "Punch"* (1947)

Drummond, J. and Upton, C. P. *The Life and Letters of James Martineau* (2 vols., 1901)

Drysdale, A. H. *History of Presbyterianism in England* (1889)

Eastlake, C. L. *A History of the Gothic Revival* (1872)

Elliott-Binns, L. E. *English Thought, 1860-1900, The Theological Aspect* (1956)

Ensor, R. C. K. *England: 1870-1914* (1936)

Ervine, St. John. *God's Soldier: General William Booth* (2 vols., 1934)

Every, George (ed.). *Herbert Kelly, S.S.M. No Pious Person* (1960)

Fairbairn, Andrew Martin. *Catholicism: Roman and Anglican* (1899)

―――. *Studies in Religion and Theology* (1910)

―――. *The Place of Christ in Modern Theology* (1893)

Fellowes, E. H. *English Cathedral Music from Edward VI to Edward VII* (1941)

Ferrey, B. *Recollections of A. N. Welby Pugin* (1861)

Forman, R. S. (ed.). *Great Christians* (1933)
Forsyth, P. T. *Christ on Parnassus* (1911)
———. *Positive Preaching and the Modern Mind* (1907)
———. *The Charter of the Church* (1896)
———. *The Church and the Sacraments* (1917, reissued 1947)
———. *The Work of Christ* (1910)
Frere, W. H. *English Church Ways* (1914)
———. *Some Principles of Liturgical Reform* (1911)
———. *Studies in the Early Roman Liturgy* (3 vols., 1930-1935)
———. *The Use of Sarum* (2 vols., 1898-1901)
(Friends, the Religious Society of.) *Extracts from the Minutes and Epistles of the Religious Society of Friends, held in London from its first institution to the present time, relating to Christian Doctrine, Practice and Discipline* (4th edn., 1864)
Froude, J. A. *Short Studies on Great Subjects* (1867-1883)

Garbett, C. F. *The Claims of the Church of England* (1947)
Gibbon, J. Morgan *et al. The Lord's Supper: Eden and Gethsemane* (Manchester, 1903)
Gillman, F. J. *The Evolution of the English Hymn* (1927)
Gore, Charles. *Anglo-Catholicism Today* (1925)
———. *The Body of Christ* (1901)
———. *The Incarnation of the Son of God* (1891)
——— *et al. Lux Mundi* (1889)
Gorham, George Cornelius. *Examination before Admission to a Benefice by the Bishop of Exeter* (1848)
Graf, Ernest. *Anscar Vonier, Abbot of Buckfast* (1957)
Grant, John W. *Free Churchmanship in England, 1870-1940* (n.d. circa 1955)
Gregory, Benjamin. *Sidelights on the Conflicts of Methodism, 1827-1852* (New York, 1899)
Guardini, Romano. *The Spirit of the Liturgy* (New York, 1953)
Gwynn, Denis. *Cardinal Wiseman* (1929)
———. *Lord Shrewsbury, Pugin and the Catholic Revival* (1946)

Halley, Richard. *Lancashire: Its Puritanism and Nonconformity* (2nd edn. Manchester and London, 1872)
Hamilton, W. K. *Cathedral Reform. A Letter to Members of his Diocese* (1855)
Hebert, A. G. *Liturgy and Society* (1935)
——— (ed.). *The Parish Communion* (1937)
Hedley, J. C. *The Holy Eucharist* (1907)
Hemphill, Basil. *The Early Vicars Apostolic of England, 1685-1750* (1954)
Henson, H. H. *Robertson of Brighton* (1916)
Hicks, F. C. N. *The Fulness of Sacrifice* (1938)
Hodder, Edwin. *The Life and Work of the Seventh Earl of Shaftesbury* (1886)

BIBLIOGRAPHY

Hole, S. R. *More Memories* (1894)
Hood, E. Paxton. *The Throne of Eloquence* (1885)
———. *Thomas Binney, His Mind, Life and Opinions.* . . . (1874)
Hoskyns, Sir Edwyn and Davey, Noel. *The Riddle of the New Testament* (1931)
Howson, J. S. (ed.). *Essays on Cathedrals* (1872)
Hughes, Dorothea Price. *The Life of Hugh Price Hughes by His Daughter* (1904)
Hunt, J. *Religious Thought in England* (3 vols., 1870-1873)
Hunter, John. *A Worshipful Church* (1903)
———. *Devotional Services for Public Worship* (1882)
———. *Hymns of Faith and Hope* (1889)
Hunter, Leslie S. *John Hunter, D.D., A Life* (1921)
Hutton, R. H. *Aspects of Religious and Scientific Thought* (1899)
———. *Contemporary Thought and Thinkers* (1899)
Hymns Ancient and Modern (official hymnbook of the Church of England, 1860 and many subsequent editions)

Ivimey, Joseph. *A History of the English Baptists* (Vol. IV, 1823)

Jackson, Thomas. *The Centenary of Wesleyan Methodism* (1839)
———. *Life of R. Newton, D.D.* (1855)
Jasper, R. C. D. *Prayer Book Revision in England, 1800-1900* (1954)
Jefferson, H. A. L. *Hymns in Christian Worship* (1950)
Jobson, F. J. *Chapel and School Architecture, as appropriate to the Buildings of the Nonconformists, particularly to those of the Wesleyan Methodists, with Practical Directions for the erection of Chapels and School Houses* (1850)
Johnson, J. O. *The Life and Letters of H. P. Liddon* (1904)
Johnson, Joseph. *George Macdonald, a Biographical and Critical Appreciation* (1906)
Jones, Sir Henry. *Browning as a Philosophical and Religious Teacher* (Glasgow, 1892)
Jones, R. P. *Nonconformist Church Architecture* (1914)
Jowett, Benjamin. *The Life and Letters of Benjamin Jowett* (ed. E. Abbott and Lewis Campbell, 1897)
——— (ed.). *Essays and Reviews* (1860)
Julian, John. *Dictionary of Hymnology* (1890 and later editions)

Kendall, H. B. *Origin and History of the Primitive Methodist Church* (2 vols., 1905)
Kerr, John. *The Renascence of Worship: The Origin, Aims and Achievements of the Church Service Society* (Edinburgh, 1909)
Kingsley, Charles. *The Good News of God* (1885)
Knox, R. A. *Enthusiasm, A Chapter in the History of Religion, with Special Reference to the XVIIth and XVIIIth Centuries* (Oxford, 1950)

Koenker, Ernest B. *The Liturgical Renaissance in the Roman Catholic Church* (Chicago, 1954)

Lake, K. (ed.). *Memorials of William Charles Lake* (1901)
Lampe, G. W. H. *The Seal of the Spirit* (1951)
Lecky, W. E. H. *Democracy and Liberty* (1896)
Lenwood, Frank. *Jesus—Lord or Leader?* (1930)
Leslie, Shane. *From Cabin-Boy to Archbishop: The Autobiography of Archbishop Ullathorne* (1941)
———. *Henry Edward Manning, His Life and Labours* (1921)
Liddon, H. P. *The Divinity of our Lord and Saviour Jesus Christ* (1866)
Lidgett, J. Scott. *The Spiritual Principle of the Atonement* (1897)
Lloyd, Roger B. *The Church of England in the Twentieth Century* (2 vols., 1946, 1950)
Loukes, Harold. *Friends face Reality* (1954)

Macdermott, K. H. *The Old Church Gallery Minstrels: 1660-1860* (1948)
Mackay, H. F. B. *Saints and Leaders* (1928)
Mackintosh, H. R. *The Doctrine of the Person of Jesus Christ* (Edinburgh, 1912)
Maclaren, Alexander. *A Year's Ministry, First Series* (1884)
Manning, Bernard Lord. *Essays in Orthodox Dissent* (1939)
Marchant, J. *Dr. John Clifford, C.H.* (1924)
Martineau, James. *A Study of Religion* (1888)
———. *Endeavours after a Christian Life* (First Series, 1843; Second Series, 1847)
———. *Hours of Thought on Sacred Things* (First Series, 1876; Second Series, 1879)
———. *Prayers in the Congregation and in the College* (1911)
———. *The Rationale of Religious Inquiry* (1836)
———. *The Seat of Authority in Religion* (1890)
———. *Types of Ethical Theory* (1885)
Martineau, James and Sadler, Thomas. *Common Prayer for Christian Worship* (1862)
Matheson, P. E. *Life of Hastings Rashdall* (1928)
Mathew, David. *Catholicism in England, 1535-1935* (1936)
Matthews, A. G. *The Congregational Churches of Staffordshire* (1924)
Matthews, W. R. and Atkins, W. M. *A History of St. Paul's Cathedral* (1957)
Mauriac, François. *Mes Grands Hommes* (transl. Elsie Pell, "Men I Hold Great," New York, 1951)
Maurice, Frederick Denison. *The Kingdom of Christ* (1842)
Maurice, Sir J. F. *The Life of Frederick Denison Maurice* (2 vols., 1884)
Maxwell, William D. *A History of Worship in the Church of Scotland* (1955)
———. *An Outline of Christian Worship* (1936)

Maxwell, William D. *Concerning Worship* (1948)
———. *The Book of Common Prayer and the Worship of Non-Anglican Churches* (1950)
McCann, Justin and Connolly, Hugh (eds.). *Memorials of Father Augustine Baker and other Documents relating to the English Benedictines* (1933)
McCrie, C. G. *The Public Worship of Presbyterian Scotland* (Edinburgh and London, 1892)
Micklem, Nathaniel (ed.). *Christian Worship* (Oxford, 1936)
Miller, Edward. *The History and Doctrines of Irvingism, or of the so-called Catholic and Apostolic Church* (2 vols., 1878)
Moberly, R. C. *Atonement and Personality* (1901)
Molland, Einar. *Christendom* (1959)
Moorman, J. R. H. *A History of the Church in England* (1953)
———. *B. K. Cunningham* (1947)
Morison, Stanley. *English Prayer Books, An introduction to the Literature of Christian Public Worship* (Cambridge, 1943)
Mozley, J. K. *Some Tendencies in British Theology, from the publication of Lux Mundi to the Present Day* (1951)
Muirhead, J. H. (ed.). *Nine Birmingham Men* (1909)

Newman, John Henry. *Apologia pro vita sua* (1864)
———. *Difficulties felt by Anglicans in Catholic Teaching considered* (4th edn., 1876)
———. *Discourses addressed to Mixed Congregations* (1849)
———. *Faith and Prejudice and other Unpublished Sermons of Cardinal Newman* (ed. C. S. Dessain, London and New York, 1956)
———. *Lectures on Justification* (3rd edn., 1874)
———. *Loss and Gain* (1848)
———. *Lyra Apostolica* (1836)
———. *Meditations and Devotions* (1903)
———. *Parochial and Plain Sermons* (8 vols., 1868)
———. *Sermons and Discourses* (ed. C. F. Harrold, 2 vols., 1949)
———. *Sermons on Subjects of the Day* (1844)
———. *Sermons preached on Various Occasions* (1857)
John Henry Newman: Centenary Essays (ed. and intro. by H. Tristram, 1945)
Nias, J. C. *Gorham and the Bishop of Exeter* (1951)
Nichols, James Hastings. *Romanticism in American Theology* (Chicago, 1961)
Niebuhr, H. Richard. *The Kingdom of God in America* (2nd edn., Hamden, Connecticut, 1956)

Oliphant, Margaret. *The Life of Edward Irving, Minister of the National Scotch Church, London, illustrated by his Journals and Correspondence* (New York, 1862)
Ollard, S. L. *The Anglo-Catholic Revival, Some Persons and Principles* (1925)

["Onesimus"] *The Pulpit, Or, a Biographical and Literary Account of Eminent Popular Preachers, interspersed with occasional clerical criticism* (3 vols., 1816)

Orchard, W. E. *From Faith to Faith* (London and New York)

Payne, Ernest A. *The Fellowship of Believers* . . . (1944)

Peaston, A. Elliott. *The Prayer Book Reform Movement in the XVIIIth Century* (Oxford, 1940)

Peel, Albert. *These Hundred Years* (1931)

Petty, John. *History of the Primitive Methodist Connexion* (1870)

Phillips, C. H. *The Singing Church* (1945)

Phillips, C. S. *Hymnody Past and Present* (1937)

Plomer, William (ed.). *Kilvert's Diary, 1870-1879* (abbreviated edn., 1944)

Pope, W. B. *A Compendium of Christian Theology* (1st edn., 2 vols., London, 1875; 2nd edn., 3 vols., New York and Cincinnati)

Prestige, Leonard. *The Life of Charles Gore* (1935)

Proctor and Frere. *A New History of the Book of Common Prayer* (1902)

Pugin, Augustus Welby. *Contrasts: or, A Parallel between the Noble Edifices of the Middle Ages and the Corresponding Buildings of the Present Day; Showing the Present Decay of Taste* (1836)

Pusey, E. B. *Remarks on the Prospective and Past Benefits of Cathedral Institutions* . . . (1833)

Quick, O. C. *The Christian Sacraments* (1927)

Raleigh, Mary (ed.). *Alexander Raleigh: Records of His Life* (1883)

Ramsey, A. M. *An Era in Anglican Theology, From Gore to Temple* (1960)

Rattenbury, J. E. *Thoughts on Holy Communion* (1958)

———. *Vital Elements in Public Worship* (1936)

———. *Wesley's Legacy to the World* (1928)

Rauschenbusch, Walter. *For God and the People: Prayers of the Social Awakening* (New York, 1910)

Reilly, J. J. *Newman as a Man of Letters* (New York, 1927)

Report of the Royal Commission on Ecclesiastical Discipline (1906)

Rhodes, Elizabeth. *Memoir of Elizabeth Rhodes by Herself* (1829)

Rickman, Thomas. *An Attempt to discriminate the styles of Gothic Architecture* (1819)

Rigg, J. H. *Comparative View of Church Organization* (3rd edn., 1896)

———. *Oxford High Church Anglicanism* (1895, 1899)

Risbrook, W. Jardine. *Anglican Liturgies of the Seventeenth and Eighteenth Centuries* (Alcuin Club, 1958)

Ritson, J. H. *The Romance of Primitive Methodism* (1910)

Robertson, Frederick W. *Sermons* (four Series, edn. of 1898)

Robinson, H. Wheeler. *The Life and Faith of the Baptists* (1927)

Robinson, William. *A Companion to the Communion Service; a Devotional Manual* (1942)

———. *What the Churches of Christ stand for* (Birmingham, 1926)

Rock, Daniel. *The Church of our Fathers as seen in St. Osmund's Rite for the Cathedral of Salisbury* (new edn. in 4 vols., eds. G. W. Hart and W. H. Frere, 1907)

[Ross, John—attributed to] *The New Apostles; or, Irvingism, its History, Doctrines and Preachers, considered by the Light of Scripture and Reason* (n.d., circa 1860)

Rousseau, Olivier. *Histoire du Mouvement Liturgique* (Paris, 1945; transl. as "The Progress of the Liturgy" and publ. Westminster, Maryland)

Routley, Erik R. *Hymns and Human Life* (1952; 2nd edn., 1959)

———. *The Music of Christian Hymnody, A Study of the development of the hymn tune since the Reformation, with special reference to English Protestantism* (1957)

Rupp, Gordon. *Thomas Jackson, Methodist Patriarch* (1954)

Ruskin, John. *The Stones of Venice* (3 vols., 1851-1853)

Sandall, Robert. *The History of the Salvation Army* (I: 1865-1876; II: 1876-1886; London and New York, 1947, 1956)

Schleiermacher, Friedrich. *Der christliche Glaube nach den Grundsätzen der Evangelischen Kirche* (1821-1822, Berlin, greatly revised, 1830-1831)

"Search, John" [Thomas Binney]. *The Great Gorham Case: A History in Five Books* (1850)

Shaw, G. Bernard. *The Complete Plays* (1931)

Shaw, P. E. *The Catholic Apostolic Church sometimes called Irvingite, A Historical Study* (New York, 1946)

Short, Ernest H. *A History of Religious Architecture* (London and New York, 1936)

Shuster, G. N. *The Catholic Spirit in Modern English Literature* (1922)

Smyth, Charles. *Simeon and Church Order* (Cambridge, 1940)

Spurgeon, Charles Haddon. *Autobiography* (4 vols., 1900)

———. *C. H. Spurgeon's Prayers* (5th edn., New York and Chicago, 1906)

———. *Lectures to My Students* (selection from original 3 vols., Grand Rapids, Michigan, 1955)

———. *Sermons* (Series I-IV, 1857, New York)

Staley, Vernon (ed.). *Hierurgia Anglicana* (3 parts, new edn., 1902-1904)

Stanford, Charles. *On Improvement in the Mode of Public Worship* (1870)

Steere, Douglas. *Prayer and Worship* (New York, 1938)

Stembridge, H. W. *A Ritual of Marriage and Burial Services designed for the use of Dissenting Ministers* (Taunton and London, 1853)

BIBLIOGRAPHY

Stephen, Sir James. *Essays in Ecclesiastical Biography* (1860)
Steuart, Benedict. *The Development of Christian Worship* (1953)
Stock, Irvine. *William Hale White (Mark Rutherford), A Critical Study* (New York, 1956)
Stone, Darwell. *The History of the Doctrine of the Holy Eucharist* (1909)
Stone, Wilfred. *Religion and Art of William Hale White ("Mark Rutherford")* (Stanford Univ., Calif., 1954)
Stoughton, John. *A Memorial of the late Rev. Thomas Binney, LL.D.* (2nd edn., 1874)
———. *Religion in England from 1800 to 1850* (2 vols., 1884)
Summerson, John. *Architecture in Britain, 1530 to 1830* (1953)

Tabor, J. A. *A Nonconformist Protest against the Papacy of Modern Dissenting Architecture imitative of Roman Catholic Churches* (Ipswich, 1863)
Taylor, Adam. *History of the English General Baptists* (2 vols., 1818)
Thompson, A. Hamilton. *The Cathedral Churches of England* (1928)
Thureau-Dangin, Paul. *The English Catholic Revival in the Nineteenth Century* (revised edn., 3 vols., 1914)
Tipple, S. A. *Spoken Words of Prayer and Praise* (1912)
———. *Sunday Mornings at Norwood* (1883)
Townsend, W. T., Workman, H. B. and Eayrs, G. (eds.). *A New History of Methodism* (3 vols., 1909)
Trappes-Lomax, M. *Pugin, a Mediaeval Victorian* (1932)
Trevelyan, Janet Penrose. *The Life of Mrs. Humphry Ward by Her Daughter* (1923)
Tribe, Rees, *et alii. Worship, its Social Significance* (1939)
Turner, W. G. *John Nelson Darby* (1944)

Ullathorne, W. B. *From Cabin-Boy to Archbishop: The Autobiography of Archbishop Ullathorne* (1941) ed. by Shane Leslie.
Underhill, Evelyn. *Worship* (1936)

Vonier, Anscar. *The Collected Works of Abbot Vonier* (Vol. 2: The Church and the Sacraments, 1952)

Waddington, John. *Congregational History: 1800-1850* (1872)
Wakefield, Gordon S. *Puritan Devotion, its place in the development of Christian Piety* (1957)
[Walker, George]. *Methodist Ritualism, or a Few Thoughts on the Methodism of Today* (n.d. but *circa* 1880)
Walsh, Walter. *The Ritualists, their Romanizing Objects and Work* (1900)
———. *The Secret History of the Oxford Movement* (1897)
Walters, J. Stuart. *Mrs. Humphry Ward and the Trend of Ethical Development since Robert Elsmere* (1912)

365

Ward, Wilfrid. *The Life of John Henry Cardinal Newman based on his Private Journals and Correspondence* (2 vols., 1912)

Ware, Bernard. *The Eve of Catholic Emancipation, 1803-1829* (3 vols., 1911-1912)

———. *The Sequel to Catholic Emancipation, 1830-1850* (2 vols., 1913)

Watford, J. *Memoirs of the Life and Labours of the late Venerable Hugh Bourne* (ed. W. Antliff, 2 vols., 1855-1856)

Watkin, E. I. *Catholic Art and Culture* (1942)

———. *Roman Catholicism in England from the Reformation to 1950* (1957)

Watson, Richard. *Theological Institutes* (1823-1829)

Webb, C. C. J. *Religious Thought in England since 1850* (1933)

Weltkirchen Lexicon Handbuch der Oekumene (Stuttgart, 1959)

White, Dorothy V. *Last Pages of a Journal, with Other Papers by Mark Rutherford* (1915)

Whitehead, A. N. *Science and the Modern World* (Cambridge, 1926)

Whitley, H. C. *Blinded Eagle, An Introduction to the Life and Teaching of Edward Irving* (1955)

Whyte, Alexander. *Newman: An Appreciation* (Edinburgh, 1901)

Wilkinson, J. T. *Hugh Bourne, 1772-1852* (1952)

———. *William Clowes, 1780-1851* (1951)

Wilkinson, W. C. *Modern Masters of Pulpit Discourse* (London and New York, 1905)

Willey, Basil. *More Nineteenth Century Studies, A Group of Honest Doubters* (London and New York, 1949)

———. *Nineteenth Century Studies, Coleridge to Matthew Arnold* (London and New York, 1949)

Wilson, Gladys. *Quaker Worship* (1952)

Wilson, Walter. *The History and Antiquities of Dissenting Churches* (Vols. ii-iv, 1808-1814)

Wood, H. G. *Belief and Unbelief since 1850* (Cambridge, 1955)

Woodgate, M. V. *Father Benson of Cowley* (1953)

Woodward, E. L. *The Age of Reform: 1815-1870* (1938)

Young, G. M. *Victorian England, Portrait of an Age* (1936)

INDEX

I. INDEX OF PERSONS

376

II. INDEX OF PLACES
(AND CHURCHES)

(Churches are assumed to be Anglican, except when otherwise indicated)